DOING
RESEARCH IN
COUNSELLING AND
PSYCHOTHERAPY

FOURTH EDITION!

DOING RESEARCH IN COUNSELLING AND PSYCHOTHERAPY

JOHN McLEOD

Los Angeles | London | New Delhi
Singapore | Washington DC | Melbourne

Los Angeles | London | New Delhi
Singapore | Washington DC | Melbourne

SAGE Publications Ltd
1 Oliver's Yard
55 City Road
London EC1Y 1SP

SAGE Publications Inc.
2455 Teller Road
Thousand Oaks, California 91320

SAGE Publications India Pvt Ltd
B 1/I 1 Mohan Cooperative Industrial Area
Mathura Road
New Delhi 110 044

SAGE Publications Asia-Pacific Pte Ltd
3 Church Street
#10-04 Samsung Hub
Singapore 049483

Editor: Susannah Trefgarne
Senior assistant editor: Ruth Lilly
Production editor: Sarah Sewell
Copyeditor: Neil Dowden
Proofreader: Thea Watson
Marketing manager: Dilhara Attygalle
Cover design: Naomi Robinson
Typeset by: C&M Digitals (P) Ltd, Chennai, India
Printed in the UK

Library of Congress Control Number: 2021940623

British Library Cataloguing in Publication data

A catalogue record for this book is available from the British Library

ISBN 978-1-5264-5948-0
ISBN 978-1-5264-5949-7 (pbk)

At SAGE we take sustainability seriously. Most of our products are printed in the UK using responsibly sourced papers and boards. When we print overseas we ensure sustainable papers are used as measured by the PREPS grading system. We undertake an annual audit to monitor our sustainability.

For Julia

Contents

About the author

John McLeod is Emeritus Professor of Counselling at Abertay University, and has held visiting professor positions at the Institute for Integrative Counselling and Psychotherapy, Dublin, University of Oslo, University of Padua and Massey University. He has had a life-long commitment to promoting the use of research as a means of informing therapy practice, improving the quality of services that are available to clients and supporting the development of a collaborative pluralistic approach to therapy. His enthusiastic search for finding ways to make research interesting and accessible for practitioners has resulted in a teaching award from the students at his own university and an award from the British Association for Counselling and Psychotherapy for his exceptional contribution to research. His writing has influenced a generation of trainees in the field of counselling, counselling psychology and psychotherapy, and his books are widely adopted on training programmes across the world.

How to use this book

This book is intended for anyone who is considering carrying out research into the process or outcome of counselling or psychotherapy. Throughout the book, the words 'counselling', 'psychotherapy' and 'therapy' are used to describe a set of activities and helping processes that are largely similar. The book is also relevant to students, practitioners, trainers, service managers in adjacent fields such as psychiatry, clinical and counselling psychology, career counselling, mental health nursing, social work and life coaching.

The book comprises two broad themes. The opening chapters address some general principles of therapy research, in relation to such activities as how to identify a research question, how to handle ethical dilemmas, and basic assumptions about knowledge that underpin quantitative and qualitative research traditions. The emphasis then shifts to explaining what is involved in conducting specific types of research study, in terms of step-by-step procedures for undertaking research projects that are feasible for novice researchers and practitioners. A closing chapter discusses the process of disseminating research findings.

Most research methods textbooks that are available in the field of therapy research and other domains concentrate almost exclusively on general methodological principles. By contrast, the present book is organised around explaining how to create different types of research product. There are three reasons why this approach has been adopted. First, I believe that it is useful to learn about research by taking the role of apprentice, and trying to produce something that is similar to existing research products that are already considered as worthwhile. Second, successfully completing a research study is greatly assisted by access to insider knowledge in the form of tips and short cuts, strategies for collaborating with others and suggestions about how to avoid pitfalls. Third, I am keen to promote an attitude to research that emphasises the achievement of a finished product that can be completed, then shared and celebrated, within a particular period of time.

In my view, it is important for those who are entering the world of therapy research to begin by developing an appreciation and understanding of the potential contribution to knowledge made by four main types of research product:

- qualitative interview studies that explore the experience of therapy for clients or therapists;
- evaluation of the outcomes of therapy in routine practice;
- systematic studies of single cases;
- studies that use personal experience as a source of information.

This book offers detailed guidance on how to carry out publishable research within each of these approaches.

Doing Research in Counselling and Psychotherapy is aimed at undergraduate and Master's degree students, as well as practitioners undertaking personal research and therapy organisations looking for ways to evaluate and improve their services. While the book may hopefully also be relevant for doctoral students and professional academic researchers, I would expect someone doing a PhD or undertaking funded research to be functioning at a more advanced level of understanding of research issues.

A key message throughout the book is that reading research papers is an invaluable means of learning about how research techniques are used, how different topics are approached and how to report research in an accessible manner. As a consequence, many research studies are cited, to function as exemplars of different types of research methodology. The intention is not that all these papers need to be read, but rather to provide a sufficient selection to allow users of the book to find studies that inspire them, and that match their own interests and research aims.

Each chapter includes a number of personal learning exercises, designed to encourage reflection on the issues that are being discussed. These exercises can be carried out on an individual basis, for example in the form of entries in a personal learning journal. Other significant research methodologies and types of product that build on these approaches but could not be addressed in detail within the present book include systematic reviews, action research studies, mixed methods research, and randomised clinical trials. Alternatively, they can be used as topics for group discussion. Some exercises may also be suitable for use or adaptation by tutors as assessment tasks or seminar topics within a research methods module or class. The book is supported by supplementary learning materials available on the online resource site: https://study.sagepub.com/doingresearch4e

I hope that you will read *Doing Research in Counselling and Psychotherapy* in the spirit in which it was written – as an invitation to participate in a collective search for knowledge and understanding. Over the course of my career as a therapy researcher and research teacher, I have personally experienced research as an activity that has helped me to be a better therapist, enabled me to develop a better understanding of myself and my place in the world, and has brought me closer to other people. I have also witnessed the same outcomes in many other researchers and students with whom I have worked. We are at a point in history where we all face massive challenges in relation to our relationship with the planet and the nature that sustains us, our relationships with each other and our use of technology. As practitioners of counselling, psychotherapy and allied disciplines, we have a responsibility to do our bit to face up to these challenges. Science is both part of the problem and part of the solution. I passionately believe that critical appreciation of how science works, its breadth, and the distinctive strengths and limitations of different methodologies, along with a much expanded voice and presence for grassroots citizen science, are how we can tip the balance in the direction of therapy practice and research as being part of the solution.

Acknowledgements

I would like to acknowledge the support I have received from many colleagues who have been willing to share their knowledge and experience around research issues, and all of the students who have allowed me to guide them and accompany me on their research journey. I would also like to thank Susannah Trefgarne, Ruth Lilly, Victoria Nicholas and Neil Dowden at Sage who have provided invaluable editorial assistance. Finally, I owe the greatest debt to my wife Julia, my daughters Kate, Emma and Hannah, my grandchildren Eva, Isaac and Ella and my sons-in-law Edd and Jack.

Online resources

Head online to https://study.sagepub.com/doingresearch4e to access a range of online resources that will support teaching and aid learning.

Counselling and psychotherapy have become an integral part of systems of health and social care in modern societies. Research in counselling and psychotherapy plays a key role in ensuring the therapy received by clients, patients and service users is responsive to their needs. This book is intended to guide and support those undertaking therapy research for the first time.

Doing Research in Counselling and Psychotherapy, 4th Edition, is accompanied by:

For lecturers

A Teaching Guide providing exercises and case studies and guidance on how to use these in your teaching.

For students

A range of resources and activities to support your learning, including examples of research, journal articles, and useful weblinks.

1

Entering the World of Research

Introduction

The aim of this book is to encourage and support individuals and groups to carry out grassroots research into counselling, counselling psychology, career counselling, psychotherapy, or related topics in fields such as social work, mental health and coaching. The book is organised around the idea of a research journey: identifying a research question, deciding on the best way to investigate it, doing the research, and then finally disseminating what has been found. The emphasis is on manageable small-scale research projects that can be completed within a year. This process involves entering the world of therapy research – directly engaging with and utilising ideas and techniques that may previously have been studied in an academic context but now need to be implemented in everyday practice. For many novice (and experienced) researchers, the notion of doing scientific research and adding to formal published knowledge can be experienced as scary, overwhelming, intimidating and potentially humiliating. The present chapter, and additional material in the online resource site, seek to make these fears more manageable by describing the landscape of research in ways that demystify and humanise it, and make it possible to recognise research as a potential arena for undertaking work that is satisfying, personally meaningful and life-enhancing, as well as contributing to the common good.

Knowledge products

There is a sense in which any therapist who takes his or her work seriously is engaged in 'research', through activities such as observing what happens in a therapy session, keeping notes, testing hypotheses or hunches about what might be helpful for a client, identifying themes and patterns, reading about the client's problem, and so on. This kind of personal research is essential to good practice. However, it is different from the type of 'research' that comprises the therapy research literature: an understanding of research that views it as a collective, rather than an individual, undertaking. Throughout human history, but particularly over the past two hundred years, knowledge has advanced through the sharing and dissemination of knowledge products such as books, articles, reports, conference presentations, and so on. What researchers do is to create knowledge products that take their place in a vast cultural marketplace of knowledge. These items may ultimately be used and traded in ways that are beyond the control or imagination of the person who carried out the study. It can be helpful to regard the distinction between personal research (small 'r' research) and formal research (big 'R' research) as similar to the difference between a writer and an author. Many people gain great satisfaction and meaning from the experience of writing. But something different happens when that same work gets published – it becomes part of a collective literature.

Within this book, there is a strong and consistent emphasis on what needs to be done to arrive at a final end product that will fulfil the standards of the relevant knowledge marketplace. Achieving these standards can be a frustrating experience. The standards that prevail within the various different subdomains of therapy research are socially constructed – they arise from a consensus about what makes sense, what is acceptable, what readers and consumers of research will 'buy'. This consensus can change over time, in response to developments in both research methodology and as a reaction to powerful social and political forces.

One of the major implications of viewing research as a matter of 'making things' lies in the area of research training. Many research training courses and modules require students to learn about a wide range of methodological issues, with the assumption that it is necessary to possess a comprehensive knowledge of research methods in order to design a study. By contrast, if the task is to create a research product, it makes a lot more sense to adopt an apprenticeship model of training, where the novice researcher seeks to copy (or create a version of) a previous product, under the close supervision of an expert. Apprenticeship learning is primarily based on practice, with occasional time out to learn about underlying principles.

Box 1.1   Making is connecting

Research is a creative process of making products that have the possibility of being useful to other people. This way of thinking about research has been influenced and inspired by the work of the sociologist and media researcher David Gauntlett (2018). His earliest studies analysed the way that the emergence of personal websites and blogs created a space on the internet through which individuals could make connection with like-minded others, rather than merely being consumers of web pages published by governments and large organisations. Further reflection led him to see similarities with a wide range of other activities such as music-making, cooking and crafts, in terms of a common thread of making connections between people, and building social capital and resourcefulness. Conducting a therapy research study provides multiple possibilities for making connection – with those who have carried out similar studies in the past, or used similar methodologies, with research colleagues and co-workers, with therapists, clients and others with an interest in therapy, and with future users of your own work.

Doing better therapy

In accordance with the procedures required in the clinic where he works, Andy invites his clients to complete a symptom measure at the start of each session, with the aim of tracking progress. The client fills in the questionnaire, hands it to Andy, and they briefly discuss the ratings in terms of implications for their work together. Andy does not find these conversations to be helpful. On reflection, he realises that he has had bad experiences in the past in relation to getting negative feedback, and is being defensive around any suggestion that his therapy approach may not be helpful for a client. At the same time, he accepts the idea that being accountable is morally the right thing to do. He knows that his clients are pleased to be completing these questionnaires, because they are familiar with such processes in other settings. He tries to make sense of what is happening in terms of the concept of countertransference, but finds that these ideas do not entirely allow him to resolve his problem. He then turns to the research literature, and finds studies that reveal that he is not alone in having these difficulties (which is reassuring), convince him that feedback tools can actually be helpful in therapy (buttressing his motivation to find a solution) and allow him to learn about how other therapists respond to negative feedback. On the basis of these ideas, he was then able to develop different ways of responding to potentially critical feedback, rehearse these strategies in supervision, and implement them in his practice.

Betty works in private practice, and sees clients with a wide range of presenting problems. A potential client contacts her, seeking to enter therapy to support them through a stressful gender transition. Following an initial meeting with this client, Betty feels confident that she would be able to help this person. However, she has relatively little knowledge of issues associated with gender transition. To prepare herself, she reads some research studies that have explored transgender client experiences of what has been helpful and not helpful in therapy, and therapist experiences of working with such clients.

A community counselling service demonstrates a commitment to research-informed practice by not only collecting outcome and satisfaction data from clients, but also holding a monthly online journal club, in which one counsellor nominates a research study that is then read and discussed by all the therapists in the organisation. In the run-up to their annual away-day, they run a staff consultation poll on whether there are any ways in which service policies might need to be reviewed in the light of research evidence. There is then a two-hour discussion slot devoted to how priority suggestions might be taken forward. At this particular meeting, it is clear that both external research and statements on client satisfaction forms indicate that the service is not sufficiently responsive to client preferences around style of therapy, session scheduling and choice of therapist. A working group is set up to review the relevant literature, consult further with clients, and identify new procedures and training requirements around this aspect of practice.

These stories illustrate some possible ways that research knowledge can help practitioners to become better therapists, and therapy organisations to offer a better service to their clients. To do good research, it is necessary to have an appreciation of what research is for – how it can be *used*. One of the key tests for any piece of research is whether it makes a difference – the 'so what?' question. Although key figures in therapy such as Freud and Rogers have generated far-reaching theories that touch on fundamental issues of human existence, at the end of the day counselling and psychotherapy are practical activities. Therapy is about helping people who are experiencing emotional pain, who are stuck in their lives, who are acting in ways that may even be destroying them. Our responsibility as therapists is to do the best job we can, to be the best therapist we can be in the circumstances in which we find ourselves. Research findings can help us to achieve this.

A crucial challenge for therapy researchers is to carry out research that facilitates productive points of contact between research and practice. There are many ways that this can happen. For example, to make a connection between the findings of a research study and what is happening in a therapy case, a reader needs to be able to answer the question 'does this apply to me?', by being able to access as much information as possible about the social and cultural context of the study, and the characteristics of the client and therapist. Similarly, data collection and analysis procedures need to be reported in such a way that a practitioner-reader can see through the text and imaginatively re-create what happened in the therapy session or research interview that is being described.

Exercise 1.1   How might your research be used?

Take some minutes to reflect and make notes on the possible practical value of your research. This could be research that you are planning to undertake, or research that has been completed. In what ways might that research make a practical difference? What can you do to draw attention to, and promote, the practical value of your work? What examples have inspired you of therapy research that has had an impact on people's lives? In what way might your research be designed or planned to maximise its practical relevance? In what way might it be written up?

Research is a collective endeavour

The reason why scientific knowledge is taken seriously in our society is that it is based on the work of thousands of investigators over many decades. The research community has generated a network of knowledge, where each specific idea, statement or assumption in a research paper is linked to, and supported by, other studies and other theories carried out by different people in different locations. This is what gives research its credibility and persuasive power. The findings of a single study can be intriguing and stimulating. But the findings of a single study will never be taken as a basis for action until they are replicated, or supported by other types of evidence.

The construction of the research literature is organised around a constant process of critical appraisal. Researchers are people who ask awkward questions: Is this true? Is this valid? Are these conclusions justified by the evidence? How can we get better evidence in relation to this issue? The research literature is organised around sustained collective effort to build knowledge. Although there also needs to be space for innovative or maverick researchers who ask new questions, or open up new possibilities, for the most part the research literature reflects a gradual, cumulative progress towards a shared objective.

One of the main tasks for any new researcher is to become familiar with the research literature around their topic of interest. The process of arriving at an understanding of any subfield within the counselling and psychotherapy literature is a complex and demanding undertaking. It can be helpful to adopt a historical perspective, looking at how knowledge has been built up over time, because in any field of research there are likely to be interesting and potentially significant findings and directions that emerged at various stages but were then never fully exploited or explored. It is also helpful to track the evolution of different research methods that have been used and essential to read the literature from a critical perspective, with a feel for what is missing and what does not 'feel right'. This can be hard, because new researchers generally do not have enough time to immerse themselves in the literature, and may lack confidence in their ability to critically evaluate what they are finding. It can be useful, again, to adopt an apprenticeship model, and work with someone who already knows the literature well.

Deep truths

Philosophy is a manifestation of the human capacity and desire to make sense of the fundamental nature and meaning of all aspects of experience. Philosophers question basic assumptions: the difference between right and wrong, the possibility of free will, the criteria for deciding what causes what. Within the field of science and research, a philosophical perspective invites reflection on two key questions: (i) what are the assumptions about the ultimate nature of reality that underpin research methodologies, and (ii) what are the assumptions about the nature of truth, evidence and knowledge that inform the criteria that are used to evaluate the validity of a study? The first set of questions concern ontology (the nature of reality); the second set of questions relate to epistemology (the nature of knowledge). These are massively complex and challenging questions, because they reach to the edges of human understanding, that do not lend themselves to fixed answers and certainties, and engage with deep truths.

Many therapy researchers have found it valuable to see their work as being informed by three broad, alternative ontological and epistemological traditions: positivism/postpositivism, constructivism/interpretivism and critical/ideological (Ponterotto, 2005). At an ontological level, positivism/postpositivism assumes the existence of a single objective real world that is in principle knowable. Constructivism/interpretivism assumes that there is no single objective reality, and that what is experienced or defined as real is constructed through the minds of individual persons, and through culture, history and language. A critical/ideological ontological position argues that scientific research should focus on challenging oppression, and creating a more equal and just world. From a critical/ideological ontological stance, evidence from both positivist and interpretivist perspectives may be relevant to an overarching socio-political purpose. In terms of epistemology, positivism is associated with measurement and experimentation, constructivism/interpretivism is associated with qualitative methodologies that analyse the ways that meaning is created through language, and critical research defines knowledge as comprising action and critical consciousness. Although these three categories represent an oversimplified summary of some very challenging issues, they do provide a reasonable starting point from which to begin to make sense of the research process. For example, research that measures change in symptoms over large client data-sets sits within a positivist paradigm, and provides a medical-scientific way of knowing that is widely acknowledged within society as being important. By contrast, research in which clients are interviewed about their experience sits within a constructivist paradigm that sees persons as active intentional agents – a way of knowing that is consistent with the way that most therapists think about their practice. Finally, critical research that seeks to develop ways that therapy can be used to combat toxic masculinity, promote feminist consciousness and empower people from minority ethnic communities to combat racism are consistent with other forms of social activism that exist within society.

Developing an understanding and appreciation of philosophical ideas can help researchers to improve their methodologies. For instance, in recent years, developments in philosophical analysis of the nature of causality have led to new ways of gathering evidence and using evidence to inform practice that have been influential across the whole field of healthcare research (Anjum, Copeland & Rocca, 2020).

Philosophy is a major academic discipline, with its own training, technical language and knowledge base. It is neither possible nor necessary for therapy researchers to be experts in philosophy. What is important, instead, is for anyone undertaking therapy research to appreciate that what they are doing is based on underlying assumptions about knowledge that can be challenged and enriched by attention to relevant philosophical concepts and debates. This process depends on the field as a whole creating opportunities for dialogue between philosophers of science, and therapy researchers.

Methodological pluralism

Methodological pluralism is the idea that there are many ways in which reliable, valid and practically useful knowledge can be attained. Within the field of research in counselling and psychotherapy there has been a growing acceptance, over the past 20 years, that a pluralistic stance in relation to knowledge is necessary if real progress is to be made in bridging the gap between research and the complexity of practice. Historically, therapy research has been dominated by the methods and assumptions of psychology, which have emphasised the use of quantitative, statistical methods to analyse data derived from the experimental manipulation of variables. The dominant role of measurement in psychology arose from the need for psychology in the early years of the twentieth century to establish itself as a scientific discipline. As a result, the first generation of researchers in counselling and psychotherapy, in the 1950s and 1960s, made use of the research tools that they had been taught as psychology students, namely quantitative methods.

What has gradually become apparent, as the psychotherapy research community has grown, and as the research literature became substantial enough to function as a credible source of knowledge for practice, is that quantitative methods could only take us so far. There are many aspects of therapy that are better understood through the use of qualitative methods, such as open-ended interviews or intensive analysis of patterns within single cases. One of the distinctive characteristics of recent research in therapy has been a search for ways of combining information that has been collected using different methods.

This book is explicitly grounded in a methodologically pluralist perspective, in aiming to provide readers with an appreciative understanding of alternative approaches to evidence and inquiry that exist within the field of contemporary psychotherapy research.

Exercise 1.2   The relevance of methodological pluralism to your own area of interest

Within the topic or area of your own research, what are the different types of insight that have been provided by different types of research (e.g. controlled outcome studies, qualitative interview-based research, case study inquiry)? If there is an absence of evidence (or limited evidence) from a particular methodological approach, what difference might it make to policy, practice and theory if more of that type of study were to be published? What are the implications of what you have learned from this exercise, for the research question and choice of methodology in the research you are doing/planning to do yourself?

Social justice

There are some branches of scientific inquiry that are driven by a simple human desire to understand and make sense of the world. This type of work is sometimes described as 'blue skies' research. Even when it yields discoveries of practical value, such as new technologies, these are by-products that do not represent the underlying reason why the work was carried out in the first place. Therapy research is not like this. It is down to earth rather than being up in the sky. Counselling and psychotherapy are forms of practice in contemporary society that aim to help people to achieve learning, personal development and emotional healing.

An emphasis on practical knowledge opens up the question of who research is *for*. An increasing proportion of counselling and psychotherapy practitioners and researchers have arrived at the conclusion that both research and practice should be informed by a social justice agenda (Goodman & Gorski, 2015; Paquin, Tao & Budge, 2019). Yes, as therapists we are working to help individuals to overcome problems in living and maximise their potential. But unless we do this in a way that takes account of the wider society, all we are doing is papering over the cracks. If therapy is not aligned with other efforts to build a more sustainable and equal society, then it can be accused of impeding these initiatives. Attention to the potential contribution of counselling and psychotherapy to finding ways of responding to climate crisis, biodiversity loss and other forms of environment destruction represents a crucial element of such an endeavour (Mustakova-Possardt et al., 2014). Other aspects of social justice include racism, colonialism, white privilege, and sexism and violence towards women. Within the present book, a social justice perspective is expressed through critical reading of research articles, qualitative research into the experiences of clients from disadvantaged groups and a broad, justice-informed approach to research ethics.

Exercise 1.3　Paying attention to how wider purpose is explained in published research studies

As you read the research studies referenced in this book or accessible through the online resource site, or studies that you find on the basis of your own literature searching, it can be useful to look for, and make a note of, the ways in which authors explain the wider purpose of their investigations. How often do authors position their work in an equality, social justice or sustainability agenda? Do they do this explicitly or implicitly? Alternatively, how often, and in what ways, do they provide rationales based in a technical, managerial or individualist perspective? What is the impact on you, as a reader, of these alternative ways of grounding a study?

Reflexivity

A commitment to the development of self-awareness represents a key value for therapists. The majority of therapists participate in personal therapy at some point in their career, as well as a range of other personal development and self-care activities. Within society, therapists can be viewed as specialists in relationships, emotions and ways of thinking. The practice of therapy involves a capacity to reflect on, and find meaning in, therapist–client interaction. It is not surprising, therefore, that therapy researchers expect each other to be aware of the personal meaning of the research that they undertake. Paying attention to researcher reflexivity comprises one of the distinctive features of all types of therapy research.

The personal meaning of the research may sometimes operate as a source of bias, for instance in studies that mainly appear to have been carried out to confirm the researcher's pre-existing beliefs. However, there are also many other situations in which the personal awareness of the researcher represents a major strength and advantage. For example, personal experience of an issue may help to sensitise a researcher to aspects of that phenomenon, or may make it more likely that research participants will trust the researcher.

The implication here is not that therapy researchers should necessarily write at length in research papers about their life experiences, feelings and expectations about the topic, and so on. Doing so may be useful in some situations, but in other contexts it will just get in the way of telling the story of what was found. What is needed is a willingness to engage in ongoing reflexive self-monitoring, pay attention to the personal meaning of research and its emotional impact, and engage in conversations with colleagues about what comes up. This holds for both qualitative and quantitative researchers. In interviews with experienced researchers across a range of areas of psychology, Levitt et al. (2021) found that all of them, in their different ways, acknowledged that the subjectivity of the researcher was always a factor, whatever the topic being investigated. What they were concerned about was not subjectivity or the existence of researcher values, but the risk of being caught up in an illusion of objectivity.

Researcher reflexivity makes a crucial contribution to the trustworthiness of a study. The main consumers of research – therapy practitioners, supervisors, trainers and service directors – are individuals who have both personally invested a great deal of time and effort on learning to use particular therapy theories and interventions, and are acutely aware of their ethical responsibility to do the best for their clients. Altering practice on the basis of reading a research article is not, therefore, an easy choice to make. Being willing to allow oneself to be influenced by a research study depends not only on the methodological rigour of the study itself, but on how much the integrity of the researcher can be trusted. Researchers who come across as too confident in themselves and their findings (i.e. who are not reflexive) are less likely to be trusted.

Collaboration

The image of the lone seeker after truth can represent an attractive metaphor for many researchers. The seeker after truth sets off alone on a long journey of discovery, or withdraws from the everyday world to meditate in a cave, or wanders dreamlike around a garden like Isaac Newton or Charles Darwin, or whatever. This is a heroic and inspiring type of image, which has some relevance to what can happen during the research process. A lot of the time, the creative process of arriving at a new understanding may be facilitated by a period of immersion in the topic, which can be greatly aided by withdrawing from everyday demands. But it is also an incomplete image. The question being investigated by the seeker after truth is never just their own personal question – it is always one that has been asked before, in some shape or form, which has then been passed on to the seeker. Even on a journey of discovery someone will be cooking the meals or on the end of the line when the time comes to phone a friend. And at the end of that journey, the truth that has been uncovered will require an audience.

Historically, the way that counselling and psychotherapy research has been organised has had a tendency to promote an individualistic model of inquiry. Most published research studies will have been conducted by students, and there is pressure on students to be able to demonstrate that what they hand in is their own individual work. There is no university regulation that prohibits a student from doing their research as part of a team. But it is generally regarded as safer and clearer, for assessment purposes, if the project has transparently been a solo effort.

On the whole, successful scientific research is carried out by teams – in labs, research institutes and clinics. Historically, research teams have been based in a single geographical location, to make it possible to engage in regular conversation. In recent times, the internet has made it possible for researchers to collaborate even when they are located many thousands of miles from each other. Even in these situations, however, international research teams will usually find ways to organise face-to-face meetings on a regular basis.

The collective nature of research can be regarded as a source of potential enjoyment and personal development. Research relationships offer opportunities to spend time with people you like, or who stimulate personal growth and learning.

Exercise 1.4   Who is in your research team?

Who are the people available to you in relation to your research endeavours, or who might be available? How satisfying and supportive is your contact with these individuals? In what ways might the collaborative dimension of your research be enhanced? If you are at the stage of planning a research study, who can you recruit to your team? As well as people you might know at a personal level, such as friends, colleagues and research supervisors, what kinds of supportive relationships might it be possible for you to access within professional organisations? How diverse is your team – does it or could it include individuals whose experience of privilege and adversity is different from your own?

Conclusions

The guiding principles outlined above offer points of reference for anyone carrying out research in therapy. The following chapters provide guidelines and information on general research skills, such as using qualitative and quantitative methods, and then show how these skills can be applied to create different types of research product. Throughout all of these chapters, it may be helpful to refer back to basic principles, by reflecting on various questions: for example, ask yourself 'How does using this research method, or recruiting participants from this population, look when considered in light of the principle of generating practical knowledge, underlying philosophical concepts, my own reflexive knowledge, my position of social justice, etc.?' Such questions make it possible to reflect critically and constructively on the many decision points that can arise throughout the course of a research project.

Suggestions for further reading

A recent example of how writers on therapy research have explicitly sought to articulate research principles can be found in:

Paquin, J. D., Tao, K. W., & Budge, S. L. (2019). Toward a psychotherapy science for all: conducting ethical and socially just research. *Psychotherapy*, 56(4), 491–502.

Further discussion of the meaning and implications of a pluralistic position in relation to research methodology:

Smith, K. et al. (2021). A pluralistic perspective on research in psychotherapy: harnessing passion, difference and dialogue to promote justice and relevance. *Frontiers in Psychology*, 12:742676.

Strategies for carrying out research that is relevant to cultural and social justice issues:

O'Hara, C., Chang, C. Y., & Giordano, A. L. (2021). Multicultural competence in counseling research: The cornerstone of scholarship. *Journal of Counseling & Development*, 99(2), 200–209.

Online resources

Further activities to support learning around the topics introduced in this chapter can be found on the online resource site: https://study.sagepub.com/doingresearch4e.

2

Reading Research

Introduction

There are four main ways to learn about how to do research. The first way is to learn from other people, through some combination of classes, supervision, mentorship, apprenticeship and being part of a network of fellow-researchers. The second pathway to acquiring research competence is independent study – spending time reading research textbooks and methodology articles, and perhaps even philosophy of science sources, in order to build a fine-grained appreciation of which methodologies and techniques are appropriate for particular questions, and how they are implemented. A third strand of learning about research arises from the experience of the work: doing a study. The final strand is to read actual research studies. A research lecture or seminar, or conversation with a research supervisor, does not mean much without being able to refer to concrete examples of published studies. The ideas in a methodology textbook only come to life when they can be related to research products that have been shaped by the application of these concepts. Doing a study involves working towards the production of a research product that resembles those that already exist in the published literature.

In the opening stages of doing a research study, it is essential to become familiar with what is already known, in relation to the topic in which you are interested. The present chapter explains what this involves, in terms of both learning how to read and make sense of research papers, and beginning to explore and map the counselling and psychotherapy research literature.

For anyone who is using this book to inform their preparation for understanding a research study for the first time, it is recommended that this chapter should be read in tandem with the next, which focuses on how to develop a research question. It does not make a lot of sense to explore the research literature in the absence of some kind of notion of an intended or hoped-for research topic or question that provides an initial entry point. Equally, it is not possible to develop a research question in the absence of an appreciation of the types of research, and types of research question, that have gone before.

Making sense of research papers

Reading research studies is a key activity for any researcher. To be able to design and carry out a piece of research, it is essential to have a detailed understanding of what you are aiming for, in terms of what your final product might look like. Reading research studies also allows you to learn about research skills and knowledge, such as how to construct a line of argument or rationale for a study, and developing an appreciation of different options regarding how data are collected and analysed, how research participants are recruited and ethical dilemmas are handled, and how conclusions are structured. Over and above these specific skills, reading research papers makes it possible to begin to appreciate the importance of coherence in a research study – how all these elements fit together.

In the field of counselling and psychotherapy research, published articles either conform to the style guidelines of the American Psychological Association (APA), or represent a close variant of that model. The APA guidelines were developed in the 1950s, in response to a perceived need to standardise what at that time comprised a somewhat eclectic (and sometimes confusing) mix of publication formats. Over the years, the APA guidelines have gradually evolved – the most recent version was published in 2020 (APA, 2020; Cooper, 2020) – and have provided a publishing framework that enables readers to know where to find different types of information within an article. It is widely acknowledged that the APA structure is not ideal for qualitative studies, autoethnographic writing or single-case studies. However, even in these genres of therapy research article, authors and journal editors tend to use formats that draw on APA principles. As a result, it is essential for anyone engaged in therapy research to be able to find their way round a typical APA-informed research paper.

Box 2.1 The structure of a typical research paper

1. Title of the article.
2. Names and contact details of authors.
3. Abstract (brief summary of the paper) – typically no more than 300 words – sometimes with structured subheadings (Background, Aims, Method, etc.).
4. Key words (in alphabetical order).
5. Introductory section, which usually includes:

   a. the 'hook': an opening statement on the general interest and significance of the topic;
   b. literature review/summary: placing the study in the context of previous research, theory and policy debates;
   c. rationale for the study (how it fills a gap on existing knowledge);
   d. statement of the aims of the present study (the research question), and sometimes also a brief summary of the design of the study.

   Note: the Introduction follows a logical progression, and tells a story that starts with a general statement of the topic, narrowing this down to specific research that has been carried out in relation to the topic, drawing some conclusions about the gaps in the literature, explaining what kind of further research is now required and introducing the aims of the current study, which has been designed to fill some of these gaps. The Introduction is mainly written in the present tense (apart from the aims bit at the end) to reflect the fact that it is a statement of established fact.

6. Methods section, which usually includes a series of sections with subheadings such as:

   a. participants: those who took part in the study;
   b. measures/instruments: the techniques by which the data were collected;
   c. procedures: how the participants were recruited, what happened to them during the study;
   d. ethical issues and how they were addressed; ethical consent procedures; source of ethical approval;
   e. the researchers: sometimes in qualitative studies there is a brief paragraph describing the background and expectations of the researchers;
   f. analysis: the procedures/strategy for analysing the data (mainly found in qualitative studies).

   Note that the Methods section is usually written in the past tense – 'This is what we did'.

7. Results section. Here the factual findings of the study are presented, with no interpretation or explanation. If quantitative/statistical data are reported, there will always be a corresponding written statement that states what the numbers actually mean. This is also written in the past tense: 'This is what we found'.

8. Discussion.

   a. brief summary statement on what the study aimed to do, and what it claims to have found;

(Continued)

   b.   comparison of the results of the study in contrast to the results of previous studies (i.e. those mentioned earlier in the literature review – no new literature is introduced here), along with an interpretation of any contradictory findings (e.g. 'Our results contradict those of Smith and Jones (2002) because ...');

   c.   discussion of the implications of the findings for theory, further research and practice;

   d.   the limitations of the study;

   e.   conclusions.

9. References.

10. Appendices – e.g. a copy of the questionnaire or interview schedule that was used to collect data.

11. Supplementary material (e.g. data files) available online at the journal website.

12. Statement of any conflict of interest.

13. Biographical and contact details of author(s).

Footnotes and endnotes are rarely used in journals that publish counselling and psychotherapy research papers.

So why are research papers structured in this kind of standard template? The advantage of a standard structure is that it allows busy people to read a paper quickly. Studies carried out on the reading strategies of experienced researchers have found that they rarely read a research paper straight through from start to finish. First, they use the title, author list (what are these people up to?) and abstract to decide whether the paper is of interest. Then, if the paper is potentially relevant to them, they sample the aims statement, the method and the start of the discussion to assess the 'guts' of the argument. Only if there is anything puzzling or unexpected about the findings will they read the paper all the way through from the start; for example, to check whether the literature review has missed anything or is biased, if the procedures or sample were unusual in some way, or whether the authors might have missed something in the analysis.

The structure of a research paper can be thought of as similar to an egg-timer shape: it starts off broad (with a general statement of interest), narrows down to very specific details in the middle and finally broadens out again to conclude with general statements that look to the future.

A key skill, in terms of being able to use research to inform practice, is to be able to critically analyse the meaning, significance and implications of a research paper. (A 'research paper' can be defined as a journal article that directly presents the findings of a research study, and includes method, results and discussion sections.) Given the massive number of psychotherapy research studies that have been published, it is vital to develop strategies for reading papers quickly. In terms of the outline provided in Box 2.1, the title and abstract of a paper are usually sufficient to indicate whether a paper is potentially relevant to your area of interest. Titles and abstracts are readily available on journal websites, bibliographic search engines used by university and college libraries, and Google Scholar. If a paper looks as though it merits closer inspection, it is then useful to scan it briefly, paying particular attention to the rationale and research question, sample and data collection procedures/measures, and the brief summary at the start of the discussion section. In some papers, the introductory literature review is worth reading on its own, as a succinct overview of research on a specific topic. This level of reading can be sufficient to grasp the gist of what a paper has to offer. Only if there is a sense that there is something not quite right about a paper, or if it is particularly relevant to your own research (or practical) interests, is it necessary to read it closely line by line.

There are two standpoints from which to read a research paper. Most of the time, papers are read in order to keep up to date about developments in the field, and to build background knowledge and awareness. Less frequently, a paper may be potentially so significant or relevant that it is necessary to read it very closely. Because research papers need to meet both of these requirements, they typically struggle to fulfil either of them in a completely satisfactory manner. Papers tend to have too much technical detail for the reader seeking awareness and background knowledge, and too little for those who might want to use the study to guide their own research or their therapy practice. In the latter case, a study should at least provide an indication of where the reader might be able to find the additional information that they require.

It can be extremely helpful to be able to discuss a paper with others who have read it, for instance in meetings of a research group, or at a journal club. Different people see different things in the same paper, with the result that sharing responses to an article generally produces an enhanced level of understanding. It can also be helpful to read particularly important papers on more than one occasion. New insights and ideas emerge on a second or third reading at a later date. It can also happen that you may realise that you have misremembered what was actually written in a paper.

An essential resource, in relation to learning how to both appreciate and critically evaluate a research article, is: T. Greenhalgh (2019). *How to Read a Paper: The Basics of Evidence-based Medicine and Healthcare*. 6th edn. Chichester: Wiley-Blackwell. Although this book is primarily aimed at doctors, its author, Trisha Greenhalgh, is a researcher whose work encompasses a broad range of medical, social science and philosophical perspectives, and is a leading figure in the current movement to develop ways to make research more relevant for practice.

Learning activities around skills for critically evaluating a research paper are available on the online resource site.

Exercise 2.1   Reading research papers

It is only by reading actual studies that you can begin to build up an appreciation of how different stages in the research process fit together, and a feel for what works and what doesn't work in respect of generating useful knowledge in relation to your areas of interest. Reading research papers quickly and effectively is a skill that takes time to develop. How many research papers do you read in an average week? Would it be helpful, in terms of deepening

(Continued)

your engagement with research, to read more research articles? How could you accomplish this? Are you able to access research articles? If you are not able to find and download relevant research papers, what can you do to make this possible?

Finding your way around the counselling and psychotherapy research literature

Becoming familiar with the research literature is an essential aspect of the planning phase of any research study (McLeod, 2013a). Thorough, appreciative, careful and critical reading of the research literature fulfils several crucial purposes:

1. *Not re-inventing the wheel.* No matter how esoteric your research topic seems to be, it is almost certain that someone has studied it (or something like it) before. It is always best to find whatever previous research has been done, and build on this, rather than designing a study completely from scratch.
2. *Ensuring that your research has the maximum impact.* Practical, research-based knowledge consists of findings from a network or web of interlocking research studies. Scientific knowledge is like a mosaic or jigsaw – each new tile or piece fills a space in a bigger picture or pattern. No single research study can ever be rigorous enough to yield reliable knowledge, taken in isolation. The existence of a rich literature of interconnected studies ensures that the findings of each study are supported by findings from other studies, and the limitations of any particular study are counterbalanced by corresponding strengths elsewhere in the literature. As a consequence, if readers cannot see how your research is embedded within the literature, they are likely to ignore it.
3. *Finding the research tools and methods that are most appropriate for your question.* It is always a challenge to collect data that do justice to the process and outcome of therapy, or the experiences and attitudes of clients and therapists. It is similarly difficult to analyse such data in a manner that arrives at valid conclusions. In response to these challenges, researchers are continually developing new methods, in the form of measures, observation rating systems, interview schedules and other techniques.
4. *Ensuring that your research meets the required standard.* It is hard to achieve reliable, valid and ethically sound knowledge in any field of inquiry. Researchers are always looking for ways to do research better. Current research is always informed by an ongoing cycle of critical debate and methodological innovation. As a result, standards change over time. What was considered good research practice 20 years ago is unlikely to be regarded as such today. If your research does not take account of such ever-shifting quality thresholds there is a risk that it may be viewed as lacking in credibility.

These factors, taken together, demonstrate why the experience of doing research always needs to involve a willingness to become immersed in the relevant literature. However, it is also vital to be realistic. For example, it is not possible for undergraduate and Master's-level researchers to gain a comprehensive understanding of the literature in their area of inquiry, because of the limited amount of time available to them. By contrast, there is a general expectation that a doctoral candidate will, at the point of submitting their thesis/dissertation, be a world expert on their chosen topic. Developing an in-depth knowledge of the literature represents an aspect of the inquiry process where it is extremely helpful to be able to function as an apprentice, and be guided through the relevant literature by a research supervisor or mentor who already possesses a close familiarity with that particular body of work.

Mapping existing knowledge: practical skills and strategies

This section primarily focuses on the kind of preparatory literature review that needs to be carried out prior to designing a research study and writing a research proposal. More advanced skills and techniques are required when conducting a research review that is intended to be published as a stand-alone paper. There is a considerable degree of overlap between the work involved in a preparatory review and a publishable review. A key difference is around how each type of review is written up and reported: in a published review paper there is an expectation that the review methodology will be transparently explained. In addition, the ultimate aim of a published review is to present a comprehensive analysis of the state of knowledge in relation to a specific question, whereas the task of a preparatory review is to provide a rationale for a new study, framed in terms of how it connects with relevant studies that are already available in the published literature.

Conducting a literature review is a practical skill. As with any other practical skill, practice is necessary to improve performance. A first attempt to conduct a research review is typically associated with frustration and wasted time. Literature reviewing is one of the most intellectually challenging aspects of the research process, because it requires an effective combination of 'big picture' conceptualisation of an area of knowledge, along with detailed critical analysis of specific papers. There are five main areas of skill that need to be developed: *searching, organising, reading research papers, quality evaluation* and *time-management*.

Searching skills consist of a set of competencies associated with the task of identifying relevant items of literature. The first step is to be able to generate appropriate search terms. A search term is a word or phrase that serves as a 'tag' or label for the topic being reviewed. The task of a reviewer involves scanning the literature looking for these tags. A lot of the time, research in a particular area of interest may have been described using a range of tags. For example, I have been interested in the topic of what clients want from therapy. Research in this area has used many different terms or concepts: attitudes, expectations, beliefs, preferences, credibility of therapy, insider knowledge. In order to find interesting studies, I need to keep a lookout for all of these terms in the titles, abstracts and key words lists of articles. The next step in searching involves deciding on where to look: online databases such as PsycInfo or Medline, general databases such as Google Scholar, and reference lists of published books and articles. The university with which I am affiliated is typical in providing a general search box that provides a single point of access to all the material in the library, and all the external databases to which the library subscribes. How far to take this? Sometimes it can be helpful to contact leading researchers, to ask them if there are any relevant studies they know about that not yet been published. Once you have made a start on a search, and are able to identify some relevant studies, Google Scholar is a valuable tool in terms of moving the search forward, and building a picture of how an area of research has unfolded over time. Entering the details of a study in the Google Scholar search box, then clicking on the 'cited by' button, leads to a list of all subsequent books and articles that have referenced the initial source article. As with any search tool, this is not infallible, and will always generate hits to studies that are not what you are looking for (as well as missing items that may be highly relevant). Nevertheless, it can be a helpful search strategy. It is important to regard literature searching as similar to detective work – there is no one method (e.g. interviewing witnesses, DNA, fingerprints) that is guaranteed to lead to the solution. Effective reviewing always depends on using multiple search strategies.

Organising skills consist of a set of competencies that are applied to the job of keeping track of the information that is generated by the search process. There are bibliographic tools, such as EndNote, Mendeley and Zotero (and many others), that are able to copy online reference details into the personal database of the researcher, where they can be organised, categorised, commented upon and reformatted. Reviews of these and similar products can be found on the internet. Alternatively, it is possible to construct a similar system just using Word files. If the intention is to publish a formal review article, a record needs to be kept of how many items were generated using each search term, and the basis on which some were rejected and others were retained for detailed scrutiny. Whether or not a detailed search log is maintained, decisions need to be made about the extent to which it is sufficient to read the abstract of a study, or whether a more in-depth appraisal of the entire document is required (and whether this is better done using a paper copy rather than on-screen). One way or another, anyone carrying out a literature review needs to develop a robust and effective filing system.

Reading skills are important, as a core skill in all of this concerns the ability to read a research paper in an efficient manner. For anyone who has not been trained in psychology or one of the sciences, the structure of a typical quantitative research paper can seem strange, confusing and mysterious. For individuals who do have a background in science or psychology, the structure and language of many qualitative research articles can be equally opaque. After a while, most readers become familiar with the way that research papers are written, and can quite rapidly extract the information they need from any paper that they come across. But to begin with, this can prove to be a slow process.

Quality evaluation skills always play a part in the review process. When drawing conclusions from the research literature, it is essential to find some way of differentiating between studies that provide strong and credible evidence, and studies that are less convincing. One way of doing this is to include only studies published in journals that use a peer-review procedure. Another way is to evaluate or screen each potentially relevant study by using a rating scale for methodological quality. A further strategy involves being as inclusive as possible, using any credible articles that can be found, then incorporating into the review a commentary on the particular methodological strengths and weaknesses of each item. Quality criteria for evaluating therapy studies are discussed in more detail in Chapter 6.

Time-management skills are often a factor in literature reviewing, for a variety of reasons. Quite often, an article or book may be identified as relevant to the review, but may not be immediately accessible, and will need to be ordered through a library, thus leading to a delay. Careful and critical reading of research articles is time-consuming. Also, reading one article may generate new ideas about further directions that the review might take, leading to a renewed search cycle. All of this may be happening right at the start of a project, when as a researcher you will be under pressure of time to meet a deadline for submitting your proposal. For these reasons, it is important to plan carefully around when and how a review is to be carried out. For example, it can be useful to devote an intensive block of time to a review as early as possible, as a means of getting into the literature and accumulating key articles or sending off for them. This makes it possible for the next available blocks of time to consist of more relaxed reading of items as they come in, culminating in a final intensive block of time when everything comes together into an actual review document.

There are many sources of training and support available to researchers, in relation to these areas of skill. University library staff tend to possess high levels of expertise around searching skills and organising skills, and may offer training workshops and/or tutorial help on an individual or small group basis. There are also websites that offer information on quality evaluation procedures, and many review articles include information on the quality evaluation approach that was adopted and the rationale behind it. Research training courses and research supervisors are good places to look for ideas about reading research papers and time management. For practitioners, practice research networks should be able to offer support in all of these areas.

Exercise 2.2 What are the key words in your area of interest?

Allow yourself at least 30 minutes to reflect in a creative way on all of the possible concepts and terms that might be relevant to your chosen research topic or question. Think about the ways in which the topic might be understood within different theoretical frameworks, and the specific terminology that may have been used within these paradigms. Also think about the way that the topic has been defined and understood within different areas of practice or professional communities. Once you have generated a list or mind-map of key words, identify the terms that are likely to have been most widely used in the literature, and which would offer the best start-points for your literature search.

What to look for

Reviewing the literature is not a matter of wandering around a body of knowledge, in the hope that some conclusions will emerge through a process of osmosis. To gain maximum advantage from time spent reading the literature, you need to be as clear as possible about what you are looking for. The following questions can be helpful in terms of organising a search process:

How is this topic conceptualised and theorised?

What are the main debates or controversies within this area of inquiry?

What are the various methodologies and research instruments and tools (e.g. specific questionnaires or interview schedules) that have been deployed within this area of knowledge?

What are the ethical issues associated with this area of inquiry? How have these issues been addressed?

Are there distinct lines of inquiry or sequences of studies that can be identified? Or: to what extent is this area of knowledge fragmented, with studies making few references to other studies?

What do we know now, in terms of conclusions that can be made with confidence?

To what extent, and in what ways, are these conclusions conditional on, or associated with, specific populations (e.g. true for people in one culture) or specific methodologies (e.g. different findings emerge from qualitative and quantitative studies, or from the use of different quantitative measures)?

What is missing from the literature?

What do we need to know next (i.e. what do authors identify as necessary directions for further research)?

From the perspective of doing a preparatory literature review, as groundwork for your own research project, a good metaphor for the review process is to view it as hunting for treasure. There are three types of treasure to look out for. The first type consists of glittering and wonderful studies that stand out from the rest. Such studies may not necessarily exist within a particular topic area, but if they do they deserve to be showcased within the review that is being compiled. The second type of treasure is a variant on the first type, namely hidden treasure. Sometimes, within studies, there will be nuggets of information that may not have been recognised by the authors as particularly glittering, but whose value shines out when seen from the context of your own particular field of interest. The third type of treasure consists of personal epiphany studies that immediately strike a chord in terms of what you as a researcher are hoping to achieve. An epiphany moment may be linked to an aspect of the design or methodology of the study, or the way that the samples were recruited, that represents a vital piece of your own personal inquiry jigsaw.

Another type of study to be treasured consists of those that are most similar to the investigation that you as a researcher intend to carry out. When the time comes to write up your study, or defend it in a viva, one of the key questions that you will need to answer will be this: 'What does your research build on, or represent the next step on from, in terms of how it connects up with previous research?'

A review of the literature involves building a general understanding of an area of inquiry that will provide a backdrop and context for your own work. But it is also, at least in part, a search for studies, or even bits of studies, that can function as templates or exemplars. To know when you have found such treasures or pearls, you need to be able to trust your own feelings and intuition about what is significant.

Box 2.2 Each study is a microcosm of the literature

The authors of research papers have been through the same process that you are following, in respect of assembling an overview of previous research to provide a context and rationale for their own study. In the introduction to any research articles they publish, they offer you a condensed version of their take on the literature. Paying close attention to intro sections of articles is one of the simplest ways to get a feel for the literature on a topic.

Issues and challenges

There are many issues and challenges that frequently arise in relation to the task of reviewing the therapy research literature. Here are some of the most frequently voiced ones.

Too much literature

Sometimes, a literature search rapidly generates several hundred items that are potentially relevant. For example, a review of 'the effectiveness of psychotherapy for depression' or 'the relative effectiveness of psychotherapy vs medication for depression' would produce several hundred hits, including a large number of empirical studies. This situation can be overwhelming and scary for novice researchers. There are, however, several strategies for dealing with this eventuality. One approach is to start by looking for existing reviews. If a lot of research has been carried out on a topic, then it is highly likely that someone, or several different research teams, will have already subjected it to a systematic review. It may then be sufficient to conduct a 'review of reviews'. Alternatively it may make sense to anchor your own review in the most recent published review, or the most rigorous review, and add on any examples of studies conducted since the cut-off date of the published review.

Another strategy is to narrow the focus of the review. For example, a search for studies on the effectiveness of therapy for depression will generate a large number of items, whereas a search for studies on the effectiveness of *psychodynamic* therapy for depression will generate a somewhat smaller number of items. Focusing on effectiveness of psychodynamic therapy for depressed *men* narrows it again – or depressed *older* men. Narrowing your review may be a good choice in any case, because the study you are planning to carry out will almost certainly inevitably consist of a specific form of therapy, or focus on a specific participant group.

Not enough literature

Another scary scenario for novice researchers arises if the review turns up nothing, or next to nothing. For example, my guess is that even the most thorough search for studies of the experience and significance of tummy-rumbling in therapy would be unlikely to produce much more than four studies (Da Silva, 1990; King, 2011; Raymond, 2017; Sussman, 2001). This is despite the fact that gut sounds are both theoretically interesting (as manifestations of transference and countertransference) and attended to in some types of body therapy practice. It is possible that these four studies could provide a sufficient platform for further research. However, it would not be a substantial platform. In this instance, it may make sense to expand the review, to include other similar phenomena. There may be studies on other bodily events in therapy sessions, such as the client feeling sick, crying or getting a headache. There is certainly a literature on the broader topic of non-verbal communication in therapy. Another strategy is to search within studies. It may be that tummy-rumbling is mentioned in passing in some studies of the client's experience of therapy, or in some case studies. Finding such evidence, when a concept is not flagged up in the abstract of a study, takes a lot of time and effort. In the end, it may be that all that can be done will be to offer a practical or theoretical rationale for investigating a neglected topic, and acknowledge that it has not been studied to any great extent in the past.

It is a mistake to regard the issues and challenges that can arise during the process of conducting a literature review as personal failings, or to fall into the trap of believing that there is one correct solution that the researcher can arrive at through personal diligence. These are problems that are part of the intrinsic messiness of the research process. In most circumstances, there will be many ways that the issue can be satisfactorily resolved. Investment in dialogue, where you can share and discuss the pros and cons of the various possible ways forward, is usually the best way to go.

Exercise 2.3   Getting inside key studies

When you search the literature, it is probable that you will find several studies that are relevant but not particularly thrilling, along with a smaller number that really capture your interest. What are the two or three essential studies that you have unearthed during your search? Read these studies carefully, and on more than one occasion. Try to get 'inside' each study. What are these studies telling you about how to go about investigating your chosen research topic? What are they saying to you about what not to do?

Conclusions

For anyone undertaking a therapy research study, placing their research in the wider context of the research literature is a vital and challenging task. It is essential both to take this task seriously and to be realistic about what can be achieved. There is a massive amount of therapy research that is published every year, and it can be hard to find an initial foothold in what can seem like a daunting and impenetrable mountain of knowledge. The message of this chapter is that reviewing the literature is a skill that gets easier with practice. The intention of the chapter has been to suggest some starting points and strategies.

Suggestions for further reading

Maps of the counselling and psychotherapy research landscape (and various territories within it) are available in:

Barkham, M., Lutz, W., & Castonguay, L. (eds) (2021). *Bergin and Garfield's Handbook of Psychotherapy and Behavior Change*. 7th edn. New York: Wiley. Chapters on current research findings and directions, written by leading figures.

Cooper, M. (2008) *Essential Research Findings in Counselling and Psychotherapy: The Facts are Friendly*. London: Sage. Provides an overview of the therapy research literature and what it contains.

Gelo, O. C. G., Pritz, A., & Rieken, B. (eds) (2015). *Psychotherapy Research: Foundations, Process, and Outcome*. New York: Springer. Includes a critical history of psychotherapy research, written by Braakmann (2015), followed by chapters written by expert researchers, surveying a broad range of methodological approaches.

McLeod, J. (2013). *An Introduction to Research in Counselling and Psychotherapy*. London: Sage. An introduction to how the therapy research literature is organised, and how it has been shaped by social and cultural factors.

McLeod, J. (2019). *An Introduction to Counselling and Psychotherapy: Theory, Research and Practice*. 6th edn. London: Open University Press. (Chapter 22: The historical context of contemporary practice.)

Midgley, N., Cooper, M., & Sparkes, J. (2017). *Essential Research Findings in Child and Adolescent Counselling and Psychotherapy*. London: Sage. Comprehensive account of topics and findings from research into therapy for children and young people.

Ochs, M., Borcsa, M.. & Schweitzer, J. (eds) (2020). *Systemic Research in Individual, Couple, and Family Therapy and Counseling*. Springer: Cham. Current research issues and directions in therapy with couples and families.

Practical guides to exploring the literature:

Aveyard, H. (2018). *Doing a Literature Review in Health and Social Care: A Practical Guide.* 4th edn. London: Open University Press.

Bell, J., & Waters, S. (2018). *Doing Your Research Project: A Guide for First-time Researchers.* London: Open University Press.

Thomas, R. (2019). *Turn your Literature Review into an Argument: Little Quick Fix.* Thousand Oaks, CA: Sage.

Online resources

The online resource site (https://study.sagepub.com/doingresearch4e) includes practical examples and exercises around reading research papers and exploring the literature.

3

Developing Your Research Question

Introduction

Research is guided by questions. The aim of research is to be able to answer questions and generate new questions that open up previously taken-for-granted areas of experience. So where do such questions come from? Some counselling and psychotherapy research is stimulated by 'burning questions' that arise from practical experience. But many other would-be researchers, particularly those faced with the demand to choose a research topic that will have to be pursued for a college or university degree, can become blocked and uncertain at this point. There are so many potential topics from which to select. Considerations of relevance, importance, practicability, legitimacy and interest value flood in, making the choice even harder. In yet other situations, the research question is given or handed over – the researcher is recruited to work within an already existing programme of research, and has relatively little scope to influence the direction that the study will take.

Formulating a research question (or set of questions) represents a key step in the research process, because it involves moving from a general topic to a specific, focused investigation of some aspect of that topic. If you are doing research, people will ask you what you are doing research *on*. They may also ask what you are *looking at*. These images imply the existence of a research topic that is something 'out there' in the external world. A research *topic* usually refers to a broad area of interest, within which many questions can be asked. By contrast, a research *question* is like a searchlight that illuminates parts of this area of interest, or like a tool for dissecting it or digging into it. Areas of interest are expressed in book titles and chapter titles. The titles of research studies are (or should be) highly focused. If you have a research question that reads like the title of a book or a chapter in a book, chances are that it is not yet sufficiently focused, concrete and specific to operate successfully as a research question.

The aim of this chapter is to offer some ideas about how to arrive at an interesting, relevant and feasible research question. We begin by thinking about where research topics come from, and how to choose a topic. The next section of the chapter introduces some strategies for refining and focusing the topic into a set of specific and researchable questions. The chapter concludes by exploring the language of research questions, and ways that different research methodologies are associated with different types of question.

For anyone who is using this book to inform their preparation for undertaking a research study for the first time, it is recommended that this chapter should be read alongside Chapter 2, which focuses on reading research articles and exploring the research literature. It is not possible to develop a research question in the absence of an appreciation of the types of research, and types of research question, that have gone before. Equally, it does not make a lot of sense to read the research literature in the absence of at least some notion of the intended research topic or question.

What follows is primarily aimed at novice researchers. By the time you have completed a research study, you will have no shortage of research questions that you will want to pursue. In research, one thing always leads to another: a research study usually generates more questions than it answers.

Exercise 3.1   Demystifying research questions

The aim of the present chapter is to provide anyone who is intending to carry out a therapy research study with an opportunity to consider the ins and outs of what is involved in formulating a research question. Different sections of the chapter invite you to look at the concept of a research question from a variety of perspectives. However, at the end of the day a research question needs to be framed as a straightforward statement that will make sense to a reasonably educated lay person. A good way to get a feel for what a research question looks like is to collect examples of research questions from published studies. There are many research studies referenced in this book, and others that can be accessed through the online resource site. In each of these studies, there will be a brief two- or three-sentence statement of the research question, or the aims of the study, that can be located somewhere towards the end of the Introduction to the paper (and just before the Method section begins). Have a look at them.

Box 3.1   What makes a good research question?

Generations of researchers have found the FINER framework invaluable as a way of reflecting on the adequacy of their research question, and where it could be sharpened up. FINER stands for feasible, interesting, novel, ethical and relevant (Hulley et al., 2007).

Deciding on a research topic

There are many sources of research ideas, and many counselling and psychotherapy research studies that need to be carried out. The choice of a research topic, from within the many possibilities that exist, is a personal matter. Before committing to a research topic, it is necessary to devote some time to exploring various possibilities.

Sources of research ideas

Possible research topics do not exist in a vacuum as abstract ideas. Rather, the meaning of any potential research idea is always embedded within a complex web of social, interpersonal and personal relationships and meanings. For anyone thinking about embarking on a research journey, unravelling this web can be helpful in clarifying the personal pay-off of alternative research directions. It is possible to identify four main sources for research ideas.

The existing research literature

There are many research possibilities to be found within the literature. Within any specific area of research, there are ongoing research programmes that cry out for the application of a particular research methodology or theory to a new population, or the replication of existing findings. It is not hard to find neglected lines of inquiry that have been opened up but not been pursued fully. Research papers often conclude by identifying areas for further research. Occasionally, leading researchers will review progress on research into a particular topic, and make suggestions regarding future research priorities. Choosing a research topic that has emerged from the research literature has the advantage of making it rather easier to justify the study, make connections to previous literature and choose a methodology – all of these factors are already taken care of.

Policy and practice initiatives

There is a continuous stream of calls for research, and funding initiatives, that emerge from government departments and other organisations. For example, in recent years the issues associated with an ageing population have resulted in many research initiatives around the care of older people. There are also many policy and practice research project ideas generated at a local level by counselling and psychotherapy agencies and service providers. For example, annual reports from therapy agencies may indicate those agencies' desire to collect information on certain aspects of their work. Alternatively, when asked, managers may have a clear idea of what it is they need to know in order to make their organisation more effective. In addition, local agencies may have ideas about research projects that they would like to develop in response to government initiatives. Choosing a research topic that fits with national or local policy and practice initiatives is a good way to ensure organisational collaboration, and perhaps even some funding. This kind of project also easily passes the 'so what?' test, as the potential social value of the study has been established by experts in the field.

Personal contact

A valuable source of research ideas comprises other people with whom one might wish to work. These individuals could be members of an existing research network or interest group, or potential research supervisors, mentors or colleagues. Selecting a research topic that is aligned with, or part of, ongoing research carried out by others may represent a particularly attractive option for new researchers, because it offers the possibility of support from others and perhaps also the chance to learn in an apprenticeship role. The disadvantage of making this kind of choice is that it may involve abandoning, or compromising, one's own personal cherished research ideas.

Personal 'burning questions'

What does the question mean to you personally? Almost all practitioner research projects, as well as many student research projects, are motivated by a burning interest, a need to know more about some area of experience. This source of research ideas may include topics associated with first-hand experience as a client or therapist, or second-hand observation of episodes in the life of a close family member. These root experiences may be positive ('I want to demonstrate the importance of spirituality as a factor in therapy') or negative ('I want to draw attention to the risks of a particular type of therapy'). The advantages of working with a research topic that is personally highly meaningful are that the researcher is highly motivated and may possess special insight into the topic. The disadvantages are that the researcher may find it difficult to make connections between their unique experience and the existing literature, may come across as biased, and may be too emotionally involved to complete the study successfully.

To some extent, the majority of research topics will connect in some way or another with all four of these sources. However, within any specific topic area, the relative weighting of the four sources is unlikely to be completely equal.

Exercise 3.2   Reflecting on the sources of your research ideas

Give yourself some time to write about, reflect or discuss with a colleague potential research topics that are associated with each of these four sources: the literature, policy and practice initiatives, people you might work with and personal interest. Map out the pros and cons, for you, of pursuing questions that originate in different sources.

The personal meaning of the research

In big, programmatic research studies, the research question may have been laid down by someone else (a principal investigator, a government committee), with the result that it might possess only limited personal meaning for the person or people actually carrying out the research. By contrast, the kind of practitioner research or student research undertaken by readers of this book tends not to be like that. Such research is much more integrated with the life of the researcher, and so it is important to be aware of the conscious and implicit meanings that such an investigation may hold. Some of the reasons for examining the personal meaning of research include:

- avoiding potential sources of bias, for example through collecting data that 'confirm' what the researcher needs to believe;
- making the research more alive and interesting, and not getting trapped into a sense that the topic is alienating and distant;
- creating the possibility of drawing on emotional and spiritual sources of understanding, to augment cognitive/intellectual analysis of the topic;
- being clear about what you want from the research – for example, are you intending or hoping that completion of the research will open up new career opportunities (and if so, how might the choice of topic and the way that topic is investigated, make the maximum contribution to accomplishing that goal)?;
- from a psychotherapeutic perspective, creating the conditions for using 'countertransference' reactions to the research in a positive or constructive way: all researchers have feelings about the work they do; therapy researchers possess the skills and awareness to begin to understand what these feelings might mean;
- acting in accordance with a view of scientific inquiry which questions the role of the detached scientific 'observer', and holds instead that knowledge is intrinsically linked to personal interests and values.

Becoming aware of the personal meaning of research can be a painful process. In my own work, for example, I know that the research I have done into experiential groups, and into storytelling in therapy, has been closely tied to areas in which I have a strong personal need to learn. It is as if there has been a personal gap that research has helped to fill. That research has been personally enabling but also disturbing. In carrying it out I have been sensitive to the danger that exploring personally meaningful issues solely through research could lead in the direction of an over-intellectualised kind of pseudo-resolution that could cut off what are much more important emotional and interpersonal dimensions of who I am, or can be, in relation to these areas of my life. Research as a way of knowing needs to operate alongside other ways of knowing, such as practical action or therapy. Other dangers include inarticulacy (learning about the research topic at a feeling level, but having difficulty putting it into words), and being personally 'thrown' by what the research uncovers.

One of the consequences of examining the personal meaning of a research topic may be a decision *not* to pursue that topic. It could turn out that opening up a set of issues by subjecting them to research inquiry could lead to so much personal material being generated that it might be difficult to complete the project in the time allocated. For example, this can happen when someone researches an issue that is linked to a problematic life episode. One student was drawn to studying the experience of people who had been hospitalised during psychological breakdown. His interest in this question was derived from a similar experience he had undergone in his adolescence. As the research progressed, he found that more and more memories of this painful episode in his life were intruding into the research process. He decided to change topics and carry out his research on a different question.

The personal meaning of a research topic may be bound up with the meaning of doing research itself. For some people, carrying out a research study for a Master's degree or doctorate may have great personal significance, in defiantly demonstrating their intellectual abilities: 'At last I'll show them that I am just as clever as my brother/sister, etc.' Other researchers may have a strong sense of responsibility towards the subjects of the research, a desire to use that research to help people in need, perhaps by using the findings to justify services and resources for those clients. Still others may be driven by a wish to be a heroic innovator, to make new discoveries (Freud was one of these). All of these factors can have an effect on the ultimate form that the research question takes.

Exercise 3.3   Exploring the personal meaning of potential research topics

What is the personal meaning of each potential research topic that you are considering? What are the points of connection between the topic and your life as a whole? To what extent might these points of connection make a positive contribution to the experience of doing the study, and to what extent might they be a hindrance?

Identifying the audience

One strategy for narrowing down the field and converging on a specific research topic is to think ahead to the end of the study and ask yourself 'Who is this for? Who is the intended audience for my research?' There are basically four audiences for counselling and psychotherapy research: the person doing the research; other counsellors, managers and policy makers; the general public; and other researchers. The interests of these different audiences are not by any means the same, although they will to some extent overlap. Research that is intended to have an impact on counsellors' practice will be likely to rely on case reports, and include detailed descriptive material on clients and interventions. Policy-oriented studies require data that can be used to address issues of cost–benefit and cost-effectiveness. Articles for the general public need to include vivid examples and case histories. Research aiming to advance the literature must be explicitly linked to issues, theories and methods already identified as important in previously published work. The anticipated audience or 'market' for a piece of research can be seen to have a crucial influence on the way a study is carried out, the type of methods that are used and the form in which this is written up.

Once a researcher has selected their audience or audiences, it will be helpful to look at the kinds of research reports that have been published for that group. If the intended audience is identifiable and accessible (e.g. other therapists in a professional association, the management executive of an agency, key contributors to the research literature), it can be productive to go and ask them about the kind of study they would like to see carried out. It is worth noting, with some regret, that at the present moment it is difficult to envisage *clients* as consumers of research, except in so far as clients or would-be clients will read popular articles in newspapers and magazines.

A key factor in the choice of audience is the function that the research is intended to have in the personal or professional development or broader 'life projects' of the person carrying it out. The choice of research question is an issue that can usefully be worked on in personal therapy, or explored with supportive friends or colleagues. It is essential to be aware, for example, of the implications of tackling an investigation into a question that is very personal. With highly personal studies, a researcher may find it difficult to gain enough distance from their own individual experience to be able to grasp the bigger picture implied in the experiences of others. Also, it may be hard to write up autobiographical material that still evokes strong, raw feelings. There are other literary forms, such as novels, autobiographies or poetry, that may be more appropriate in allowing a voice to the person. On the other hand, a research study that does not connect with any personal experience runs the danger of becoming dry and lacking in motivation and sparkle. If a research project is to be located within the context of the career development of the person carrying it out, then it is necessary to look at what this will entail in terms of how the findings might be presented to managers and interview panels, and to shape the study accordingly.

Exercise 3.4   Choosing a research topic: consulting other people

The preceding sections of this chapter have offered some ideas about where to look for research topics, and perspectives on factors to take into account when deciding on whether a particular topic is right for you at this stage of your life. In addition to thinking it through on your own, it will also be valuable to discuss these options with other people who know you well, or with whom you are involved in research roles (e.g. fellow students, academic advisers, research mentors and supervisors).

Arriving at something that you can work with

The earlier sections of this chapter have suggested various ways of deciding on a possible research topic or question, and then looking at that question from all possible angles in order to develop as complete an understanding as possible about what the question might mean, and how it could be tackled. In the end, however, it is necessary to arrive at a clear and final statement of your research question. You will need to arrive at something you can work with, and which works for you. Your research question is the key point of contact with the research literature. The question reflects your understanding of a desirable and justifiable next step in the research literature that builds on what has gone before. The research question is also a kind of promissory note: this is what my study will deliver. Most forms of research product, such as journal articles, are organised around a research question, and tell the reader why that question is important, how it was addressed in terms of evidence (method), and ultimately how it was answered (the results of the study).

The closing section of this chapter considers the issue of how to phrase a research question, and offers some practical suggestions for how to formulate and use research questions. The key message, as we approach the end of this chapter is this: be guided by the literature, and do not try to invent your own research language.

Different types of question

There are different types of research question. Sometimes questions may be intentionally open-ended, as in qualitative research. Examples of this type of question would be 'What is the client's experience of a therapy session?' or 'What is the experience of being really understood?' These are open, exploratory questions. In other research situations, for example in most quantitative research, questions will be formulated as precise hypotheses of the type: 'Is behavioural counselling more effective than client-centred counselling for students with study skills problems?'

This is a more precise question, which seeks to confirm the truth (or otherwise) of a proposition, rather than opening up an area for exploration.

There are many different research 'action words', such as 'explore', 'describe', 'analyse' and 'predict', that have subtly different meanings. For example, a researcher might be interested in therapist empathy and how it facilitates client change. Consider the following research questions:

- 'Do levels of therapist empathy *predict* client outcomes in early sessions of client-centred therapy for depression?'
- 'Are levels of therapist empathy *associated with* client outcomes in early sessions of client-centred therapy for depression?'
- 'Do clients *perceive* therapist empathy as contributing to outcomes in early sessions of client-centred therapy for depression?'
- 'How do clients *experience* therapist empathy as contributing to outcomes in early sessions of client-centred therapy for depression?'

Each of these questions refers to the same basic idea, but each leads to a fundamentally different research design. The first question ('predict') requires some sort of quantitative experimental design, in which the causal impact of empathy can be controlled and measured. By contrast, the final question ('experience') is consistent with the use of open-ended qualitative interviews. Using interviews to investigate a 'predict' question does not work, nor would using a controlled study to investigate an 'explore' question.

Further discussion around how to develop research questions in qualitative studies can be found in Agee (2009) and McCaslin and Scott (2003), as well as in many qualitative research textbooks. It can be useful to contrast these sources with the approach taken by Riva et al. (2012), who describe the PICOT framework for formulating research questions in quantitative RCT studies of therapy outcome (P – Population; I – Intervention; C – Comparison or reference group to compare with the treatment intervention; O – Outcome; T – Time duration of data collection).

Exercise 3.5   Reflecting on how the scope and focus of a research question depends on the methodology being used

Later chapters in this book introduce a wide range of different types of research methodology – qualitative interviews, quantitative measures, professional knowledge studies, autoethnography, case studies, measure development and more. As you learn about these research approaches it can be useful to reflect on how your research question might be explored in the context of each method, in terms of the type of data that might be collected, the participant sample and research context, and the distinctive knowledge and insights that might eventually be produced.

Using exemplar studies

One of the strong recommendations made in Chapters 1 and 2 was that the best way to acquire research skills, and to conduct a successful first publishable study, is to adopt the role of apprentice. Within such a role, a key task, when searching the literature, is to identify 'exemplar' studies that might function as templates or guides to investigations that 'fit the bill' in terms of what you want your research to achieve. An exemplar study may not necessarily be a study of the specific topic that you intend to pursue. For example, a researcher who is interested in clients' experiences of bereavement counselling may have difficulty in locating good-quality studies of that particular topic, but might discover a study of therapy for depression or anxiety that deployed a methodological approach that you can adapt for your own purposes. Each of the exemplar/template studies that you harvest will provide you with an example of how research questions are phrased and handled in that type of study.

Practical considerations

There are some further practical considerations that are worth bearing in mind when arriving at a final formulation of a research question:

- A research proposal will always require a clear statement of the research question (or set of questions).
- Typically, somewhere in a research proposal there will be a requirement that the research question is explained at three levels: (i) the aim of the research; (ii) the main question; and (iii) specific sub-questions. For example:

  o aim: to examine the effectiveness of CBT for depression in a community setting;
  o main question: is short-term CBT for clients seen in a low-cost community counselling clinic as more effective than treatment as usual (TAU) from their GP?;
  o specific questions:

    - is reduction in depression scores, measured by the Beck Depression Inventory, more likely to occur in patients who receive CBT, compared to those who receive TAU?;
    - are clients who receive CBT more likely to report reliable and clinically significant change at the termination of therapy and three-month follow-up?
    - what proportion of clients drop out of treatment?
    - is the level of severity of the depression associated with the outcome?

- Traditional or conventional Master's and PhD dissertations and theses (i.e. long research reports that are not written in an immediately publishable form) will usually include a statement of the research questions at the end of the literature review chapter, or the start of the method chapter. These questions may be re-presented at the start of the discussion chapter, as a means of structuring the discussion of findings in terms of how the original questions have been answered. A dissertation or thesis will also usually include a more general statement of aims in the abstract and in an introductory chapter.

- In research proposals, statements of research aims such as 'to review the literature' or 'to contribute to better treatment' are not needed – these can be assumed as general goals for any project.
- Published papers do not always make use of the term 'research questions', but instead may make use of terms such as 'aim', 'objective', 'purpose' or 'intention'. Different journals tend to be associated with different forms of words in this respect.
- In general, the aims and questions in quantitative studies and qualitative papers tend to be framed in rather different ways. It is helpful to develop an appreciation of both styles.
- The aims of a study, and research questions, need to be consistent with, and implicit in, the title of the study.
- In a published research article, the abstract, at the start, will usually include a succinct statement of the aim of the study.
- It is not unusual, particularly in large or complex studies, for some questions to turn out to be unanswerable (for instance, if some data were lost, or a questionnaire or interview schedule turned out not to make sense to participants). In addition, occasionally it turns out that the original way a question was phrased could be improved. In these situations, researchers will proceed on the basis of what makes most sense in the circumstances. Sometimes it will make sense to readjust the questions retrospectively. In other situations, the fact that the initial question did not work out is an interesting finding in itself, and needs to be reported.

Conclusions

In this book, research is understood as an activity that contributes to the development of a *collective* knowledge base. In the field of counselling and psychotherapy, potential consumers of research encompass therapists, therapy educators and trainers, the managers and administrators of therapy clinics, agencies, clients, potential clients, policy makers, the general public, and academic theorists and researchers both within the field of counselling and psychotherapy as well as in cognate disciplines such as psychology, sociology, management studies, nursing or social work. Each of these audiences has different interests, and looks for different things in what it reads (and in fact reads quite different kinds of publications). At some point, all researchers are faced with the challenge of conveying the results of their work to different audiences. It is inevitable that many members of these audiences will be somewhat shaky regarding the technical aspects of a study. The aspect of a study that has to be communicated clearly and convincingly to readers from all backgrounds is the research question. In the end an interesting question, which has a plausible rationale, and which evokes curiosity and interest in the mind of a reader or listener, lies at the heart of all good research.

Suggestions for further reading

O'Leary, Z. (2018). *The Research Question: Little Quick Fix*. Thousand Oaks, CA: Sage. A short and stimulating book on how to develop a research question.

Riva, J., Malik, K. M. P., Burnie, S. J., et al. (2012). What is your research question? An introduction to the PICOT format for clinicians. *Journal of the Canadian Chiropractic Association*, 56: 167–171. Introduction to the PICOT model.

Vandenbroucke, J. P., & Pearce, N. (2018). From ideas to studies: how to get ideas and sharpen them into research questions. *Clinical Epidemiology*, 10, 253–264. Discussion of the process of developing productive research questions.

White, P. (2017). *Developing Research Questions*. 2nd edn. London: Palgrave. The go-to source for all aspects of how to formulate research questions, and how questions contribute to the design and conduct of a study.

Online resources

Further activities to support learning around the topics introduced in this chapter can be found on the online resource site: https://study.sagepub.com/doingresearch4e.

4

The Research Proposal

Introduction

This chapter explains what is involved in writing a research proposal, and the part that a proposal plays in the life-cycle of a research project. Research proposals may sometimes be described as research protocols or plans, depending on the context. The primary purpose of a research proposal is to describe and justify what it is that the researcher intends to do. The proposal can be viewed as a 'plan of action' or a 'blueprint'.

Why do you need to write a research proposal?

There are two main functions of a research proposal. The first function is to force a researcher or research team to decide what the research is intended to achieve, and how it will be carried out. In this sense, constructing a proposal follows on from identifying a topic and narrowing that topic down to a set of research questions. A research plan is similar to any other design task in that it requires different kinds of information and activity to be brought together. When designing a house, an architect needs to achieve a balance between the wishes of the client, the cost envelope, the materials and workforce that are available, and government building regulations. All of this needs to fit into a sequence of activities – the roof needs to be on before the wiring can be installed. Similarly, a researcher or research team must achieve a balance between a range of factors. Constructing a research plan operates as a reality check for a researcher, which may lead to some rethinking about research priorities.

The second function of a research proposal, plan or protocol is that it serves as the basis for a contract between the researcher (or team of researchers) and the other people who may be involved. These people may include:

- providers of funding for the study;
- academic committees whose role is to decide whether, once completed, the study is in principle appropriate for the award of a degree;
- the academic supervisor(s) of the study;
- ethics committees or Institutional Review Boards who give ethical approval for the study to go ahead;
- managers of agencies that are being asked to provide access to informants;
- primary informants/participants, such as members of the public, therapists and therapy clients;
- colleagues who may be asked to help with aspects of data collection and analysis.

These different audiences have different interests and requirements. For example, primary participants in a study are not likely to want to read through a lengthy proposal. Institutional audiences, such as funding agencies, university project approval panels and ethics committees, will almost always require a proposal to be written in accordance with their specific requirements regarding length, subheadings and referencing. It is therefore sensible to think in terms of creating a general proposal document that can be edited and reshaped for a variety of purposes.

In relation to the process of submitting a proposal to external gatekeepers, it is crucial to develop an understanding of what that agency or committee is looking for, in terms of both the content and style of the proposal. It is not uncommon for a research project to falter or stall at the proposal stage, either because the proposal is turned down by a committee, or because of a failure to resolve issues that are raised by the committee. It is important for researchers to retain a sense of perspective around the interpersonal dynamics of this process. The researcher is usually operating from a place of passionate personal interest. By contrast, a funding agency, ethics committee or similar group will usually be struggling to process a backlog of applications. Its members are unlikely to have a personal stake or interest in any particular project that is submitted – their interest is in dealing with the paperwork with the minimum amount of fuss, consistent with maintaining standards.

Because a proposal is a complex document, it is extremely difficult to get it right first time. It is important to allow time for draft proposals to be read by supervisors, peers and other interested parties, and for subsequent revisions to be recirculated for comment. Even when a final version of a proposal is submitted to a funding agency or ethics committee, it is common for further modifications to be required.

Exercise 4.1   The heart of your proposal

A research proposal inevitably includes a lot of detailed information. However, at the heart of a good proposal is a simple idea. Once you have developed a clear idea of what you plan to do in your research, try to explain the core idea, or heart of the proposal, to various people. With each person or group, summarise the proposal in less than two minutes, using non-technical language. Listen carefully to the questions that they then ask you – these will be indicators of how successful you have been in communicating your ideas. It can be valuable to try out this exercise with people who know nothing about your research area, as well as with those who possess expertise and experience. Ethics committees and research boards will often include 'lay' members, whose role is to determine whether proposals pass the 'common-sense, plain English' test.

What a proposal looks like

This section offers an outline of the types of information that may be included in a research proposal. It is necessary here to keep in mind that different audiences or organisations may stipulate other subheadings or domains of information. In such circumstances, it would be unwise to include domains or subheadings that have not been specifically asked for – this can be confusing and the people assessing the proposal will already have enough material to work through without having to take account of even more stuff. Research proposals will usually consist of information under the following headings:

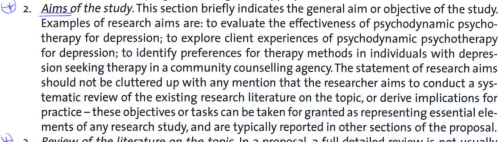

1. *Cover sheet.* Name(s) or researcher(s), date, title of study, your postal and email address, title of the research programme/degree (if appropriate).
2. *Aims of the study.* This section briefly indicates the general aim or objective of the study. Examples of research aims are: to evaluate the effectiveness of psychodynamic psychotherapy for depression; to explore client experiences of psychodynamic psychotherapy for depression; to identify preferences for therapy methods in individuals with depression seeking therapy in a community counselling agency. The statement of research aims should not be cluttered up with any mention that the researcher aims to conduct a systematic review of the existing research literature on the topic, or derive implications for practice – these objectives or tasks can be taken for granted as representing essential elements of any research study, and are typically reported in other sections of the proposal.
3. *Review of the literature on the topic.* In a proposal, a full detailed review is not usually required, due to space restrictions. However, a researcher does need to demonstrate that

they have read widely enough on the topic to provide an authoritative and convincing rationale for the research, in terms of how it builds on previous studies or fills a gap in the research literature. It can be particularly worthwhile to briefly describe two or three previous papers that are most directly similar and relevant to the study which is being proposed. The literature review may need to discuss not only the findings of previous research into the topic, but also the use of different research methods applied in the investigation of the topic. Ultimately, this section will be evaluated on how well the review is able to establish (a) what is currently known about the topic, and (b) why the proposed study is necessary, in terms of what it adds to previous knowledge. It is unlikely that there will be enough space in this section to allow for an exploration of theoretical issues or clinical examples. The focus needs to be very much on research that is directly relevant to the proposed study. It can be helpful to describe the search strategy and quality criteria used to identify items included in the review.

 4. _Methodological issues._ There is not always a separate subheading provided for this theme, but it is worthwhile to try to weave it in somewhere. Readers/reviewers of a proposal may well respond to the research plan with a view that 'this is interesting, but it won't work because ...'. A brief discussion of the main difficulties or challenges associated with the study, and how they will be addressed, can go a long way towards alleviating any anxiety around the feasibility of a study that is being felt by readers and gatekeepers. Common methodological issues include: defining, observing or measuring the key phenomena, gaining access to informants, the ethical sensitivity of the topic and the lack of previous research on the topic.

5. _Research questions or hypotheses._ What are the actual research questions or hypotheses you intend to investigate? These need to be established early in the proposal, and the reader needs to be able to see, in later sections of the proposal, exactly how these questions will determine the sample, the data that are collected, how these data will be analysed and the conclusions of the study. For example, a study that aims to evaluate the effectiveness of psychodynamic psychotherapy for depression may break down into the following questions: (a) what proportion of clients completing psychodynamic psychotherapy for depression record clinically significant and reliable levels of change on a standard depression scale, the Beck Depression Inventory?; (b) how does the success rate for this form of therapy compare with improvement rates reported in relevant benchmark studies?; and (c) to what extent are therapy outcomes related to the number of sessions, age and gender of the client, and their previous experience of therapy? These research questions will allow the reader of the proposal to gain a clear appreciation of what the study will deliver. The rationale for the questions also needs to be outlined in the literature review – for example, evidence from previous studies that gender, age, length of therapy and previous therapy have been found to be linked to outcome.

 6. _Design of the study._ Usually a brief description of the type or genre of the study – e.g. survey, grounded theory, naturalistic outcome study. This section may also include a brief description of what will happen in the study, suitable for a lay reader (for example: 'The study will consist of a naturalistic, practice-based evaluation: all clients applying for psychodynamic therapy for depression at a community counselling centre will be invited to complete a depression scale at the start of each weekly session of therapy, and at a three-month follow-up'.

7. _Prior work/pilot study._ This section includes (if available) information about any previous research or publications by the researcher or research team that have provided a rationale or background for the present study. For example, a counselling clinic may have been

using weekly questionnaire completion for several years, and be able to point to annual reports which show that this practice has been acceptable to clients.

8. *Sample/participants*. The information you can give about your research sample: number of participants, demographic characteristics, inclusion and exclusion criteria, arrangements for recruiting participants. If access requires permission from an external agency, a letter from the manager of that agency must be provided in an appendix. Similarly, if participants are to be recruited through a poster or newspaper advertisement, this also needs to be available in an appendix. A rationale needs to be provided for the sample size. In qualitative research, it is usually acceptable to refer to sample sizes in existing published studies that made use of the same methodology. In quantitative studies, sample size is justified by a statistical power calculation or accepted practice (i.e., sample sizes in previous published studies). Procedure for dealing with attrition rates (drop-out) from the study needs to be explained, if appropriate. Sampling strategy should be explained and justified – e.g. random sample, stratified sample (for instance, certain number of people in each age band), a homogeneous vs a heterogeneous sample.

9. *Intervention.* If the aim of the study is to explore or evaluate some form of therapeutic intervention, then information about the therapy should be provided.

10. *Ethical procedures.* The measures that will be taken to ensure informed consent, confidentiality, security of data, avoidance of harm, etc. Copies of participant information sheets, consent forms, letters, etc. may be included in an appendix. Information should also be included about the procedure through which ethical consent is obtained, such as the length of time the participant has to decide whether to be involved, and what happens if a participant quits the study; about how the participant can complain if something goes wrong; about actions taken to ensure the safety of the researcher; arrangement to de-brief participants. For some purposes (e.g. a proposal to a funding body) it is sufficient to indicate that ethical consent has been received, or specify the ethics committee by which the proposal will be scrutinised.

11. *Equal opportunities and social inclusion*. Information about how the research is open to people with disabilities, for example participants who require wheelchair access or have reading difficulties. It may be necessary here to explain any special action taken to respect the rights and needs of children or vulnerable adults who may be taking part in the study.

12. *Procedures for data collection*. Details of the interview schedule, questionnaire, rating scales, etc. that are used in the study. Indication of when, where and how these instruments will be administered. Be clear about exactly what will happen to participants, and what they will be asked to do. Copies of questionnaires, rating scales or interview schedules must be provided in an appendix. Details should be given about the reliability and validity of all data collection tools, in terms of previous studies in which these attributes have been established. If a purpose-designed questionnaire or interview schedule is to be employed, information should be provided about how it was designed, and (if appropriate) any pilot work that has been carried out.

13. *Method of data analysis*. How the data will be analysed, explaining the statistical or qualitative methods that will be applied. Information about who will be involved in data analysis, and their roles/responsibilities.

14. *Dissemination of findings*. Will informants be offered a copy of the report – and if so, how will this be accomplished? To which journal(s) will the study be submitted? Information about other forms of dissemination – conferences, seminars, internet, etc. The rationale for the dissemination strategy. Time scale to publication.

15. *The social and/or clinical value of the study/consultation with service user groups.* Account of how the findings of the study might contribute to enhanced treatment, or quality of life, for a particular client group, or how this might be of benefit to the sponsoring organisation. Such statements are more credible if they are based on evidence of active involvement of service users and other stakeholders, for example through membership of a steering group, or focus group interviews).

16. *Background and qualifications of the researcher(s).* This section may consist solely of factual information, such as the qualifications or CV(s) of researcher(s) and any training they have received in relation to the research techniques used in the study. In some circumstances it may be appropriate to use this section to reflect on the meaning of the research for the researcher (researcher reflexivity).

17. *Training and support.* Information about research training courses that the researcher may be required or expected to attend, as well as research conferences, seminars and workshops. Description of supervision arrangements and the qualifications and experience of members of the supervisor team. If the project is not part of an academic degree, then this section may include information about any external consultants involved in the study, and the extent and nature of their engagement.

18. *Timeline/Gantt chart.* Specifies the target dates for the completion of different aspects of the study.

19. *Resources.* Information about the costs of the study, including materials, travel, staff time, equipment, licences, consultancy fees, payments to participants, etc.

20. *References.*

21. *Appendices.* Ethics and risk assessment checklists, client information sheet and consent form, questionnaires, interview schedules, etc.

Many organisations (e.g. universities and funding bodies) require separate ethics, risk assessment and health and safety forms or checklists to be completed and submitted alongside a proposal. The purpose of such forms is to make it easier for assessors to quickly evaluate whether all relevant ethics and safety issues have been addressed.

What makes a good research proposal?

The criteria that are used to evaluate research proposals will depend on the terms of reference of the individual or group being consulted. Ethics committees are mainly interested in the ethical soundness of a proposal. However, some ethics committees will also make some evaluation of the scientific merit of a proposal, on the grounds that a study that has no hope of producing meaningful or valid findings is ethically problematic because it is a waste of participant time. By contrast, academic panels will tend to look for intellectual rigour, while funding bodies are often more interested in practical relevance and value for money. At the same time, there are also some more general criteria, described below, which would normally form part of any appraisal of a proposal.

Does the proposal describe a relevant topic that is being investigated at an appropriate level? Sometimes a proposal can be sound, in research terms, but not on track in terms of topic and context. For example, some students on counselling and psychotherapy training programmes will submit research ideas that are more appropriate for health psychology or developmental psychology programmes. Likewise some proposals will describe projects that are too ambitious for the level of competence of the researcher, the resources that are available or the level of degree that is being sought, or are not ambitious enough.

Does the proposal give a clear account of what is intended to happen (who, where, when and how), and why? It is essential that someone reading a proposal is able to gain a clear understanding of what it will be like for a participant to be involved in the study, and the roles, tasks and responsibilities of all members of the research team. The reader needs to be able to mentally track through the unfolding process of the study, all the way from start to finish. Any gaps in the narrative, or contradictory information in different sections of the proposal, will undermine the confidence that a reader has in the viability of the project.

Other important criteria include:

Is the proposal sufficiently informed by knowledge of previous research in this area (including knowledge of alternative methods)?

Is the proposal internally consistent? Do the methods and sample enable the research question(s) to be answered?

Is the study ethically sound? Has everything possible been done to ensure that no harm comes to the participants?

To what extent will the study add significantly to previous knowledge of the topic? How creative or innovative is it?

Is the plan realistic? Have costings and a timetable been calculated so that there is a reasonable chance of completing the study on time and within budget?

Does the researcher possess the experience and skills that are required to carry out this study? Are appropriate supervision and training available, to ensure that the researcher develops appropriate skills and knowledge?

In many instances, the committee or organisation to which a proposal is being submitted would have published their own evaluation criteria. It is always worth looking closely at these documents. It is also valuable to talk to people who have experience of making proposals to these agencies. Typically, officers within committees and funding agencies are willing to respond to requests for clarification of their procedures, but are reluctant to enter into a detailed discussion of proposals that could be construed as comprising selective coaching that would disadvantage other candidates.

The main reason why a research proposal is referred back to its author for revision is because particular information has not been supplied, or aspects of the procedure have not been explained clearly enough. This kind of outcome can be regarded as useful 'critical friend' feedback that helps a researcher or research team by offering external scrutiny that tightens up their plans.

In some instances a proposal is referred back because of more serious problems that call for a more fundamental re-think. These problems tend to take the following forms:

- lack of coherence, focus, organisation and structure – the proposal rambles, is hard to follow or may include unnecessary detail;
- does not provide a coherent and persuasive argument for the study – important background studies have not been cited, too much emphasis on secondary sources;
- what is being proposed is not practically feasible (e.g. will not be completed within the time/financial resources available; assumes access and collaboration that may not be forthcoming or sustainable);
- researcher does not possess the skills and experiences necessary to conduct the study;
- presents fundamental ethical issues around confidentiality of participants, wellbeing of participants and researcher(s), or legality of procedures.

The criteria outlined above operate within a somewhat broad set of parameters. For example, an undergraduate research project is primarily intended as a learning experience for the student. By contrast, Master's or doctoral projects are judged in terms of whether they have the potential to lead to publications in peer-reviewed journals. Funded projects are evaluated against more challenging and complex criteria, such as excellence, value for money and societal impact. Most funding sources operate competitive bidding for research money, with the result that the likelihood is that even exceptional proposals from experienced research groups may not be supported.

Box 4.1   Published research protocols as learning resources

The majority of research proposals, for example those written by students or to support funding applications, have a very limited circulation and are not written for general dissemination. However, there is a growing literature that consists of research protocols that are published as journal articles prior to the commencement of a study. The largest group of such articles consists of research protocols/plans for randomised controlled studies (RCTs). Increasingly, researchers using RCT methods publish their research protocols ahead of carrying out the study, as a means of being transparent about what they intend to do. These protocols can be found in several places, including open-access journals such as *Trials* and *BMC Psychiatry*. Protocols for qualitative studies are also beginning to be published. Published research protocols can function as a useful learning resource, even for those researchers whose own proposals are not expected to meet the same level of detail or quality threshold that would be required in a published article. They provide valuable insights into both the range of issues that need to be taken into account when designing a research study, and the ways that experienced researchers provide a rationale for investigations. Examples of published research protocols are available on the online resource site.

Conclusions

This chapter has looked at various aspects of the process of constructing a research proposal. This element of a research study closely aligns with the concept of research *design*: a proposal can be viewed as hinged around a research question that is designed to progress knowledge in relation to a particular topic or area of practice, and a set of data collection and analysis procedures that are designed to ensure that the question is answered in a credible manner in the context of the resources and stakeholder permissions that are available. It is not possible to be prescriptive about what a research proposal should look like – a proposal is always written for a particular purpose and in response to particular organisational requirements. It is therefore essential, when writing a research proposal, to pay close attention to, and adhere to, the format and guidelines that you are being asked to follow, and to consult with others who have prior experience of the research approval system within which you are operating.

Suggestions for further reading

Guidance on how to write a research proposal can be found in:

Bell, J., & Waters, S. (2018). *Doing Your Research Project: A Guide for First-time Researchers*. London: Open University Press.
O'Leary, Z. (2018). *Research Proposal: Little Quick Fix*. Thousand Oaks, CA: Sage.

Online resources

Further activities to support learning around the topics introduced in this chapter can be found on the online resource site: https://study.sagepub.com/doingresearch4e.

5
Ethical Responsibility

Introduction

Being able to deal with ethical issues, and making sure that research is conducted within a sound moral, ethical and legal framework, are essential elements of researcher competence. The aim of this chapter is to provide an overview of the kinds of ethical issues that arise in research on counselling and psychotherapy, and how these issues can be addressed.

Why is ethical responsibility important?

Ethical responsibility lies at the heart of any research. There are several reasons why it is necessary to take ethical issues seriously:

- There is a broad social consensus, backed up by law, around the freedoms and rights of individuals as regards the research process, in terms of factors such as voluntary participation, informed consent, avoidance of harm and confidentiality of information. This consensus is reflected in the insistence on the part of universities and other research institutions that all research projects need to undergo ethical approval prior to the commencement of data collection, and the fact that research journals will only publish studies that have been ethically approved.
- Researchers have a responsibility to the research community to act in an ethically appropriate manner – if members of the public get the impression that researchers exploit or deceive participants, then it will become much harder to recruit participants, or to argue for public funding for research.
- Researchers who are not secure in relation to the ethical probity of their work may feel anxious and guilty, and ambivalent about publishing their findings.
- Research participants who feel safe and who trust the researcher are more likely to respond to research questions in an open and honest manner. In therapy research, access to clients or patients is controlled by professional gatekeepers such as agency or clinic managers, and therapy practitioners, who are always cautious and wary in respect of any possibility that clients will be harmed or confidentiality will be compromised.
- Ethical clarity enables clients to participate more fully in therapy (Trachsel & Grosse Holtforth, 2019).

These considerations, taken together, mean that it is vital for therapy researchers to develop skills and knowledge in relation to the ethical dimensions of the research process.

What do you need to know?

There are basically four levels or layers of knowledge that are required, in respect of research ethics:

1. *An understanding of basic ethical principles.* Within the broad arena of social research, and studies of health and social care, there is general agreement on a set of core ethical principles: *beneficence* (acting to enhance research participant wellbeing); *nonmaleficence* (avoiding doing harm to participants); *autonomy* (respecting the right of the person to take responsibility for themselves); and *fidelity* (treating everyone in a fair and just manner). All therapy researchers should already be familiar with these principles in the context of their primary training as therapists. However, it is necessary to extend this clinical knowledge of ethical issues by reflecting on the implications of ethical principles for the research process.
2. *Routine procedures for implementing ethical principles within research studies.* There are a number of standard methods through which ethical aspects of research are typically handled: information leaflets for participants, informed consent forms, strategies for dealing with participant distress and procedures for ensuring data security. These techniques form part of the design of a study, and are included within the research proposal.
3. *Strategies for responding to ethical dilemmas that arise during the research process.* Even when robust ethical measures are in place, such as consent procedures, it may be necessary for a researcher to deal with ethically sensitive situations during the process of recruitment, data collection and data analysis.

4. *Strategies for dealing with ethical issues associated with sensitive research topics and groups of participants.* There exists a category of ethically sensitive research topics that are associated with a higher level of risk. Researchers working in these areas need to be familiar with specific ethical debates and solutions around their topic, and possess sufficient experience and confidence to be able to handle whatever comes up.

These areas of ethical knowledge and competence can be viewed as existing on a continuum or dimension. It is important to recognise that this dimension does not merely refer to increasing cognitive and theoretical knowledge, but also takes account of what Carroll and Shaw (2012) describe as 'ethical maturity' based on personal experience and a capacity to reflect on practice. For example, it is not sensible for a novice researcher to undertake research that is highly ethically sensitive, such as interviews with vulnerable participants. Such projects may be ethically viable and defensible, but are better carried out by researchers who have more experience of how to respond effectively to any ethical dilemmas that may arise.

There is a further aspect of what a researcher needs to know about ethics: *knowing how to consult.* Ethical good practice does not arise from the application of a set of rules that can be learned or worked out by an individual researcher in isolation. This is because the ethical rules or principles may be in conflict with each other or lack clarity. For example, how much information do research participants need in order to guarantee that informed consent has taken place? How do you know that they have understood the information that has been provided? Deciding on how best to proceed, in relation to ethical issues, requires a willingness to engage in a dialogue with others: research colleagues and supervisors; professional gatekeepers; ethics committee members; advocates for groups of clients.

It is important to become familiar with the research ethics codes of major therapy organisations such as the British Association for Counselling and Psychotherapy, the British Psychological Society, the American Psychological Association, or whatever other national professional body has jurisdiction within your area of practice. These documents are available online.

Exercise 5.1   Using your existing knowledge of ethical issues

Take a few minutes to reflect on your knowledge and experience of ethical issues, in relation to your practice as a therapist. Make notes about the key themes and events that have been most important for you in relation to this aspect of your practice. Having carried out this piece of self-reflection, move on to consider the implications for your research project of each item that you have included in your notes. For example, if you have learned in your work with clients to be highly sensitive to possible breaches of confidentiality, how can you apply this knowledge to your research? Finally, reflect on whether you can identify any ethical issues that might arise in your research, that are not informed by your pre-existing ethical understanding derived from therapy training and practice. It can be useful to carry out this exercise with a group of colleagues, as a means of developing a more comprehensive appreciation of the connections between practice ethics and research ethics.

Box 5.1   The professional misconduct dimension of research ethics

The focus of the present chapter is mainly on the kinds of procedures that are required to ensure the wellbeing of research participants. A further level of ethical practice relates to researcher professional misconduct. Researchers may sometimes fail to acknowledge the contribution of junior (especially female) colleagues, or may pass off the work of other people as their own, distort research findings, misuse research funds, and even invent whole studies and datasets. These problems have become more acute in recent years, across all academic disciplines, as competitive pressures in universities have become more intense (Gross, 2016; Pratt et al., 2019; Swift et al., 2020). Within psychology, the topic of research fraud has been linked to a research culture that rewards novelty and originality, and downplays the importance of replication studies that allow findings to be directly compared (thus making it easier to detect deception). Strategies for reducing research fraud include publication of research protocols (to make it easier for readers to check whether the ensuing research report has ignored key data) and expectations that data will be lodged in open access depositories where they can be analysed by other researchers. So far, there have not been any widely publicised research fraud scandals in the field of psychotherapy research. However, anyone engaging in research needs to be aware that such things may happen.

Gaining ethical approval

There is a standard set of hurdles that any research project needs to negotiate, in order to gain approval from the relevant ethics committee, Institutional Review Board (IRB) or organisational management committee. The basic steps involve:

- carrying out an audit of the potential risks to any participants (including possible risk of harm to the researcher);
- taking account of relevant legal issues, for example around secure storage of personal data;
- designing a participant information leaflet that explains what the study is about, what the person will be asked to do, what will happen if they decline or withdraw, what will happen to the data and what to do if they wish to make a complaint;
- designing a form that the participant can sign to indicate that they agree to take part (or otherwise);
- constructing a set of procedures for ensuring data security;
- working out how the various ethical procedures fit together, perhaps using a flow diagram. For example, it is necessary to give participants enough time to think about their

decision to take part, an opportunity to ask questions and possibly also the option to review their decision at various stages. It is also necessary to be clear about who handles the data, and how long these will be stored.

The process of gaining ethical approval usually consists of sending a package of information, including consent forms and leaflets, along with a version of the research proposal, to an ethics committee or other suitable mode of external consultancy. The task of the ethics committee is to look at the project from the point of view of the participant. The committee may then make recommendations or require alterations, to make sure that the interests of participants are being looked after to the maximum extent. For a researcher or research team, this is usually a helpful and illuminating process. It is very hard for those on the 'inside' of a project (the researchers) to ever fully appreciate what the project is like from the perspective of an 'outsider' (the participants). It is the job of the research committee to supply that critical outsider perspective. In projects that are particularly ethically sensitive, it is good practice for the researcher or research team to consult with potential participants, or those who can speak for them, from the earliest stages of the research planning process.

When working out these procedures, it is important to keep in mind that in some studies the therapist will be a participant (for instance, their performance is being evaluated). Also, it is possible that third-party individuals, such as family members, may be affected by the research, and may need to be consulted.

Basic ethical tools

In the process of obtaining ethical approval, and carrying out a study, there are various ethical tools or procedures that you will almost certainly need to develop, for administration to research participants:

- invitation to participate in research (letter, leaflet, email, talk, notice, video, or combination of these elements);
- participant information sheet;
- informed consent form;
- debrief/sources of further support leaflet (Sharpe & Faye, 2009).

Examples of these documents can be found in the section of the online resource site that provides supplementary material and learning activities relevant to the topics covered in the present chapter. When consulting these specimen documents it is important to keep in mind that each research situation has distinctive features, and different ethical approval committees may have slightly different priorities and concerns – it is always necessary to adapt documents to fit your specific needs.

Responding to ethical issues once research is under way

There are many ethical dilemmas and choice points that can arise once participant recruitment and data collection have commenced, no matter how much thought and care have gone into the formulation of the ethical procedures that are being applied. These dilemmas represent decisions that need to be made by the researcher, in respect of situations that could not be precisely anticipated in advance. Examples of such situations include the following:

- A client in a therapy outcome study has completed a lengthy assessment before commencing therapy. By the third session, it becomes clear that he was never really interested in receiving therapy, but believed that being seen to seek therapy would convince his estranged wife to come back to him. Is it ethically acceptable to drop him from the sample?
- A client has completed therapy and is being interviewed about her experience. Towards the end of the interview she starts to get very upset. What should the interviewer do?
- A client is being interviewed about her experiences in therapy over the past decade. She starts to talk about an episode of therapy that the interviewer regards as having been exploitative and abusive.
- Employees in a large organisation are asked to complete a stress questionnaire, to evaluate the potential need to introduce a counselling service. One of them writes in the margin that he is feeling suicidal.
- In a randomised trial, clients are randomly allocated to either CBT or psychodynamic therapy at the end of a screening interview. The researcher has spent over an hour listening to a person who desperately needs therapy, but who has had a previous negative experience of CBT. On opening the random number file, the researcher sees that this individual would be allocated to CBT.
- A PhD student carries out an autoethnographic study in which he carefully documents and analyses his personal experience of sexual abuse in childhood. The thesis is then made generally available through the university online archive. His mother reads this and gets very upset, even though she knew what his research was about, and had signed a consent form.

These scenarios represent what are described as ethically important moments in the research process (Guillemin and Gillam, 2004). Useful guidelines on how to apply ethical principles in order to arrive at the best response to these situations can be found in Danchev and Ross (2014). Such research ethics dilemmas are similar, in many respects, to the kinds of ethical challenges that arise in counselling and psychotherapy practice. The ethical decision-making strategies that therapists already possess, arising from basic training, are therefore highly relevant.

However, these scenarios can also be viewed as calling for a different kind of ethical response. The common thread that joins together most of the ethical dilemmas that arise during the process of doing a research study is the notion of the researcher–participant *relationship*. These dilemmas are difficult to deal with because what is happening is that there is a conflict between general ethical principles, such as autonomy and avoidance of harm, and the in-the-moment connection that the researcher has with the research participant. This connection encompasses a set of relational values, such as care, mutuality, respect and dialogue. A concern to do justice to these values has led contemporary ethicists in the direction of developing a distinctive form of *relational ethics* (Gabriel and Casemore, 2009), informed by feminist and multicultural perspectives, and the writings of the postmodern philosopher Emmanuel Levinas.

A relational ethical perspective has been particularly influential within the field of qualitative research (see Chapter 8).

Critical ethical challenges

Earlier sections of the present chapter have explored general ethical issues that arise in therapy research, and standard strategies for managing such dilemmas. The following sections examine additional critical ethical challenges that may need to be considered in particular research contexts.

Practitioner research

There are two distinctive ethical challenges associated with practitioner research: doing research on your own clients, and ethical support and scrutiny when a study is conducted outside of a university environment.

One of the most basic processes that occurs in psychotherapy is that the client forms a particular type of relationship with their therapist. This relationship can consist of many disparate elements, including an emotional bond, trust and sharing of sensitive information. Even though it may be that in some, or even most, cases the client retains a capacity for autonomy, it is also clear that a temporary loss of autonomy is something that may occur in therapy – it goes with the territory. What this means, in respect of ethical decision-making, is that studies where the researcher is also the therapist are ethically problematic. For example, a client who is asked by their therapist to take part in a research study may agree because they want to please their therapist or are grateful to them. It is therefore important, when designing a study in which the therapist is also the researcher, to make sure that, as far as possible, the participant consent-taking process incorporates a strong degree of externality, or (even better) is wholly separate from the therapist. Therapist research on their own clients is ethically possible, but requires careful planning. The area of therapy research where this issue is most acute is in the field of case study research. Strategies for doing ethically sound case study research, and examples of what can go wrong, can be found in McLeod (2010). An example of ethical good practice in this kind of practitioner research can be found in Fleet et al. (2016).

It is widely accepted that ethical standards in research require evaluation and approval of research protocol by a group that comprises experts and (ideally) lay people which functions independently of the researcher or research team. This kind of scrutiny and consultation is usually provided by a university or health service ethics committee or review board. There are many therapists who work in private practice, or non-statutory services that do not have ready access to this kind of ethical expertise. On the whole, universities are not keen to offer ethical approval to practitioner studies that are not supervised by a member of university staff, because of the costs and risks that are entailed. This situation functions as a significant barrier to practitioner research, and has contributed to a lack of studies of therapy conducted in private practice and community-based agencies. Possible solutions to this problem are discussed by Osborne & Luoma (2018; Osborne, 2018), including the establishment of an ethical approval system developed within a consortium of therapy clinics.

Impact of research on the process of therapy

A key area of ethical complexity in therapy research concerns the impact of research on the therapy process. In medical research, there are many situations where research can be carried out on data that are routinely collected as part of treatment, such as blood tests or heart monitoring. In these situations, the fact that research is being carried out has no impact on treatment at all. The growing popularity of practice-based research in counselling and psychotherapy (see Barkham, Hardy & Mellor-Clark, 2010, and Chapter 12 of the present book) is partly due to possibilities around this kind of normalised data collection within routine practice. However, most counselling and psychotherapy research involves some degree of alteration or intrusion to treatment as usual. This intrusion may not necessarily have a negative impact. Up to a point, clients find personal meaning and benefit in taking part in research activities such as filling in questionnaires or being interviewed (Marshall et al., 2001; Stone & Elliott, 2011). Clients report that these activities help them to reflect, help them to monitor their progress and give them a sense of making a contribution to the greater good. These positive reports raise the question of whether, in some cases, it may be ethically wrong to deny clients these potential benefits by excluding them from research. But it is also indisputable that there are some occasions when research activities may have a negative impact on therapy; for example, by taking up time in the hour that could be spent on therapeutic work, inhibition of client and therapist openness in response to recording devices, questionnaire items that ask the client to report on scary symptoms that they did not think they had, or concerns about how research data might be used in future.

Vulnerable participants

Within the broad field of research ethics, a great deal of attention is devoted to how to act responsibly in relation to the rights of people who are considered to be vulnerable. An individual may be deemed to be vulnerable if they have difficulty understanding what they are consenting to, lack confidence or authority to refuse to participate in research, or are likely to be upset or harmed by the research process. The scope and implications of this kind of vulnerability reach back into basic principles of human rights, and are interpreted in a range of ways in different countries and by researchers in different fields (Bracken-Roche et al., 2017; Finnegan & O'Donoghue, 2019; Lajoie, Fontin & Racine, 2020). The issue of participant vulnerability is problematic in psychotherapy research, because most therapists would consider their clients to be responsible adults who are capable of making consent decisions. However, even clients who are successful and far from vulnerable in many areas of their life, may be emotionally or interpersonally diminished at the point of entry into therapy. In addition, there are specific groups of clients, such as children, or people with dementia, who clearly meet the criteria for vulnerability. As a result of these factors, most university ethical approval procedures operate on an assumption that therapy clients are a vulnerable population. It is therefore necessary for researchers to acknowledge this possibility in proposals, and show that they have put measures in place to address it. A key requirement is to think carefully through all aspects of the research pathway, from the perspective of a participant, in terms of what might need to be put in place to keep them safe. A paper by Butler, Copnell and Hall (2019) provides a good example of how to do this, in the context of their research into the experiences of a highly vulnerable group of participants – parents in the months following the death of a child. It can be helpful to undertake this kind of auditing of the research pathway in consultation with members from the vulnerable group, or their representatives. Other procedures include rewriting the consent form and information sheet to make them more accessible, and arranging for a supporter or advocate to be involved in the consent-making process. Draucker, Martsolf and Poole (2009) describe the use of a distress checklist that interviewers are trained to use, to reinforce their sensitivity to potential negative effects of an interview. A further strategy to address distress during data collection is to offer participants a debrief, information about sources of ongoing assistance, or researcher contact details if they need a further debrief or support at a later stage. In many situations, a capacity to demonstrate sensitive and effective responsiveness to participant vulnerability is a condition for getting a research proposal accepted, not only by an ethics committee but also by service gatekeepers. An example of this is in the field of research on therapy for children and young people (Fried & Fisher, 2017).

Decolonising research

Research into the experiences of people from indigenous and First Nations communities involves awareness of vulnerability that is grounded in historical institutional oppression. The New Zealand educational researcher Linda Tuhiwai Smith has been a catalyst for drawing attention to this issue, and her work is key reading for all therapy researchers (Smith, 2021). There have been three main ethical issues associated with research on indigenous people (Tauri, 2018). First, a great deal of research has been carried out that has served the interests of white researchers, and left indigenous participants feeling exploited. Second, indigenous cultural values and worldview require attention to ethical considerations that are not generally considered to be important in Western culture – for example, the protected status of sacred knowledge, or the requirement for collective consent. Third, relationships between indigenous and white peoples take place against a backdrop of brutally destructive colonialism and racism – a context that needs to be taken into account in all aspects of a study. An example of the type of disconnect that has existed between therapy research and indigenous communities can be found in a study by Giordano et al. (2020) that reports on what indigenous people believe that white researchers need to learn. Important ethical strategies in decolonising research are an emphasis on collaborative research planning and research ownership, and publication in specialist indigenous journals (e.g. *Journal of Indigenous Research*; *AlterNative: An International Journal of Indigenous Peoples*) that function as guardians of ethical good practice.

Online research

The kinds of ethical procedures that are highlighted in the present chapter are based on research practice over many decades that took it for granted that there would be an actual face-to-face encounter between researcher and informant. However, in recent years, and more intensively in the light of the Covid-19 pandemic, there has been a major expansion in online research in which all communication is through remote contact using telephone, online interviewing, social media and online survey questionnaires. At an ethical level, this shift has important implications in terms of such aspects as recording participant consent in the absence of a written signature, certainty around the actual identity of a participant, difficulty in supporting vulnerable participants, security of online data, reduced capacity to detect participant distress, and territorial jurisdiction of ethics committees/review boards and other relevant professional bodies. There are also new and emergent ethical dilemmas associated with social media use – a reflection by Søndergaard (2019) on her experience of conducting research into sexualised social media communication in young people offers a glimpse of the moral complexities that can be involved. A valuable source for starting to think about strategies for addressing ethical issues associated with different types of online and distance research is Colson (2015). Additional recommended reading is British Psychological Society (2017) and Hunter et al. (2018). This is an area in which new data collection techniques are constantly being developed, and new ethical procedures are being devised to handle them – as with other areas of research ethics, it is always necessary to pay attention to how these areas are addressed in recent studies.

It is important to acknowledge that the ethical dilemmas outlined in the previous paragraphs are not insurmountable. Even a brief look at the therapy research literature will reveal many published studies in which therapists were involved in collecting data on their own clients, the research had an influence on the therapy process, clients were randomised to different forms of manualised intervention, studies were conducted of therapy with indigenous clients, and so on. What is concealed by the existence of these studies is the number of potentially valuable projects that were abandoned because such ethical issues could not be resolved, or the hours of negotiation and the compromises that shaped the design of the studies that were eventually carried out. When undertaking research that touches on any of these areas of ethical sensitivity, it is important to look at how the ethical issue has been addressed in published studies, consult widely, and show the ethics committee that you have taken the issue seriously and have been guided by best practice examples.

Research into ethical issues

Most of the literature on research ethics is written from a philosophical perspective, and consists of rational argument interspersed with occasional case examples. However, there also exists a substantial amount of research into various aspects of ethical good practice in research on psychotherapy and mental health issues. Studies have looked at the effect on vulnerable people of taking part in research that asks them to explore difficult life experiences. For example, research has explored the experiences of people who have been suicidal (Biddle et al., 2013), bereaved by suicide (Dyregrov et al., 2011), carers of those who have attempted suicide (Maple et al., 2020) and in recovery from trauma (Jaffe et al., 2015) or mental illness (Lajoie, Fortin & Racine, 2020). Such studies consistently find that the majority of participants view such research involvement in positive terms, because any distress that is felt is transient and balanced against the possibility of allowing them to give something back and make a contribution to service enhancement, and having an opportunity to reflect on their experience in a non-judgemental and supportive context (Lakeman et al., 2013). These outcomes are encouraging for anyone planning to undertake research with vulnerable participants, because they indicate that the appropriate implementation of wellbeing and confidentiality safeguards enables this area of inquiry to have the potential to be a meaningful and positive experience for informants.

Box 5.2   Beyond ethical codes

In practice, ethical decision-making in psychotherapy research is ultimately guided by ethical codes published by relevant professional bodies in such disciplines as psychology and psychiatry, social work and education. The ethical guidelines produced by these organisations are continually being reviewed and revised in response to critique. For example, Teo (2015) has identified important gaps in the research ethics codes of the psychology associations in the

USA and Canada. Journals such as *Ethics and Behavior* and *Research Ethics* explore the growing edges of ethical practice, where established ethical procedures and principles can be questioned and rewritten.

Conclusions

This chapter has provided an overview and introduction to the main ethical issues associated with research in counselling and psychotherapy, and the ways in which these issues can be addressed. To a large extent, knowledge and skills in relation to ethical issues can be regarded as a rather neglected area of the research literature. Typically, ethical issues receive scant attention in research articles. Most researchers are keen to get on with the actual research, and are reluctant to write or read about ethics. What this means, in practice, is that ethical know-how tends to be located in individuals and organisations. In a university or healthcare system, the research ethics committee, the people who sit on it, and those who submit research projects to it function as an informal repository of ethical knowledge. The extent and complexity of this knowledge are rarely apparent in any written documents. Instead, ethical knowledge takes the form of a set of shared understandings around what is possible, often connected to specific examples of research proposals that presented particularly thorny ethical dilemmas. It is important to realise that ethics books and chapters serve only as a means of learning the language of research ethics, as a means of being able to enter into the conversation. It is only then, by talking to other people, that it is possible to decide what needs to be done.

Suggestions for further reading

Further exploration of the issues outlined in the present chapter can be found in:

Danchev, D., & Ross, A. (2014). *Research Ethics for Counsellors, Nurses and Social Workers*. London: Sage.

Finlay, L. (2020). Ethical research? Examining knotty, moment-to-moment challenges throughout the research process. In S. Bager-Charleson & A. McBeath (eds), *Enjoying Research in Counselling and Psychotherapy Qualitative, Quantitative and Mixed Methods Research* (pp. 115–135). Basingstoke: Palgrave Macmillan.

Patel, T. (2020). Research in therapeutic practice settings: ethical considerations. In R. Tribe & J. Morrissey (eds), *The Handbook of Professional Ethical and Research Practice for Psychologists, Counsellors, Psychotherapists and Psychiatrists*. 3rd edn (pp. 191–205). London: Routledge.

Sieber, J. E., & Tolich, M. B. (2013). *Planning Ethically Responsible Research*. 2nd edn. Thousand Oaks, CA: Sage.

Srinath, S., & Bhola, P. (2016). Research ethics in psychotherapy and psychosocial interventions: role of institutional Ethical Review Boards. In P. Bhola & A. Raguram (eds), *Ethical Issues in Counselling and Psychotherapy Practice* (pp. 219–238). New York: Springer.

Online resources

The online resource site (https://study.sagepub.com/doingresearch4e) includes learning activities on ethical issues in therapy research.

6

Criteria for Evaluating the Quality of a Research Study

Introduction

There are several ways in which an understanding of the criteria for evaluating research studies can be helpful to someone who is planning to embark on their own research project. Being guided by a sense of what makes for quality and excellence in research provides a basis for critical and appreciative reading of research articles. Being able to identify appropriate standards of good research practice is also necessary during the research planning and proposal-writing process. A thorough knowledge of criteria of research quality is vital at the stage of writing up the findings of a study, and submitting a thesis or dissertation, or a paper for journal publication. Finally, familiarity with quality criteria makes it possible to play a role within the research community, in supporting colleagues who are planning or writing up their own studies, and acting as a reviewer of journal articles and research proposals.

In this chapter, the issue of quality criteria for evaluating research is approached from three perspectives. First, there is a discussion of some general quality criteria that are widely accepted across the whole field of science. The focus then turns to specific criteria that are associated with quantitative and qualitative research methodologies, and finally how research quality is assessed within the psychotherapy professional community.

Exercise 6.1   Exploring your own quality criteria

Identify some therapy research studies (or studies in other fields) that have been meaningful and inspiring for you. Then identify other studies that have left you feeling bored, annoyed or frustrated. What are the key attributes that you associate with each group of studies? What have you learned from this exercise, about the quality criteria that are most important to you?

General criteria for evaluating research

Research consists of a process of knowledge-building through collective critical debate. Scientific research can be regarded as a core aspect of modern democratic societies that are based on values such as freedom of the press and universal human rights. The corruption of scientific transparency, such as the distortion of science for political purposes in Nazi Germany and Stalinist Russia, or the abuse of science for commercial purposes by drug companies who conceal negative results, strikes at the heart of democratic society.

Critical debate needs a shared language, and institutional structures within which dialogue around competing ideas can be safely conducted. In relation to research, that shared language consists of a complex network of values and principles around what counts as acceptable and useful knowledge, and the basis for rejecting certain knowledge claims as unreliable or wrong. What lies behind this is a big question: what is true? Taken far enough, this question will always dissolve – ultimately, we can never know what is true. But, to thrive and evolve, any community needs to be able to operate on the basis of an agreed set of principles for deciding whether a statement is true or false.

Within the field of counselling and psychotherapy research, as well as elsewhere in the natural and social sciences, it is possible to identify some general quality criteria or 'truth tests' that are applicable to all research products:

Coherence refers to the extent to which each element of a study or research article is connected to each other element. Does the literature review provide a credible rationale for the research question? Does the methodology represent an appropriate means for collecting data that are relevant to the research question? Are the conclusions justified in terms of the evidence? A good piece of research fits together – it offers a logical line or argument all the way through. By contrast, when a reader gets lost reading a study, and unsure of how one aspect of it leads to the next, they are unable to respond to it as an overall unit of knowledge (even if specific parts of the study may be meaningful and valuable).

Communicability. Any piece of research consists of a complex set of procedures that rests upon an even more complex set of assumptions and theories. It is therefore not an easy matter to communicate research findings in a clear and concise manner. Lack of clarity makes it hard, or impossible, for a reader to judge whether the conclusions of a study are valid or reliable, or even what they mean. In practice, communicability depends on two skills: an ability to provide straightforward descriptions of what was done and what was found, and an absence of rhetorical language that goes beyond the information given. Ideally, sufficient information should be provided about method and results to enable the reader to come to their own conclusions about the study, for example by developing an alternative interpretation of findings.

Replicability refers to the possibility that a study could be repeated, by another researcher or research team and in a different setting. The principle of replicability is integral to the whole notion of science: a result that can only be obtained by one researcher or research team lacks credibility until it has been verified in other studies conducted elsewhere. The replicability criterion means that a reader of a research article should be provided with sufficient detail regarding what happened to participants, and how the data were collected, to be able to be in a position, in principle, to carry out the study for themselves. An importance aspect of replicability relates to the technical competence with which data were analysed: if the researcher has not followed accepted procedures then their work cannot be regarded as either a useful addition to the existing literature, or as a basis on which future studies might build.

Moral integrity refers to the ethical soundness of a study, in terms of safeguarding the confidentiality and wellbeing of participants. A more subtle level of moral integrity relates to the good faith of the researcher. Is the researcher trying to put a 'spin' on the findings, in order to provide evidence for his or her theory or therapy approach? If you read a research paper and end up not trusting the intentions of the researcher, there will always be a question mark over the findings and conclusions that it is offering.

Contextualisation within the relevant literature is particularly relevant at three points in a research study or paper: (i) providing a rationale for the study in terms of how it builds on existing knowledge; (ii) how the methodological approach adopted, or specific data collection techniques deployed, reflect current good practice within a field of inquiry; and (iii) how the findings of the study add to previous knowledge, in terms of confirming and challenging results of earlier studies.

Theoretical clarity is an evaluative criterion that reflects the importance of theory in any form of systematic inquiry. Although careful and accurate observation and description of phenomena are hugely important, it is only when we are able to make connections between disparate observations, by using concepts and theories, that we will be able to develop a form of knowledge that makes a difference to our lives. Every piece of research is informed, to a greater or lesser extent, by theory.

In good research, which is easy to read and makes sense, concepts are used appropriately and explained in a way that can be understood by the reader.

Originality refers to the capacity of a study to add something distinctive to the literature. In school, science classes are organised around demonstrations that re-run classic experiments. While such demonstrations of research techniques are essential teaching activities, they do not count as actual research. To be considered as research, a procedure needs to add something new to the stock of knowledge. There are some studies that provide, or contribute to the development of, a radically new way of making sense of a phenomenon. However, this is rare. More typically, originality takes the form of incremental progress, such as showing how an approach to therapy is effective (or needs to be adapted) with a new client group.

Acknowledging limitations. Any piece of research can only provide one piece of a much bigger picture. An indicator of research quality is the capacity of an author to be clear about the contribution that a study has made, while acknowledging its limitations and the types of further research that are required to fill gaps in knowledge of the topic that has been investigated.

Impact comprises an evaluation criterion that considers the extent to which a study or paper has made a difference in the world. There are many ways in which this benchmark has been defined. Impact on the scientific community and the literature can be assessed through counting the number of times a study has been cited or referenced in other articles or books. Google Scholar provides an estimate of this (other search engines can also be used for this purpose) – it is easy to see that some articles have been cited thousands of times, and others not at all. Impact also refers to the social and practical consequences of a study. To what extent, and in what ways, has a study or research programme made a difference to policy in relation to health and social care, or education? To what extent has it resulted in therapists changing their practice?

The application of these criteria is seldom clear-cut. Difficult judgements need to be made in relation to whether an adequate standard has been reached in each area. For example, one reader may find a study easy to follow, whereas another may not. Social and clinical impact of research is easier to demonstrate in a well-established and clearly definable therapy approach that gets rolled out at a health-service level, such as CBT, compared with a more integrative and flexible approach such as feminist therapy. The final section of the chapter, on how research quality is assessed within the psychotherapy professional community during the journal review process, explores how these general principles are applied in practice.

Exercise 6.2   Evaluating research papers that you read

Taken together, coherence, communicability, replicability, moral integrity, contextualisation, theoretical clarity, originality, acknowledging limitations and impact provide a matrix through which you can assess research papers that you read. You might want to add further personal criteria to this list. As you read research papers through the lens provided by these principles, it is valuable also to be curious about *how* authors accomplish them. What is it that a researcher is doing that leads you to regard their work as coherent, replicable, etc.? If you have doubts about the coherence, replicability, etc. of a study, what would the author need to do (or have done in the process of collecting and analysing data) to convince you?

The big divide: evaluative criteria associated with quantitative and qualitative research

The field of counselling and psychotherapy research can be divided, for the most part, into studies that look for patterns in numbers (quantitative methods) and those that look for patterns in words and stories (qualitative methods). In Chapter 1, it was argued that both of these approaches are necessary in therapy research. However, it is important to recognise that qualitative and quantitative methodologies generate different types of knowing that are associated with different quality criteria. A useful perspective on this divide was offered by one of the leading figures in the twentieth century, Jerome Bruner, who made a distinction between 'narrative' and 'paradigmatic' forms of knowing. Narrative knowing is based on stories through which people share their experience of specific events, typically using evocative language and vivid imagery that convey emotional meaning. By contrast, paradigmatic knowing reflects rational, abstract if–then general statements. For Bruner (1990), both types of knowing are essential aspects of being human.

Qualitative research can be viewed as broadly representing a narrative way of knowing, while quantitative research reflects a paradigmatic mode of understanding. However, quantitative research can be more appropriately regarded as a particular form of paradigmatic/abstract knowing that is expressed through numbers. While paradigmatic knowing, in the form of a capacity to operate in terms of abstract categories, is a general human attribute, number-use only emerged fairly recently in human history, in conjunction with money, trade and taxes. Using numbers to regulate social life, through such means as the census, or intelligence tests, only developed in the nineteenth century. As a result, quantitative research needs to be seen as a special type of paradigmatic knowing that depends on a double abstraction: not just the use of an abstract numerical label in itself, but a further step of comparison across a population through the calculation of averages and other statistical concepts. The point being made here is that the introduction of numbers takes paradigmatic knowing into another level. For example, psychoanalytic theory is a form of paradigmatic knowing that does not depend on numbers.

In relation to the issue of research quality, what makes quantitative research distinctive is that it assumes that there exists an objective reality that can be measured. At the end of the day, the adequacy of a quantitative study is evaluated in terms of how accurately it has reflected that reality. By contrast, qualitative research seeks to make sense of the stories we tell ourselves and each other, in terms of understanding how meaning is created and communicated. While correspondence with objective reality is relevant to qualitative research (was the account of therapy generated by a client interview an accurate depiction of what happened, or was it shaped by a wish to please the interviewer?), what is more important is whether a qualitative study helps to make an aspect of human experience more meaningful. As a consequence, evaluating the adequacy of a qualitative study is not straightforward, because the issue of meaningfulness inevitably refers to personal and subjective judgements and also to contrasting moral and value positions that exist within a culture or community.

For example, it is widely accepted that quantitative research produces more reliable findings if there is a large sample of participants. Basically, this is because the average or mean score reported in a large sample is less influenced by outliers and as a result is more likely to be the 'true' average (with the further consequence that statistical operations based on this array of data are more likely to be meaningful).

By contrast, qualitative research yields more meaningful findings with a small or moderate number of participants (for example 1–20). Basically, this is because it is harder to convey rich detail and nuanced descriptions of individual experience if the sample is too large: qualitative studies with larger samples either report meanings (i.e. themes or categories arising from analysis of qualitative data) in the form of abstract themes that are distanced from lived experience, or (in an attempt to stay close to informant experience) become so complex that they are difficult to understand. In a qualitative study, a participant who is an 'outlier' (e.g. someone whose interview generates themes that differ from those contributed by other informants) is a gift – the data they provide stimulates the researcher to think more deeply about the topic being investigated.

Criteria for quantitative studies

Quantitative psychotherapy research makes use of an array of strategies for assessing and ensuring the quality of a study. The key concepts that underpin all of these approaches are *validity* and *reliability*. Validity refers to the extent to which a measurement, or set of conclusions derived from analysis of quantitative data, corresponds to the true or real state of affairs. For example, does a measure of depression actually capture levels of depression, or are its scores also influenced by the person's level of anxiety? Or: when a study shows that therapy X is more effective than therapy Y, is this a true result or is it error? Reliability refers to the question of whether a measure or study will produce the same result on a different occasion. For example, if a person reports a high score on a depression measure, and their life situation remains stable, will they record the same score (or a very similar one) three months later? Or: will the superiority of therapy X over therapy Y be found in a different clinic in a study run by different researchers?

In quantitative research, validity and reliability are never absolute. Instead, statistical procedures are used to estimate the level of confidence with which we can accept a particular set of data, or conclusions, as being valid or reliable. These procedures operate at different levels:

The validity and reliability of a measure. There are several statistical techniques for establishing the validity of a measure (e.g. a self-report questionnaire through which clients can indicate the severity of depression). Scores on the measure can be compared to an external criterion. For instance, depression scores can be compared with results of an in-depth psychiatric interview. Scores can be compared against scores from measures of other variables (construct validity): one would expect a low correlation between depression and intelligence, but a higher correspondence between depression scores and self-esteem scores. Reliability can be determined by administering a measure on different occasions, and estimating the stability of scores over time (test re-test reliability). The internal reliability (or consistency) of a scale can be calculated by analysing the extent to which each item correlates with other items. These are just some possibilities; many other validity and reliability procedures are described in the literature. Each of these validity and reliability procedures yields a score of strength of validity/reliability. This makes it possible to study the extent to which improvements to a measure have the effect of enhancing its accuracy. None of these procedures require personal judgement on the part of the researcher – they are entirely based on the application of standardised statistical techniques.

The appropriate use of statistical methods. In any area of quantitative research, there exist established rules regarding which statistical test or technique is appropriate, and how the outputs of these tests should be interpreted.

The design of a study. The purpose of quantitative research is to establish patterns or regularities within the real world. Sometimes these patterns refer to the structure of a phenomenon – for instance, is intelligence a unitary phenomenon (i.e. are people simply more intelligent or less intelligent?) or does it break down into a set of sub-factors (e.g. verbal intelligence, emotional intelligence, kinaesthetic intelligence)? Hundreds of studies have shown the latter is the case, even if they do not entirely agree on how best to describe what these factors are. Sometimes the aim is to identify causal links between factors. For example: is CBT an effective therapy for depression? Or to identify the relative strength of causal links, as in: is CBT more effective than psychodynamic therapy, *or* what contributes more to outcome – therapist technique or the therapeutic alliance? In order both to detect patterns, and to be confident that the patterns that emerge from a quantitative study actually reflect patterns in the real world, it is necessary to create a situation in which extraneous factors are controlled. For example, in research on intelligence, you probably do not want some of your participants to be fatigued (e.g. just completed a night shift) and others not fatigued. Similarly, in a study of the effectiveness of therapy for depression, you do not want some of the therapists to be offering different styles of CBT, or some clients to be struggling with trauma symptoms alongside their depression, and so on. Over time, quantitative researchers have developed sophisticated criteria for evaluating the design of studies in terms of the degree to which non-relevant factors have been controlled or eliminated. For example, randomised controlled/clinical trials of health interventions (such as psychotherapy) are evaluated using the CONSORT (Consolidated Standards of Reporting Trials; www.consort-statement.org) guidelines. A researcher would not be able to receive funding for an RCT if their research design did not adhere to CONSORT standards, and their eventual report of findings would not be taken seriously if it was apparent that they had diverged from these standards in the conduct of the study.

Because of the intensity of global research effort associated with quantitative methodologies, and the unifying effect of a common commitment to mathematical reasoning, all aspects of quantitative research are covered by well-understood evaluative criteria that can be applied in a systematic and objective manner. This does not mean that these criteria are fixed in stone – they are constantly being debated and refined – but they do provide researchers with a secure, agreed framework to inform research practice.

Box 6.1   Therapist criteria for evaluating research

Although the ultimate purpose of psychotherapy research is to support more effective practice, research studies are generally written for an audience of other researchers, rather than for practitioners. A particularly interesting study on this topic was conducted by Stewart, Stirman and Chambless (2012). Although the therapists interviewed in this study were clear that research was a potentially valuable source of learning, they regarded the majority of studies that they read as being too remote from practice to be of any use to them.

Criteria for qualitative studies

The situation in *qualitative* research is quite different. Qualitative inquiry consists of a family of methodologies that draw on contrasting philosophical principles. Although quantification does happen in qualitative research (e.g. number of participants contributing to a particular theme), it is not a central aspect of this approach to knowledge, and it is not possible to generate numerical evaluation metrics.

A further challenge for the evaluation of qualitative research is that it has not been easy to move beyond the concepts of validity and reliability. For most people, these concepts make a lot of intuitive sense as ways of talking about whether a study is any good. However, these ideas have become firmly anchored in statistical procedures that are not applicable in qualitative research. As a consequence, a major challenge for qualitative researchers has been to develop an alternative language for evaluating research. Terminology that has been used includes words such as trustworthiness, credibility, practical utility, plausibility, heuristic value, transferability and integrity, or phrases that tweak quantitative language, such as consequential validity, transgressive validity and transformational validity. Another approach has been to discuss research quality in relation to the criterion of 'publishability' (Elliott, Fischer & Rennie, 1999).

Many papers have been written on how to evaluate qualitative research. Within the field of qualitative research in counselling and psychotherapy, influential contributions have been Stiles (1993), Elliott, Fischer & Rennie (1999) and Morrow (2005). The broad themes outlined in these (and other) reviews of qualitative validity were condensed by Tracy (2010) into a set of eight 'big-tent' criteria for excellence in qualitative research:

- *worthy topic*: the research focuses on an issue that is timely, significant and interesting;
- *rich rigour*: all aspects of the study (e.g. the sample, time spent in the field, data collection and analysis) reflect close, intense commitment;
- *sincerity*: the researcher positions themselves in the study, and is open about the challenges they have faced;
- *credibility*: rich description and carful reporting enables the reader to get close to the topic being investigated; showing as well as telling; evidence that study was meaningful for participants;
- *resonance*: study is capable of moving the reader, and offering them insights that they can apply in practice;
- *significant contribution*: offers an advance on existing knowledge (theoretical, methodological, practical);
- *ethical*: shows sensitivity to ethical dimensions of the research process, and addresses them effectively;
- *meaningful coherence:* consistency between the goals of the study, and methods used.

An example of how these criteria were applied in a research study can be found in Gordon and Patterson (2013).

A different approach to determining what makes an exceptional qualitative study was taken by Jonsen, Fendt and Point (2018), who selected papers in their own field (organisational research) that had touched them personally and that they regarded as being highly meaningful and persuasive. They then looked closely at how these papers were written, to see if they could discover how the authors had worked their magic. In addition to the criteria identified by Tracy (2010), they came up with the notion that the researchers in their sample of studies all exhibited a capacity to use imagination and creativity.

An important development within qualitative research in psychology and psychotherapy was the establishment of a special task force of the American Psychological Association (APA), set up to try to bring together ideas about standards for qualitative articles in a way that would offer guidance to both researchers and reviewers. This group aimed to develop a framework for understanding what made a piece of qualitative research rigorous or trustworthy (Levitt et al., 2017). They suggested that trustworthiness arose from a combination of how the study was carried out (method) alongside other factors such as the reputation of the researcher, the way the study was written and how well it connected with the personal experience of the reader. They decided that what was particularly important for APA to be able to advise on was the methodology of a study. The task force therefore identified one broad criterion as an indicator of rigour: *methodological integrity* (consistency between all aspects of a study, particularly in relation to how methods of data collection and analysis align with underlying philosophical/epistemological assumptions). Integrity was seen as comprising two dimensions: *fidelity* to the subject matter of the study, and *utility* in relation to achieving the goals of the study. As well as providing a detailed analysis of how methodological integrity, fidelity and utility permeate all aspects of qualitative research (Levitt et al., 2017), the task force also produced an itemised guide to how to write a paper that conformed to these principles (Levitt et al., 2018; Levitt, 2020). The influence of the ideas and criteria developed by this APA task force fairly soon became apparent in qualitative therapy research papers, particularly those published in APA journals such as *Journal of Counseling Psychology*, for instance through much more frequent reporting of how underlying philosophical/epistemological assumptions were articulated in the design of a study.

Practical strategies for enhancing the credibility of a qualitative study

As well as paying attention to evaluative criteria such as integrity, fidelity, utility, and so on, another way of thinking about what makes for a good piece of qualitative research is to consider what researchers actually do in practice to fulfil these principles. Many strategies have been developed for enhancing the rigour, trustworthiness or validity of a qualitative study:

- transparent paper-trail that allows the reader to follow the process that took place between data collection, analysis and conclusions;
- rich description of data, in the form of informant quotes, observations, segments of transcript, etc. ('showing' rather than just 'telling');
- providing information on number of participants who contributed to each theme;
- researcher reflexivity/positioning: providing the reader with information about the background, pre-expectations, etc. of the researcher(s); using a research journal and supervision to enhance this process;
- verifying themes: analysing a set of interviews, then applying the themes to additional interviews;
- reliability of analysis: independent auditor given set of participant statements and themes – do they allocate statements to the same themes as main researcher?;
- auditing and dialogue in which other people (usually research colleagues and research supervisor, but sometimes also research participants) read and analyse the data, and compare perspectives;
- consultation with participants at end of interview about their experience of being interviewed;
- member checking: presenting findings to research participants, and asking them to comment on whether themes match their own experience;
- catalytic validity: collecting evidence on whether findings are meaningful to target audience (e.g. by giving talks and asking for feedback);
- secondary analysis (another researcher or team conducts a completely independent analysis of the entire data set).

There exists an extensive literature (and debate) on the use of each of these strategies. It is also valuable to pay attention, when reading qualitative studies, to which validity strategies are selected in specific studies (no one ever uses all of these techniques) and how they are implemented or adapted in different contexts. An important aspect of these strategies for enhancing trustworthiness is that they are valuable no matter what underling epistemological position is adopted by a researcher. For example, if a researcher is operating from a realist or objectivist approach to knowledge, the techniques listed above can be used to establish consensus (i.e. convergence on a single 'true' set of findings). Alternatively, if a researcher is influenced by a constructivist, interpretivist or critical perspective, the same techniques can be used to promote dialogue that supports a 'multi-voiced' presentation of findings.

How research quality is assessed within the psychotherapy professional community

The preceding sections of this chapter have introduced the main criteria that are used to evaluate the quality, truth-value and practical utility of therapy research studies. It is clear that there are a wide range of criteria, many of which are difficult to define in a precise manner, and may be in tension with each other. To be able to answer the question 'Is a research paper any good?' it is therefore necessary to understand not only what the relevant criteria are, but also how these standards are applied in practice.

Technical criteria and guidelines

There exists a wide range of specific technical criteria associated with the use of different research techniques. For example, there are generally recognised conventions, defined by the American Psychological Association (APA), in relation to the reporting of statistical analyses (Appelbaum et al., 2018; Cooper, 2020). Most approaches to qualitative research have generated books and articles on how they should be used – see, for example, the criteria for Interpretative Phenomenological Analysis (IPA) published by Smith (2011a). There are detailed style guidelines for how articles should be written for APA journals (APA, 2020). All research measures are supported by manuals that describe how they should be administered and analysed.

Rating scales

In some situations, it can be useful to be able to apply a standard set of criteria to the assessment of research papers. For example, when conducting a literature review on a topic where a lot of research has been carried out, it may be necessary to impose a quality threshold, and only consider papers that reflect a higher level of methodological rigour. In such situations, the team conducting the literature review will normally employ a rating scale or checklist, through which they can quantify the degree of adequacy of various aspects of the study, and compare their judgements. Examples of research quality rating scales are Deeks et al. (2003), Downs and Black (1998), and Hong et al. (2018). There are also many rating scales for evaluating the extent to which a therapist in a research study had adhered to a specific model of therapy. Although, as seen above, there are many different criteria that can be applied when assessing the quality of research, and many different ways of interpreting these criteria, what a rating scale does is simplify all of this into a set of maybe 10–12 summary statements.

The journal review process

All of the perspectives and criteria discussed in the present chapter come together in the process of reviewing research articles submitted for publication in a journal. Anonymous peer review of papers represents a cornerstone of contemporary scientific practice. The version of an article that is sent to a journal includes no information that might allow its authors to be identified. The manuscript is then sent to three or more experts in the field, for anonymous peer review. Reviewer feedback and suggestions are collated by the journal editor and sent to the author(s) of the article, along with a recommendation that the paper is either accepted or rejected, or can be revised and corrected. Typically, reviews draw on any or all of the general and specific criteria that the reviewer feels may be relevant. The purpose of this procedure is to exert the highest possible standard of quality control for articles that enter the literature, in a context in which reviewers are not influenced by the reputation of the author, or whether they personally like or dislike them.

Journals tend to publish fewer than half of the manuscripts that are submitted to them. Even though some of these papers are then subsequently resubmitted to another journal and eventually published elsewhere, a considerable proportion of potentially valuable studies end up never being published. In addition, there are many studies (e.g. student dissertations, practitioner research, reports by community agencies) carried out by researchers who lack the confidence, time or motivation to embark on the publication pathway at all. Also, there are often quite significant disagreements across reviewers regarding whether a study has reached the standard required for publication. Finally, there are concerns about the robustness of the review process. Some studies are published with gaps and flaws that ideally should have been picked up by the review process. An overview of these issues can be found in Oddli, Kjøs and McLeod (2020).

A key point here is that despite the vast array of quality criteria, checklists and guidelines that are available, there are still considerable legitimate differences across expert reviewers regarding whether a study is good enough.

Conclusions

This chapter has explored the various kinds of evaluative criteria that can be applied when assessing the merit of research proposals and publications. Sometimes, it can happen that the more a person reads about methodology, the more critical they become of the research that is carried out. This tendency can even give rise to a form of nihilism or deep scepticism about research, in which all research is irredeemably flawed. In my view, this is a trap. My own position is that any research that has been carried out with integrity, and from a position of genuine curiosity, will almost always have something interesting to offer. It is essential to be able to affirm the value and contribution of a study, while at the same time recognising its limitations. All research has its limitations: there exist a wide range of criteria for answering the question 'Is it any good?', and no study is perfect.

Suggestions for further reading

Further exploration of the issues discussed in the present chapter can be found in Barker, C. and Pistrang, N. (2005). Quality criteria under methodological pluralism: implications for conducting and evaluating research. *American Journal of Community Psychology*, 35, 201–212. Although this paper discusses quality criteria from a community psychology perspective, and does not specifically refer to psychotherapy research, its line of argument and conclusions are highly relevant for the study of therapy.

Online resources

The online resource site (https://study.sagepub.com/doingresearch4e) includes further learning activities related to the issues discussed in this chapter.

7

Using Quantitative Methods

Introduction

Historically, research in counselling and psychotherapy, along with research in psychology, social science and the health sciences, has largely consisted of quantitative studies. The use of measurement to carry out comparisons between different groups or interventions, or to identify patterns and causal linkages, has proved to be an essential tool in the development of research-based knowledge. The present chapter provides an overview of the role of quantitative methods in therapy research, what novice researchers need to know in order to make use of such methods and how statistical skills can be acquired.

Why is it important to know about quantitative methods?

There has been a degree of resistance to quantitative methods within some areas of the counselling and psychotherapy professional community. Part of this resistance arises from a view that the translation of the therapy experience into numbers involves losing the real meaning of what happens in therapy. Those who espouse this position tend to argue that quantitative methods have only a very limited relevance to the advancement of practical knowledge about therapy, and that we would be better served by pursuing other forms of inquiry, such as qualitative research, clinical case studies and philosophical critique.

I would strongly encourage all readers who are resistant to quantitative methods to reconsider their position. Avoidance of studies that use quantitative methods means cutting oneself off from around 90 per cent of the therapy research literature. It also means cutting oneself off from dialogue and debates with groups of colleagues who carry out quantitative research and use it to inform their practice. Within the field of contemporary research in counselling and psychotherapy, there is a broad consensus that qualitative and quantitative methodologies represent distinct and complementary approaches to inquiry, and that both are necessary. It is therefore important for each approach to be able to engage with the other.

Exercise 7.1   Your attitude to quantification

How do you feel about the practice of measuring aspects of therapy? Does it fill you with excitement, around the possibility of developing a more rigorous evidence base? Or do you have more ambivalent or even negative feelings and images around this kind of approach? It can be valuable, in relation to your development as a researcher, to explore the origins and basis for these attitudes. Where do these attitudes and beliefs come from? What were the critical events and relationships that shaped the way you think about numbers? Once you have mapped your own stance in relation to quantification, it can be instructive to engage in dialogue with individuals whose position on quantification is different from your own. What can you learn from them? What can they learn from you? To what extent does the attempt to engage in dialogue lead to a modification of your position?

What do I need to know?

It is possible to identify three levels of statistical knowledge: reading-level knowledge, novice user and advanced user. It is important for all counselling and psychotherapy practitioners to possess sufficient understanding of statistical concepts to be able to read and make sense of quantitative research papers. This is not a particularly difficult hurdle to negotiate, because in any quantitative research paper, any tables of numbers, or passages describing statistical techniques and results, will always be accompanied by a non-technical narrative account of the same information. To be able to read a quantitative paper, therefore, it is only necessary to be familiar with basic statistical terminology (such as 'mean' and 'standard deviation' – see following section), along with a grasp of what the researcher is trying to achieve by carrying out a statistical analysis (e.g. looking at whether one group of clients has better therapy outcomes than another group). The possession of a basic reading-level competence does not allow the reader to evaluate whether the right statistical techniques have been applied, or whether the appropriate conclusions have been drawn. This is not a major problem, because any published article should have been carefully reviewed by independent referees who know about these things. The most important step in the development of reading-level competence is to read quantitative papers, if necessary looking up the meaning of terms that are unfamiliar, and to persevere. It is also helpful to be able to talk to colleagues who are a few steps further down that road. Sometimes, it may be less helpful to talk to advanced experts in statistical methods, because they know too much and find it hard to get on the same wavelength as statistical beginners.

Being able to take the further step of using statistical techniques in a piece of research requires training. There is a wealth of statistics tutorials online, which allow basic stats skills to be acquired through independent study. Another way of learning statistics is through assisting with a research study and being taught by whoever is carrying out the statistical analysis of data collected in the study. That kind of apprenticeship training is probably the best way to learn, because it is tailored to the learner and goes at the learner's pace. However, it is somewhat time-consuming for the teacher. An option that is available in most universities is to sign up for a statistics class that offers structured, step-by-step training, accompanied by assessment of learning, support and feedback. All universities and most colleges offer statistics training, usually at all levels from introductory to advanced, and may allow learners to enrol in these classes even when they are not registered for a specific degree.

Typically, a statistics class will be organised around a specific textbook, which will be used by all students. There are many excellent statistics textbooks on the market. A statistics textbook that has been particularly well received by novice therapy researchers is Field (2017). This book is very widely used, and therefore likely to be available in a local library. It is written with a fair amount of humour, and supported by a well-planned and comprehensive website that includes video demonstrations of key statistical skills.

An alternative strategy, for anyone thinking about carrying out a quantitative study, might be to join a research team that includes a stats specialist, or find someone who will do the stats for you. This is a perfectly legitimate solution which is widely used in many areas of medical and social research. For example, university-affiliated teaching hospitals will normally employ statisticians whose job it will be to take responsibility for analysing quantitative data collected in medical studies.

Advanced users of statistical methods are people who are particularly interested in statistical techniques, and who have undergone training in sophisticated methods such as regression, complex analysis of variance, factor analysis and multilevel linear modelling (Field, 2017). Advanced statistical methods are typically covered in doctoral-level training in clinical or counselling psychology.

The Statistical Package for the Social Sciences (SPSS) is a popular downloadable, user-friendly statistics package which is available in most universities and health services. However, an individual user licence to use SPSS is fairly costly, and as a result a number of open source/free statistics packages have become available, such as GNU-PSPP. Reviews of statistic software packages, and stats video tutorials, are readily available on the internet.

An introduction to basic statistical concepts and terminology

The purpose of this section is to enable people who are not familiar with statistical concepts to be able to read and make sense of counselling and psychotherapy research papers that make use of quantitative analysis. It includes brief explanations of basic concepts and terminology. Information about more advanced concepts can be explored through consulting statistics textbooks and internet resources.

In any well-written quantitative paper, in the results section the author should provide a plain language account of findings, alongside the numbers and reports on statistical analyses. It should always be possible to 'skip' the stats, and pick up the thread of the study and its results by reading the non-statistical sections of the report.

When reading a quantitative study, it is important to take account of the fact that therapy researchers tend to make use of the most advanced and sophisticated forms of statistical analysis that are available to them, in order to extract the fullest value out of complex data sets. Quite often, in the pressure to report these advanced analyses, they may neglect to provide more basic information regarding the actual average scores different groups of participants recorded on different measures. This can be frustrating for practitioners who are reading a paper and want to know about such matters as the degree to which participants in a study reported symptom severity scores that were comparable with the clients with whom they work on a day-to-day basis in their own practice.

Much of the time, the majority of readers do not fully understand the stats that are used in a quantitative article – even people who have had some stats training. It is not unusual for the researcher themselves to not fully understand what the stats are about, because they work in a university where they have expert statisticians to advise them on what to do. On the whole, experienced readers are not bothered by any of this. It is very unlikely, in an article published in a reputable journal, that the stats have been calculated wrongly. This is because the figures are checked carefully before the paper is published. Occasionally, arguments break out in the literature around the best way to analyse particular types of data.

It can be useful to view statistics as a language that includes new ideas and words. As with any language learning, it takes a bit of time to get to grips with it and feel comfortable using it. Regular practice is important. And there is always more to be learned.

Numbers and statistical tests are a really good way of summarising information that has been collected from groups of people, and looking for patterns in that information. Essentially, that is what it is all about. A typical scenario is that a sample of people complete a questionnaire. By using stats, it is possible to look at questions such as:

- What is the average score?
- What is the range of scores (i.e. highest to lowest)?
- How spread out are the scores (i.e. are the scores spread out across the whole scale, or have all the participants obtained fairly similar scores)?
- Do different groups (e.g. men vs women; CBT clients vs psychodynamic clients) have different scores?

Statistical methods used in therapy research can be divided into *descriptive* and *inferential* statistics. Descriptive statistics provide a description of the people in the research sample, in terms of the information collected on these people by the researcher. Inferential statistics, by contrast, enable the researcher to test hypotheses, and assess the confidence with which statements made about the sample being investigated will also be likely to hold true for the population as a whole.

Descriptive statistics

The most basic piece of descriptive terminology is 'n' or 'N' – the number of people in a sample.

In almost all research that uses measurement, the average or *mean* score is reported. This is simply calculated by adding up everyone's score and dividing it by the number of people. The mean score for a sample is usually symbolised as 'm'. Other ways of reporting on the 'central tendency' in a set of data are through the *median* score (the middle of a set of numbers/scores) or the *mode* (the single most frequently recorded number/score).

It is also interesting to know about the *variability* of scores – the amount of spread in the distribution of scores. The *standard deviation* statistic (abbreviated as s, s.d., sd or S.D.) is almost universally given in research reports as a measure of variability. The SD figure summarises the spread of scores: two-thirds of people in a sample will have scores that are one SD above or below the mean (this proportion included is an arbitrary convention and has no deeper meaning in itself). Another way of reporting on the spread of scores is to report minimum and maximum scores, or percentiles (e.g. the highest or lowest 10 per cent of scores). In some studies variance is described through *z-scores*. A z-score of +1 indicates that a case is 1 standard deviation above the mean; a z-score of −0.5 means that the case is half a standard deviation below the mean.

Mean and standard deviation figures are most meaningful when a graphical plot of scores resembles a 'normal' distribution. The concept of normal distribution refers to a widely observed phenomenon that, when something occurring in nature (such as the height or weight of a group of people) is plotted on a graph, it ends up looking something like a bell-shaped curve, with a big cluster of cases toward the centre, and tailing off on either side towards extreme high or low scores.

A lot of statistical analysis techniques depend on being able to demonstrate (or reasonably assume) a normal distribution of scores. Situations where the distribution of scores is skewed to one end of the range, were the peak is very sharp or very flat, or where there is more than peak, generally cause problems in quantitative research. For example, if you use a five-point (1–5) rating scale to ask people about their attitude to CBT, what you are hoping will emerge is a graph where few people score 1 or 5, and most are somewhere in the middle of the range. If almost everyone scores 5 (extremely positive) or 1 (extremely negative), then you are likely to be left wondering whether your results are an accurate representation of attitudes, or whether they just mean that your questionnaire item was phrased in a way that was not sufficiently sensitive to a range of views. Alternatively, if a big group of respondents tick the '1' box and a similarly large group tick '5' (i.e. two peaks with a dip in the middle rather than a single high point in the graph) it may mean that question was ambiguous, and was phrased in a way that resulted in it being interpreted differently by different groups of people. Or, that attitudes to CBT are not distributed along a smooth pro/con continuum, but instead comprise a split between some people who are strongly pro and others who are strongly against.

Inferential statistics

The purpose of inferential statistics is to enable the researcher to *test hypotheses*. For example, a researcher may hypothesise that clients will report higher levels of satisfaction in sessions where the counsellor displays a higher proportion of accurate empathy responses. Or the hypothesis may be that group therapy is more effective than individual counselling for students with loneliness problems. Statistical analysis of scores collected from groups of clients makes it possible to confirm/accept or refute/reject these hypotheses.

The way that inferential statistics operate is not to test a research hypothesis directly, but to calculate the confidence with which the null hypothesis can be rejected. The null hypothesis is a statement that the sets of scores that have been obtained for different groups are *equal* (e.g. that the high- and low-empathy groups are no different in satisfaction, or that individual counselling and group therapy are equally effective). If it turns out that the scores are unequal, then this is evidence to support the research hypothesis.

The null hypothesis is a precise and exact statement: there is *no* difference between the groups. In reality, there will always be *some* difference in the scores on a test or measure that two sets of people have completed. What needs to be known is whether this difference that has been found is due to random or chance factors (i.e. fluctuations in scores that could occur for myriad reasons), or whether it is a sufficiently large difference to indicate that a meaningful effect has been observed. The statistical formulae used in inferential statistics essentially give the researcher a way to ascertain the level of *probability* (p) that a particular result could have been obtained by chance.

The concept of probability refers to the likelihood of occurrence of an event. A high probability would mean that the event was almost certain to happen. A low probability indicates that the event is very unlikely indeed. The convention in mathematics is to report probability on a scale of 0 to 1, with a probability of 0 being equivalent to 'never' and a probability of 1 meaning that the event was certain. A probability of 0.5 would reflect a 50 per cent, or one time in two chance of the event occurring (as with tossing a coin – over a series of tosses, heads and tails each come up half of the time). A probability of 0.1 would suggest a 10 per cent or one time in ten chance. A probability of 0.01 would suggest a 1 per cent or one time in a hundred chance.

In the studies of empathy or student counselling mentioned above, from a statistical point of view the question that is being asked is: what is the probability that the difference between the two groups is due to chance? If the scores from each group are quite similar, this suggests that the difference between them is due merely to chance. When this happens, the null hypothesis is supported (or, strictly speaking, cannot be rejected) and the research hypothesis (i.e. that there is a meaningful difference between the groups) is not supported.

By contrast, if the differences between the two groups are large, it is unlikely that this has occurred due to random fluctuations in, say, how much attention that participant Z was paying to the answers he was giving to questionnaire items. In such a scenario, null hypothesis can be rejected and the research hypothesis supported.

Although students designing experiments in lab classes are drilled to present their findings in terms of testing the null hypothesis, this phrase is rarely found in published studies. However, it remains a crucial underlying logical principle in all statistical techniques.

Statistical tests are formulae or equations for calculating the probability of a set of scores or numbers appearing by chance. These formulae need to take account of various aspects of the data: the variability of scores (e.g. presence of outliers that skew the average/mean score); the magnitude of the differences observed between groups; and, the size of the sample (if there is a small sample, there is more chance that one additional case might change the whole picture – by contrast, in a large sample an additional case is unlikely to make much difference).

There are many different statistical tests, because there exist many different research contexts. For example, in relation to the discussion of variability, above, there are different formulae for analysis of normally distributed data and for skewed data. There are also different formulae (tests) for data that reflect different levels of measurement. *Categorical* measurement involves numbers being used as labels (male = 1 and female = 2). There is a limited amount of statistical wizardry that can be carried out at this level (e.g. *chi-square* analysis of male–female difference in completing therapy vs unplanned ending). An *ordinal* level of measurement is like lining up children in a playground in height order (1 is less than 2, which is less than 3, but no assumptions that the difference between 1 and 2 is the same as between 2 and 3). A therapy research example of ordinal scaling might be if you were to ask clients to prioritise the importance of therapist attributes such as qualifications, age, gender, ethnicity and warmth. The ultimate level of measurement involves the construction of an *interval* scale which is like a metre stick or stop-watch in which the interval between each unit is exactly the same. Interval measurement is jackpot territory for statisticians, because it makes it possible to carry out more sophisticated types of analysis because the numbers behave like numbers rather than like labels.

In a research study, the investigator is looking for low probabilities that findings can be attributed to chance. But, for a probability estimate, how low is low enough? Again, this is another situation where there exist generally accepted conventions. Usually, a probability of less than 0.05 (or one time in 20) would be considered as the threshold for statistical acceptability. If a result is likely to happen more than one time in 20 simply because of random error or chance factors, it is not a very robust or meaningful finding. In research studies, therefore, statistical significance values are usually reported in a form such as $p < 0.05$, which would indicate a probability of less than 1 in 20 that a result has been obtained by chance. Other probability threshold levels commonly employed are 0.01 (one in 100) and 0.001 (one in 1000). Some researchers prefer to report the exact probability value obtained, rather than a 'less than' figure. Increasingly, researchers report probability in terms of *confidence intervals*: for example, 95 per cent confidence (i.e. $p < .05$) that the true result lies somewhere between two figures.

A statistical test that is widely used in therapy research is the *correlation coefficient* (reported as 'r'). This is a statistic that shows the strength of relationship between two variables. The value of a correlation coefficient (r) can range from +1.00 to −1.00 (this is another example of a statistical convention). A positive (plus sign) correlation means that there is a positive linear relationship between two variables (i.e. higher scores on one variable are associated with higher scores on the other). A negative correlation means that high scores on one variable are associated with low scores on the other: a negative linear relationship. The nearer r is to plus or minus 1.00, the stronger the relationship is between the two variables. An example of how this statistic is used can be found in studies in which multiple measures of client symptoms and other characteristics are administered. Often, such studies will include a matrix that displays the degree of correlation between different measures. For instance, a (very high) correlation of 0.8 between anxiety and depression suggests that these measures are essentially measuring the same thing (e.g. level of general distress). By contrast, a low correlation of 0.1 between intelligence and depression would suggest that these are quite separate variables that overlap in relatively few cases (i.e. high intelligence is found in people who are depressed and also in those who are not depressed). A negative correlation indicates an association between two variables, but in a reverse direction. For example, a negative correlation between depression and self-esteem suggests that they are fundamentally the same construct (i.e., people who score high on depression also tend to score low on self-esteem).

A wide range of statistical techniques can be used to decide whether to reject the null hypothesis when comparing scores for two or more groups. Some of the main hypothesis-testing techniques used in therapy research are:

- chi-square (X squared);
- t-test;
- analysis of variance (ANOVA) and multiple analysis of variance (MANOVA);
- linear regression.

The results of t-tests and ANOVA/MANOVA calculations are sometimes reported as F ratios (or as F = …) or as t = …. This is sometimes also accompanied by a figure for 'df' (degrees of freedom: a statistical concept that refers to the influence of sample size on the calculation that has been reported). In some studies, the F ratio (or other statistical test results) are reported, while in some other studies only p values are reported.

Any statistical test is based on a formula or equation for calculating probability. Statistics textbooks generally provide details of these equations, because they are of interest to readers with a mathematical background. However, in practice most researchers conduct statistical analyses using software packages that do not require the user to know anything about the underlying formula that is being applied.

This discussion of some of the statistical techniques employed in counselling and psychotherapy research is intended to do no more than supply an initial basis for understanding the role of statistics in studies of therapy, to the extent of being able to make sense of quantitative research articles. There are many more statistical tests than could possibly be covered here – when you come across them in an article you are reading, you should be able to find a definition and explanation through an internet search, or in a stats textbook.

In summary: the key things to look for when reading a quantitative study of therapy are the mean (m) scores that are reported, and which of the analyses that have been carried out have produced statistically significant results ($p < .05$). You also need to be aware that the use of statistical significance, on its own, as a rationale for arguing that a result is real and meaningful (i.e. not due to chance) is increasingly viewed as questionable in therapy research. This is because statistically significant differences can be generated by quite small between-group differences as long as the sample size is big enough. The therapy research community has become more interested in differences that are not just statistically significant, but are also clinically significant (i.e. let you see whether clients have actually recovered). As a consequence, in addition to statistical significance, most therapy studies now also report effect size (ES), and metrics for estimating clinically reliable change. These techniques are discussed in Chapter 12. An implication of the use of ES and reliable change figures is to be slightly suspicious of studies that only report statistical significance (Balkin & Lenz, 2021; Lenz, 2020).

What practical skills do I need to develop?

Training in quantitative methods and statistics always involves a considerable amount of hands-on experience in relation to the intricacies of entering data into SPSS or an equivalent statistics package. Learning how to make sense of the various menus and options that are available, and the outputs that they produce, also requires concrete practice guided by someone who is familiar with these topics. These hands-on practical aspects of using quantitative methods are not covered in the present book. To develop such skills, readers are advised to consult Field (2017), and the website supporting that book, for a taste of what is involved in this kind of learning, enrol on a course, or find a tutor or mentor. However, there are also vital conceptual skills that need to be acquired. To do good quantitative research involves thinking like a quantitative researcher. Some of the main principles of a quantitative mind-set are outlined in the following sections. To anyone who has been trained in a scientific discipline, these principles will seem utterly obvious. However, many counsellors and psychotherapists have backgrounds in the arts and humanities, and can find it hard to connect with the logic of quantitative inquiry.

Thinking like a quantitative researcher

Quantitative research methods form part of a broader movement within science, sometimes described as 'positivism'. The image of scientific knowledge that emerged in Europe in the seventeenth century regarded nature as obeying cause-and-effect laws. The task of science was to uncover these laws. Mathematics – the 'queen of sciences' – provided a universally applicable language within which the logical structure of scientific laws could be expressed. Ultimately, everything could be represented in numbers. This philosophical and cultural shift encompassed a rejection of religious beliefs. No longer was everything driven by a prime cause (God's will). Instead, the world operated like a machine. The notion of a 'positive science' referred to the assumption that the mechanical, cause-and-effect laws that were so readily applicable in fields such as physics and optics, could also be applicable in domains of social life, such as economics, sociology and psychology. As a reflection of these underlying beliefs about science, quantitative researchers do not see the world in terms of personal choice and intention. The world is made up of 'factors' or 'variables' that have an 'impact' on each other, or that can be used to 'predict' other factors. So, for example, therapy outcome predicts later use of medical care (i.e. means that the person visits their GP less often). Quality of therapeutic alliance predicts therapy outcome. Fulfilment of therapy preferences predicts therapeutic alliance. Previous experience of therapy predicts therapy preferences. The job of the researcher, from this perspective, is to contribute to the development of a reliable and valid matrix of cause-and-effect linkages. These cause–effect linkages exist in an abstract mathematical space, defined in terms of statistical averages. This way of looking at the world can be hard for some therapists, who are accustomed in their clinical work to understanding causality in terms of concrete choices and actions undertaken by actual persons.

Hypothesis testing

There are two ways in which cause-and-effect matrices can be explored and identified. One way is to measure a lot of variables or factors, and then look at the patterns that emerge. This is the basis of statistical techniques such as correlation, factor analysis and regression. There are many valuable studies that have followed this general strategy and have produced practically useful results. However, there are some notable logical limitations associated with this approach. Co-variance (things clustering together in a pattern) does not necessarily imply causality. For example, imagine that client satisfaction data are available from questionnaires completed at the end of counselling. It is then possible to analyse many potential correlations and patterns in that data set. It may emerge that (a) female counsellors receive higher satisfaction ratings than male counsellors, and (b) that there is no difference in the satisfaction ratings received by more experienced counsellors, and trainee counsellors. These are interesting findings. However, it is not reasonable to argue, on the basis of these results, that counsellor gender influences client satisfaction, while therapist experience-level has no effect. Both of these linkages could be the result of at least one (and maybe several) other causal factors, such as the assessment and case allocation system used in the counselling service. It may be that the more hostile or potentially violent cases are allocated to male counsellors, and the more straight-forward (i.e. higher likelihood of success) cases are allocated to trainees. While correlational studies may provide valuable insights, and indications of possible causal linkages, they cannot in themselves provide evidence of causality.

A better way to investigate such causal linkages, leading to more confidence about results, is to design a study in which specific factors are controlled, and then followed up over time. This is usually called a 'quasi-experimental' study or a 'randomised controlled trial'. To test the hypothesis that gender of counsellor has an effect, clients would need to be randomly allocated to either male or female counsellors. To test the hypothesis that experience-level had an effect (or had no effect), clients would need to be randomly allocated to a group of experienced therapists, or a group of trainees. The key point here is that thinking like a quantitative researcher involves looking at research as a process of hypothesis testing. On the whole, statistical tests have been developed to allow researchers to test hypotheses. A quantitative study therefore should, if possible, be driven by a hypothesis or hypotheses. (By contrast, most qualitative studies are driven by curiosity – for example, the intention to explore, in as open a manner as possible, the experiences of a group of clients. For most qualitative researchers, the aim is to contribute to enhanced understanding and awareness.) In a quantitative study, the heavy lifting takes place at the start, in the form of identifying a hypothesis and then devising a set of procedures through which that hypothesis can be subjected to a fair test. This aspect of quantitative research has significant implications – the researcher needs to demonstrate, before any data are collected, that their hypothesis is warranted in terms of a combination of previous research and theory.

Probabilistic thinking

A further key aspect of thinking like a quantitative researcher involves embracing the concept of *probability*. In some areas of science, it is possible to determine cause-and-effect relationships with a high degree of certainty – for example, the boiling point of water at a certain atmospheric pressure. The situation in psychology, social science and therapy research is quite different. In these domains, the researcher is dealing with complex real-world phenomena, in which each factor or variable is subjected to multiple sources of causal influence. Also, the phenomena that are being investigated are not amenable to precise measurement – it is not possible to measure 'depression' with anything approaching the same level of precision as 'length'. As a consequence, the results of therapy research studies can never be reported in the form of simple assertion such as x causes y under condition z, but instead need to be reported in probabilistic terms (there is a high/low probability that x causes y under condition z).

In quantitative studies of therapy, this is reported in terms of the 'p' (probability) value, or confidence limits, of findings. As a rule, a finding is generally considered as credible if it can be shown that it occurs less than one time in 20 ($p < .05$) by chance. (The probability level/confidence limit that is considered acceptable will depend on the type of study that has been carried out – more highly controlled studies allow stricter probability/confidence levels.) A key implication of this facet of quantitative research is that it demonstrates the importance of identifying the research hypothesis from the outset. In a 'fishing expedition' investigation, in which the researcher measures a range of variables and then looks for patterns, it is likely that several statistically significant findings will emerge, purely by chance. For example if you measure 40 variables and use a $p < .05$ significance threshold, then you will get two statistically significant findings. It is then usually possible to produce a plausible interpretation of why this pattern of results is meaningful. This is poor science. In statistical terms, this kind of situation is defined as a 'Type 1' error – appearing to detect an effect when in fact no real effect has occurred. Being clear about the primary hypotheses that are being tested represents a crucial means of avoiding Type 1 errors – the researcher concentrates their attention on the data relating to that hypothesis, and regards any other, unanticipated patterns as being of secondary importance. Alternatively, in a study where quantitative data have been collected on a wide range of factors (e.g. in a survey or audit), it is sensible to restrict the analysis as far as possible to providing a descriptive account of what was found, along with a report on any patterns or trends that have emerged, very clearly in the data, and avoid any temptation to over-analyse.

Exercise 7.2   Thinking like a quantitative researcher

To what extent do you make use of hypothesis testing and probabilistic thinking that occur in your practice as a therapist, or in other areas of your life? What have you learned about these ways of thinking, in the context of non-research situations, that could be relevant to your work as a researcher?

Designing and planning a study so that statistical data are meaningful: statistical power/sample size

The way that a statistical technique operates is that it identifies a 'signal' in a mass of background 'noise'. The assumption is always that a pattern of results will consist of a certain proportion of random error (noise) along with some real effects (signal). In order to increase the likelihood that the signal will be detected, it is necessary to increase the power of the transmitter (size of the sample) or the sensitivity of the detector (accuracy of measurement). Sample size is therefore of paramount importance in quantitative research. The concept of *statistical power* refers to the interplay between the validity and reliability of measures, the predicted effect size of findings, and the sample size that will be necessary in order to achieve a sufficient level of statistical probability/confidence. There are several free, open-access statistical power calculators available on the internet. The concept of statistical power is explained in more detail in Field (2017) and other statistics textbooks. To gain an understanding of how statistical power operates in research, it is necessary to pay attention to the sample sizes in published studies, as a rough guide to the kind of sample size that is required to carry out different types of investigation. It can be very frustrating to complete a study that is 'under-powered': a great deal of time and effort may have been expended on setting up the study and collecting data, only to find that the results are statistically inconclusive because the sample size was insufficient.

Choosing the appropriate stats technique

There exists a massive statistical toolkit that is available for quantitative researchers – different statistical techniques that have been developed for different tasks. A key skill for any quantitative researcher involves selecting the appropriate statistics technique for the specific study and data-set that have been compiled. All statistics textbooks provide guidelines and criteria for the use of different techniques. Many researchers acquire this kind of knowledge in apprenticeship mode, through guidance from research mentors and supervisors, or being part of a research team. It is also helpful to pay attention to the statistical techniques used in recent published studies, as a way of learning about current good practice: guidelines provided in statistics textbooks tend to reflect general principles, rather than specific technical solutions and adaptations that have emerged within particular disciplines or professional communities. The present chapter has focused on relatively simple statistical procedures that are feasible for novice and practitioner researchers. Further information on more adavanced statistical techniques is available in Limberg et al. (2021), Watson et al. (2021) and Wood et al. (2021).

Handling data

In any quantitative study, there is a lot to think about in respect of the process of collecting data. Usually, paper or online questionnaires and rating scales will be completed by a large number of people. It is necessary to work out robust and ethically sensitive procedures for making sure that all of this information is collected in a standard fashion, and entered onto a database. For many researchers, SPSS (Field, 2017) functions as a flexible database that enables many different kinds of data analysis. However, in some situations it may be preferable to use a simpler database, such as an Excel spreadsheet. Companies that publish widely used outcome measures, such as CORE-OM (see Chapter 9), also usually supply custom-designed database systems. It is important to think in advance about whether the chosen database will be sufficient for the amount and type of data that will be collected, will be secure, will allow the kind of analysis that the researcher plans to carry out and is affordable. Increasingly, therapy researchers are using online 'crowdsourcing' techniques for data collection, which tend to be linked to specific database packages (Mullen et al., 2021). Whatever database is chosen, it is also important to give consideration to the amount of time it will take to enter data, and who will undertake this task. Once data are entered, they will need to be checked for errors. Decisions need to be made about how to handle missing data. Most ethics committees will require a researcher to clarify the length of time that the database will be maintained, and what will happen to the data at the end of that period. None of these tasks are particularly difficult, but they do require attention to detail.

Carrying out statistical analysis

A detailed account of how to carry out a statistical analysis is provided in Field (2017) and other stats textbooks. In practice, statistical analysis involves being able to find one's way around a software package with multiple drop-down menus. It is important to be able to access tutorials that explain how to navigate a specific package in a step-by-step manner. Generally, in a quantitative study, there is not much point in running a full analysis of the data until all of the information has been collected. In fact, in some types of study, such as randomised controlled trials (RCTs), it is considered poor practice to analyse early returns, because this could act as a source of bias. For example, if a researcher finds that his or her preferred therapy is not producing good results, he or she may subtly manipulate the remaining stage of the study to remedy this situation, perhaps by subverting the randomisation procedure to ensure that more difficult clients are allocated to the comparison therapy condition. The exception to the general principle of not looking at the data until the end occurs if a study involves risk and side-effects. For example, in an RCT some participants may use their questionnaire responses to indicate suicidal tendencies, or early results may reveal that one of the therapy conditions is associated with an unacceptably high level of drop-outs. It is good practice, in such studies, to build in some minimal monitoring of information as it comes in, to safeguard against risk and harm. The good news about quantitative research is that once all the data have been entered onto a database, the ensuing statistical analysis can be carried out quite quickly. Typically, data can be analysed and the results section of a thesis or research article can be finalised within one or two days of concentrated effort.

Reporting quantitative findings

Quantitative researchers have developed standardised protocols for presenting complex data and findings in succinct and accessible ways. As always, it is helpful to look at how this is accomplished in published studies. Usually, statistical data are presented in tables, accompanied by a brief descriptive account in the main text. It is useful to look at recently published articles, in terms of getting a feel for options around how to format and organise tables of results. Most therapy journals adhere to the American Psychological Association (APA) guidelines around how to report quantitative findings (Cooper, 2020).

Conclusions

Quantitative methods have proved to be an essential strategy for investigating many aspects of the process and outcomes of therapy. In order to use quantitative methodologies appropriately, it is necessary to appreciate that they comprise an array of approaches that serve different scientific functions, ranging from collecting factual descriptive information, through identifying trends and patterns, to developing complex models. The general principles of quantitative research introduced in the present chapter provide a platform for understanding the application of quantitative techniques within specific types of research product discussed in later chapters, such as evaluations of the outcomes of routine practice (Chapter 12) and single case studies (Chapter 13).

The statistical methods used in psychotherapy research continue to evolve. In recent years, within the field of applied statistics there has been a steady movement in the direction of approaches that take more account of the practical implications of findings (Appelbaum et al., 2018; Calin-Jageman & Cumming, 2019; Cumming, 2014; Wasserstein, Schirm & Lazar, 2019).

Suggestions for further reading

Further discussion of how to use quantitative methods in research in counselling and psychotherapy can be found in:

Barker, C., Pistrang, N., & Elliott, R. (2016). *Research Methods in Clinical Psychology: An Introduction for Students and Practitioners*. 3rd edn. Chichester: Wiley-Blackwell (Chapters 4 and 12).
McBeath, A. (2020). Doing quantitative research with statistics. In S. Bager-Charleson & A. McBeath (eds), *Enjoying Research in Counselling and Psychotherapy Qualitative, Quantitative and Mixed Methods Research* (pp. 161–173). Basingstoke: Palgrave Macmillan.

Twigg, E. (2015). Quantitative methods. In A. Vossler & N. Moller (eds), *The Counselling and Psychotherapy Research Handbook* (pp. 131–150). London: Sage.

Twigg, E. & Redford, P. (2015). How to use t-tests to explore pre-post change. In A. Vossler & N. Moller (eds), *The Counselling and Psychotherapy Research Handbook*. (pp. 151–163). London: Sage.

Online resources

The online resource site (https://study.sagepub.com/doingresearch4e) includes articles and learning activities on quantitative methods issues and topics.

8

Qualitative Methods

Key Principles

Introduction

In recent years, a steadily growing proportion of research studies on counselling and psychotherapy topics make use of qualitative methods. The aim of qualitative research is to describe, explore and analyse the ways that people create meaning in their lives, through analysing meaning-making activities such as talk, stories and cultural objects such as photographs. Qualitative research provides a different perspective to quantitative research. For example, a quantitative study might show that 60 per cent of clients who receive a particular form of therapy report a substantial shift in levels of symptoms of depression. However, the meaning of their therapy, for clients who have undergone that type of intervention, may be quite different. It may be that some of those whose symptoms were reduced were nevertheless dissatisfied with the therapy they received. Or some of those whose symptoms remained high were able to point to other ways in which the experience of therapy was meaningful and helpful. It is not that the quantitative evidence is correct and the qualitative evidence is false (or vice versa). Instead, each approach offers complementary insights.

This chapter begins with an overview of the key methodological principles that underpin qualitative research. The emphasis then shifts to examining the various specific qualitative approaches that have been developed, such as grounded theory, interpretative phenomenological analysis and thematic analysis. Later chapters in the book explore how these principles and approaches have been applied to different types of research question relating to client and therapist experiences of therapy.

The primary focus in the present chapter, and throughout the whole book, is on qualitative research that uses interviews and written accounts to investigate participant experience of therapy. In addition to these methods, there also exist important genres of qualitative inquiry that analyse data from transcripts of naturally occurring talk (e.g. conversation analysis), documents such as diaries or official case records, or collected through direct observation of behaviour (ethnographic research). Although these other qualitative approaches are valuable, and have the potential to make a significant contribution to knowledge about therapy, they require additional specialist training, and for reasons of space are not discussed in detail within this book.

Why is it important to know about qualitative methods?

Qualitative methods play a significant role within the counselling and psychotherapy research literature. To be a research-informed practitioner, it is necessary to understand what qualitative research can and cannot do, and to be able to arrive at a balanced appraisal of the value of qualitative studies that are published. Researchers who specialise in quantitative methods still need to know about qualitative methodologies, because at least some of the relevant literature on their topic of interest will be based on qualitative approaches. Both researchers and practitioners seeking to gain an understanding of the development of research in a particular topic need to be able to appreciate the interplay between qualitative and quantitative methodologies over the course of a programme of research. For example, some programmes of research begin with qualitative research that generates themes and hypotheses that are then tested using quantitative techniques.

Qualitative research makes a major contribution to therapy practice, and well-conducted qualitative studies have the potential to be highly relevant for therapy practitioners. Good qualitative research takes the reader closer to the phenomenon or topic being investigated, and can offer new ways of seeing the process of therapy. Some qualitative studies explore the meaning of an experience: what it is like to be depressed, what it is like when therapy ends. Other studies seek to gain an understanding of how people do things: what clients do to enable their recovery from chronic anxiety, how therapists manage the challenge of working with clients with autism. Yet other qualitative studies make connections between therapy and broader dimensions of human experience, such as agency, reflexivity, intimacy and identity.

What do I need to know?

In order to make effective use of qualitative approaches to research, it is important to appreciate that there exist a variety of qualitative traditions, which reflect different research aims and philosophical positions. The territory of qualitative research is a bit of a jungle, so it is essential to go in there with a map. Once inside that territory, there are some key issues that need to be confronted. All qualitative research needs to take account, one way or another, of the subjectivity, personal involvement and reflexivity of the researcher. And all qualitative research needs to be based on a clear understanding of the validity criteria that can be applied to the work that is being done. Finally, there are some practical skills that qualitative researchers need to possess. These aspects of qualitative research competence are discussed in the following sections.

The territory of qualitative research

There exist a wide range of qualitative methodologies, reflecting different ways of doing qualitative research. Widely used qualitative methodologies include grounded theory, ethnography, autoethnography, participative inquiry, conversation analysis and discourse analysis. Each of these approaches consists of a distinctive bundle of philosophical assumptions, types of questions that are asked, techniques for collecting and analysing data, and ways of disseminating findings. The scope and complexity of contemporary qualitative research is examined in the authoritative *SAGE Handbook of Qualitative Research* (Denzin & Lincoln, 2017). Some influential figures in qualitative psychotherapy research such as Brinkmann (2017), Morrow (2005) and Ponterotto (2005) regard different qualitative methodologies as reflecting different underlying philosophical positions. It can also be valuable to adopt a historical perspective that makes it possible to make sense of why each research approach developed at a particular stage (McLeod, 2011).

Exercise 8.1   Being interested in conversations and stories

How interested are you in stories? All forms of qualitative research are based on a process of collecting stories and looking at the ways in which stories are constructed in conversations or written texts. What are the strengths and limitations of client and therapist stories as a means of learning about what happens in therapy? In what ways does your own preferred mode of involvement in narrative (as a storyteller, and/or as a consumer of narratives) shape and influence your attitude to qualitative research? What kind of skill, knowledge and experience do you already possess, in relation to making sense of stories?

Thinking like a qualitative researcher

There is a distinctive way of thinking that tends to be found in people who specialise in carrying out qualitative research. To some extent, this can be summed up as a 'discovery-oriented' mind-set. For the most part, qualitative research does not aim to test hypotheses or assess the validity of existing theories. Instead, qualitative research tends to be about *exploring* the meaning of different kinds of experience or ways of interacting with others. The aim is to develop understanding. The concept of understanding refers to a state of knowing in which the person already possesses some degree of understanding, but at the same time has a sense that this understanding could be extended, deepened or 'thickened'. This process never ends – as soon as a new way of understanding has emerged, it invites curiosity about the limits of that way of seeing things.

It can be helpful to break down the concept of understanding into some of its constituent parts. Wolcott (1990) and other qualitative researchers have characterised the process of developing understanding as consisting of three stages: *description*, *analysis* and *interpretation*. In qualitative inquiry, there is an expectation that the researcher will *describe* the phenomenon being studied in detail and with memorable clarity. This is a crucial step, because conveying understanding requires that the phenomenon being studied is evoked in the mind of the reader or consumer of a study. The next step, *analysis*, involves identifying patterns that appear within the phenomenon being studied, in terms of recurring themes and categories. The analysis of a qualitative interview or written text understanding that has been attained by the researcher or research team – how they have made sense of what they have observed and described. Finally, *interpretation* involves making connections between these patterns and observations, and the findings of other studies. Interpretation also involves making sense at a broader level, in terms of theoretical perspectives that allow further conceptualisation of the topic. The step of interpretation can be seen as a movement of reaching out to the reader, inviting them to consider the value of the study as a means of deepening their pre-existing understanding of the topic.

Viewing the nature of understanding as an interplay between description, analysis and interpretation leads to consideration of what it is that a qualitative researcher can do to promote and cultivate skills in these areas. For example, philosophical concepts from phenomenology (the practice of rigorous description) and hermeneutics (the practice of rigorous interpretation) are highly relevant (McLeod, 2011). Many qualitative researchers also become interested in the act of writing, and the many ways in which meaning can be conveyed in writing. There are some respects in which qualitative research is similar to journalism and other genres of non-fiction writing.

There are other respects in which qualitative research can be similar to poetry. In recent years, some qualitative researchers have begun to move beyond the text, and started to look at the ways that meaning can be conveyed through other means, such as art and drama.

Thinking like a qualitative researcher means being interested in *particular* examples or instances of a topic (Flyvbjerg, 2001). For instance, to appreciate the human impact of war, it can be useful to compile statistics on death and injury rates and economic impact, read the diaries of combatants, and so on. However, gaining a more complete understanding of the meaning of war can also occur through spending time reflecting on the significance of a single painting or photograph. The principle of particularity has implications for the way that qualitative researchers think about sample sizes. On the whole, qualitative studies with large sample sizes do not work very well, because making sense of a massive amount of data has the inevitable effect of distracting the researcher from allowing the meaningfulness of particular examples or cases fully to emerge. There are many excellent qualitative studies that are based on a single case or example, or a handful of cases.

Sample sizes in qualitative research

Decisions about sample size inevitably arise when planning or designing a qualitative study. In their review of 109 qualitative studies of the client's experience of therapy, Levitt, Pomerville and Surace (2016) found that sample size ranged from 3 to 77 cases, with an average of 13. The majority of studies had a sample size of between 4 and 20 participants. In a survey of qualitative studies published in healthcare journals, Vasileiou, Barnett, Thorpe and Young (2018) found a similar range of sample sizes. They also analysed the types of sample size rationale provided by authors, and reported that many different criteria were utilised, including saturation (stopping recruitment of further informants when additional interviews cease yielding new themes), pragmatic reasons (e.g. time constraints, or number of suitable informants) and adherence to sample sizes laid down in guidelines/previous research. The most widely reported rationale was saturation. Certain qualitative methodologies are associated with particular ranges of sample size. For example, interpretative phenomenological analysis (IPA) emphasises the theoretical value of looking at single cases, and being able to compare cases. As a consequence, many IPA studies have relatively small sample sizes (5–8 participants). By contrast, grounded theory studies aim to generate a theoretical model (set of categories) that can accommodate all aspects of a phenomenon or topic. To achieve this objective, it is normally necessary to interview 10–20 participants. Some researchers establish the validity of themes or categories by generating a set of themes based on an initial set of interviews, then testing them out on a further set of cases. Further perspectives on sample size can be found in Braun and Clarke (2016, 2021c), Fugard and Potts (2015), Malterud, Siersma and Guassora (2016) and Sim et al. (2018). There is no simple answer to the question of what is the right sample size for a particular qualitative study. However, readers of a study will want to know the reasoning behind sample size decision-making, because it helps them to gain a clearer idea of the underlying assumptions that have informed the study as a whole.

Researcher reflexivity

In quantitative research, it is possible to collect data through questionnaires or even direct measures of behaviour or physiological function, using techniques that are largely free of the interest or influence of the researcher. It is also possible to analyse quantitative data using pre-determined statistical procedures. These strategies are not available to the qualitative researcher. In qualitative inquiry, the main instrument of the research is the researcher, and it is inevitable that the person of the researcher will exert some kind of influence. For example, interviewee participants may be more willing to say certain things to some interviewers rather than others. When analysing interview transcripts or other forms of qualitative texts, one researcher may be sensitive to meanings that might never occur to one of his or her colleagues. As a result of these factors, the issue of researcher *reflexivity* plays a key role in all qualitative work. Reflexivity refers to the capacity of the researcher to reflect on and take account of their personal and subjective involvement in the process of carrying out a study, and report in a transparent and informative manner on aspects of these experiences that may be relevant for readers. Researcher reflexivity encompasses all aspects of personal identity, ranging from moment-by-moment thoughts and feelings, through to social role and status. The topic of researcher reflexivity in qualitative research can be understood from different perspectives. Useful sources of further reading in relation to this issue can be found in Finlay (2002, 2012), Frost (2016), Granek (2017), Hofmann and Barker (2017), Smith and Luke (2021) and Tuval-Mashiach (2017).

It is important to appreciate that the concept of reflexivity can also be used in relation to the experience of research participants. For example, a person being interviewed continually engages in a process of self-reflection as they consider what to say or not say in response to questions. A key aspect of researcher reflexivity consists of the awareness of participant reflexivity. Qualitative research can be regarded as based in what has been called a 'double hermeneutic' (Smith, Flowers & Larkin, 2009): the research interprets the words of the informant, which are in turn an interpretation of the informants' experience.

Although the identity of the researcher is ever-present during all stages of the research process, it is possible to identify some specific 'moments' within the conduct of qualitative research when a capacity to be reflexive is particularly relevant:

- the choice of research topic;
- relationships with research participants and colleagues;
- emotional responses to any aspect of the research;
- analysing data;
- selecting particular examples to highlight in a paper or report.

In relation to each of these aspects of a research study, it is helpful to take account of two key questions. To what extent did your personal interests and beliefs influence what you did? In what ways might these personal factors have shaped the conclusions of the study?

In practice, addressing the issue of researcher reflexivity in an effective manner requires the incorporation into the research process of specific procedures. Many qualitative researchers will keep a reflexive journal or diary, in which they will do their best to document their experiences and reflections in relation to moments when the personal meaning of the research became apparent. For example, it is usually helpful, at the start of a study, to take time to write about what one expects to find. It is also usually worthwhile to keep a note of feelings and images that were triggered by the experience of interviewing a person, or reading a transcript or other text. In addition to keeping a research journal, it is also useful to enlist other people, for example research colleagues or supervisors, in conversations about the personal meaning of the research. Other people can offer a crucial external perspective, and typically will draw the attention of the researcher to personal dimensions of the research that they had not considered, or were reluctant to admit. It is then a good idea to incorporate the product of these conversations in a journal. The value of a journal is that it then provides the researcher with a document from which they are able to quote, in subsequent articles and reports. Observations made at the time tend to be more convincing than reflections that take place months after an event. Using a journal also makes it less likely that important personal meanings are lost – sometimes these insights are ephemeral, and are hard to recall if not written down.

A further aspect of researcher reflexivity concerns the inclusion of personal and reflexive writing in dissertations, theses and articles. At the present time, there is a lack of clear consensus across the field of qualitative research as a whole, as well as within therapy research, about how such forms of writing are to be handled. For example, some journals will restrict reflexivity to a brief section within the methods part of a paper, on the identity and expectations of the researcher(s). Some journals will encourage or allow the use of 'I' and 'we'; other journals will discourage these uses. Some journals (e.g. *Qualitative Inquiry*) actively promote innovation and experimentation in terms of forms of researcher reflexivity. Building in reflexivity procedures from the start, such as journal writing and conversations, makes it possible for a qualitative researcher to have choices regarding reflexive writing when the time comes to publish their work.

Researcher reflexivity is not a matter of bias. Part of the ability to think like a qualitative researcher is an appreciation that this kind of research does not seek to produce 'objective' truth. Instead, qualitative research generates an understanding of a topic that is inevitably shaped by the identity and position of the researcher. Taking account of researcher reflexivity allows the researcher to make the most of what they bring to the research process. For example, previous personal experience of a topic may sensitise the researcher to the deeper significance of that topic in the lives of informants, and may make the researcher more credible and trustworthy to informants. Taking account of reflexivity also makes it possible for readers or consumers of research to make up their own minds, and interpret findings in the context of an informed knowledge of who did the study and what it was like for them to do so.

Exercise 8.2   Being a reflexive researcher

What are the implications of researcher reflexivity, in the context of the research that you are planning, or are already conducting? In what ways do you monitor and record the personal dimension of your involvement in research? How do you intend to use this information? What are the challenges associated with this process? Find examples of research reflexivity in published studies that are meaningful or inspiring for you. How might they serve as models for how you might handle this issue in your own work? How could you implement, or adapt, the reflexivity strategies adopted by these researchers?

Validity issues in qualitative research

Criteria for establishing the trustworthiness and credibility of a qualitative study, and how they fit into broader debates about how to evaluate the quality of scientific work, are discussed in Chapter 6. It is essential for anyone planning to undertake a piece of qualitative research to become familiar with relevant criteria as early as possible, to be able to incorporate them into the design of the study. Practical procedures for enhancing the credibility of a qualitative study include:

- transparency and clarity around the way in which data were analysed;
- providing vivid and convincing examples of themes and categories;
- disclosure of relevant aspects of the identity and experience of the researcher(s);
- external auditing of data analysis.

Ethical issues in qualitative research

As with any other type of study, qualitative research needs to take account of the wide range of ethical issues discussed in Chapter 5. In addition, it is crucial to be aware of specific areas of ethical sensitivity associated with qualitative inquiry. A key ethical factor is that qualitative data-collection techniques such as interviewing, participant observation and diary keeping inevitably involve some form of relationship being developed between the researcher and research participants, in which the latter disclose personal information about topics and experiences that may be embarrassing or emotionally painful. Participants may be emotionally and socially vulnerable and be at risk of harm to their wellbeing by being interviewed. An informant may also disclose ethically sensitive information (e.g. an account of illegal or abusive behaviour) about other people in their life. Typically, when qualitative data are analysed, this information is then presented in a report in terms of lengthy quotes from participants that may make them identifiable (particularly to those who know them well). Each of these processes creates possibilities for breaches of confidentiality, and harm to participants. There can also be harm to researchers who may be exposed to stories of trauma and suffering, or may feel a sense of responsibility for helping needy participants. Many qualitative researchers are motivated by a commitment to social justice, in the form of conducting research that gives a voice to oppressed groups – this position sets a high ethical standard to live up to. The quality of research data that are collected may be influenced by the level of ethical trust that exists between the researcher and research participants.

As a consequence of these factors, qualitative researchers have found it helpful to emphasise the distinction between 'procedural ethics' and 'ethics in practice' (Guillemin and Gillam, 2004). Procedural ethics refers to the ethical procedures that are required by institutional ethics committees and boards, in terms of participant information sheets, consent forms, and the like. By contrast, ethics in practice, process ethics or 'microethics' refer to the moment-by-moment ethical decision-making that takes place in interaction with research participants, in the form of difficult and unpredictable situations that may arise in the practice of doing research (Guillemin and Gillam, 2004). In some respects, these situations are similar to the kind of things that can happen in therapy, and researchers who are also therapists are in a good position to know how best to respond. One of the key factors in the management of ethics in practice is to have access to effective supervision, from an experienced researcher or peer group (or preferably both). Qualitative researcher practice is also informed by ideas from relational ethics. On the whole, ethics committees and review boards are well aware of the ethical sensitivities associated with qualitative research, and expect qualitative ethics protocols to include a comprehensive and informed analysis of risk, along with a clear specification of robust strategies for mitigating them. There exists an extensive literature about ethical issues in qualitative research, that should be consulted by anyone who is intending to undertake this type of study. Key sources include Iphofen and Tolich (2018), Ponterotto, Park-Taylor and Chen (2017) and Tolich (2016). There are further distinctive ethical dilemmas that can arise in autoethnographic studies and other forms of qualitative personal experience research that are discussed in Chapter 14.

Practical skills and time management

There are many practical skills associated with the use of qualitative methods, for example, in such areas as conducting interviews, preparing transcripts of interviews, working with analysis of texts and creating systems for managing textual data. Developing competence and confidence in these areas is a matter of learning-through-doing, preferably in the context of an apprenticeship relationship within which the novice researcher can observe how these tasks are accomplished by more experienced colleagues.

A key aspect of the practice of qualitative inquiry is a willingness to become *immersed* in the task of making sense of the data. The personal and time demands of qualitative research are rather different from those of quantitative research. Research is always hard work. The work of quantitative research can be fairly readily parcelled up into blocks of time; for example, checking the accuracy of the data on one evening, running a particular stats test on another evening, and so on. By contrast, qualitative research has a tendency to take over a researcher's life. Talk to anyone who has completed a qualitative study, and they will describe occasions when they listened to interview recordings while on the running machine at the gym, while driving their car, or lazing on the beach on holiday. They will also describe scenarios in which the walls of their spare room, or all available surfaces in their dining area, were covered with post-it notes and bits of text. This kind of personal immersion is necessary because there is a point at which a qualitative researcher needs to be able to hold the totality of the material at the forefront of their attention and allow the meaning of that material to be tested against his or her imagination and inner emotional life.

Exercise 8.3   Stretching exercises

A book by Janesick (2016) offers a series of 'stretching exercises' for qualitative researchers – learning tasks and activities that introduce creative ways of observing and listening that are necessary for qualitative work. Working your way through these exercises provides excellent preparation for doing a qualitative study.

A step-by-step guide to doing a qualitative interview study

At the beginning of a qualitative interview study, it is necessary to assemble appropriate research support (e.g. supervision), and identify the aims and research questions that are being pursued. In relation to undertaking a qualitative interview study, it is also wise to decide early on which method will be adopted (e.g. thematic analysis, grounded theory, IPA, CQR). The choice of method is determined partly by the aim of the study, and partly by the research supervision, training and expertise that are available. The issue of choosing a method (e.g. grounded theory, IPA, thematic analysis) is discussed in a later section of this chapter. Once these elements are in place, it is possible to construct a research proposal, and receive ethical approval to collect data. The research proposal or plan needs to take account of validity criteria for qualitative research. In the process of designing a study, it is helpful to identify one or more published studies that can serve as 'templates' for the proposed research.

Keeping a research journal

Alongside the general research tasks mentioned already, it is also advisable to begin to keep a research diary or journal. A research journal is particularly necessary in qualitative interview research because it serves two vital functions: deepening researcher reflexivity, and building an analytic framework. Researcher reflexivity is a central aspect of qualitative research, because it acknowledges the personal involvement of the researcher in the research process, and seeks to use this involvement to sensitise that researcher to aspects of the phenomenon being studied. By contrast, a lack of attention in researcher reflexivity can lead to research that is perceived by readers as biased. Qualitative research requires summarising or condensing a lot of verbal material, such as interview transcripts, into a succinct statement that will highlight key themes or categories. In order to do this, it is necessary to conceptualise the material in some way. It is a mistake to think that these concepts will only emerge after all the data have been collected, and the researcher is sitting in their study reading through the transcripts line by line. Useful concepts can come to mind during or after an interview, while transcribing, in conversation with a colleague, in a dream – that is to say, anywhere. Keeping a journal allows these ideas to be harvested and then fed into the final data analysis stage.

Deciding on an interview strategy and schedule

The most frequently adopted interview strategy is to use a semi-structured interview schedule, in the context of a one-to-one interview that lasts for about an hour. Ethically, participants need to have received information about the study in advance. It can also be helpful to devote some time at the start of an interview to checking out that the person has understood what is involved, and is still willing to proceed. This can take a few minutes. Also, some participants may have a lot to say, take time to warm up, or talk slowly. For these reasons, even if the aim is to conduct a 50–60-minute interview, it will be sensible to have a contract with participants that allows for a longer period of time. There are then some choices that need to be made about how to organise the interview:

- Will the participants receive the questions in advance?
- Should the interview begin with neutral/factual questions, such as age, occupation and so on, or will it be more effective to go straight into the topic, and leave the factual questions until the end?
- How many questions can be asked? Is it helpful to organise these in themes, or as a narrative timeline?
- Is it better to follow a script, in the form of a fixed set of questions, or would it be more effective to begin with a general or 'grand rounds' question and then only use other questions as prompts if the participant misses something that is important to the study?

- How interactive, or personally involved, should the researcher be?
- What does the researcher do if the participant (or the researcher) gets upset, or the participant discloses information about unethical or illegal conduct?
- How does the interview end? Is it useful to know about how the participant experienced the interview? Is it helpful to leave open the possibility of further contact (e.g. if the interviewee has any further thoughts, or the interviewer wants to check on any details)?
- Does the interviewer write notes after the end of the interview about their experience (e.g. points at which they felt angry, moved, confused), and what that might signify?

There are no right or wrong answers to these questions – each one represents a genuine methodological choice-point. What is important is to take the time to consider these possibilities, and consult with others, during the research planning stage. It is also important to remember that the perfect research study does not exist: research always involves arriving at a compromise between competing possibilities and objectives. In deciding on an interview strategy and schedule, it is wise to be guided by exemplar/template studies on similar topics, and build on what has worked for these predecessor researchers.

Refining the interview strategy: carrying out a pilot interview

It is never possible to know whether an interview strategy and schedule will work in the field, without trying these out in a safe situation. Even highly experienced researchers are capable of designing interview schedules that are too lengthy to cover in the time available, or research questions that are not understood by informants. Pilot studies can be carried out with colleagues who play the role of participant (e.g. most therapists can usually get into the role of being a client for interview purposes), or with potential 'real' participants with whom the researcher has a sufficiently robust relationship. It can be illuminating to invite pilot interviewees to act in a difficult or resistant manner. When asking pilot participants for feedback, it is useful to ask them not only about their response to the interview, but also how they believe that other people might respond. It is easier to say 'someone else might have been irritated by that question' rather than 'I was irritated'. It is useful to record pilot interviews, and review them (or parts of them) with a supervisor or members of a peer support group. It is also useful to reflect on the material generated by the interview in relation to the aims of the researcher. For example, it may be that some questions elicit information that is not required, while other questions need to be deepened in order to gain access to the phenomena that matter most. Another aim of the pilot interview phase is to allow the researcher to become more comfortable, confident and fluent in the interviewer role.

A further possibility, at the stage of developing the interview schedule and strategy, is for the researcher to be interviewed by a colleague. It is likely that the researcher will be able to draw on some areas of personal experience that are relevant to the topic of the study. Alternatively, the researcher can role-play an imagined informant. This exercise provides a researcher with a valuable alternative perspective on the interview process, as well as contributing to the enhancement of researcher reflexivity.

Doing the interviews

To a large extent, the success of a qualitative interview-based study will depend on the richness and authenticity of the interviews. Even the most expert and careful analysis can only work with what is in the transcript. If informants have not felt safe enough to open up, or have been asked irrelevant questions, the resulting transcripts and analysis will inevitably be somewhat limited.

In principle, counsellors and psychotherapists have the potential to be highly effective research interviewers, because they are good at listening, have a capacity to tune in to non-verbal cues, and are practised in using their own emotional response to the person as a source of information. Some people, confronted by the task of carrying out a semi-structured interview, will resort to a kind of market research strategy of rattling through a fixed set of questions. Therapists doing research interviews are not like this – they are generally able to create space for the person to tell their story. Nevertheless, there are two important areas in which therapist-researchers can find it hard to make the transition from therapy dialogue to research interviewing. Sometimes therapists will allow themselves to be drawn in to responding therapeutically, for example by helping the informant to resolve an issue. Sometimes therapist-researchers can be too non-directive, and come away from an interview having neglected to ask certain key questions. These are areas that can readily be addressed in research supervision.

It is important to recognise that there are many different styles of qualitative interviewing, and that it is necessary for each researcher to find a style with which they are comfortable. For example, some interviewers find that it is helpful for them to take notes, or draw diagrams during an interview (in addition to recording the interview), because doing so helps them to keep track of what is being covered. For other interviewers, taking notes would be an intrusive distraction. Some like to start with a 'grand rounds' general question ('I'd like to know what this episode of therapy meant for you'), and then use further probe questions if there appear to be key areas or issues that the informant may seem to have skipped. Other interviewers are more comfortable adopting a step-by-step approach, working through a set of questions. For some interviewers, it is useful to share some of their own experience of the topic being explored. It is useful to take some time to study qualitative interview textbooks, guidelines and published studies, and practise interview skills with/ on colleagues.

A crucial aspect of any qualitative interview is the commitment to take care of the informant, in terms of time boundaries, confidentiality, monitoring level of distress in relation to sensitive topics and making sure that there is a sufficient degree of closure at the end of the interview. It is always useful to include, at the end of an interview, an invitation to the participant to add anything that has not been covered and which they feel might be relevant to the study, and to ask about what it was like to be interviewed and how the interview approach might be improved for future participants. A useful technique here is to ask not only whether the person found any of the questions confusing or difficult, but also whether they think that another person might find them confusing or difficult; there can be a certain amount of embarrassment about admitting to not personally understanding something. These closing questions can also provide useful information about the authenticity and meaning of the interview for the informant. If an informant states that they found the interview to be an interesting experience, which helped them to look at a topic in a fresh way, then this usually indicates that the information they provided was a genuine reflection of how they feel. If, on the other hand, an informant does not convey a sense of having been involved, during the interview, in a genuine process of inquiry and exploration, then this may indicate that the informant was holding something back, or was ambivalent about some aspect of the topic of the research.

Taking care of the informant may be facilitated by the order in which questions are asked. For example, many interviewers will begin with relatively factual questions, which are easy to answer, before moving into more sensitive areas of questioning. Questions about the interview experience, and then the collection of demographic information, can be used right at the end to close off the interview. Taking care may also be facilitated by using early, pre-interview contact to begin to establish a research relationship or research alliance; for example, by personalising communication and being sensitive to participants' needs around the venue and timing. Another element of taking care is to invite a participant to make contact after the interview, if there is anything further they wish to add to what they have said. In some studies, it can also be appropriate to provide details of counselling and support services, helplines, and so on, that the person might wish to consult.

In qualitative interview-based research, the researcher is the main research instrument or tool. The previous paragraphs in this section have looked at ways in which the interview schedule and strategy can be designed to be consistent with the style and personal values of the researcher. There is also a more direct way of using the interviewer as an instrument, which is to pay attention to one's own responses to the interviewee, and note these down after the end of the interview. The kind of things that might be useful to note include: feelings, emotions, images and fantasies that came into awareness during the interview; the appearance, voice quality and physical presence of the interviewee; the impression that the interviewee seemed to be trying to convey. This kind of information can be really helpful in enabling a deeper understanding of the material in an interview transcript, by sensitising the researcher to the implicit or hidden dimensions of an informant's account.

A final point is that not all interviews are equally informative. In most studies, there will be some interviewees who talk vividly and honestly about their experience, and contribute a wealth of insights and quotable statements. Other interviewees will offer less, either because they do not feel safe, do not develop rapport with the interviewer, are not ready to talk, or because of innumerable other factors. This is just the way it is. Obviously, it is essential for a researcher to give equal consideration to the contribution of every informant. Sometimes, there can be massively important ideas buried in throwaway comments by informants who have not said much.

Strategies for enhancing the interview process

Most qualitative interview studies are based on single, face-to-face interviews with informants, using an interview schedule. While this remains a robust and time-effective means of collecting data, there are many ways in which it can be intensified and expanded. One strategy is to conduct two (or more) interviews. This allows the researcher to analyse and reflect on what has been offered in the first interview, and follow up on statements or themes that might repay further exploration or clarification. It also allows the informant to continue to think about the research topic, possibly leading to further things they might want to add to their initial account. Meeting more than once may help some informants to trust the researcher, and as a result talk more freely. Examples of using multiple interviews in therapy research include Bolger (1999), Morrow and Smith (1995) and Sørensen et al. (2020). Some researchers augment standard descriptive questions with other questions that invite the person to think about images or metaphors for the experience they are being interviewed on. It is possible to use material objects to trigger memories. For example, if a client is being interviewed about their experience of starting therapy, it may be useful to show them a copy of a symptom measure that they completed at that time. There are many examples in qualitative research of informants either bringing in photographs, or taking photographs, as a means of symbolising a particular set of experiences. The informant may be asked to talk about the events surrounding the taking of the photography, why they selected that particular image to bring in, or how they feel when looking at the picture. Photovoice represents a well-established research (and therapy) technique that makes use of this approach (Gupta, Simms & Doherty, 2019; Sutton-Brown, 2014; Wester et al., 2021). A further interview strategy that draws on the meaning of the informant's life context is the walking or 'go-along' interview (Kinney, 2017).

Interpersonal process recall (IPR) is an augmented interview method that has been specifically developed within the field of therapy research to collect information on client and therapist moment-by-moment experience of the process of therapy (Larsen, Flesaker & Stege, 2008; Macaskie, Lees & Freshwater, 2015). A session is audio or video recorded. Then, within 24 hours, the client or therapist is invited to replay the session (or segments of the session pre-selected by the researcher) and pause it whenever they recall what they had been experiencing at that moment. The assumption behind this technique is that soon after an event a person will be able to access a vivid internal memory of what actually happened, whereas an interview conducted at a later date is more likely to access a mix of actual recall and reconstruction. IPR evolved out of training methodologies, and was first used in psychotherapy process research by David Rennie in the 1980s (McLeod, 2011). Although it is somewhat intrusive on the therapy process, and thus ethically sensitive, IPR has been implemented in a wide range of research settings. Examples of IPR studies include investigations of trainee information processing (Burgess, Rhodes & Wilson, 2013), experience of empowerment in psychotic clients (Baker et al., 2019), feeling vulnerable in couple therapy (Egeli et al., 2014, 2015), shared decision-making (Gibson et al., 2020), using a feedback system (Solstad et al., 2021) and client inner struggles (Kleiven et al., 2020). A structured version of IPR was developed by Swift, Tompkins and Parkin (2017).

There are also important developments in the use of on-line interviewing, that may need to be taken into account when face-to-face meetings are not possible (Iacono, Symonds & Brown, 2016; Lobe, Morgan & Hoffman, 2020).

Transcribing

Interviews need to be transcribed. It is possible to take notes while listening to a recording or watching a video of an interview, but it is then awkward to check back to the source, when comparing ideas from different interviews. Also, taking notes when listening to a recording usually involves transcribing passages that are of special interest. So, in the end, most qualitative researchers will convert recordings into transcripts.

Transcripts can also be readily made ethically safe, in terms of confidentiality, because names, places and other identifying information can easily be redacted or changed.

If possible, it is a good idea for the researcher to do the transcribing, and to make notes as they go along. The discipline of transcribing forces one to listen closely to what was said, enabling immersion in the data. Sometimes, because of time pressure, or lack of typing ability, transcribing will have to be done by someone else. It is essential that the person doing the transcribing fully appreciates the confidentiality of the material with which they are working. Ethics committees will sometimes want the transcriber to be named, so they can be sure that ethical considerations will be handled properly. For example, sending recordings to be transcribed by a commercial office services company would seldom be appropriate. It is necessary to decide, at the outset, on the transcribing rules that will be followed. In conversation analysis studies (not the type of study being described in the present chapter), it is essential to use a complex, detailed and time-consuming set of transcribing rules that convey information about voice quality, exact length of pauses, talkover sequences, and much else. This level of detail is required if specific linguistic and conversational processes are being analysed. However, qualitative interview-based studies are usually more concerned with analysing meaning, rather than analysing linguistic features. It is therefore sufficient, when transcribing, to include the words that were said, and to indicate silences and emotions (e.g. if the person seemed angry or was in tears). Transcribing rules need to be defined to ensure consistency across a series of transcripts.

Some researchers will send a copy of the transcript to each interviewee, with a request to make corrections and indicate any passages that they would not want to be quoted in research reports. Sending a transcript opens up the possibility of the person being upset when they see what they said in the interview. This occurs in a situation where the researcher is not on hand to offer support. Also, there is a possibility that the transcript may be read by another member of a person's family. It is therefore important to consider these factors, and discuss them with informants, before agreeing to send out transcripts. Some informants may strongly wish to receive a transcript, as a form of documentation of a significant experience in their life.

The format and layout of a transcript need to be prepared for analysis. It is useful to insert line numbering, so that the location of interesting quotes, or instances of codes/themes, can be readily identified. If coding/analysis is carried out on paper copies, it may be helpful to display the text double-spaced, or to use wide margins, to allow notes to be written on to the page.

Transcribing takes time. It is important to include a realistic estimate of the time requirement during the planning phase of a study. If time constraints are a significant issue, it may be better to choose a different type of research or method of data collection. Within a qualitative research approach, it is possible to collect data using diaries, open ended-questionnaires, or other forms of written report that do not need to be transcribed.

Analysing

The process of analysing transcripts of qualitative interviews should adhere to the procedures specified within the qualitative method that is being followed (e.g. grounded theory, IPA, CQR). All of the widely used methods are supported by clear instructions and worked examples around how transcript data should be analysed. These instructions need to be studied carefully, and discussed/practised with a research supervisor or mentor. The comments below are intended as a supplement to the guidelines associated with grounded theory, IPA, CQR or other established qualitative methods, and not as a replacement for them.

The first step in qualitative analysis is to become immersed in the data, to upload these into your imagination and working memory. This happens by doing interviews, transcribing interviews and reading transcripts. This process can also be aided by constructing a physical location for the data. Paper-based analysis may involve spreading notes or file cards on the floor, on a table top, attaching them to walls, or clipping them to loops of string stretched across a room. Screen-based analysis may involve creating and organising folders in Word, or becoming familiar with the operation of a qualitative analysis package such as NVivo.

It is then necessary to make best use of the time available. Arriving at a robust and coherent analysis of qualitative transcript texts takes a lot of time. Typically, students who are under pressure to complete their dissertation or thesis do not have a lot of this, and in some cases may not have enough to get to a point of being fully satisfied with the job they have done. There are two types of analytic time. There is a kind of rhythmic use of time, where the researcher dips in and out of the material for fairly short periods, for example when transcribing, or discussing specific transcripts with their supervisor or peer group. It is important to keep a note of the analytic ideas (codes, themes, connections with theory and previous studies) that arise during or following each of these visits to the data. These notes constitute the elements or building blocks of the ultimate analysis. At the time of making the notes, it may not be clear where they fit into an overall scheme. That does not matter – the overall scheme comes later.

The other type of time is a block of time, of at least several days, towards the end of the project. Some researchers will go away for a few days, or take a holiday from work, to make sure that they have a block of undisturbed time. (This can be unpopular with family members.) By this point, all the interviewing and transcribing will have been done, and a great many notes compiled. The task now is to connect everything together and begin to write it all down. It is probable that most of what is written will need to be edited and polished. The aim is to emerge from this block of time with a version or working draft. In my experience, qualitative researchers who manage to create this kind of block of time report that they are excited and energised by the experience, and feel that they have achieved something worthwhile. Those who proceed on the basis of analysing the data on two evenings each week, or every second Saturday, tend to accumulate high levels of stress and frustration. This is because it is enormously difficult, at a cognitive and emotional level, to re-enter this material at depth over and over again.

In terms of the actual process of analysing transcript data, all of the widely used methods of qualitative analysis, such as grounded theory or IPA, require researchers to work through the material, on a line-by-line or statement-by-statement basis, and allocate a code or descriptive label (or multiple codes/labels) that convey the possible meaning of that little segment of the data. The idea is that the interview as a whole has given the person an opportunity to express what it means to him or her to be a client, or a therapist, or to sit in silence, or write answers to a feedback questionnaire or whatever the research topic might be. Within that totality, each line of transcript or statement reflects a fragment of the total meaning. This procedure lies at the heart of qualitative analysis. A good way of thinking about what happens next is that each meaning-code is then written on a card. These cards are then compared with one another to allow all the cards with a similar meaning to be together to form categories or themes. In practice, not all researchers use actual cards – an equivalent process can be replicated with computer files, diagrams and other means of display.

However, qualitative analysis is not merely a matter of accumulating and sorting out codes. These codes come from the mind of the researcher, and the words, concepts and metaphors that are available in the wider culture. One of the major lessons of cognitive psychology is that, confronted by a complex array of information, people tend to see patterns and jump to conclusions. In such a context, the discipline of coding line by line is an effective means of subverting and challenging any pre-existing or early assumptions and imagined patterns that the researcher might hold. Micro-coding forces the researcher to pay attention to what is there, or more probably, *what else* might be there. Within the phenomenological tradition, this is the activity known as 'bracketing-off' (Fischer, 2009; Tufford & Newman, 2010). It is only very rarely, or perhaps even never at all, that a researcher is able to lay aside all of their assumptions, and be fully open to the essential meaning of something said by a research participant. But each moment of willingness to bracket-off gives a researcher the opportunity to make a new discovery, learn something new, extend their interpretive horizon, deepen their understanding.

This kind of micro-coding is primarily cognitive: it involves thinking, reasoning and using concepts and words. However, it also involves emotional responses to the material and 'felt sense' of the message that the participant was communicating. These are bodily phenomena. It can be valuable for qualitative researchers to make use of their physical, bodily response to what they hear in a recording or read in a transcript. Rennie and Fergus (2006) have written about coding 'from the gut'. What they mean is that, by being immersed in the data, the researcher develops a gut feeling around what the speaker might have meant. The task is then to find the words, phrases or images that best capture this felt sense.

It is important to accept that the process of qualitative analysis is not linear. It is not a matter of gradually accumulating more and more codes and meanings, until a structure or overall picture emerges. Unfortunately, it is a process that goes backwards as well as forwards. In any qualitative research, the investigator begins with some kind of pre-existing understanding of the phenomenon being studied. A genuine process of exploration and discovery requires that this prior structure of understanding should be dismantled and rebuilt. This can be scary. Many qualitative researchers report that, during data analysis, they went through a period or periods of what some therapists describe as 'not-knowing' and what ordinary people describe as 'getting really confused'. This is scary because by that point the researcher will have invested many hours on the project, and will be aware that they need to 'come up with something' if they are to get their degree or produce a publishable study. It is crucial in this situation to accept that being confused is actually a good sign, a progress marker. It is also crucial to recognise that the way forward may not necessarily be to work harder at the analysis. It may be useful to keep going with the analysis, because there may be a little nugget of a quote in the next transcript that triggers an 'aha' moment. But it is also a good idea to pay attention to one's own sources of creativity, whatever these might be – art, music, dreams, nature, reading, meditation. Another way of looking at it is that arriving at a coherent and satisfying analysis of interview data calls on a belief in, and acceptance of, one's own capacity to understand.

A final practical tip in relation to data analysis is to make use of other people. An activity that can be extremely useful, following a period of immersion in the data and coding, is to meet with others and just talk about what has been found, with no requirement to label any of this as categories or different levels of category. It can also be helpful if a member of the group writes down what the researcher says, and how he or she responds to questions. The act of just freely talking about what has been found, calls for the researcher to articulate ideas that up to that point were implicit. Talking in a non-judgemental environment means that self-censorship is minimised, and self-contradiction is permissible. After such a conversation the researcher will need to sift through what has emerged, including systematically checking on whether what they were able to say represented all of the data, and whether there might be counter-instances in the data that did not fit into the implicit themes that were articulated.

There are many other ways that other people can play a part in data analysis. It is instructive for a small group to spend at least 90 minutes sharing their interpretations of a portion of a transcript. It is certain that an enormous amount of ideas will be generated, and that some of these ideas will be completely new to the researcher, no matter how much time he or she has already spent on that material. It is then up to the primary researcher to determine whether these ideas are relevant to the dataset as a whole. The members of a discussion group need not all be other researchers, or from the same discipline. Academic researchers, particularly within a single discipline, tend to make reference to the same set of ideas – lay people, inexperienced students or people from other areas of the university are likely to offer interpretations that are more creative and diverse. A further way in which other people can be involved is by acting as auditors. At the point where a reasonably complete draft of an analysis has been assembled, it will be helpful for a 'critical friend' to go through this to check whether the quotes/examples are convincing as illustrations of themes/categories, and whether the themes/categories that have been clustered together into main/superordinate groupings seem to be plausibly connected to each other. This task needs to be carried out by someone who is an experienced researcher, but is not necessarily all that time-consuming. For example, if a quote that is used as evidence to back up a category can readily be interpreted as carrying a meaning that has not been picked up by the researcher, then something is badly wrong. Auditing could involve the auditor analysing one or more transcripts, and then comparing their themes/categories with those of the primary researcher.

The involvement of other people in the process of qualitative analysis is only effective if they are genuinely interested in, and respectful of, the researcher and what they are trying to achieve. They also need to be willing to challenge the researcher, in terms of questioning how statements have been coded, and offering alternative interpretations.

Box 8.1 Creative approaches to data analysis

The process of qualitative data analysis can be time-consuming and tedious. Qualitative researchers have devised many techniques to help them to remain on task. One strategy is to be on the alert for informant statements that are particularly luminous and powerful, that are candidates for being used as theme titles, quotes in a paper, or that stimulate a deeper level of reflection on the meaning of findings. In a paper that is full of practical hints, Smith (2011b) calls such statements 'pearls' and 'gems'. Metaphors and images offer a valuable source of such treasure. A potentially useful way of 'hearing' multiple meanings being expressed in an interview is to read the transcript aloud, listen while a colleague reads it back, or listen while different colleagues read the same passage aloud. The 'listening guide' technique

(Continued)

aims to access implicit meaning in transcript through multiple readings, each of which focuses on a different aspect of the informant's world (Gilligan, 2015). The first reading involves paying attention to the story being told; the second reading is attuned to examples of the subjective 'I' voice of the informant; a third reading collects examples of the voices of others. The 'empathic bridges' approach invites the researcher (or, even better, several members of a research team) to read a transcript and then transform it into a first-person statement, as a means of bringing forward the unique identity and life story of each interviewee. Stanza analysis makes use of the poetic quality of spoken communication, by displaying key segments of research transcripts as poems (McLeod & Lynch, 2000). Finally, some qualitative researchers believe that transcript analysis on its own can never adequately convey embodied, relational and unconscious dimensions of the researcher–participant encounter. In response to this dilemma, many researchers write personal reflective notes immediately following each interview, in an attempt to capture the emotional and interpersonal meaning of what happened, to sensitise them to possible themes in the transcript data: 'I recall feeling really energised at that point in the interview – what was it that the participant was saying that triggered that response?' Beyond this type of enhancement to the craft of qualitative inquiry, some researchers have sought to use psychoanalytic concepts to harness unconscious, unspoken and implicit interview communication in a more systematic manner (see, for example, Hollway and Jefferson, 2013; Midgley & Holmes, 2018; Stänicke et al., 2015; Strømme et al., 2010).

Box 8.2   Using a computer programme to assist qualitative analysis

Many qualitative researchers make use of qualitative analysis software packages to assist in the process of data analysis. Such packages display the text on screen, and provide quick ways of assigning passages of text to category files, which can then be arranged in hierarchical order or as a meaning network (Gibbs, 2014; Humble, 2019; Oswald, 2019). They also make it possible to compare the analyses produced by multiple coders working. It is important to emphasise that these programmes do not actually analyse the data – they just make it easier to organise and retrieve codes, themes and text segments. Most qualitative researchers who use software tools undergo training in how to use them. Anyone undertaking a small-scale project needs to calculate the trade-off between the benefits of using a software tool, and the time spent mastering it. In addition to qualitative analysis tools, there are also text analysis programmes that make it possible to identify recurring types of words or phrases in transcripts (see, for example, Smink et al., 2019). There is also commercially available software that will transcribe spoken conversation. At the time of writing, neither of these technologies have been applied in qualitative research. However, given the pace of technological advance, it seems inevitable that at some point this will occur.

Writing

Writing a qualitative paper or dissertation/thesis comprises an extension of the process of data analysis. The stage of writing up a study functions as a test of the coherence of the analysis that has been carried out. A structure of themes or categories that make sense on the whiteboard or during conversations within a research team can fall apart when it begins to be articulated on paper. A written report requires a logical sequence or narrative flow from one idea to another. Sometimes it can be hard to arrive at a satisfactory way of structuring the material to achieve an acceptable degree of linearity. This is a fundamental issue in all qualitative research, rather than being a sign of the inadequacy of any particular researcher. Qualitative interview-based research asks participants to share their experience of some specific part of their life. The themes that are then generated can be viewed as different aspects of that experience, which do not necessarily have a causal or linear relationship with each other. However, a results/finding section in a paper that jumps abruptly from one theme or category to the next will prove hard to read.

The most effective strategy for writing a results/finding section is to begin by offering the reader a brief summary of what was found as a means of orienting and preparing them for what is to follow. Sometimes this summary will take the form of a table made up of themes/categories, or a diagram showing how the themes/categories are connected with each other. Sometimes the summary will just consist of a brief paragraph. The actual presentation of findings, which comes next, is then structured in terms of the story that the researcher has decided to tell. This story might start by explaining the key 'headline' finding of the study in some detail, before moving on to describe less important themes/categories in less detail. An alternative story structure is to organise the material around stages or phases in an unfolding experience. Results/findings sections in which the researcher does not tell a story, but instead offers a list of themes/categories in no particular order, or (worse) zig-zags back and forward between themes, or (even worse) relies on long quotes with little or no commentary, will have the effect of leaving the reader with a sense that the researcher has only collated the material and then left it up to the reader to analyse this.

In a qualitative article there are two stories that are being told. The first story is an account of what participants had to say on the topic under investigation. The second story consists of a narrative of how these findings fit into, confirm or contradict previous knowledge of the topic. In well-written qualitative articles, these different levels of narrative will dovetail together in a seamless fashion. In poorly written papers, these narratives will either be awkwardly bolted together or one of them will be subjugated to the other. When writing a qualitative paper, it is therefore particularly important to pay careful attention to the points of connection between the 'literature story' and the 'participant story' – the bridge passage between the introductory literature review and the method section, and the part of the discussion section where the findings of the study are looked at in relation to previous research. These transitions are handled very well, in my view, in most articles published in

Qualitative Health Research, and in many IPA articles. By contrast, these transitions are deeply problematic for many authors publishing in therapy journals, because it is almost certain that the background/introductory literature will consist of quantitative studies. In such a situation, it is possible to deal with the first transition by arguing that qualitative research has the potential to open up new ways of understanding a topic that has hitherto been studied using quantitative methods. But it is much harder, towards the end of a paper, to do the comparing task. It is like comparing apples and oranges, but without the space to clarify or explain the concept of an apple or the concept of an orange. As always, it is vital for novice researchers to look at how these technical writing tasks are handled by more experienced authors. These are not always done well.

There is, of course, a third story that can be told in a qualitative study – the researcher's story. The issues outlined in the previous paragraph should help to make it clear why it is so hard to integrate researcher reflexivity (the researcher's story) into a conventional research paper. This third narrative thread introduces a degree of complexity that is hard for most writers to handle. As a result, most journals have over the years arrived at their own specific 'house style' in respect of reflexive writing. This can be frustrating for qualitative therapy researchers who accept the role of reflexivity but are aiming to publish in therapy journals that have opted for minimal researcher self-reference in the form of a brief section in the method part of an article. It can be easier to include reflexive writing in a dissertation or thesis, because there is enough space to include different forms of writing, and also enough space to explain the rationale for these rhetorical choices.

It is worthwhile paying attention to the challenges of qualitative writing from the outset of a project. When reading the literature and compiling a literature review, it is useful to reflect on the effectiveness with which different articles are written, and build up a catalogue of 'good ideas for writing'. It is also valuable to write as you go along. It is easier, at the end, to be in a position of editing text that already exists, rather than staring at a blank laptop screen.

In the findings/results section of a paper, a powerful and persuasive way of communicating qualitative insights is to look for ways of combining 'telling' (information about themes/categories) and 'showing' (brief stories that capture and exemplify that theme).

At the point of actually writing a qualitative paper, it is important to be mindful of the aims of qualitative inquiry and the type of knowledge that is generated. The quantitative, 'positivist' tradition is based on an underlying model of the world as consisting of causal 'factors'. The counselling and psychotherapy research literature is largely organised around this way of thinking. Examples would be research into the *effect of* interventions on outcome, or the *impact of* working alliance on dropout. Qualitative research, by contrast, is based on a rather different set of underlying assumptions, which posit the world (or at least, the social world) as organised around purposeful collaborative action carried out by self-aware agents. The report of a qualitative study needs to be written in a way that reflects this philosophical stance. Careful reading of well-written qualitative articles will reveal the many ways in which this has been accomplished. Themes and categories are best formulated as action statements or 'doing' words. For example 'search*ing* for a therapist voice' works better than 'counsellor identity' as a label for a theme. Although both labels are accurate, and convey meaning, the former implies a self-initiated process, while the latter comprises a static concept. A paper by Sandelowski and Leeman (2012) provides an invaluable account of the subtle implications of different ways of labelling themes and categories. An example of a qualitative therapy research study that has explicitly adopted an 'action language' approach to theme-labels (i.e. using words that end in '...ing') can be found in Levitt, Butler and Hill (2006). Another form of writing that conveys lived experience involves the judicious use of statements from informants, not only to illustrate themes and categories, but also as the titles of themes and categories and possibly also within the title of an article. Images or phrases from informants can be highly evocative. Such category labels also function to remind the reader that the research is based on the experiences of specific people rather than a 'sample'.

Box 8.3   Learning the craft of qualitative research

There is a worldwide community of qualitative researchers who are keen to share their experience – a Google search on any aspect of qualitative inquiry will generate multiple hits. The open-access *Qualitative Report* journal runs a series of short 'how to' articles that are particularly helpful. In relation to research training, for example within a university programme, the current evidence suggests that the best way to learn about qualitative research is through hands-on practice (Levitt, Kannan & Ippolito, 2013; Neal Kimball & Turner, 2018).

Deciding on the method

There is a large body of research that uses open-ended or semi-structured interviews with individuals, followed by analysis of interview transcripts in terms of themes or categories. There are different ways in which this general research task can be handled. These approaches have tended to have been described in terms of specific 'brand names', such as empirical phenomenology, thematic analysis or grounded theory. This section offers a brief review of the key features of each of these approaches. They are treated here as 'methods' – sets of procedures that are used to organise a study and are reported in the 'method' section of a journal article. It is important to keep in mind that these approaches can also be considered 'methodologies' because each of them is broader than just a set of procedures, and in fact draws on a somewhat different set of underlying philosophical assumptions. For the purpose of undertaking this kind of research, as a novice or apprentice researcher, what is essential is to be able to understand and follow the relevant procedures.

Phenomenology

One of the longest established approaches to qualitative research is *phenomeno-logical analysis* (Wertz, 2005, 2015). To distinguish it from phenomenology as a school of philosophy, some qualitative researchers will describe what they do as *empirical phenomenology* (Finlay, 2011; Giorgi, 2009). Although all forms of qualitative analysis are informed by phenomenological principles, a study that adopts a specific phenomenological stance is distinctive in aiming to develop a description of the 'essence' or essential features of an experience. Compared to other qualitative methods outlined in this section, phenomenology is probably somewhat more challenging, and harder to do well, because it requires at least some degree of engagement with philosophical ideas, and is associated with quite demanding requirements around the depth of analysis that is carried out (Van Manen, 2014). Conducting a pure phenomenological study is therefore not necessarily a sensible choice for a novice researcher, unless their chosen topic or question is particularly well suited to phenomenological analysis. However, the writings of leading phenom-enological researchers, such as Finlay (2011) and Fischer (2009), have been highly influential within the field of qualitative research as a whole, with the consequence that all of the approaches discussed in the present chapter are 'small-p' phenomeno-logical in differing degrees.

Grounded theory

Another long-established qualitative method is *grounded theory*. Initially developed by Glaser and Strauss (1967), the grounded theory approach is probably the most widely used method in the field of qualitative research. Because it has been applied by so many researchers and research groups, what has happened is that slightly dif-ferent versions of grounded theory have emerged (see McLeod, 2011, for further discussion). Nevertheless, all grounded theory research follows the same set of basic procedures. The researcher is advised against reading or reviewing the literature ahead of collecting the data, in order to remain as open as possible to subtle mean-ings conveyed by interview participants. The method is open to any type of qualitative data that might be available, including interviews, observation and docu-ments. Ideally, each interview is analysed before the next one is carried out, so that the interviewer is sensitised to emerging themes that can be explored further in later interviews. As a result, this method uses a flexible, adaptable interview schedule rather than a fixed set of questions. Transcripts are subjected first of all to open coding, in which potential meaning(s) conveyed by 'meaning units' (e.g. phrases, sentences, longer passages) are noted. These codes undergo a process of constant comparison to identify similarities and clarify differences. Through this activity a set of categories will emerge, which are then clustered into a smaller set of perhaps four or five main organising categories. Finally, a 'core category', which captures the meaning of the phenomenon being studied as a whole, is formulated. Grounded theory adopts a distinctive approach to sampling. Rather than deciding the sample size (number of participants) in advance, the aim is to continue collecting data until 'theoretical saturation' has been achieved – in other words, no new codes or categories are being discovered. In the later stages of data collection, 'theoretically interesting' participants are sought out in order to test the robustness of the emerging category structure. The end-point of a grounded theory analysis is a theoretical framework (set of concepts) that is grounded in the everyday experience of participants. In many studies this framework or theory will be expressed in the form of a diagram. The grounded theory method is flexible, well understood, and supported by a range of textbooks and websites, as well as a critical methodological literature. It has also been used in many influential studies of counselling and psychotherapy (see, for example, Rennie, 2000). The downside of grounded theory is that it calls for certain procedures that can be difficult to follow in practice (for example, continuing with theoretical sampling long enough to achieve saturation, finding a plausible core category). Not reviewing the literature in advance can create difficulties in academic settings where students will need to submit a review before commencing data collection. A further limitation of grounded theory, for some researchers, is that like phenomenology it has an arms-length relationship with theory. Allowing pre-existing theoretical concepts to influence data analysis is not part of a grounded theory approach. It is only when an entire grounded theory has been constructed that the links with pre-existing theory are supposed to take place. Information on how to carry out a grounded theory study is available in Charmaz (2014) and Levitt (2021). Because grounded theory is such a long-established and influential approach, it has generated a considerable literature around what it means and how it should be carried out. Useful entry points to these debates are Bryant and Charmaz (2019) and Charmaz and Thornberg (2021).

Interpretative phenomenological analysis (IPA)

Interpretative phenomenological analysis (IPA) is an approach that was developed by Jonathan Smith and his colleagues (Smith, Flowers & Larkin, 2009) in the 1990s. In many ways, the IPA method is similar to grounded theory, particularly in terms of initial line-by-line open coding of the possible meaning of informant statements. However, unlike grounded theory, IPA does not require researchers to keep recruiting additional research participants until they have reached a state of 'saturation' (i.e. no further categories are emerging). On the contrary, IPA encourages the use of small samples (often around six participants) and analysis on a case-by-case basis, leading to a discussion of differences across cases as well as common themes. IPA also incorporates analysis of informant language use (e.g. repetition, metaphors), and encourages researchers to develop theoretical interpretation of findings. The IPA tradition has evolved a style of reporting results of studies in terms of themes that flows well and in many respects is more direct than the category structure used in grounded theory. IPA is supported by a textbook that elegantly and accessibly explains the philosophical rationale for the approach (Smith, Flowers & Larkin, 2009), and by useful online learning materials. The clarity of exposition in these sources, allied to flexibility over sample size, has made IPA an attractive choice for many novice researchers.

Reflexive thematic analysis

Reflexive thematic analysis is a method that has been influenced by descriptive content analysis approaches to analysis of qualitative data, alongside the more interpretative and phenomenological focus found in grounded theory and IPA. It gained prominence following the publication of a highly influential paper by Braun and Clarke (2006) which described a set of procedures which could be followed. At that point, the approach was described as thematic analysis. More recently, the term reflexive thematic analysis has been preferred, in order to emphasise that it is different from more objectivist content-oriented theme-based approaches. Reflexive thematic analysis is a highly flexible way of working with qualitative data, and allows the researcher a great deal of freedom to analyse qualitative data in a form that is appropriate to their own purposes. It is applicable in a wide range of research situations, and supported by a rich array of texts and online resources (Braun & Clarke, 2013, 2019, 2021a,b; Braun et al., 2019; Clarke & Braun, 2018).

Consensual qualitative research (CQR)

Consensual qualitative research (CQR) is mainly an approach to qualitative analysis that is similar to phenomenology, grounded theory, IPA and thematic analysis, but which includes two additional elements. Unlike other qualitative approaches, which assume that the researcher is working alone, CQR explicitly consists of a team approach. Data are parcelled up to be analysed by members of a small team made up of perhaps three or four people. In addition, the results of these analyses are audited by an expert researcher from outside the team. The intention is that the contributions of all members of the research team combine to yield a consensus analysis which is richer and more plausible than an analysis carried out by an individual working on their own. The other distinctive element of CQR is that theory informs analysis from the start, rather than being considered only at the end. The research team takes existing theory into account when deciding on the 'domains' that will be used to organise the process of data analysis. Interview transcripts are first chunked in terms of domains. Following this, blocks of text within each domain are subjected to open coding and the identification of themes and categories, along the lines of grounded theory. This strategy makes it much easier to make links between the aims and findings of a study, and previously existing theory and research findings. On the other hand, it can have the effect of restricting the potential creativity of the research process. CQR has been immensely productive, with many counselling and psychotherapy studies completed in recent years using this approach (see Hill, 2012). It fits very well into situations in which there exists a potential pool of researchers, such as a therapy training course or doctoral programme. The role of auditor is also consistent with an apprenticeship-oriented model of research training. Alongside its use with groups of student researchers, CQR is a method that meets many of the needs of experienced practitioners seeking to carry out research-based continuing professional development within a peer group. The CQR research community has generated very clear guidelines about how the method can be applied to different types of research question (Hill, 2012; Hill & Knoz, 2021).

Narrative analysis

The concept of narrative refers to the activity of telling a story about some aspect of personal experience. Storytelling represents a basic mode of human expression and communication, acquired at an early age. All of the qualitative methods described above can be regarded as adopting a narrative approach, in the sense that the informant is invited to tell their story. However, in requiring responses to specific questions, these methods may restrict the extent to which participants can tell their whole story. In addition, data analysis typically deconstructs participant stories into themes or meaning categories, rather than retaining complete stories as units of analysis. As a result, narrative analysis has emerged as a distinctive approach that seeks to retain the storied nature of participant data. There are a number of styles of narrative analysis, rather than a single narrative methodology that adheres to a single protocol (De Fina, Georgakopoulou & Barkhuizen, 2015; Wong & Breheny, 2018). Compared to thematic and category-based forms of qualitative analysis, narrative studies have the potential to be more evocative, in the sense of bringing readers closer to concrete examples of lived experience (Reynolds, Lim & Prior, 2008). On the other hand, themes and categories may provide a more clearly defined means of conveying findings. Analysis of narrative is particularly sensitive to capturing processes that unfold over time – a well-formed story will always have a beginning, middle and end.

Choosing a method

The above list of methods for analysing qualitative interview data reflects only the most widely adopted approaches. Many other qualitative methods have been used by therapy researchers. For example, the method of systematic text condensation (Binder, Holgersen & Nielsen, 2009; Malterud, 2011) is a phenomenological-interpretive form of analysis that has been widely used in Nordic countries. Framework analysis is an approach that involves creating a pre-determined starting point set of categories, derived from research goals and relevant theory

(Parkinson et al., 2016). The Ward method is a highly disciplined way of combining interpretations made by different members of a research team (Schielke et al., 2009, 2014). A generic approach to qualitative data analysis, which integrates elements from grounded theory and CQR, has been developed by leading therapy researchers Robert Elliott and Ladislav Timulak (2021). It is also possible to adopt a 'bricolage' perspective, which brings together analytic ideas and techniques from a range of methods (McLeod, 2011).

A comparison of the key features of phenomenological, grounded theory and narrative analysis is available in Wertz et al. (2011). Comparison of practical and conceptual aspects of using reflexive thematic analysis, grounded theory, IPA and discourse analysis can be found in Braun and Clarke (2021b). Other useful evaluations of the pros and cons of contrasting qualitative traditions are offered in Barker, Pistrang and Elliott (2016) and Prosek and Gibson (2021). A clear and helpful guide to differences in the philosophical underpinning of qualitative methods can be found in Ponterotto (2005).

The choice of method will depend on a number of factors. Some research questions will be better suited to some methods. For example, questions that involved describing or uncovering the meaning of a specific type of experience, such as 'anger', 'understanding' or 'forgiveness', lend themselves to phenomenological inquiry. Questions that explore action sequences or processes, such as 'living with depression' or 'using metaphor in therapy', are a good fit for grounded theory, IPA and CQR. However, each method can be applied to a range of research topics and questions; it is important to take time to search in the literature for examples of how different methods have been used in relation to one's own research question, or similar types of question.

Another factor to take into consideration when selecting a method is the nature of support that is available, in particular the experience and interests of possible research supervisors or mentors.

Having decided on a method, it is necessary to allow sufficient time to learn the method, by reading textbooks and chapters, talking to supervisors, mentors and research colleagues, attending training workshops (if available), and reading and reflecting on articles that have employed that approach.

What can go wrong?

The criteria for evaluating qualitative research discussed in Chapter 6 provide a framework for understanding what a good piece of qualitative work might look like. These criteria also highlight things that can go wrong. For example, a qualitative study is unlikely to be seen as credible and trustworthy if it lacks researcher reflexivity, the method of data analysis is not explained clearly, or if there are not enough examples and participant quotes (or the ones that are provided do not match analytic themes). There are also many ways in which practical arrangements often can go wrong in interview-based qualitative studies: participants do not turn up for interviews, recording devices break down and transcribing takes much longer than anticipated.

Box 8.4 Where to find qualitative research

Almost all counselling and psychotherapy research journals publish qualitative papers. Some authors of qualitative articles in these journals respond to the lingering resistance among editors and reviewers to qualitative inquiry, by ramping up the methodological detail. This can make such papers difficult to read. By contrast, studies published in journals that more actively embrace qualitative methodologies, such as *Qualitative Health Research, Qualitative Social Work, Frontiers in Psychology* and the *International Journal of Qualitative Studies on Health and Well-being,* are often more confidently written and impactful, in part because the review process in these journals helps authors to showcase their work to best advantage. Even though these are not specialist psychotherapy journals, they do publish studies on therapy, recovery and experiences of specific disorders. *Qualitative Inquiry, Qualitative Research in Psychology, Qualitative Psychology,* the *European Journal for Qualitative Research in Psychotherapy* and *Qualitative Report* are valuable sources of methodological innovation.

Conclusions

From one perspective, interview-based qualitative research is an impossible task. It involves asking informants to report coherently and concisely on perhaps years of personal life experience. The researcher then needs to be able to do justice to the complex, nuanced meanings that are embedded within interview transcripts, and find a way to convey what they have found within the constraints of the results section of a research paper. On the other hand, this kind of process is something we are all familiar with in our everyday lives: we talk to each other about what has happened to us, and are usually well able to summarise and convey what we have understood to an interested third party. The principles of qualitative inquiry outlined in the present chapter represent the accumulated wisdom and skill of several generations of qualitative researchers around how to build on common-sense, everyday accomplishments in ways that are sufficiently credible and trustworthy to inform the practice of therapy.

To be able to carry out qualitative research in therapy it is not only necessary to have a grasp of basic principles – it is also essential to have an appreciation of how these strategies have been applied in the context of specific types of therapy research products. Later chapters in this book explore how qualitative methods have been used in studies of the client experience of the process and outcomes of therapy, therapist professional knowledge and as an element of systematic case study research.

Suggestions for further reading

A book that captures the spirit of qualitative inquiry, and has inspired several generations of researchers, is:

Brinkmann, S., & Kvale, S. (2014). *InterViews: Learning the Craft of Qualitative Research Interviewing*. 3rd edn. Thousand Oaks, CA: Sage.

Fascinating and insightful accounts of the experience of doing qualitative research:

Minichiello, V., & Kottler, J. A. (Eds.). (2009). *Qualitative Journeys: Student and Mentor Experiences with Research*. Thousand Oaks, CA: Sage.

A comprehensive analysis of the current state of qualitative research in psychotherapy can be found in:

Levitt, H. M., McLeod, J., & Stiles, W. B. (2021). The conceptualization, design, and evaluation of qualitative methods in research on psychotherapy. In M. Barkham, L. Castonguay, & W. Lutz (ed.) *Bergin and Garfield's Handbook of Psychotherapy and Behavior Change*, 7th edn. New York: Wiley.

McLeod, J., Levitt, H. M., & Stiles, W. B. (2021). Qualitative research: Contributions to theory, policy and practice. In M. Barkham, L. Castonguay, & W. Lutz (ed.) *Bergin and Garfield's Handbook of Psychotherapy and Behavior Change,* 7th edn. New York: Wiley.

Online resources

The online resource site (https://study.sagepub.com/doingresearch4e) provides access to qualitative research resources.

9

Basic Research Tools

Introduction

It is not easy to investigate the process and outcome of therapy, or the ways in which therapy is understood and organised within different social settings. Counselling and psychotherapy are complex activities that take place at various levels – cognitive, physical, emotional, interpersonal – over varying periods of time. One of the primary achievements of the counselling and psychotherapy research community over the past 70 years has been to construct reliable tools and methods that can be used to gain access to aspects of what happens in therapy. This chapter provides an introduction to some of the most widely adopted therapy research tools. Within a chapter of this length, it is not feasible to offer a comprehensive listing of all the scales, instruments and forms that are in circulation. The intention, rather, is to illustrate some of the main possibilities and where they can be located, discuss how they can be applied and indicate some of the criteria against which their value can be assessed.

Why do I need to know about basic research tools?

There are several reasons for being interested in research instruments and techniques. First, these products represent the 'tools of the trade' – in order to carry out one's own personal research, it is necessary to be able to use one or more of these tools in a competent and thoughtful manner. The techniques described in this chapter all 'work', in the sense of forming the basis for successful, publishable and influential pieces of research. Appropriate deployment of any of these techniques allows a researcher to build on the achievements of the researcher or team who developed the method, and of subsequent researchers who have used it within published studies. For example, collecting outcome data using a particular questionnaire, such as the CORE-OM, not only means that you are employing a credible, client-friendly research instrument – it also makes it possible to compare findings with the innumerable other studies that have gathered similar data.

A second reason for learning about research tools is that it is hard to read and appreciate research papers in the absence of an understanding of the techniques that were used to collect information. Typically, in a research paper, only very brief information is provided about questionnaires or other research tools that were used. It is assumed that the reader will already be familiar with these instruments, or, if not, will be willing to go off and read about them. A third way in which an interest in research tools is important is concerned with the necessity to take a critical and questioning approach to all knowledge claims. For example, there are many therapy studies that have examined outcome in terms of change in client scores on the Beck Depression Inventory (BDI). A full appreciation of the meaning of the results of these studies requires understanding of how the BDI is constructed, the items included in it, and what it can and cannot do. Closer reflection on the ways in which knowledge is constructed or 'operationalised' through the implementation of various data collection techniques can be surprisingly informative and interesting. In respect of the BDI, for instance, anyone who looks closely at how it was constructed and how it operates will realise that it captures certain aspects of depression but not others. Thinking about whether these missing aspects are important enough to make a difference to how the results of a study could be interpreted invites consideration about the very nature of depression and its treatment.

A further facet of why it is important to know about research tools relates to the possibility of designing new research measures and instruments. In most research projects, it is not a good idea for a novice researcher to devise their own questionnaire or rating scale, because a satisfactory scale will almost certainly already exist in the literature. Developing a new tool takes a lot of time and effort, and needs to be seen as a research project in itself, rather than as merely a preliminary step.

A final reason for leaning about research tools is that they are increasingly used within therapy practice. Many of the tools described in this chapter are used by therapists to collect information on the progress of therapy, and form the basis of client–therapist exploration around whether their way of working needs to change, or whether it might be time to plan to bring therapy to a close. Research tools can also be used for screening and assessment purposes, for example feeding in to case formulation and contracting. There are research tools, such as client diaries and projective techniques, that can have a facilitative effect in relation to helping the client to reflect and be aware of issues in their life. Increasingly, clients self-monitor their mood, mental state and behaviour using apps that allow them to complete brief questionnaires in their own time. To be able to use scales and questionnaires sensitively and ethically for therapeutic purposes, it is essential to understand the strengths and limitations of such instruments, and be able to interpret the data that they produce in a balanced and informed manner.

Using research tools – general principles

When using any of the techniques introduced in this chapter to collect research information that might be included in a published study, it is essential to seek approval from the client before the commencement of therapy. It is also important to consider practical issues associated with the use of a data collection technique, such as the amount of time it will take to complete.

Some of the scales and instruments discussed in this chapter are copyrighted, and can only be used with the permission of the author or the organisation that owns the copyright. Sometimes a fee will need to be paid for each questionnaire or scale that is used, or for a licence to use the instrument for a specific period of time. Occasionally, access to a scale is restricted to users who have undergone specific training. However, there are also many research tools that are freely available, and are accessible either through the websites of researchers or research teams/organisations, or within the text of research articles. Some researchers are willing to allow anyone to use their research instruments, but only on the basis of a personal request – this allows them to keep track of who is using the instrument, and inform those users about updates. On the whole, it is in the interests of those who develop research tools to promote and support the use of their products on as wide a scale as possible, so such requests almost always receive a favourable response. It is always necessary to provide reference details for any research tools that are used in a study.

On the whole, once a research tool has been developed, there is an expectation that it will be used as it is, without alteration. It is important to proceed with caution in any situation where it may seem desirable to change the items, instructions or format of a research tool. With standardised, psychometric measures such as the BDI or CORE-OM, any change will mean that it is not possible to compare findings with the results of previous studies that have used the intact, published version of the scale. Tampering with such a scale may even be regarded as a breach of copyright. Some other data collection techniques, such as the Change Interview or any qualitative interview schedule, or survey questionnaires, tend to be more flexible: the original version is understood to be a template that can be adjusted according to circumstances.

Many research tools have been translated into different languages, with data available on scale reliability and validity, and norms, in a range of language communities. Translating a scale is a complex endeavour because of the ways in which the meaning of emotional and psychological terms may be subtly different in different languages. Good practice around guidelines and procedures for translating measures is exemplified in the literature on the development and dissemination of the CORE-OM – for instance in reports on how it has been translated into Italian (Palmieri et al., 2009) and British Sign Language (Rogers et al., 2013).

A crucial aspect of deciding whether a research tool is worth using is to evaluate the extent to which it is fit for purpose, in terms of actually measuring what it claims to measure. There are three key criteria through which measures and other research tools can be assessed: *validity*, *reliability*, *sensitivity to change* and *heuristic value*. Deciding on the best tool to include in any particular study means finding the most appropriate balance between these factors.

Validity

The concept of validity refers to the ability of the test, questionnaire, rating scale or other type of instrument to measure the actual construct it claims to be measuring. Strictly speaking, all techniques or tools employed in research studies should be backed up by data demonstrating acceptable levels of reliability and validity. For the most widely used method, data are made available from the publishers of the instrument in the form of a test manual, or are reported in a journal article by the author of the technique. If an instrument or test has been created for use in a specific study, reliability and validity information should be provided in the report on the study.

Many tests used in counselling research have been applied in the absence of basic information about reliability and validity. A researcher utilising an instrument that has not been shown to be reliable and valid runs the risk of producing results that are meaningless or lacking in credibility.

In relation to quantitative methods, the main forms of validity include:

Face validity. The instrument, measure or test appears to measure what it claims to measure. This can be helpful in gaining acceptance for the test in some groups, but can be a hindrance if it allows respondents to guess what the test is about, and shape their answers to achieve 'impression management'.

Content validity. The items in the instrument comprehensively reflect the domain of meaning that is intended to be measured. For example, an instrument designed to assess depression will have items relating to all aspects of depression.

Criterion validity. An estimate of whether the instrument differentiates between people in the same way as other types of measures. For example, concurrent criteria for a social anxiety scale might include observations made by nurses. Predictive criteria refer to measures taken at a later time. For example, the predictive validity of a social anxiety scale might be future level of participation in a discussion group.

Construct validity. Scores on the test correlate (or otherwise) with scores on other tests in accordance with theoretical predictions. For example, measures of social and manifest anxiety should correlate more highly with each other (convergent validity) than they do with measures of depression (divergent validity).

There are some rather serious issues associated with the validity of the kinds of self-report questionnaires and rating scales that are widely used in counselling and psychotherapy research. Research in social psychology has established that when people evaluate a situation or action, their judgements are heavily influenced by a general, evaluative, good–bad dimension. This has important implications for therapy research. For example, when a client completes a questionnaire that is intended to measure a specific factor such as depression, anxiety or wellbeing, it is probable that their responses will largely reflect their sense of overall distress. As a result, there tend to be high correlations between scores on different problem areas. In other words, it is hard to differentiate between theoretically interesting dimensions of distress – what you tend to get is a picture of overall unhappiness. The other difficulty associated with the validity of self-report scales is concerned with the fact that completing a questionnaire or other instrument is a social act or performance. The person is not merely reporting on, say, how depressed they feel, but is also at the same time engaged, at some level, in a process of impression management. This dilemma is often discussed in the context of the concept of *social desirability* – when a person completes a questionnaire, is he or she describing how depressed they are, or do their responses say more about how willing they are to admit that they are depressed? Further discussion of these issues can be found in Galasiński and Kozłowska (2013), McLeod (2001), Paz, Adana-Díaz and Evans (2020) and Truijens et al. (2019).

Reliability

The concept of reliability refers to the robustness of a test, questionnaire, rating scale or other type of instrument. A high level of reliability means that the technique produces similar results in different situations or when administered by different people or at different times. The concept of reliability is particularly associated with quantitative research tools, and the main forms of reliability which need to be established by those who have developed such tools can include:

Test–retest reliability. An assessment of the extent to which similar scores are recorded when the measure is administered to the same person or group of people on two (or more) occasions.

Alternate form reliability. The same group of people are given parallel versions of the instrument on different occasions, and their scores are compared.

Internal consistency. A reliability coefficient that estimates the extent to which different items in a test are in agreement with each other (Leech, Onwuegbuzie & O'Conner, 2011).

Inter-rater reliability. The level of agreement between different raters who have coded or categorised the same set of data.

These concepts of reliability are applicable in qualitative research, but with some caveats. For example, in an interview study, it can be very useful to conduct more than one interview with participants. However, if a person says something different in a second interview, compared with the first meeting, this may not mean that one of these statements is wrong, and the other is correct (although that may occur). It may be that the development of a stronger relationship of trust allows the informant to go deeper into their experience at the second interview. Similarly, when two researchers arrive at diverging interpretations of a segment of a transcript, it may indicate a lack of reliability (i.e. each researcher is operating from a different idea of what the research is trying to achieve) but it may equally serve as a trigger for further dialogue between the researchers that will eventually lead to a more complete or deeper interpretation of the material.

Sensitivity to change

One of the main reasons for using process and outcome measures in therapy is to be able to detect change over time, for example in terms of whether the client has shifted in the severity of their depression, or their perception of the therapy relationship. How sensitive a measure is in respect of detecting change is therefore a significant issue. If a measure is so sensitive that if it picks up transient mood changes, then it is likely to lack reliability (see above). Conversely, if it is more oriented to tapping into relatively unchanging personality traits, the researcher may end up missing evidence of changes that have occurred. It can be hard to access information about relative levels of sensitivity to change of different measures. As a rule of thumb, measures that have been widely used in therapy research tend to be the ones that are most sensitive to change. Although a symptom measure such as the General Health Questionnaire (GHQ) may appear to be relevant for therapy research, and can boast good reliability and validity, it is not sensitive to change, and functions best as a screening or assessment tool. A good indicator of sensitivity to change of an outcome measure is whether it asks the client to report on how they have felt over the last week or two weeks (i.e. since the previous therapy session). By contrast, measures that ask the client to rate how they 'generally' feel are less likely to pick up change from one session to the next.

Heuristic value

Even when a research tool possesses only marginal validity or reliability, or where reliability and validity are hard to establish, the instrument or technique may nevertheless possess a high level of *heuristic* value. The concept of 'heuristic value' (sometimes also described as 'clinical utility') refers to the capacity to generate new insights and understanding, or contribute to a process of discovery. Heuristic value can apply to the use of research tools strictly in relation to research purposes, and also to the use of tools as a means of enhancing the process of therapy. The easiest way to understand this concept is through examples. For instance, the *Helpful Aspects of Therapy* (HAT) instrument, described in more detail later in the chapter, consists of a form that clients and/or therapists complete after the end of a therapy session, where they are invited to identify and briefly describe a helpful and hindering event or episode in the session. It is extremely difficult to determine whether these accounts are valid, in the sense of reflecting everything that was helpful (almost certainly not), or even what was most helpful (the person may not have been aware of what 'really' helped). The instrument is also somewhat unreliable, because sometimes a person may write a lot, and other times much less, and what is written may be cryptic or hard to interpret. Nevertheless, the information it produces is interesting and meaningful, and in case study research (see, for example, Elliott et al., 2009; Smith et al., 2014) can be triangulated against other sources of data that may be available (e.g. shifts in scores on outcome measures). In other words, as a stand-alone measure, the HAT does not work very well, but when used alongside other sources of information, its availability makes it possible to see patterns that would otherwise have been hidden from view.

Quantitative methodologies, and associated concepts of validity and reliability, have dominated the field of counselling and psychotherapy research. As a result there has been little explicit discussion or acknowledgement within the literature around the concept of the heuristic value of research tools.

Widely used research instruments

The following sections of the chapter provide an introduction to various types of research tool or instrument that have been used, or could be used, in therapy research.

Exercise 9.1   Learning about research tools from the inside

As you learn about new research tools in later sections of this chapter, try to find copies of at least some of them, and try them out on yourself. Many of these measures are available on the internet, or can be accessed through the online resource site. As you complete each measure, do so mindfully – be aware of the thoughts, feelings and fantasies that are triggered for you. Imagine what it would be like to complete the scale if you were a client. Look closely at the instructions and format of the measure – what implicit meanings and messages are conveyed by these aspects of the instrument?

Outcome measures

An enormous amount of effort has been expended, over many years, on the task of evaluating the outcomes of therapy. Within the research community, every decade or so, complaints arise about the proliferation of outcome measures, and the need to concentrate efforts on using an agreed 'core battery' of scales. Inevitably, this is followed by a renewed outpouring of new scales. It seems highly unlikely that an agreed core battery will ever be adopted. There are a great many theoretically interesting and practically important aspects of therapy outcome. Scale developers are continually finding ways to enhance the reliability, validity and usability of measures. There are also commercial pressures in play – there is profit to be made from outcome packages that can be sold to healthcare providers. This section focuses on describing the most widely used outcome scales. At the present time, there is no single review or online resource that brings together information on all the outcome measures that are available.

When selecting an outcome scale for use in a research study, there will be a number of factors that will need to be taken into consideration:

- Does the instrument assess an outcome factor that is relevant to the goals of the study?
- Have the reliability and validity of the scale been established?
- Do norms exist that can be used for differentiating between 'clinical' and 'non-clinical' populations or cases, and thus making it possible to engage in benchmarking comparisons and estimating the cut-off points for clinically significant and reliable change?
- Has the instrument been used in other studies with similar client groups or therapy approaches, thus allowing the results to be compared?
- Is the questionnaire acceptable to clients (e.g. clarity of questions, cultural sensitivity, length of time to complete)?
- Is the scale sensitive to change, or does it assess enduring personality characteristics that are unlikely to be affected by therapy?

Outcome assessment can be achieved through standardised questionnaire measures of symptom or problem areas such as anxiety or depression, or by using individualised personal questionnaires or target complaints scales, in which a client describes their goals for therapy in their own words. It can be valuable to use both methods together, to capture any personal or idiosyncratic dimensions of change, as well as more general problem areas. Outcome data can also be collected through interviews (see the later section).

Therapy outcome measures administered on multiple occasions

A selection of self-report therapy questionnaire outcome measures is provided below. These are all instruments that ask the client to report on more than one occasion (e.g. start and finish of therapy, or every session) about how they have been feeling and acting over a recent period of time; change is assessed by comparing scores across time periods. A more detailed appraisal of the most widely used measures is available in Tarescavage and Ben-Porath (2014).

Clinical Outcomes Routine Evaluation – Outcome Measure (CORE-OM) is a 34-item, self-report questionnaire which measures general client psychological distress (Barkham, Mellor-Clark & Connell, 2006; Evans et al., 2000; Mellor-Clark et al., 1999). This scale was originally designed to yield scores on four subscales: wellbeing, symptoms, functioning and risk. However, further research suggests that these subscales do not represent distinct factors; in recent studies, only the overall score has tended to be reported. The CORE-OM questionnaire is easy to understand, and has been found to be acceptable to the majority of clients. Brief ten-item and five-item versions are available. Typically, the CORE is administered at the start of each therapy session, so that change scores can be calculated on a weekly basis, or across the whole of treatment. Client scores on entry into counselling can be used to examine the profile of clients seen by an agency. There are also assessment and end of therapy forms completed by the counsellor, with the result that the CORE system can operate as a comprehensive evaluation package. Versions for children and young people, and those with learning difficulties, are available, at a cost. CORE materials can be downloaded from the CORE-IMS website, and copied without charge. Software analysis packages and computer-based questionnaire administration are available. The CORE questionnaire has been widely adopted by counselling, psychotherapy and clinical psychology service providers in Britain and other countries, and many translations have been carried out. A great deal of data have been collected on the progress of therapy with clients in a range of settings, enabling the 'benchmarking' of standards of effectiveness (Barkham et al., 2001).

Outcome Questionnaire (OQ-45) is similar to CORE, and is widely used in the USA. The OQ comprises a 45-item scale which provides a measure of overall disturbance, as well as subscale scores of subjective distress, interpersonal relations, social role functioning, suicide, substance abuse and workplace violence. A version of the scale for use with children and adolescents has also been produced. As with CORE, software packages and benchmarking norms are available. Further information on the OQ can be found in Lambert (2015). Access to the OQ-45 requires paying a licensing fee to its distributors.

Treatment Outcome Profile (TOP) is a 58-item symptom scale that generates a client profile in relation to 12 domains: sexual functioning; work functioning; violence; social functioning; panic/anxiety; substance abuse; psychosis; quality of life; sleep; suicidality; depression; mania. Versions are available for children, young people and older people, and the scale has been translated into several languages. Further information is available in Kraus and Castonguay (2010). A unique feature of this scale is that it makes it possible to analyse client outcomes in terms of broad, quasi-diagnostic categories. This can be useful for therapy services that are required to collect information on their effectiveness with different groups of clients. A further unique feature is that the scale can only be analysed by sending the data (online) to a central office – it is not possible for the researcher or practitioner to work out the score by himself or herself, because items are weighted according to an algorithm. Access to TOP requires the payment of a licence fee.

Outcome Rating Scale (ORS) is a four-item visual analogue scale of global psychological difficulties (Miller, Duncan & Hubble, 2005). It is simple, free to use, very acceptable to clients and available on the internet.

Beck Depression Inventory (BDI-II) is a 21-item scale designed to assess depression. Each item comprises a set of four or five self-statements of increasing severity (e.g. 'I do not feel sad', 'I feel blue or sad') that can either be read out to the testee or administered as a self-rating questionnaire that the person completes on his or her own. The person selects the statement that best fits the way he or she feels at 'this moment'. The BDI is used in research as a screening and outcome measure. Beck, Steer and Garbin (1988) provide a review of developments in the validation and use of this scale. Access to the BDI is only available by paying a licensing fee to its distributors.

Patient Health Questionnaire (PHQ-9) is a nine-item depression scale (Kroenke et al., 2001). Widely used in the UK, it is included in the evaluation package for the Improving Access to Psychological Therapies (IAPT) programme. It is free to use and downloadable from the internet.

Generalised Anxiety Disorder scale (GAD-7) is a seven-item anxiety measure (Spitzer et al., 2006). Widely used in the UK, it is included in the evaluation package for the Improving Access to Psychological Therapies (IAPT) programme. It is free to use and downloadable from the internet.

Hospital Anxiety and Depression Scale (HADS) is a 14-item scale of depression and anxiety (seven anxiety items; seven depression items) (Bjelland et al., 2002; Zigmond and Snaith, 1983). Widely used in therapy research, it is free to use, and downloadable from the internet.

Systemic Clinical Outcome and Routine Evaluation (SCORE) is an outcome scale for evaluating the effectiveness of systemic family therapy (Carr & Stratton, 2017; Stratton et al., 2010). Available in 15-, 29- or 40-item versions. It measures three dimensions of family functioning: strengths and adaptability; overwhelmed by difficulties; disrupted communication. It is free to use.

Inventory of Interpersonal Problems (IIP) is a questionnaire that assesses the patterns of interpersonal problems that are causing difficulties in a person's life (Horowitz et al., 2008; Woodward, Murrell & Bettler, 2005), and 32- or 64-item versions are available. The IIP is structured around eight sub-scales: domineering/controlling; vindictive/self-centred; cold/distant; socially inhibited; non-assertive; overly accommodating; self-sacrificing; intrusive/needy. This has been widely used in counselling and psychotherapy research studies. It requires the payment of a fee for access.

Hopkins Symptom Checklist (SCL-90) was initially developed at Johns Hopkins University. The aim of the test is to detect levels of psychiatric symptomatology. The standard 90-item version of the test has nine sub-scales: depression, anxiety, somatisation, obsessive-compulsion, interpersonal sensitivity, hostility, phobic anxiety, paranoid ideation and psychoticism. There also exist shorter versions of the test. The format of the SCL-90 presents the respondent with a list of symptoms, such as 'heart pounding or racing' or 'trembling' (both anxiety items) and the instruction to indicate the severity of these on a four-point scale ranging from 'not at all' to 'extremely'. Derogatis and Melisaratos (1983) provide further details on the operation of this test. The SCL-90 is highly regarded, but less widely used in recent years because of the cost of the licence.

Shorter Psychotherapy and Counselling Evaluation (sPaCE) is a 19-item self-report instrument to measure depression (general and self-harming), anxiety (general and phobic), apathy and functional cognitive problems. A copy of the scale, and validity data, are available in Halstead, Leach and Rust (2007). Further validity data can be found in Jimenez-Arista et al. (2020).

Norwegian Outcome Response System for Evaluation (NORSE: Hovland & Moltu, 2019) is a personalised online feedback system that adapts the questions presented to clients depending on their responses on previous occasions, thus enabling a closer focus on key problem areas. It is distinctive in being designed on the basis of extensive consultation with clients and therapists around what they would want an outcome measure to do for them. It is only available as a paid-for package.

The scales listed above are all broadly similar, in requiring participants to respond to a set of statements within the questionnaire that are indicative of general symptomatology, depression, anxiety, stress or some other general dimension of distress or wellbeing. An important strength of these instruments is that all participants are responding to exactly the same items, with the result that cross-case or cross-group comparisons can be made without difficulty. In addition, each of the scales is supported by data regarding cut-off thresholds that differentiate between clinical 'caseness' as against the range of scores that can be found in the 'normal' range, and number of scale points that are necessary in order to categorise a client as having demonstrated a 'reliable' level of change (i.e. degree of change beyond mere random fluctuation in scores).

Personalised or individualised outcome measures

A drawback to the measures listed in the previous section (with the exception of NORSE) is that some items may not be relevant to particular individuals, and issues that are central to a person's difficulties may not be included at all. In a scale such as the CORE-OM, for example, it may be that only four or five items are directly relevant for a particular client, with all the other items functioning as 'filler'. If this occurs, it is likely that significant change may be missed, in terms of their effect on the overall score on a measure, a shift in a positive direction on only a few items may look as though only a minimal amount of change has occurred, whereas in reality their answers on these specific items may represent a massive breakthrough for the client. Also, any questionnaire with a pre-determined set of items runs the risk of not referring to an area of concern that may be crucially important for a particular client. For example, none of the measures reviewed above include items on the experience of spiritual crisis, climate change anxiety or moral injury – issues that certainly trouble at least some clients. A methodological strategy that directly addresses these limitations is to use individualised measures, in which the client writes down (or the researcher writes down, following an interview) the client's self-defined key concerns, issues or goals for therapy. The client can then carry out ratings, week by week, of the degree to which these issues are still bothering them, or the degree to which goals have been attained. Individualised measures have been found to be more sensitive to client change on a case-by-case basis, compared with standardised self-report measures (Lindhiem et al., 2016). In recent years, several individualised outcome measures have been devised. These include a variety of forms that invite clients to identify their goals for therapy, and rate how close they are to attaining them:

- *personal questionnaire* (Elliott et al., 2016; Elliott, Shapiro & Mack, 1999);
- *target complaint rating scale* (Deane, Spicer & Todd, 1997);

- *CORE goal attainment form* (details available on the CORE-IMS website);
- *goals form* (Cooper, 2014);
- *goal-based outcomes form* (Law, 2011).

A review of the pros and cons of these (and other) goals measures can be found in Lloyd, Duncan and Cooper (2019). A further personalised measure, the *Psychological Outcome Profile* (PSYCHLOP; Ashworth et al., 2004), which emerged from the *Measure Yourself Medical Outcome Profile* (MYMOP; Paterson, 1996), includes self-defined goals statements and ratings alongside other items designed to access the client's views about the therapy they have received.

The use of goals forms and other types of individualised measures is backed up by a considerable amount of research in recent years on the nature of goal consensus and attainment in psychotherapy (Law and Cooper, 2017), and the methodological and practical rationale for individualised assessment (Sales & Alves, 2012).

Retrospective outcome measures and interview schedules

An alternative approach to evaluating the outcome of therapy is to invite the client to complete a questionnaire, or be interviewed, after they have completed their course of treatment. There are advantages and disadvantages associated with both longtitudinal data from clients (the strategy underlying the measures outlines in the previous section) and retrospective data. Although comparison of pre-therapy and post-therapy measures makes a lot of intuitive sense (it is like measuring how much one's children have grown year by year), there are also good reasons to believe that the ratings made by at least some clients at the start and then the end of therapy may be influenced by extraneous factors such as an over-exaggerated sense of crisis at the start and then cognitive dissonance at the end ('I must be better now because I have invested a lot of time and energy in therapy'). Retrospective ratings of change may also be shaped by extraneous factors, such as gratitude to a caring therapist even if the therapy itself has not yielded much benefit. However, through judicious question design, it is possible to overcome gratitude effects and collect useful retrospective information about the change (or otherwise) that the client has observed in their life and their capacity to cope.

The most straightforward retrospective outcome evaluation tool is a brief client satisfaction measure. Typically, such an instrument will ask the client to use a five-point scale to rate how satisfied they are with various aspects of the therapy (e.g. waiting time, the therapy room, number of sessions, their relationship with the therapist) and also to give a rating of overall satisfaction and whether they would recommend the service to a friend or family member. Such forms usually include space for open-ended comments and suggestions for how to improve the service. A widely used satisfaction scale is the one developed by Oei and Shuttlewood (1999). Information about other satisfaction scales is available on the online resource site.

Beyond satisfaction scales, there exist a group of retrospective outcome measures and interview schedules that explicitly probe for specific changes. The *Patient*

Estimate of Improvement scale (Hatcher & Barends, 1996) and the *Bochum Change Questionnaire 2000* (BCQ-2000; Willutzki, et al., 2013) are questionnaires that the client completes at the end of therapy. Although these scales have not been widely used in research, there is evidence that they have the potential to provide accurate outcome estimates (Flückiger et al., 2019).

A further type of retrospective outcome assessment tool involves interviewing the client either after a pre-determined number of sessions, or following the end of treatment. Two interview formats have been devised:

- *Change Interview* (Elliott , Slatick & Urman, 2001; Rodgers & Elliott, 2015; http://www.drbrianrodgers.com/research/client-change-interview)
- *Change After Psychotherapy* (CHAP) interview (Sandell, 1987a, 1987b, 2015; Sandell & Wilczek, 2016).

These interview guides have provided valuable insights into the ways that clients evaluate therapy. The Change Interview has served as the cornerstone for many important and influential therapy case studies (see Chapter 13). Clients generally describe the experience of participating in such an interview as meaningful and facilitative, in helping them to reflect on and make sense of the therapy they have received.

Outcome measures for evaluating therapy for children and young people

It is generally understood that outcome measures that are relevant for adult clients may not be appropriate for younger people. Children and adolescents may need or want different things from therapy, compared with adult clients, and are likely to respond better to scales that are shorter, written in a more direct language, and are visually more attractive. Separate child and young person versions of the CORE-OM and the ORS have been developed. There are also some specially developed scales for evaluating therapy for young people, such as the *Strengths and Difficulties Questionnaire* (SDQ; Brann, Lethbridge & Mildred, 2018) and *MyLifeTracker* (Kwan & Rickwood, 2021; Kwan, Rickwood & Telford, 2018). An accessible and informative guide to therapy measures for young people (*A toolkit for collecting routine outcome measures*) has been produced by the Children and Young People Practice Research Network within the British Association for Counselling and Psychotherapy (BACP) and is available free to download from the BACP website. Systematic reviews of outcome measures for young people have been published by Kwan and Rickwood (2015) and Bentley, Hartley and Bucci (2019). In recognition that it may not be helpful to medicalise difficulties experienced by young people, there has been a movement to avoid describing measures in terms of medical diagnostic categories; for example, a widely used measure of depression in young people is titled the *Mood and Feelings Questionnaire* (MFQ; Burleson Daviss et al., 2006). Individualised goals ratings have been extensively used in research and practice around therapy for young people (Law, 2011; Rupani et al., 2014).

Other tools for evaluating outcome

There are many worthwhile, valid and reliable measures that could not be included in this chapter for reasons of space. In particular, there are measures that have been developed to assess levels of functioning and distress (and change in distress/functioning resulting from therapy) in relation to specific problem domains such as post-traumatic stress disorder, self-harm, eating disorders, loss, sexual functioning, marital satisfaction and many other factors. Further information on disorder-specific research tools and measures can be found in Bowling (2001, 2017), Maruish (2017) or by looking at recent studies on therapy for such issues. A further approach, used in some studies, has been to conduct a diagnostic interview of the client before therapy and again at the end of treatment. The most widely used technique for this purpose is the Structured Clinical Interview for the DSM (First, 2014; see also https://www.appi.org/products/structured-clinical-interview-for-dsm-5-scid-5).

Process measures

The topic of therapy process encompasses a large number of aspects of therapy, including relational processes such as the quality of the therapist–client relationship and repairing ruptures in the therapeutic alliance, and facilitative or helpful/hindering processes, including analyses of what happens during significant moments of change in terms of elements of therapy such as experiential processing, therapist empathic reflection or interpretation of transference. An overview of counselling and psychotherapy process research can be found in Cooper (2008). Constantino, Boswell and Coyne (2021) have authoritatively reviewed current research trends and evidence around relational processes, and Crits-Christoph and Connolly Gibbons (2021) have similarly reviewed how various process factors contribute to eventual outcomes. Contributors to Norcross and Lambert (2019) and Norcross and Wampold (2019) comprehensively explore how this body of research knowledge translates into practice.

Within a student or practitioner research toolkit, a particularly useful process tool is a measure of the strength of the therapeutic relationship or working alliance, such as the *Working Alliance Inventory*, *Helping Alliance Questionnaire*, *Barrett–Lennard Relationship Inventory* or similar measure. Each of these measures has therapist and client versions, to elicit perceptions of the relationship from both perspectives. These relationship scales allow statements to be made in case studies regarding how the quality of the therapeutic relationship in the case being investigated might compare with norms for clients as a whole. If administered on a regular basis (e.g. weekly or bi-weekly) these scales can also be employed to identify shifts in the relationship (e.g. 'ruptures' in the therapeutic alliance). Another process research technique that is particularly valuable from both a research and practice perspective is the *Helpful Aspects of Therapy* (HAT) form, which is completed after each session, and asks the client to describe the most and least helpful or significant events that took place within that session, and then rate these events on a scale of helpful/hindering. The *Session Rating Scale* (SRS) also collects information on the extent to which the client found the session to be helpful or hindering.

The type of preferences that a client has for therapy, and the extent to which these preferences are matched in the therapy they receive, represents an increasingly important area of inquiry. There is consistent evidence that therapy that corresponds to client preferences is associated with better outcomes and lower levels of client premature ending (Swift et al., 2019). Specific measures that have been developed in relationship to this topic include the *Patient Expectation* scale (PEX; Berg, Sandahl & Clinton, 2008) the *Therapy Preferences Form* (TPF; Bowens & Cooper, 2012) and the *Cooper–Norcross Inventory of Preferences* (C-NIP; Cooper & Norcross, 2016). Vollmer at al. (2009) have developed a client preference interview schedule that can be used for both research and practice purposes.

Further information on the first generation of process assessment tools can be found in Greenberg and Pinsof (1986) and Toukmanian and Rennie (1992). Over the past 20 years, many additional measures have been developed to augment the tools described in these seminal texts. Process measures that are currently widely used in research include:

Working Alliance Inventory – a short-form, 12-item scale: client–therapist agreement around *bond, goals* and *tasks* and overall quality of alliance (Hatcher and Gillaspy, 2006).

Helpful Aspects of Therapy (HAT) – form that invites the client to provide open-ended descriptions and ratings of most/least helpful events in session (Llewelyn, 1988 and also freely available online).

Barrett-Lennard Relationship Inventory (BLRI) – client and therapist forms. Subscales cover: level of regard, congruence, empathic understanding, unconditionality of regard (Barrett-Lennard, 2014).

Session Evaluation Questionnaire (SEQ) – client and therapist forms. Subscales cover: depth, smoothness, positivity, arousal (Stiles, Gordon & Lani, 2002; see also the homepage of William B. Stiles - http://www.users.miamioh.edu/stileswb/).

Agnew Relationship Scale (ARM) – client and therapist forms with five, ten or 28 items, rated on a seven-point scale. Subscales cover: bond, confidence, partnership, openness, client initiative (Agnew-Davies et al., 1998; Cahill et al., 2012).

Session Rating Scale (SRS) – client form. Four-item visual analogue measure of client satisfaction with the process of therapy (Duncan et al., 2003; Miller, Duncan, & Hubble, 2005).

Relational Depth Frequency Scale (RDFS; Di Malta, Evans & Cooper, 2020). Client and therapist forms. 16-item measure of occurrence of deeply meaningful relational connection in therapy sessions.

Recent years have seen a shift in focus in therapy process research, away from the measurement of general process dimensions or factors, such as the bond, goal and task scales of the Working Alliance Inventory, and in the direction of seeking to capture the actual activities in which clients and therapists engage in order to accomplish these factors. In other words, 'how' processes are created rather than 'what' the processes are. Examples of this movement are the *Alliance in Action* (Owen et al., 2013) and the *Therapeutic Agency Inventory* (Huber et al., 2019).

Rating scales for therapy recordings and transcripts

Transcripts of therapy session recordings are the one data source that most effectively provides readers of case studies with authentic insights into what actually happened between therapists and clients. Transcripts of sessions capture the lived complexity of the therapy encounter, and can be analysed in many different ways, depending on the aims of the investigation. It is always necessary to be sensitive to the needs of the client around making recordings of sessions, for example by asking permission each time the recorder is switched on, and letting the client know that they can switch it off at any point, or ask for the recording to be deleted. Video recordings can be valuable in terms of analysing factors such as body posture, direction of gaze and interactional synchrony. However, video cameras may be regarded by clients as more intrusive, and video data can be time-consuming to analyse as well as hard to summarise in a written report. There are various formats that can be used to transcribe audio recordings, depending on the level of detail that is required (e.g. length of pauses, ascending/descending voice tone). A useful introduction to methods of transcript analysis can be found in Lepper and Riding (2006).

Anyone embarking on research that involves analysis of transcripts needs to consider the amount of data, and corresponding workload, arising from the use of session recordings. In this context, it is important to recognise that it is not always essential to listen to, or transcribe, every session. If all sessions have been recorded, it may be sufficient to analyse only those that are theoretically interesting or clinically significant (or even only to analyse segments of these sessions). Indicators of significant sessions can be found in therapist notes, HAT data, interviews with the client or therapist, or sudden shifts in scores on weekly process or outcome monitoring scales.

Some widely used observational measures of therapy process include:

Accurate Empathy Scale – a nine-point scale, applied by trained observers to tape segments. Similar scales exist for non-possessive warmth and genuineness (Truax and Carkhuff, 1967).

Experiencing Scale (EXP) – a seven-point scale, applied by trained observers to 2–8-minute tape segments, transcripts or written materials. This scale measures depth of experiencing in client, counsellor or group (Klein et al., 1986).

Client and therapist vocal quality – coding made by trained observers. Each client/therapist statement is coded. Four categories of vocal pattern: focused, externalising, limited, emotional (Rice & Wagstaff, 1967; Tomicic, Martinez & Krause 2015).

Client perceptual processing – trained judges rate seven categories of perceptual processing, using both transcript and audiotape (Toukmanian & Rennie, 1992).

Verbal response modes – trained judges rate 14 categories of verbal behaviour, using transcripts of whole sessions (Elliott et al., 1987).

Vanderbilt Psychotherapy Process Scale (VPPS) – 80 Likert-scaled items used by trained raters. Scales cover: patient exploration, therapist exploration, patient psychic distress, patient participation, patient hostility, patient dependency, therapist warmth and friendliness, and negative therapist attitude (Suh et al., 1986).

Narrative Process Coding Scheme (NPCS) – Trained judges code therapy transcripts in terms of topic shifts, and internal, external and reflexive modes of narrative processing (Angus, Levitt & Hardtke, 1999).

Assimilation of Problematic Experiences Scale (APES; Stiles, 2001) – protocol for rating session transcripts for level of client assimilation of problematic experiences and the emergence of suppressed 'voices' that allow these experiences to be brought into awareness and worked through.

Psychotherapy Process Q-Sort (PQS; Jones, 1985). Observers watch or listen to recordings of therapy sessions (or transcripts) and rate them in terms of 100 items that describe client and therapist actions across an entire therapy session. Scoring is based on Q-sort methodology. Rater manual is available on the internet. Has been widely used, and adapted for different research purposes.

Innovative Moments Rating Scale (Gonçalves et al., 2011) – guidelines for identifying and analysing points in therapy when the client introduces new ideas or reports on novel actions.

Transference Work Scale (TWS; Ulberg, Amlo, Critchfield, Marble & Høglend, 2014; Ulberg, Amlo & Høglend, 2014). Procedure for identifying and analysing different types of transference interpretation made by therapists.

There are important practical and validity challenges associated with the use of these instruments. An essential characteristic of this type of measure is the construction of a training manual for observers to ensure that each observer is employing the same definitions of constructs in a systematic manner. It is also necessary to check the performance of observers at regular intervals, to safeguard against 'drift' away from the procedures and criteria specified by the manual. The degree of agreement between observers is assessed by calculating an *inter-rater reliability* coefficient (Hallgren, 2012) which to be acceptable would normally be expected to reach 0.7 or above (+1 indicates complete agreement between ratings; −1 indicates that the ratings are similarly in agreement but in opposite directions; 0 means no agreement at all). As with other tests, the instrument cannot be regarded as valid unless it also demonstrates sufficient reliability.

Treatment manuals and adherence scales

In many therapy research studies, the reader will want to know about the type of therapy that was provided, and how closely and competently therapists delivered the therapy approach that was meant to be delivered. Although this issue is particularly important in randomised controlled/clinical trials (RCTs), it is also relevant to other research designs, including practice-based studies and case studies. Within RCT research, the use of meta-analysis involves very close scrutiny of the methodological quality of RCTs, which in turn gets translated into expectations for greater levels of methodological rigour, for example through the CONSORT (Consolidated Standards of Reporting Trials; www.consort-statement.org/) guidelines

(Trudeau, 2007). In the first generation of therapy RCTs, in the period up to 1980, it had been hard to interpret the meaning of findings because of lack of certainty over whether therapists were actually delivering the specified treatment. As a consequence, it became standard practice to define therapy in terms of a treatment manual, employ therapists trained and supervised to operate according to the manual, and check whether they were adhering to the model, usually by rating sessions using an adherence or fidelity scale.

Treatment manuals have been published as books and articles, and usually focus on the application of a specific form of therapy (e.g. psychodynamic, CBT) to a specific disorder (e.g. depression, panic, PTSD). A good manual provides a richly described account of what a therapist needs to do, in the form of a theoretical rationale, description of specific techniques, frequently encountered problems in using the treatment, contraindications of the treatment or some of its techniques.

The broad concept of treatment *fidelity* refers to the extent to which a therapist's actions correspond to those recommended by a theory or manual. It can be divided into:

- *treatment adherence* (assessment of the degree to which a therapist intervenes in specific ways as prescribed by the protocol or manual);
- *treatment competence* (assessment of the adequacy with which the therapist applies the prescribed techniques). Competence can be divided into generic competence (e.g. common factors) and competence that is specific to the particular approach being delivered.

A valuable introduction and overview of issues involved in constructing and using adherence procedures is available in Nezu and Nezu (2007). A detailed example of how one research team constructed a treatment fidelity scale (for gestalt therapy) can be found in Fogarty, Bhar and Theiler (2020).

Treatment manuals and adherence scales are important research tools in relation to research questions in which it is necessary to be clear about what is happening in the therapy room (e.g. studies that compare the effectiveness of different types of therapy). These tools also have value for therapist training and professional development, because they provide detailed descriptions of what particular groups of therapists (who use a specific approach) actually do in practice. Examples of treatment manuals and adherence scales can be readily located through an online search with Google Scholar. Many studies that employ treatment manuals make them freely available on the internet.

Formats for analysing therapist notes and client records

There are many good-quality case studies that have been published on the basis of detailed therapist notes, sometimes including near-verbatim accounts of therapy dialogue. Other research that has been based on analysis of clinical records includes studies of reasons for ending therapy or psychological autopsies (retrospective analysis of the processes leading to client suicide). If it is anticipated that notes may be used for research purposes at some point, it may be valuable to develop a structured format for writing therapist notes, to ensure that essential information is comprehensively and accurately collected after every session. At the present time, there are no standardised tools that have been developed or widely adopted for collecting this kind of data.

Client diaries and other written documents

Client and therapist diaries may be used to collect information on the week-by-week experience of engagement in therapy. Studies by Mackrill (2007) and Kerr, Josyula and Littenberg (2011) provide examples of some of the ways in which diaries can be used. A review of the use of diary methods in counselling and psychotherapy research can be found in Mackrill (2008).

A way of collecting data that is similar in some respects to diary-keeping is to invite the participant to write or talk about their life-story, for instance in terms of discrete chapters or phases. Studies by Adler (2012, 2019) and Lind et al. (2019) provide useful introductions to this approach.

Experience sampling and mood tracking

Experience sampling is a technique that involves participants making observations of their experience, through ratings of emotional states and behavioural activities, at regular intervals during their day-to-day lives. This approach is sometimes also described as *ambulatory assessment* or *Ecological Momentary Assessment* (EMA; Heron et al., 2017). The attraction of experience sampling is that in principle it allows access to how people actually feel and act, rather than relying on their recollection of these states. Typically, participants are reminded by some kind of pager, handheld device, digital wristwatch or mobile phone app when it is time to enter data into an online form. Studies by Ellison et al. (2020) and others have found that experience sampling can produce more accurate estimates of mood and stress levels, and occurrence of problem behaviour, than can be achieved through the kind of retrospective weekly self-report forms used in most therapy research studies and clinical practice. Experience sampling has been used to collect information about such factors as emotion differentiation (i.e. being aware of different emotions vs existing within a single homogenised emotional state) and time orientation (whether the person is thinking about things in the past, or in the future) (Beaty, Seli & Schacter, 2019). The rapid commercialisation and dissemination of experience sampling in the form of smartphone apps has resulted in a situation in which there is not only a wide choice of such tools for therapists to draw on, but also that an increasing number of people use mood tracker apps on their own initiative, whether or not they are seeing a therapist at all (Areán, Ly & Andersson, 2016). There is no point in trying to list such apps in the present chapter; the pace of development of such tools is so rapid that any listing would soon be out of date. Finding information on EMA apps through an internet search is a straightforward matter.

Projective techniques

Projective techniques operate in a quite different way from the other research tools reviewed in this chapter. In a projective test the participant is asked to respond to a relatively unstructured, ambiguous stimulus in an open-ended way. Typical projective techniques are the Rorschach Inkblot Test, in which the person is invited to report on what they see in each of a set of symmetrical inkblots, and the Thematic Apperception Test (TAT), where the person tells or writes imaginative stories in response to a set of pictures. Another widely used projective test, the sentence completion technique, involves writing endings to incomplete sentence stems (Clarke et al., 2017). The Early Memory Technique (Fowler, Hilsenroth & Handler, 2000) invites the person to write or tell their story of their earliest memories. The Lowenfeld World Technique enables a person to use a sand tray, figures and objects to express their current state of being in an imaginative and expressive manner. The assumption underlying these techniques is that the person will project their characteristic way of thinking and feeling into the way they react to the open-ended projective task. For example, in a TAT story, the respondent may unconsciously invest the hero or heroine of the story with their own personal motives and patterns of behaviour. A person with a strong need for achievement may write stories that all make reference to winning or doing well. Conversely, a person with a strong need for sociability may write stories emphasising relationships and friendships. A key feature of projective techniques is the intention to gain access to fantasy and imagination rather than consciously processed 'socially desirable' responses.

Projective techniques have in the past been widely used within clinical and occupational psychology for such purposes as personality assessment, clinical diagnosis and appraisal of managerial potential. Projective techniques were extensively used in the early research into client-centred therapy carried out by Rogers and his colleagues at the University of Chicago (Rogers & Dymond, 1954). In recent years, however, there has been increasing scepticism over the validity of these instruments (Lilienfeld, Wood & Howard, 2000). The current lack of interest in projective techniques may be misguided. It could be argued that questionnaires evoke only the capacity of a person to respond passively to a stimulus. By contrast, the projective situation forces the person to engage in active, purposeful, problem-solving behaviour. In addition, when a person answers a questionnaire item, they are not merely reporting on what they know about their behaviour, but are drawing upon their image or concept of self. In a projective technique, the person usually has no idea of what the test is about, and answers spontaneously without reference to attitudes and self-images. Both these factors lead to a conclusion that, in a projective test situation, the person being tested is displaying patterns of behaviour and feeling that are similar to those they exhibit in actual real-life situations.

Box 9.1   Psychoanalytic research tools

The concept of the unconscious is a central construct within the theoretical approach that underpins psychoanalytic and psychodynamic practice. Belief in the central importance of the operation of unconscious processes inevitably leads to an awareness of the limitations of self-report measures. The psychoanalytic and psychodynamic professional community has been highly active in developing research tools that are consistent with its theoretical stance (Leuzinger-Bohleber et al., 2020; Levy, Ablon & Kächele, 2012).

Conclusions

This chapter has provided an overview of some of the main 'off the shelf' research tools that have been created to collect data about the process and outcomes of counselling and psychotherapy, and how these instruments have been used. It is important to emphasise that many highly valuable tools have not been included, due to space constraints. It is also essential to be aware that the chapter has focused on specific, named tools, and that a great deal of research is conducted on the basis of data collection using general methods such as interviews. In addition, there are many variables that are highly relevant to the progress of therapy, such as exam results, school attendance, sickness absence from work, hospital visits, frequency of alcohol or drug use, binge eating episodes, and so on, that are usually measured using locally constructed scales developed by a particular researcher for a specific purpose. Some studies also collect data in the form of therapy artefacts that are created, such as drawings, photographs, sculptures or poems, and referral letters or other forms of communication from outside agencies – all of which can become part of a case record or be studied in their own right. Finally, it can be helpful to view research tools as not just resources to be deployed in one's own research, but as potential points of connection with other researchers and research groups. The development of a research tool sends a message and invitation to others: 'this is how we can collect information on an important issue – why don't you try it out?' There are many examples of how lateral adoption of a research tool, across a global network, has leveraged the efforts of a small research team into an international programme of investigation around a topic.

Suggestions for further reading

A comprehensive overview of the issues involved in using tests and questionnaires in counselling and psychotherapy research and practice can be found in Maruish, M. E. (2017). *Handbook of Psychological Assessment in Primary Care Settings*. 2nd edn. New York: Routledge. Other volumes by the same author examine the use of measures in relation to specific populations, such as children.

The state of the art in psychotherapy outcome measurement is discussed in a Special Issue of *Psychotherapy* (volume 52, issue 4, 2015), and in a chapter by Lutz et al. (2021). Measuring, predicting and tracking change in psychotherapy. In M. Barkham, W. Lutz, & L. Castonguay (eds), *Bergin & Garfield's Handbook of Psychotherapy and Behavior Change*. 7th edn. New York: Wiley.

A classic source on questionnaire and coding systems for measuring therapy process variables is Greenberg, L. S. and Pinsof, W. M. (eds) (1986). *The Psychotherapeutic Process: A Research Handbook*. New York: Guilford Press.

The instruments discussed in the present chapter represent only the tip of a vast iceberg, in respect of techniques for assessing aspects of health and wellbeing. Information about other tools that may be of interest can be found in:

Bowling, A. (2001). *Measuring Disease: A Review of Disease-specific Quality of Life Measurement Scales*. 2nd edn. London: Open University Press.
Bowling, A. (2017). *Measuring Health: A Review of Quality of Life Measurement Scales*. 4th edn. London: Open University Press.
Liamputtong, P. (ed.) (2019). *Handbook of Research Methods in Health Social Sciences*. New York: Springer.
McDowell, I. (2006). *Measuring Health: A Guide to Rating Scales and Questionnaires*. New York: Oxford University Press.

Online resources

Further activities to support learning around the topics introduced in this chapter can be found on the online resource site: https://study.sagepub.com/doingresearch4e.

10

Using Qualitative Interviews to Explore the Client's Experience of Therapy

Introduction

The most straightforward way to find out about therapy is to ask people. There exists a massive and fascinating literature consisting of research studies based on interviews with clients, which has made a significant contribution to the development of therapy theory and practice. Chapter 9 introduced the fundamental principles and aims of interview-based qualitative research, and provided a step-by-step guide on how to conduct this type of study. The present chapter explores how these principles and methods may be applied in research on the client's experience of therapy.

What is qualitative research into the experience of therapy?

Qualitative research is an approach to inquiry that collects data in the form of personal accounts, stories and descriptions of experience, and seeks to identify themes or patterns within the information that has been collected. Usually, this type of research makes use of one-to-one interviews as the primary means of data collection. Qualitative accounts can also be obtained through the use of diaries, group interviews and participant reflections on visual data (e.g. photographs or drawings).

There are three key tasks in a qualitative interview study: deciding on which questions to ask and how to ask them; conducting interviews in a way that allows the person to tell their story; and analysing the meaning of the material that has been collected. In addition to these tasks, there is usually a substantial amount of work involved in setting up interviews and transcribing interview recordings.

Qualitative interview-based research in counselling and psychotherapy comprises part of a broader and highly influential tradition of qualitative research in health and social care. Researchers within these fields have used qualitative methods to provide service users with a voice, in order to enable their experiences to have an impact on professional training and practice and public policy (Ryan, Hislop & Ziebland, 2017). This kind of evidence has been invaluable as a means of making health and social care more user-focused.

Why would I want to do this kind of research?

There are several reasons why counsellors and psychotherapists find it meaningful and satisfying to be involved in this type of research. At a basic level, research interviews can be regarded as an extension of therapy interviews, and analysing research interviews is similar to arriving at a case formulation. Qualitative research therefore builds on the skills, knowledge and experience that therapists already possess – it is an obvious next step. It is also a next step that provides substantial opportunities for personal learning, and becoming a more effective therapist. There are important practical and ethical differences between research interviews and therapy interviews, and as a result doing this kind of research can generate valuable reflection around the question of what is therapeutic about a therapy conversation. For example, many research participants report that taking part in a research interview had been personally meaningful and helpful, despite the fact that the interviewer had made no attempt to use any therapy interventions. Another major source of personal learning is associated with the process of transcribing and analysing interviews in which people have been invited to talk about their experience of therapy. What becomes clear, most of the time, is that what people experience, and the way they understand that experience, will not map on to theories of therapy in any straightforward manner. Doing this kind of research has the effect of inviting therapist-researchers to examine their basic assumptions about therapy, and arrive at a deeper understanding.

Research that makes use of qualitative interviews also provides an ideal entry into the field of therapy research as a whole. The experience of undertaking this kind of research project forces a novice researcher to think seriously about a whole range of basic methodological issues, from ethical concerns around confidentiality and avoidance of harm, through to questions of reliability (would that person have told a different story to a different interviewer?) and validity (how can I know whether the themes I have identified in the data are a true reflection of participants' experiences?). Analysing qualitative interviews makes it possible to see why quantification of experience makes sense – yes, every research participant has a unique story to tell, but at the same time there are common themes that can be identified and added up. It also makes it possible to appreciate the limitations of self-report, in terms of the ways in which any source of information about therapy is shaped by the context within which it is collected. Finally, for most people, analysing qualitative interviews leads to a realisation that there exists a level of meaning beyond the overt content of what is said, and that there are significant research possibilities in analysing the structure of a conversation, or the intricate ways that a person uses language.

There are also important reasons for *not* doing qualitative interview research. This is a type of research that can be highly time-consuming. For example, each hour of recorded interview may require up to eight hours to transcribe. It is also a type of research that tends to be a bit messy. Sometimes, what a person says in an interview can be interpreted in several different ways, or may not make sense at all. Also, it is never possible to be absolutely confident that a set of categories or themes comprises a wholly adequate means of representing the data. Embarking on this kind of research therefore requires a sufficient level of tolerance for uncertainty, ambiguity and anxiety.

Exercise 10.1   Investigating your research question

Reflect on how you might investigate your research question by using each of the types of client experience research introduced in this chapter. What would your study look like? What would be the advantages and limitations of different client experience research designs and methods, and the unique or distinctive insights yielded by each of them?

What kind of skills and support do I need?

The most important source of support, in relation to undertaking a qualitative interview study of the experience of therapy, is a supervisor, mentor or colleague who knows what to do, and is willing to pass on practical knowledge. It is helpful to envisage this as an expert–apprentice relationship. In other words, the supervisor or mentor is not just someone who tells the novice researcher what to do. Instead, they work together on specific tasks (such as designing an interview schedule, listening to a pilot interview, or analysing a transcript). The apprentice then goes off and does the next bit on his or her own, and brings it back to show what they have done.

It is also very useful to assemble a group of colleagues or friends who would be willing to provide support over the course of a study, as sounding boards for ideas, acting as role-play subjects for pilot interviews, offering their interpretation of segments of interviews and reading draft reports. Sometimes, students undertaking research studies at the same time will organise themselves into informal peer support and consultation groups. In some academic programmes, research groups are formally organised by academic staff. Such groups may also form part of practitioner research networks.

The process of carrying out qualitative, interview-based research consists of a mix of intense personal immersion in the data, accompanied by dialogue and contact with others.

Exercise 10.2   The interview style that is right for you

In order to use the interview to best effect, it is necessary to ensure that the interviewee is relaxed and comfortable. One of the factors that has a major influence on this process is the capacity of the interviewer to be 'centred' and to come across as genuine rather than playing a role. It can be useful to reflect on your style of being with clients, in your role as a counsellor or psychotherapist, and consider how this way of relating could form the basis for your style as an interviewer. It is also helpful to take part in interviews with colleagues, from both sides of the fence, to develop a first-hand sense of what works for you.

Client experience research in action: key questions and areas of focus

The studies outlined in the following sections offer a wide range of exemplars of how well-established qualitative methods, such as grounded theory, empirical phenomenology, IPA and CQR, have been used to generate research into the client's experience of therapy. Within each domain of qualitative interview-based study of an aspect of client experience of therapy, selected articles have been high-lighted to provide a flavour of different approaches that can be adopted within that area of research. This list of studies is not intended to be comprehensive – many other excellent studies can be found in the literature, and continue to be published every year.

The client's experience of the process of therapy

Interviewing clients about their experience of therapy presents a number of meth-odological challenges. It may not be easy to get clients to agree to give up time to be interviewed. Less-satisfied clients might be particularly reluctant to take part in research. The actual task of reflecting on the experience of therapy is not straight-forward. There may be many weeks of therapeutic involvement to sift through. Some informants may find it hard to explain what happened in therapy without telling the story of what led up to their decision to enter therapy in the first place. The interviewer needs to strike a balance between keeping the informant on track, rather than heading off at tangents, while at the same time allowing the participant sufficient space to tell their own story in their own way. A further challenging aspect is that the researcher is usually a therapist (or therapist in training) who will have their own ideas about the therapy processes that they are asking their research par-ticipants to talk about – it is no simple matter to bracket these assumptions to a sufficient extent to be genuinely open to what an informant is trying to say. For these reasons, qualitative research into the client's experience of therapy tends to produce more interesting findings when it focuses on a specific aspect of therapy, rather than trying to capture the client's story as a whole.

Several contrasting areas of focus that have been pursued in research on client experience follow. When reading the exemplar studies highlighted within each area, it is valuable to pay particular attention to key methodological choice-points, such as the recruitment of participants, development of interview strategies to help their informants to explore specific aspects of their experience, and approaches to analys-ing data and presenting findings.

The experience of disadvantaged or marginalised clients

Generating knowledge about the needs and experiences of 'seldom heard' voices comprises one of the most important functions of qualitative research. The therapy research literature as a whole largely consists of studies of white, middle-class, able-bodied clients. Qualitative interview-based research has made a major contribution to the field, by giving a voice to clients who do not fit into these mainstream catego-ries. For example, there have been many powerful studies on the experiences of black and minority ethnic clients. Significant exemplar studies within this literature include Chang and Berk (2009), Chang and Yoon (2011), Tarabi, Loulopoulou and Henton (2020), Thompson, Bazile and Akbar (2004) and Ward (2005). Several qualitative studies have also focused on the therapy experience of economically disadvantaged clients (Krause, et al., 2018; Pugach & Goodman, 2015; Thompson, Cole & Nitzarim, 2012). Other qualitative studies have explored the experience of therapy of people with disabilities of various kinds. Further examples of qualitative research into the experiences of disadvantaged and marginalised clients, and methodological strategies associated with such studies, can be found in Levitt, McLeod and Stiles (2021) and McLeod, Levitt and Stiles (2021).

The ideas of clients around what makes therapy helpful

An important and influential subset of qualitative interview-based studies consists of investigating the views of clients around what has been helpful or unhelpful to them in their therapy. Many helpfulness studies have analysed client accounts in terms of general themes (Bowman & Fine, 2000; Clarke, Rees & Hardy, 2004; Göstas et al., 2013). Levitt, Butler and Hill (2006) reported client views of helpful aspects of therapy in terms of therapeutic principles intended as a guide for therapists. Studies by Lilliengren and Werbart (2005) and Philips et al. (2007) approached the construct of helpfulness through identifying client theories of change. An emergent approach within this field of inquiry involves analyses that seek to identify helpful sequences, for instance around what is experienced as helpful (or not) in response to particular client concerns, and what that helpful response leads to in terms of immediate benefits or outcomes (Simonsen & Cooper, 2015; Thurston & Cooper, 2014). Research into the broad topic of helpfulness also incorporates studies of what clients find unhelpful (Bowie, McLeod & McLeod, 2016; Burton & Thériault, 2020; van Grieken et al., 2014). A discussion of methodological issues and choices in qualitative client helpfulness studies has been produced by Cooper et al. (2015).

The client's view of therapy approaches

Many qualitative studies have used interviews to explore what it was like for clients to receive particular types of therapy from the client perspective. These investigations have looked at a wide range of therapy models. Exemplar studies include: CBT for fear of flying (Borrill and Foreman, 1996); CBT for depression (Glasman et al., 2004); psychodynamic therapy for eating disorders (Poulsen, Lunn & Daniel, 2010; Proulx, 2008; Toto-Moriarty, 2013); minimal therapy based on a self-help manual (Macdonald et al., 2007); psychotherapy for chronic pain (Osborn & Smith, 2008); psychotherapeutic support in cancer care (MacCormack et al., 2001); dynamic interpersonal therapy for anxiety and depression (Leonidaki, Lemma & Hobbis, 2016). Perhaps because mindfulness training is a therapeutic method that has emerged in recent years, at a time when qualitative research was becoming more widely accepted, a substantial proportion of the qualitative studies into the experience of a specific therapy in respect of mindfulness interventions have been published (Chadwick et al., 2011; Fitzpatrick, Simpson & Smith, 2010; Hanssen et al., 2020).

Experience of specific therapy activities and processes

Qualitative research has explored the client's experience of particular activities and moments within therapy, such as receiving a letter from their therapist (Hamill, Reid & Reynolds, 2008), missed appointments (Snape et al., 2003), moments of therapist self-disclosure (Audet & Everall, 2010; Hanson, 2005), giving the therapist a gift (Knox et al., 2009), the influence of the design of the therapy room (Fenner, 2011), filling in feedback questionnaires (Unsworth, Cowie & Green, 2012), exploring therapy goals (Di Malta, Oddli & Cooper, 2019), receiving a case formulation (Redhead, Johnstone & Nightingale, 2015), deciding whether to quit therapy (D'Aniello et al., 2019), and feelings about the ending of therapy (Knox et al., 2011). Other studies have explored client experience of processes within therapy, such as whether or not to be honest with their therapist (Blanchard & Farber, 2016, 2020). These are just some of the many therapy activities, procedures and processes that have investigated using qualitative interviews with clients. Such topics are well suited to qualitative inquiry, because they represent reasonably clearly defined blocks of lived experience that informants can access and report on without too much difficulty. The purpose of this kind of study, in terms of helping therapists do a better job, is readily grasped by participants, with the result that they are generally willing to engage with the research process in an active and open manner.

The experience of the relationship with the therapist

The therapy relationship or alliance is one of the most widely researched topics in the therapy literature. The vast majority of such studies have used quantitative questionnaires completed by clients or their therapists, or researcher-administered quantitative rating scales. A consistent finding across this body of research has been that it is the client's alliance ratings (not those of the therapist or researcher) that predict eventual therapy outcome. However, despite this clear signal that the client's view of the therapy relationship may be reflecting something that is not readily detectable by therapists and researchers, there have been relatively few qualitative studies of client experience of the relationship with a therapist. This is a pity, because the studies that have been carried out make it possible to see the therapy relationship in a different light. A particularly fine example of this kind of study is an investigation by Binder et al. (2011) in which adolescent therapy clients were interviewed about their feelings about their therapist. Other notable research into the experience of a therapeutic relationship includes studies by Kastrani, Deliyanni-Kouimtzi and Athanasiades (2015), Nødtvedt et al. (2019), Sagen et al. (2013), and Sandberg, Gustafsson and Holmqvist (2017). Other studies in this area have focused on failed client–therapist relationships (Bacha, Hanley & Winter, 2020; Bowie, McLeod & McLeod, 2016). In addition, valuable ways of understanding the therapy relationship from the point of view of the client may be embedded within the findings of qualitative studies that have not primarily focused on this topic (see, for example, von Below, 2020).

How clients define and evaluate the outcomes of therapy

An area of qualitative research that has significant implications for policy and the provision of services, consists of interview-based studies of the ways in which clients assess the outcomes of the therapy they have received. This area of qualitative research has yielded a picture of therapy outcome that in many respects is quite different from the findings of quantitative outcome studies. Exemplar studies within this area include Binder, Holgersen and Nielsen (2010), Gibson and Cartwright (2014), Knox et al. (1999), Kuhnlein (1999), Lavik et al. (2018), Løvgren et al. (2020), Nilsson et al. (2007), Perren, Godfrey & Rowland (2009), Werbart, Bergstedt and Levander (2020) and Valkonen et al. (2011). The findings from these studies have made it possible to see that it is not adequate to define outcome purely in terms of a change in scores on quantitative symptom measures (McLeod, 2011). For example, outcomes reported in post-therapy client interview studies include a sense of disappointment with therapy despite some helpful experiences (Nilsson et al., 2007), an enduring supportive inner image of the therapist that can be accessed at times of stress (Knox et al., 1999) and an enhanced sense of personal agency (Gibson & Cartwright, 2014). An important sub-set of qualitative outcome studies has explored client experience of negative outcomes (De Smet et al., 2019; Radcliffe, Masterson & Martin, 2018). Hardy et al. (2019) identified five themes in client written accounts of harmful therapy: feelings of failure, loss of hope, loss of coping skills, loss of confidence and regret.

Qualitative outcome evaluation research is technically challenging. A researcher undertaking such a study needs to navigate their way through issues such as:

- the difficulty faced by the interviewee in retrospectively reviewing extensive memories of what happened in therapy, and condensing this information into a succinct report on how they have changed;
- the problem of recalling what life was like before entering therapy;
- the participant feeling that they need to tell their life story in order to explain why certain changes were significant for them;
- determining the extent to which reported changes are attributable to therapy or to other factors;
- the likelihood that the interviewee may be trying to please the interviewer (or justify their own investment in therapy) by reporting a good news story;
- dissatisfied clients or those who have dropped out of therapy are less likely to be willing to be interviewed.

In response to these methodological issues, some researchers have developed interview formats and questions that support the research participant to provide detailed, relevant outcome information. The main research tools that have been devised for this purpose have been the *Client Change Interview* (CCI; Elliott , Slatick & Urman, 2001; Rodgers & Elliott, 2015) and the *Change After Psychotherapy* (CHAP) interview (Sandell, 1987a, 1987b, 2015; Sandell & Wilczek, 2016). An example of how the CCI has been used in a qualitative outcome study can be found in De Smet et al. (2019, 2020).

In addition to interviewing clients after therapy has ended, some qualitative researchers have approached the question of how clients make sense of outcome by investigating how they make sense of, and decide how to respond to, items on symptom scales used in quantitative outcome research (Galasiński, & Kozłowska, 2013; Rodgers, 2018; Truijens et al., 2019).

The experience of living with a diagnosis or disorder

As psychotherapy practice has become increasingly medicalised and biologically informed, and both clients and members of the public have become more familiar with the terminology of psychiatric diagnosis, it has been valuable for qualitative research to explore the experience of receiving or living with a diagnosis. Such research offers a bridge between the application of diagnostic categories by mental health professionals and care systems, and the actual lived experience of the people who are being categorised. A large proportion of therapy clients have either received a diagnosis, or have given serious consideration to whether such a move might be helpful for them. Interview-based studies have been able to identify aspects of the meaning of a diagnosis, and the strategies adopted to come to terms with it. Some studies have explored how individuals respond to a psychiatric diagnosis, in terms of such themes as acceptance, ambivalence, rejection and coping with stigma (Hundt et al., 2019). Other studies have investigated the process through which a diagnosis is personalised by constructing one's own explanatory account of how a condition has developed (Sørensen et al., 2020). There have also been qualitative studies in which interviews have been used to investigate participants' accounts of how the implications of a diagnosis unfold over time, for instance in relation to a shift in sense of self, the reactions of significant others or access to services (Johansson & Werbart, 2020). Typically, a psychiatric diagnosis leads to a prescription of some kind of medication. A further strand of qualitative research has comprised studies of the personal meaning of taking psychiatric medication (for example, antidepressants: Gibson, Cartwright & Read, 2016; McMullen & Herman, 2009).

The experience of recovery

The concept of recovery refers to the processes and activities through which individuals and groups take responsibility for addressing mental health issues in their lives. Although there exist several alternative perspectives for making sense of recovery, a central element of this approach is an acknowledgement that the effect of professional interventions (e.g. counselling, psychotherapy and medication) needs to be viewed in the context of other healing activities such as self-help, mutual support and use of transformational activities such as art, spirituality and time in nature.

Studies by Hänninen and Valkonen (2019) and Wilson and Giddings (2010) provide an example of how these themes can be explored in interviews on the experience of recovery from depression. Recovery is understood by those involved with it to be much more than symptom amelioration (Moltu et al., 2017). An important strand of research into the experience of recovery has focused on what people do to live with, and move on from, a diagnosis of a long-term 'personality disorder' such as bipolar (Billsborough et al., 2014; Borg et al., 2013; Veseth et al., 2012) or borderline (Kverme et al., 2019; Ng et al., 2019). Motivated by the wish to avoid being constrained by a purely professional perspective, an important methodological direction taken by research on recovery from long-term mental health conditions has taken the form of initiatives to plan, conduct and analyse studies in collaboration with service users (see, for example, Moltu et al., 2012; Veseth et al., 2017). Qualitative research into the experience of recovery has the potential for enhancing an understanding of the processes and outcome of psychotherapy in at least two ways: (i) by comparing their therapy involvement with other sources of help, participants offer valuable insights into the role of therapy that might not have emerged from just asking them about the therapy on its own; (ii) by drawing attention to the agentic ways that individuals draw on multiple sources of support and learning in actively addressing problems in living.

Box 10.1   Other perspectives on the experience of therapy

In addition to interviewing clients, important insights into how non-therapists view therapy can be derived from interviews with client 'significant others' (Roberts, 1996; Stapley, Target & Midgley, 2017) or members of the public (Weatherhead and Daiches, 2010). Studies of therapist experiences of working with different client groups can also make a valuable contribution to understanding the process of therapy (see Chapter 11).

Client and therapist experiences of the same therapy

All of the studies outlined so far in this chapter have focused on the experience of the client, without reference to what the process of therapy was like for the therapist in the same dyad. Although some studies have sought to incorporate dual (client and therapist) perspectives on the same therapy, this approach remains unusual. Dual or parallel perspective investigations are methodologically challenging, for several reasons. It can be hard to align client and therapist accounts. For example, the client and therapist may describe the same phenomenon, but use different language to describe it. Alternatively, one or other participant may describe an aspect of therapy that was not mentioned by the other, but may potentially have been mentioned if their attention had been drawn to it. A classic finding, from such a study, is that clients say that they really appreciated the 'advice' offered by their therapists – but the therapists do not mention 'advice' at all. It is then not at all easily to find a credible way of reconciling these contrasting perspectives while at the same time honouring the standpoint of both parties. This type of design can leave the reader frustrated, because they have not been able to get close enough to the experiences of either group of informants. In addition, such research can be ethically sensitive, in terms of the therapist or client disclosing information that they would not want the other to learn about. Finally the rationale for conducting a dual perspective study is to develop new insight into some aspect of the interaction between client and therapist: self-contained analyses of client and therapist data may end up merely wrapping up what could be two separate studies in one publication. For these reasons, while a dual perspective study may seem like an exciting and interesting thing to do, it is not necessarily a good choice for an inexperienced researcher, and is best restricted to situations or research questions where it is really necessary.

A classic example of a dual perspective study is a piece of research conducted by Dos Santos and Dallos (2012), in which members of therapy dyads consisting of white therapists and clients of African-Caribbean descent were interviewed about their experiences of engaging in therapy with someone from a different culture to their own. Therapists described high levels of sensitivity to be seen to be culturally insensitive and 'not politically correct', which resulted in them avoiding talking about issues around cultural difference or racism. From the point of view of the client, such therapist behaviour conveyed an unwritten rule that there could be 'no race talk in therapy'. As a consequence, clients actively implemented strategies to distance racial experiences from therapy, which meant that a wide range of significant personal issues were not discussed. This detailed interweaving of client and therapist reflective accounts, within this study, makes a powerful and theoretically significant contribution to the field of multicultural therapy. Other studies that have made good use of a dual perspective approach include a study by Small et al. (2018) that explored the difficulties of providing individual therapy in an acute inpatient setting, an analysis by Råbu and Moltu (2021) of the process of mutual interpersonal engagement in therapy, and an intensive case-by-case investigation by Werbart, Annevall and Hillblom (2019) of the differences between good- and poor-outcome cases within a larger study. A study by Krause et al. (2020) compared client, therapist and parent criteria for evaluating the outcome of therapy for depressed adolescent clients. Each of these studies effectively navigated the complexities of dual/parallel perspective inquiry by starting with a clear rationale for undertaking this kind of study, and devising an approach to data analysis that was appropriate to the aims of their investigation.

Client experience of researcher-defined concepts or phenomena

A general characteristic of qualitative interview-based research in therapy is that it tends to invite the client to talk about a specific and concrete aspect of the lived experience and practice of therapy that can be described in everyday language, such as 'the first session', 'the ending' or 'whether it helped you'. While it is possible to use qualitative reviews to explore the meaning for clients (or therapists) of theoretically defined phenomena such as 'empathy' or 'transference', it is typically quite difficult for the informant to talk about such entities because they lack any concrete experiential anchor from which to speak. There is a risk, as a result, that participants being interviewed about 'conceptual' phenomena will draw on their (implicit or explicit) theoretical understanding, rather than their lived experience, or try to figure out what it is that the interviewer wants to hear. Examples of studies that have been able to overcome these issues include Cooper (2005), Knox (2008), MacFarlane, Anderson & McClintock (2017) and Schnellbacher and Leijssen (2009). On the whole, qualitative interview-based research into the experience of clients and therapists is a methodology that is best suited to investigating concrete moments in therapy or broader themes that can be described in ordinary language (e.g. 'What was helpful?'). Within such an approach, the role of therapy theory and concepts is to provide a basis for designing theoretically relevant interview questions, or to facilitate the interpretation of findings within the discussion section of a paper or dissertation.

Variants on interview-based qualitative research into the experience of therapy

The step-by-step guidelines and exemplar studies that have been suggested in this chapter have centred on the use of individual, face-to-face interviews in which the participant, drawn from some kind of representative group, responds to a set of questions. Within this broad approach, there are several important additional strategies that can be adopted:

Visual techniques. It can be valuable, in enabling informants to generate richly described accounts of their experience, to make use of visual imagery and methods. Many interviewers include, in their list of questions, invitations to 'imagine' – for instance, if your therapist was an animal, what kind of creature would they be, and what would they look like? McKenna and Todd (1997) used a visual timeline to help clients map out the sequence of multiple therapy experiences over their lifetime. Rodgers (2006, 2018) invited clients to depict their 'life-space' in the form of a map or drawing, and then talk about the image they had created. These applications of visual methodologies reflect a wider movement within the field of qualitative research as a whole.

Interpersonal Process Recall (IPR)/Stimulated Recall. Several studies have made use of a technique known as Interpersonal Process Recall (IPR) to make it possible for informants to talk in detail about specific moments or episodes in therapy. IPR involves making a recording (usually audio) of a session, and then asking the client or therapist to listen to it, with a request that they pause the recording whenever they recall what they were thinking or feeling at the time. If carried out soon after a session, the assumption is that this kind of 'stimulated recall' technique will make it possible for the person to re-enter their original experience and describe it in detail. Further discussion of IPR can be found in Chapter 8.

Focus group interviews. In a private one-to-one interview, the informant may be strongly influenced by the presence of an authoritative expert other (the interviewer). The *focus group* technique (Bloor et al., 2000; Krueger and Casey, 2008) is a means of conducting systematic small group interviews with sets of around seven to twelve people. In these groups, the interviewer acts as a facilitator to draw out the beliefs and attitudes of group members concerning the topic under examination. The group discussion is tape recorded and represents a rich source of qualitative data. In the focus group setting each member of the group is exposed to an open social situation, one in which the views of the researcher will be less significant as a potential source of influence. The group facilitator or director must, of course, skilfully conduct the session to prevent any members of the group dominating the discussion. A study by Karakurt et al. (2013) provides a typical example of the application of focus group methodology to the investigation of therapist experiences in working with a specific client group. A valuable reflective account of using focus groups in a therapy research study is available in Pearson & Vossler (2016).

Open-ended qualitative questionnaires can be a valuable research tool in some circumstances. Because questionnaires are easy to distribute, for example in an online survey format, a wider coverage of informants can usually be achieved by using this technique compared with the use of interviews. Short, open-ended questionnaires are normally experienced by research participants as straightforward, unintrusive and unthreatening. From the point of view of the researcher, there is also the major advantage that qualitative questionnaire data do not need to be transcribed. Open-ended questionnaires have been used in several studies of the experience of therapy (for example, Anker et al., 2011; Bachelor, Laverdière & Gamache, 2007).

Box 10.2   Comparing client experiences of different types of therapy

It is standard (good) practice in quantitative research to compare scores and ratings from clients who have experienced different types of therapy. Quantitative scaling techniques are ideally placed to explore such research questions. By contrast, comparing experiences across groups is not straightforward in qualitative research, because it is hard to determine whether informants are referring to the same process (e.g. clients from psychodynamic therapy may say that it was helpful to develop insight, whereas those who have undergone humanistic therapy may use the term 'understanding' – are they the same thing?). It is also hard to detect gradations or differences in the intensity or frequency of experiences on the basis of verbal accounts. To be able to arrive at credible cross-group comparisons, a qualitative researcher

(Continued)

needs to be able to define themes/categories, and estimate their prevalence, with a higher degree of rigour than is required in single-group studies. For anyone considering carrying out a comparative qualitative study, it is useful to pay close attention to the study by Nilsson et al. (2007) comparing client experiences of the outcomes of either psychodynamic psycho-therapy or CBT, and the investigation by Steinmann et al. (2017) of family-based vs individual therapy for anger, as examples of how to handle such analyses. It is also important to be aware that qualitative research has often found that different therapies are experienced by clients in rather similar ways (see, for example, Göstas, Wiberg & Kjellin, 2012).

How to get published

The majority of counselling and psychotherapy journals, and journals in cognate disciplines, publish qualitative interview-based research.

Writing up a qualitative research study for publication presents a number of challenges:

- Condensing many thousands of words of interview transcript into a results/findings section that is perhaps no more than 1,500 words in length, and at the same time providing enough examples of informant statements to ensure that the conclusions are grounded in data.
- Making sure that the 'voice' and standpoint of participants are honoured.
- Reporting on the reflexivity of the researcher, and how this has influenced various aspects of the research process – it can be awkward to combine first-person ('I') writing with the kind of third-person, distanced form of writing that predominates within most scientific articles.
- Reporting on method (how the data were collected and analysed) in sufficient detail to satisfy the needs of researcher-readers who may be considering replicating your study, without losing the interest of the general or practitioner reader.
- Writing a paper that commences with a review of the literature, following a study that started with an exploratory question and in which it was only possible to identify the relevant literature after the data had been analysed.

As a response to these issues, guidelines have been produced about how to write qualitative articles (see online resources).

It is always helpful to look at the writing style adopted by authors who have used the same method, and who have published in potential target journals where you might seek to place your own work. There are distinct differences between the reporting style of grounded theory, IPA and CQR studies, and in the way qualitative material is handled in various journals. Some of these differences are very obvious – for example, the highly reflexive articles published in *Qualitative Inquiry*, compared with the minimally reflexive writing in most counselling and psychotherapy journals. Other differences are more subtle, such as conventions around how to report on the proportion of participants who contributed to a particular category, the number of participant quotes that are provided, or the use of figures and tables. For a novice researcher, it is sensible to find a published article that could function as a template, and then use that structure to organise one's own material.

Suggestions for further reading

This chapter has included many suggestions for how to use qualitative methods to explore different aspects of the client's experience of therapy. For anyone who is planning to undertake this type of investigation, a priority is to find exemplar studies that are inspiring and offer a framework for how to proceed.

Online resources

The online resource site for this book (https://study.sagepub.com/doingresearch4e) includes learning activities related to different types of qualitative interview-based study of client experience.

11

Research on Professional Knowledge

Introduction

In the course of their professional work with clients, any counsellor or psychotherapist will develop a rich practical understanding of how to handle particular issues and respond effectively to the needs of different client groups. This way of knowing can be described as a form of 'professional knowledge' that overlaps with, but is distinct from, ways of understanding that are informed by theory, research and personal life experience. Informal sharing of professional knowledge and wisdom takes place in multiple ways, for example supervision, conversations between colleagues, and in anecdotal examples that live 'in margins' of books and articles. Some therapists write books or articles that specifically aim to allow the reader to look over their shoulder at their practice. Examples of this genre of therapy literature include Elton (2021), Shahar (2013) and Yalom (2001). Another way that this kind of knowledge can be disseminated is by formally documenting and analysing it in research; for example, by conducting interviews with therapists who have interesting and relevant things to say about specific aspects of practice. Such research provides a valuable complement to other types of inquiry, such as outcome studies, case studies and client experience research. Research into professional knowledge is particularly interesting and relevant for practitioners, because it gives access to how colleagues think and act.

At a broader societal level, members of all occupational groups operate within networks of colleagues who share stories about good and bad practice, how to deal with things that go wrong and similar issues. Such networks have been described as 'communities of practice' (Lave & Wenger, 1991). An influential study of how GPs use conversations with colleagues as a means of participating in a community of practice was conducted by Gabbay and le May (2011). The concept of a community of practice refers to everyday learning, outside of classrooms, colleges and universities, through which people in a particular line of work share their experience in order to develop a broader understanding of issues and strategies related to their job. Therapist professional knowledge research studies make an important contribution to building communities of practice, by carefully documenting, analysing and disseminating what therapists have learned in relation to working in particular settings, or around particular presenting problems and dilemmas.

Although communities of practice definitely exist within the world of therapy, they have received relatively little attention (for an exception, see Landes, Smith & Weingardt, 2019). Similarly, 'professional knowledge research' is not a phrase that is widely used in the therapy literature. However, a large number of studies have been published in which therapists have been interviewed about their experience of working with specific issues and client groups. More widespread use of the term 'professional knowledge' as a tag for this genre of research would greatly facilitate efforts to collate and review this body of work.

Research on professional knowledge can be defined as comprising any form of systematic inquiry that seeks to analyse the knowledge, understanding, practical skills and strategies, challenges and dilemmas arising from therapeutic work. Most professional knowledge studies have used individual or focus group interviews, followed by qualitative analysis of transcripts, to explore professional knowledge topics. This chapter concentrates mainly on that type of study. Other approaches to conducting such research – surveys, pragmatic case studies, and autoethnographic research – are discussed towards the end of the chapter.

Exercise 11.1   Mapping your own community of practice

Either through making notes, or drawing a map on a piece of paper, itemise the sources of professional knowledge that are available to you. Looking at this array as a whole, reflect on its strengths and limitations as a means of support for your practice. In what ways might reading professional knowledge studies, of the type described in the present chapter, deepen your involvement in a professional community of practice?

Carrying out a qualitative interview study on therapist professional knowledge

Conducting a professional knowledge study can be personally rewarding: it is intrinsically interesting to listen to colleagues talking about how they work, and writing and publishing an analysis of such material offers an opportunity to make a valuable contribution to the literature. Professional knowledge research also makes it possible to explore questions that are hard to investigate using other methods. It is usually much easier to get ethical approval for a study of therapist views, rather than any study that involves collecting data from actual clients. It is also usually much easier to set up interviews. For students working within time constraints, these practical factors make professional knowledge research an attractive option.

The skills and support for this type of study are similar to those required in a client experience study. There are four distinctive sets of issues that need to be taken into account during the planning and conduct of a professional knowledge study:

1. *Recruitment of participants.* For the most part, participants in studies of the client experience of therapy are recruited from the clinic or service where they have received therapy. Depending on the aims of the study and the amount of client information that is available, it may be possible to focus on a sub-group of clients, such as those who have improved, or have dropped out of therapy. In contrast, professional knowledge research tends to be conducted with informants who are selected and recruited because they possess special insight and experience in relation to the topic being investigated. This can make recruitment a more challenging process. One strategy is 'snowballing': starting with one or two informants who are known through personal contact, and then asking them to recommend other potential interviewees. An additional strategy is to circulate information about the study through social media, emails, notices in professional journals and similar outlets. It is necessary to be able to provide possible interviewees with a clear and succinct explanation of what it is you are looking for.

2. *Ethical sensitivity.* The aim, when interviewing a therapist, is to develop an appreciation of how they work. As a means of describing how they practise, it may be valuable for an informant to talk about specific examples of what happened with particular clients. Ethically, it is essential that this is done in a way that does not compromise the client's identity. Usually, the best way to address this ethical issue is to emphasise the necessity of client confidentiality in the information sheet that the participant reads before agreeing to join the study, reinforcing this message at the start of the interview, and possibly also reminding the informant again at the point where they start to provide concrete examples of their practice. Another distinctive ethical issue relates to safeguarding the identity of informants. For example, it is likely that a professional knowledge study will be read by other colleagues in that field of practice, or who are geographically located in the same city or region as the researcher. Such readers may be able to jigsaw identify informants through piecing together subtle clues within the study. Given that the purpose of such a study is to facilitate participants in sharing their experience in an open and unguarded way, any uncertainty around possible identification risks undermining the viability of the whole project. It is therefore important to clearly explain all confidentiality

procedures and choices to participants, let them edit the interview transcript, and ask them to read a draft of the final report and make suggestions around any further action that needs to be taken to maintain their anonymity. It is also very important to be ultra-cautious when talking about the study to others, or when presenting findings at seminars or conferences.

3. *Working collaboratively with research participants.* Unlike the majority of clients or members of the public who might be interviewed in research studies, professional colleagues are better informed about the topic (and probably also the methodology) and interested in knowing about the findings. These considerations mean that it is often appropriate to approach the study in a collaborative manner, viewing participants as co-researchers. There are many ways in which such a stance can be implemented, such as asking the participant to read interview questions in advance, asking them at the end of the interview what they would want to add, sharing personal experience, involvement in the process of analysing data, inviting feedback and comment on the analysis and the final paper, and so on. Although not all of these strategies will be feasible in every situation, it is helpful to think through with a supervisor or research colleagues how a collaborative approach might be sustained. A further aspect of professional colleagues as research participants is that it is probable that there will exist a degree of professional transference/counter-transference. For example, a young student interviewing a respected older member of the profession may be in awe of their reputation, while the interviewee may treat the researcher as naïve, or as a threat.

4. *Dealing with the complex structure of professional knowledge.* When interviewing a client about their experience of therapy, the research participant is almost entirely drawing on their feelings, and their memory of key incidents within one therapy relationship. By contrast, a participant who is a therapist will not only be drawing on their personal experience, but also, to some extent, on their theory of therapy. The knowledge that they share is not a static entity, but a form of understanding that is constantly changing as they see more clients, or attend training courses. In telling stories about their practice, they will be aware of the difference between narratives that will make them look good, and those that reveal uncertainty, lack of competence, or even ethically questionable behaviour. The design of an interview schedule needs to take these issues into account.

A useful guide to handling these distinctively challenging aspects of professional knowledge research is to study how they have been addressed in published studies.

Exercise 11.2 Approaches to exploring professional knowledge

Reflect on how you might investigate your research question by using each of the approaches to exploring professional knowledge introduced in this chapter, such as interviews and surveys. What would your study look like? What would be the advantages and limitations of different professional knowledge research designs, and the unique or distinctive insights yielded by each of them?

Methodological challenges

Therapist professional knowledge reflects an ongoing, fluid intersection of personal experience (feelings and responses to client), practice (doing the job) and theoretical perspectives, within a specific organisational and cultural context. Therapists being interviewed about their practice are likely to draw on all of these strands of knowledge. Professional knowledge is organised around scripts or sequences of thought/action: an unfolding sense of how a response or intervention might have an effect on a client, in ways that either open up or close down possibilities. Typically, a therapist is seldom required to explicitly articulate their professional knowledge – for the most part, it represents an implicit or background set of concepts, ideas, memories and action tendencies. In important respects, professional knowledge is a collective as well as an individual construct. For example, when faced with a problem, a therapist may not know the answer but they might know who to ask. Knowledge is also in a constant state of renewal and repair – the majority of therapists are avid learners, readers and workshop attendees, and their way of understanding the process of therapy gradually shifts over the course of time.

These aspects of professional knowledge represent challenges for researchers. Most therapists are happy to talk about their work, and, when informed about the aims of a study, will expand at length about their experience. However, to make sure that data adequately captures implicit, sequential and collective dimensions of knowledge, it is necessary to develop an interview strategy that helps the informant to explore these themes. An important aspect of such a strategy is a focus on concrete examples. The interview transcript of a therapist who mainly answers in general terms (i.e. 'this is what usually happens') is likely to be dominated by theoretical abstractions. By contrast, asking a participant to talk about a specific case (e.g. 'can you tell me about a recent case, or the most recent case, when …?') is more likely to get closer to actual moment-by-moment experience of the work, including points of uncertainty or ambiguity. To collect rich data on professional knowledge it is necessary to spend time developing interview questions that highlight areas that are important in terms of the aims of the study, but might not be mentioned by the interviewee unless prompted. It is also important to conduct the interview in such a way that the participant is given sufficient space to formulate replies in areas around which they only have a vague sense of what their answer might be. Analysis of interview transcripts needs to be able to take account of subtle, emerging themes as well as areas in which the informant is confident about what they think and believe. At the end of a good interview, an informant will typically say that they have learned something about themselves in the process of responding to the researcher's questions.

Box 11.1   The distinction between knowledge and wisdom

The majority of therapist professional knowledge research is based on practitioner reflective accounts of the everyday experience of engaging in a particular form of practice. Beyond such studies, there exists a further type of professional knowledge study that seeks to document therapist wisdom: hard-learned lessons arising from the struggle to reconcile competing demands and tensions within professional roles. Examples of therapist wisdom research include studies by Levitt and Piazza-Bonin (2016) and Råbu and McLeod (2018). Although wisdom is hard to pin down, it represents a crucial aspect of any kind of collective capacity to respond to the challenges of cultural and technological change. The therapist wisdom literature also connects with initiatives around wisdom-oriented therapy, and research into wisdom in other professional fields.

Exemplar studies

A recurring recommendation to those wishing to learn about therapy research, repeated throughout the present book, is the advice to read actual research studies. The professional knowledge research studies highlighted below exemplify the kinds of insights that can be achieved from this type of investigation, the types of research question that have been pursued within this area of inquiry and the methodological strategies that are available. The content of these studies – what they have found – is undoubtedly of interest. However, from the perspective of doing research it is vital to pay heed to *how* the study was carried out, in terms of how interviews were set up in order to make sure that they allowed the participant to share their experience of implicit aspects of their practical knowledge.

A valuable function of research into therapist knowledge and experience is to draw attention to aspects of practice that are rarely discussed. A notable example of this type of study explored therapist experiences of clients that they frequently thought about between sessions and who almost seemed to force their way into the personal inner world of the therapist (Bimont & Werbart, 2018). In-depth qualitative interviews with therapists who had first-hand experience of this phenomenon revealed a set of recurring themes. These therapists described themselves as carrying the client's problems, and being caught between powerful feelings of love and care for these clients, alongside fear, worry and concern. They described various ways in which they handled these situations. This study did not prescribe any single best way to deal with such experiences. Instead, what it offered was an account of a set of possible ways in which therapists might respond to this issue, and an invitation to join a reflective conversation. A valuable facet of the Bimont and Werbart (2018) paper – typical of articles that report on investigations of professional knowledge – is that it provides an accessible and relatively brief introductory literature review that places a specific set of therapist accounts in a broader context of relevant theory and research. The Bimont and Werbart (2018) paper also includes a detailed interview schedule that shows how a set of questions can be developed that allow the participant to tell their story, while respectfully and carefully probing for implicit threads of experience. Other examples of professional knowledge research into seldom discussed topics include studies of what it is like to receive negative feedback from a client (Brattland et al., 2018), or to feel embarrassment and shame about something that happened in a session (Klinger, Ladany & Kulp, 2012).

Another way that professional knowledge research can contribute to a community of practice is to serve as a channel for disseminating the cumulative experience of practitioners who have expertise arising from specialising in working with a specific client group. Aherne, Coughlan and Surgenor (2018) interviewed therapists working in a suicide prevention service in Ireland around what they had learned concerning the therapeutic relationship with suicidal clients, in particular the experience of connection/disconnection. Vulcan (2016) interviewed therapists about their experiences of working with children diagnosed with autism spectrum disorder, and found that a common theme was a capacity to use bodily responses and reactions as a way of developing a sense of the inner world of the client. Veseth et al. (2016) carried out interviews with therapists who had worked extensively with clients diagnosed with bipolar disorders. Quinn, Schofield and Middleton (2010) documented the professional knowledge and learning of therapists who had supported individuals struggling to cope with psychogenic non-epileptic seizures. This type of study provides insights that are not only valuable for colleagues beginning to work with such clients, but also offer a practice-based perspective that can inform other forms of inquiry, such as randomised clinical trials.

One of the great strengths of contemporary therapy is the degree of innovation that exists. However, when a novel approach to therapy begins to emerge, it can be hard to know how useful it may turn out to be, or to assess the pros and cons of adopting it in particular settings. In such scenarios, professional knowledge research can play a vital role in allowing pioneers of such approaches to report on their experience in using innovative methods. For instance, in recent years there has been a move to bring some aspects of specialist therapies conducted out of doors, such as wilderness and adventure therapy, into routine practice. This is sometimes described as 'walk and talk' therapy. Professional knowledge studies by Asfeldt and Beames (2017), Jordan (2014) and Revell and McLeod (2017) have analysed the experience of therapists who have experimented with offering outdoor therapy sessions to clients. These interview-based studies allow other members of the profession to get a sense of what is involved in this way of working, and help them to decide on whether this might be something that they would wish to incorporate into their own practice, and to be aware of what kind of training and preparation might be required.

Research into professional knowledge sometimes has the effect of challenging taken-for-granted assumptions. For instance, it is widely accepted that it can be highly stressful to be a therapist for clients who have been subjected to traumatic and cruel treatment from other people, in the form of violence, sexual abuse or torture. While there is substantial evidence that such negative effects do occur, studies that have allowed therapists to talk openly about all aspects of their work with individuals who have been subjected to extreme adversity have also found evidence of positive impacts on therapists. Therapists interviewed about their work with refugees in Australia (Puvimanasinghe et al., 2015) and child victims of sexual abuse in Ireland (Wheeler & McElvaney, 2018) reported a sense of privilege at being allowed to hear their stories, and an enormous amount of personal learning arising from witnessing the courage and resourcefulness of their clients. These therapists strongly believed that their work with traumatised clients had made them more resilient both as therapists and as people.

What can go wrong?

A professional knowledge study is a relatively straightforward type of research, and a good opportunity for a novice researcher to acquire research skills and confidence. Research participants are usually eager to talk, and are sufficiently aware and resilient to not be put off by researcher insecurity. Nevertheless, there are some hazards to be avoided. Some researchers are so preoccupied by the task of exploring the informant's story that they neglect to collect crucial background information about the setting where the therapist works, their previous training, the models they use, what they read, how many clients in a particular category that they have worked with, how many sessions the clients are offered, client outcomes, and so on. The absence of this kind of contextual information can leave readers unsure of how to interpret professional knowledge themes that have been identified, because they are unable to place what they read within their map of professional practice as a whole. Another hazard, discussed earlier in the chapter, is allowing interviews with practitioners to be dominated by abstract theorising or the desire of the participant to portray themselves as wise and competent. A key methodological message of this chapter is that it is necessary to plan and conduct professional knowledge interviews in a way that makes it possible to collect information on not only the expertise of the informant, but also the uncertain, implicit and emergent aspects of their practice.

A further hazard for professional knowledge research is associated with the way it is written up. It confuses and antagonises readers if findings from such studies are reported as being in some sense objectively 'true'. It is essential to be more modest, and always emphasise that what is being reported is therapists' accounts, ways of understanding and ways of talking about their practice, and not the practice itself. This issue is illustrated in debates over the years over the status of research into the attributes of 'master therapists'. Jennings and Skovholt (1999) asked therapists in a city in the USA to nominate colleagues who they regarded as 'the best of the best' – the therapists they would consult themselves, or would recommend to members of their own family. They then interviewed the most frequently nominated individuals. Over the last 20 years, the themes that they generated have proved to be an invaluable and inspiring source of insight into therapist development and the qualities of exceptional practitioners (Hou & Skovholt, 2020). But, of course, critics have pointed out that we cannot really know whether those nominated as master therapists are in fact any more effective than other therapists. It may be that they are put forward because they are particularly likeable or charismatic individuals, or avid self-publicists. The enduring influence of this body of work has depended on the willingness of Thomas Skovholt and his colleagues to acknowledge these methodological limitations, and to show how the findings of their interview-based studies are consistent with results from other types of investigation.

Other approaches to investigating professional knowledge

Interview methods have proved to be a robust and flexible way of building an understanding of professional knowledge. However, other methodologies have also been used in this field, such as surveys, case studies and autoethnography:

Practitioner surveys. The professional knowledge research studies that have been discussed so far have all been based on qualitative interviews with therapists. An alternative approach, which is highly time-efficient and has the potential to draw on large numbers of informants, is to use online survey methodology. A particularly notable example of this kind of investigation can be found in a project initiated by Marvin Goldfried and other leading members of the CBT community in the USA. CBT practice is largely dominated by the use of treatment manuals that have been developed in research contexts, and there was some concern that these protocols might not always be appropriate in everyday clinical practice. Surveys were carried out that asked CBT practitioners to rate their experience in using research-based CBT protocols with clients with a range of different presenting problems (Goldfried, 2011; Goldfried et al., 2014; Jacobson, Newman & Goldfried, 2016; McAleavey, Castonguay & Goldfried, 2014; Pittig, Kotter & Hoyer, 2019; Szkodny, Newman & Goldfried, 2014).The findings of these studies raised important questions about the use of CBT in routine therapy practice. It turned out that many CBT practitioners found it necessary to adapt standardised protocols to meet the needs of clients with co-morbid conditions or chaotic social lives, and reported that a significant minority of clients reject CBT ideas and techniques. These studies illustrate how professional knowledge research can supplement other types of study (e.g. RCTs of therapy effectiveness) to provide a more complete understanding.

Delphi technique. The Delphi technique (or Delphi poll) is a structured method for exploring and synthesising professional knowledge using a series of survey questionnaires. Whereas interview studies of professional knowledge primarily focus on the lived experience and learning arising from working with a specific client group, a Delphi study aims to condense such reflections into recommendations for policy and practice. The first step in conducting such a study is to identify a group of practitioners with relevant expertise, who would be willing to participate in the project. Typically, a Delphi study would then consist of three cycles of inquiry. First, an open-ended, exploratory survey is sent to participants to elicit their initial views on the topic. The results of this survey are analysed and sent back to participants in the form of levels of agreement around various themes and conclusions. This allows informants to see how their views correspond with those of colleagues. The final stage involves further ratings to arrive at an agreed set of recommendations. West (2011) provides an example of how this approach has been used in a therapy research study. Further information about the origins and application of Delphi methodology is available in Diamond et al. (2014), Keeney, Hasson and McKenna (2010) and Linstone and Turoff (2002). Delphi surveys have been carried out to analyse practitioner views on such therapy topics as how to supervise counsellors and psychotherapists who work with trauma (West, 2010), developing culturally appropriate therapy in Iran (Rezaie et al., 2020), how to describe and report how therapy is delivered (Sündermann, See and Veale, 2019), therapy approaches that are not helpful (Norcross, Koocher & Garofalo, 2006), and identifying competencies for psycho-therapeutic practice with eating disordered clients (Williams & Haverkamp, 2010), therapy for psychosis (Kongara et al., 2017), therapy for men (Seidler et al., 2019) and blending online with face-to-face therapy (van der Vaart et al., 2014). An alternative approach that is similar to Delphi, is the nominal group technique (Harvey and Holmes, 2012).

Pragmatic case studies. Another way of sharing professional knowledge and sup-porting a community of practice is to let colleagues see how you work with a particular client. The format of the pragmatic case study provides a rigorous frame-work that requires a therapist to present a comprehensive analysis of all aspects of their work with a client. *Clinical Case Studies* and *Pragmatic Case Studies in Psychotherapy* are journals that are devoted to publishing this kind of study. Further information of case study approaches to professional knowledge can be found in Chapter 13.

Autoethnographic research in which therapists explore their experience rep-resents a potentially valuable source of professional knowledge. Examples of such studies are Chigwedere (2019), Falzon et al. (2020), King and Jones (2019), Råbu et al. (2021) and Stirling (2020).

How to get published

Most therapy journals are open to publishing professional knowledge studies. The studies cited in the present chapter and in the online resources provide an indication of the range of journals that have carried such work.

Suggestions for further reading

At the present time there are no reviews of research into professional knowledge, or critical analyses of methodological issues associated with this area of inquiry.

A book that offers a coherent analysis of the nature of professional knowledge in psychotherapy is: Fishman, D. (1999). *The Case for a Pragmatic Psychology*. New York: New York University Press.

A comprehensive account of how to understand the way that practitioners synthesise multiple sources of knowledge in the service of clinical decision-making can be found in: Gabbay, J. & le May, A. (2011). *Practice-based Evidence for Healthcare: Clinical Mindlines*. Abingdon: Routledge. Although primarily focused on medical practice, the concepts and examples discussed by Gabbay and le May are highly relevant to psychotherapy.

Online resources

Further examples of professional knowledge studies and activities to support learning are available in the online resource site for this book: https://study.sagepub.com/doingresearch4e.

12

Evaluating Outcome

Practice-based Research

Introduction

Evaluating the outcome of therapy has represented the single most important research topic within the counselling and psychotherapy research literature. Many organisations, institutions and governments have invested substantial resources on research into the effectiveness of therapy. Partly, this investment has been motivated by a desire to ensure that the kinds of therapy that are offered are both helpful and cost-effective. This line of research has also reflected the reality that the field of psychological and mental healthcare comprises a crowded and contested marketplace.

There are many competing ideas about why people become depressed or anxious, and how these difficulties can be alleviated. Outcome research can be used to develop an appreciation of which approaches to therapy might be most effective for particular types of problem.

Historically, randomised controlled/clinical trials (RCTs) have been regarded as the most reliable source of evidence in respect of therapy outcome. In an RCT, clients are randomly assigned to different treatment conditions (e.g. psychodynamic vs CBT, or face-to-face vs online therapy). The aim is to discover whether clients in one of the intervention conditions demonstrate higher levels of improvement, compared with those who have received other types of therapy (or have been assigned to a 'no treatment' waiting list condition or a 'treatment as usual' condition such as routine GP care). If one of the intervention conditions is associated with significantly higher levels of change, there is a strong logical case to be made for the efficacy of that model of therapy, because the randomisation process has ensured that all other relevant factors have been held constant. While the RCT design remains hugely influential within the field of counselling and psychotherapy research, there is also a growing appreciation of the limitations of this type of study:

- The procedures that are necessary in order to ensure rigorous randomisation can mean that clients in RCTs tend to be rather different from clients seen in routine practice.
- The need to closely define and monitor the type of therapy that is delivered may leave little space for therapist flexibility, responsiveness and use of clinical judgement.
- Researchers conducting RCTs typically have a strong personal and professional allegiance to one of the models or treatment conditions being evaluated; several studies have found that this kind of allegiance is associated with a tendency to produce research that yields results that support the favoured model of therapy (see McLeod, 2016, Chapter 5);
- RCTs are expensive to run, with the consequence that many plausible and probably effective therapy interventions have never been evaluated in this way.

As a result of these factors, a great deal of effort has been devoted to the development of reliable, valid and economically feasible methods that can be used to evaluate the effectiveness of therapy in everyday routine practice, rather than in the artificial conditions of an RCT. The debate over the pros and cons of RCTs as a methodology for determining the relative efficacy of different types of therapy has raged for many years, and is a central preoccupation of the international psychotherapy research community. Points of entry into this debate can be found in many places (Carey & Stiles, 2016; McLeod, 2011, Chapter 8; McLeod, 2016, Chapter 5; McPherson et al., 2020).

Practice-based or *naturalistic* research consists of studies that analyse data within routine practice. Applied to studies of the outcomes of counselling and psychotherapy, such an approach has typically used brief self-report symptom questionnaires to monitor client outcome over the course of therapy. The strength of such studies is that they provide evidence of the effectiveness of therapy as it is generally practised. The limitation of naturalistic studies is that they lack the level of control that is inherent in an RCT design, with the result that there may be a lack of certainty about how findings should be interpreted. However, in recent years a range of methodological innovations has been introduced to strengthen the methodological robustness of practice-based research.

There are two types of practice-based outcome research that have been developed. The first type makes use of massive databases consisting of data from thousands of clients receiving therapy within large-scale healthcare systems. Examples of such studies include a large-scale investigation of therapist differences in effectiveness conducted by Kraus et al. (2011) and an analysis of relative levels of effectiveness of different therapy approaches across the NHS in England (Stiles et al., 2006, 2008). The organisational complexity and time-scales associated with this form of 'data-mining' research mean that it is beyond the scope of novice or practitioner-researchers. This chapter focuses instead on a second type of practice-based outcome research which analyses the outcomes of therapy delivered within a specific agency or local/regional network of practitioners. This second type of practice-based outcome research provides many opportunities for novice researchers to make a contribution to the literature on the effectiveness of therapy, while at the same time providing valuable feedback for the therapy clinics or agencies sponsoring the research. The primary focus of the present chapter is on this kind of grassroots research. Where relevant, reference will be made to large-scale data mining studies to exemplify potential research questions that could be explored at a more local level by practitioner researchers.

What is a practice-based outcome study?

A practice-based outcome study usually involves the collection of data on the symptoms, problems, wellbeing or goals of clients before they commence therapy, at various points over the course of therapy, at the end of therapy, and perhaps also at follow-up. The primary aim of this sort of research is to provide evidence of the effectiveness of therapy. This evidence may relate to the effectiveness of a particular approach to therapy (e.g. person-centred therapy) or to the work of a particular therapy clinic or service.

Box 12.1   Other ways of describing a practice-based outcome study

The kind of study described in this chapter refers to investigations that seek to measure outcome in a sample of clients, without using a comparison or control group against which results might be contrasted. This type of research is described in several different ways in the literature: quasi-experimental design, open trial, naturalistic study, pre-post design, single group design and effectiveness study.

Why would I want to do this kind of research?

There are strong organisational reasons for undertaking this type of study. Most counselling and psychotherapy services and agencies need to be able to demonstrate, for example in annual reports, bids to funding agencies and client publicity, that they are achieving a satisfactory level of results. In addition, evaluating the outcomes of routine practice can enable a service to do better work, for example by identifying groups of clients who may need longer therapy or a different approach. The skills and knowledge that are required to carry out a practice-based outcome study are relevant for therapists in respect of evaluating their own work with clients, and using feedback from clients to guide the therapy process.

Undertaking a practice-based outcome study, or studying and learning about how such studies are carried out, can also inform therapy practice. Such experience provides an appreciation of the complexity of outcome, in terms of different outcome indicators and evidence that can be used to monitor whether work with a particular client is going well, or whether it is time to stop. Understanding the challenges involved in collecting reliable information about outcome allows practitioners to develop a balanced sense of humility and health scepticism around the success of their own efforts with clients, and the claims made by proponents of leading 'brand name' therapies.

What kind of skills and support do I need?

This type of study requires competence in basic statistical techniques, either on the part of the lead researcher or another member of the research team. Collecting data requires a sustained level of collaboration and commitment from the counsellor or psychotherapists who are seeing the clients, and administration and reception staff within the service. A sufficient degree of organisational ability is also necessary to design and implement the systems for storing data and checking that forms have been distributed to the relevant people and then completed on time and filed.

Exercise 12.1　Mapping stakeholder priorities – who wants what?

If you are considering introducing practice-based outcome monitoring into an established counselling or psychotherapy service, a valuable early step is to construct a stakeholder map. Take a large piece of paper. Around the outside edge place all of the key stakeholders – the management, the funders, clients, counsellors, other interested parties. Beside each group, make a list of (a) what they might want in terms of information and possible eventual improvements to the service, and (b) what they may be willing to give in terms of time and resources. Use the centre of the page to identify areas of agreement and areas in which further discussion and negotiations will be required. Direct consultation with representatives of each stakeholder group is then necessary to clarify details and establish an agreed set of procedures.

A step-by-step guide to doing a practice-based outcome study

It is important to allow time, and consult widely, on the aim and purpose of a practice-based outcome study. Some of the factors that will need to be considered are as follows:

- What research questions are being pursued?
- Which clients are being targeted?
- What kind of consent will clients be asked to provide?
- Which outcomes are being measured?
- Are all possible therapists, and cases, included in the study, or just a sample?
- How will the data be collected and stored?
- How will any missing data be handled?
- What is the time-period for the study?
- How much will it cost?
- How will the data be analysed?

As with any other type of research, it is vital to be guided by examples from studies that have already been completed and published. Rather than attempt to design a practice-based outcome study from the ground up, it is sensible to look at what has worked (or not worked) in previous studies, and assemble a research protocol that comprises, as far as possible, proven elements. These issues are explored in more detail below.

Identifying research aims and questions

The main aim of a practice-based outcome study is to evaluate the effectiveness of the therapy that is being offered. In many studies, this aim translates into a research design in which all clients, over a specific period of time, are invited to complete a general symptom measure such as the CORE-OM, ORS, OQ-45, PHQ9, GAD-7 and/or a goals form (see Chapter 9 for further information on these and other measurement scales). However, there are many secondary research questions that may also be relevant. For example, it may be of interest to look at the outcomes of trainee counsellors, or counsellors who have received different forms of training or supervision.

It may also be of interest to focus on outcomes in clients with different types of problem, such as eating disorders or depression, or who vary in problem severity, or who require a greater or lesser number of sessions. These are just a few of the many theoretically interesting and practically relevant types of question that can be asked with a standard practice-based outcome design. To explore these questions it is necessary to be able to think ahead and anticipate the types of analysis that might be carried out on the data, and then ensure that the relevant information on these factors has been collected. For example, if the aim is to discover whether clients with eating disorders (or whatever) achieve outcomes that are better or worse than those for other clients, it will be necessary to (a) be able to identify which clients have eating disorders; (b) make sure that enough of this type of client are captured in the sample; and (c) use a measure that is credible as a way of assessing change in clients with dysfunctional eating.

Some of the main research questions that have been explored in practice-based outcome studies include the following:

1. *How effective is therapy?* The intention to document the effectiveness of therapy underpins the whole practice-based evidence movement. In many practice-based outcome studies, the aim is merely to evaluate the overall effectiveness of the particular form of therapy being offered by a counselling centre or therapy provider (see for example Archer et al., 2000; Balfour & Lanman, 2012; Gibbard & Hanley, 2008; Lindgren, Werbart & Philips, 2010; McKenzie et al., 2011; Ogrodniczuk et al., 2012; Weersing & Weisz, 2002; Westbrook & Kirk, 2005). In other studies, the aim has been to compare the effectiveness of alternative therapy approaches (e.g. person-centred and CBT; individual vs group therapy) offered within the same service (see, for example, Marriott and Kellett, 2009; Stiles et al., 2006, 2008; van Rijn & Wild, 2016; Werbart et al., 2013). A further variant around the question of effectiveness involves focusing on the outcomes associated with a particular group of therapists, such as novice/trainee counsellors (Armstrong, 2010; Owen et al., 2016).

2. *Are there subgroups of clients who are more or less likely to find therapy beneficial?* If a practice-based database includes a sufficient number of cases, it may be possible to identify groups of clients who do better in therapy, or report lower levels of benefit. For instance, in practice-based research, Weersing and Weisz (2002) found that ethnic minority clients recorded lower levels of change than white clients, and studies by McLeod , Johnston and Griffin (2000) and Saxon, Ivey and Young (2008) found lower levels of change in clients who were unemployed. Cairns (2014) used practice-based research to explore the characteristics of clients who found it hard to engage with therapy. In practice-based studies where clients complete measures at each session, it has been possible to identify characteristics of those clients who exhibit sudden gains (Stiles et al., 2003). In client surveys (i.e., not practice-based outcome studies), around 5 per cent of clients have experiences of therapy that they regard as having been harmful to them (see, for example, Crawford et al., 2016). Even if this is a small proportion of all clients, such events may have very significant long-term consequences for individuals and their families. Being able to identify negative outcomes, and the conditions under which they are more likely to occur, is an important goal for any practice-based outcome study.

3. *What proportion of clients drop out of therapy?* Clients who do not attend (DNA) therapy, drop out of therapy or do not have planned endings have represented a

significant focus for practice-based research. It seems probable that the majority of clients in this category are not being helped by the therapy they have been offered, or do not perceive it as being potentially helpful to them. The occurrence of missed sessions represents a major cost to services, which has the effect of increasing waiting times for those who are seeking therapy. Practice-based studies have made a major contribution in drawing attention to the high DNA levels associated with some services and client groups (for example, Connell, Grant & Mullin, 2006; Gilbert et al., 2005; Scheeres et al., 2008; Schindler, Hiller & Witthöft, 2013).

4.   *What are the characteristics of clients who receive therapy?* The planning, co-ordination and funding for therapy services require information about the types of clients who use various services. Practice-based studies have shown that clients who are seen within voluntary sector counselling agencies in the UK are similar in symptom profile and severity to patients within National Health Service (NHS) outpatient services (Caccia and Watson, 1987; Moore, 2006). Werbart and Wang (2012) have used practice-based data to analyse the attributes of clients who are not accepted for therapy within a specific service.

5.   *How many sessions do clients need?* Analysis of practice-based data can be used to explore questions around the number of sessions used by clients, and the number of sessions that are necessary in order for meaningful change to occur. It can be useful for a practice-based study to provide information on the number of sessions used by clients, and examine the relationship between length of therapy and outcome. This information can be valuable for therapy clinics and agencies looking to make decisions about whether to introduce limits on the number of sessions.

6.   *How can practice-based evidence be used by a therapy agency to inform the design of more effective services for clients?* Ultimately, the aim of practice-based research is to contribute to the development of better services. For example, if routine outcome monitoring identifies unemployed clients as a group that does not do particularly well in therapy, it would be possible to offer some kind of augmented model of therapy to this set of clients, such as a support group alongside one-to-one sessions. It would then be possible, in the next time period, to look at whether this initiative had made a difference to the outcomes of therapy for this client group.

These questions represent the primary areas in which practice-based methodology has been applied within the field of counselling and psychotherapy research. Later in the chapter, we also consider some examples of how practice-based outcome research can be augmented through the concurrent use of other research approaches, such as qualitative interviews and case studies.

Exercise 12.2   Using practice-based outcome research to explore your research question

Reflect on how you might investigate your research question by conducting a practice-based outcome study. What would the study look like? What would be the advantages and limitations of this kind of approach?

Choosing outcome measures

Within the wide range of methodologies that are used in counselling and psychotherapy research, the key distinctive feature of practice-based research is that it aims to capture information about what is happening in routine practice. It is therefore essential that the data collection procedure intrudes as little as possible into the naturally occurring process of therapy. What this means, in practice, is that data are collected through a combination of forms filled in by staff (therapists and administrators) and brief self-report measures completed by clients. One of the goals of this type of research is to allow connections and inferences to be made between a particular set of data and broader trends within the field. As a result, it is best if data are collected using standardised, validated measures that allow comparison with other studies and data-sets. In general, it is not sensible to try to design one's own outcome questionnaire, or to modify existing questionnaires – either of these strategies will mean that it is difficult or impossible to compare one's findings with the results of other studies. In addition, developing a new measuring instrument is a highly time-consuming task. However, if there are specific questions that are highly relevant to the aims of a practice-based outcome study, but not included within pre-existing validated measures, it is possible to develop custom-designed items that are used in addition to (but not instead of) standardised forms.

Before embarking on a practice-based outcome study, it is important to look carefully at the intended use of the data. It is also helpful to imagine what a subsequent article or report might look like. It can be frustrating for all concerned to collect data that are not subsequently used. It can also be frustrating to realise, at the end, that important data have not been gathered.

Describing the therapy

From the point of view of supporters of RCT methodology, one of the main weaknesses of the practice-based outcome literature is that studies do not provide sufficient information about the therapy that is being delivered. In RCTs and also in case studies, a lot of attention is devoted to defining the therapy that is offered and the characteristics of therapists (e.g. training and experience). By contrast, such information tends to be missing, or thinly reported, in practice-based studies. This is doubly unfortunate, because (a) the distinctive contribution of practice-based research is diminished if the actual practice is not described, and (b) this makes it hard for practitioner-readers to know whether the results of a study apply to their own practice setting.

Domains of factual information that can contribute to providing a richly described account of practice include:

- How clients make contact, how they are assessed, how client preferences are accommodated.

- Location, duration and frequency of therapy, cost of therapy, therapy modality (individual, couple, group).
- Client demographic characteristics, presenting problems/diagnoses, chronicity of problems, adversity issues (e.g. poverty, disability), client past/current use of therapy and other services.
- Therapist demographic characteristics (age, sex, ethnicity), training, experience, supervision.
- Type(s) of therapy being delivered.
- Values/principles espoused by the organisation.

It may be useful to refer readers to publications or websites that describe the work of the agency or clinic. In some instances it may be relevant to invite therapists to describe their practice using a brief questionnaire. The CORE outcome evaluation system includes forms completed by therapists that cover many of these areas. These forms provide a useful starting point, but it may be that in particular circumstances additional information needs to be collected.

An associated issue, which also needs to be considered at the outset, is how the ending of therapy will be defined, and how information on that ending will be collected. Knowing about the proportion of DNAs and unplanned endings is important information for therapy organisations, because missed sessions represent a resource cost. Typically, however, such data are not collected in a reliable or consistent way that would allow comparison with other services. A useful discussion of how to collect data on unplanned endings is available in Connell, Grant and Mullin (2006).

When describing the therapy that is offered, it is valuable to think about the ways in which readers of an article will seek to assimilate the findings of the study into their interests and their existing 'map' of therapy. For example, readers will want to know about aspects such as 'Is this CBT?', 'Are these minority/disadvantaged clients?' or 'Were these people depressed?'

Addressing ethical issues

Clients are entitled to receive an explanation of why they are being asked to complete questionnaires, and what will be done with the information they provide. It should always be made clear that a client has the right not to complete questionnaires, without prejudice to their entitlement to therapy. It is good practice to offer appropriate assistance to people who have difficulty in completing questionnaires, for example because of literacy problems or visual impairment.

In most therapy settings, the collection of routine outcome data is defined as an 'audit' rather than 'research', with the consequence that formal ethical approval is not required. However, it is always important to check this out. Any research, including analysis of an existing data-set, being carried out by a student will always require ethical approval from the relevant university committee. Research designs that go beyond a routine audit (e.g. interviewing clients, or randomly assigning clients to alternative therapies) always require formal ethical approval.

No matter whether formal ethical approval is obtained or not, it is always essential to collect and store data in a manner that respects client confidentiality, autonomy, wellbeing and human rights and adheres to current legal requirements.

A specific ethical issue that may need attention is the inclusion in many scales of 'risk' items (e.g. the intention to do harm to the self or others). It is reasonable for clients to expect, no matter what they are told about how questionnaires are processed, that if they indicate an intention to harm on a questionnaire then someone will pay attention to their distress and respond appropriately. This issue does not arise often, because relatively few therapy clients are suicidal or otherwise at risk. But it certainly can happen that a client will indicate risk, on a measure, while not disclosing this issue to their therapist.

A further ethical issue associated with practice-based outcome research arises when data are analysed in relation to the relative effectiveness of different therapists. Therapists have a right to be consulted on whether such analyses are to be carried out, and to have the option to opt out.

Collecting data/minimising attrition

It is instructive to look closely at the method sections of practice-based outcome studies to learn about how the data were collected. One approach is for questionnaires to be completed just before or at the end of the first meeting with a therapist (which could be an assessment session or a first therapy session), and then at the end of the final therapy session. Often the questionnaire will be collected by a receptionist or administrator. If it is collected by the therapist, the client is usually told that the therapist will not read it, and it is placed by the client in a sealed envelope. A variant on these arrangements can involve the client completing a questionnaire on a PC or laptop, rather than being given this in paper form.

While this kind of procedure is relatively straightforward to administer, it is problematic on research grounds. The main limitation is that many clients (as many as 40 per cent) may have unplanned endings, and as a result will not complete end-of-therapy measures. This means that it becomes difficult to interpret the meaning of any change statistics that are generated by the study. The probability is that the majority of clients with unplanned endings are dissatisfied with therapy. But you never really know. A second limitation is that nothing is known about the lasting effects of therapy. At least some clients benefit from regular supportive contact, and the presence in their calendar of a predictably positive experience of meeting with a counsellor gives helpful structure to their life. For such clients, these effects may disappear as soon as therapy is over. Their end of therapy scores may therefore provide an overestimate of the benefits of therapy. In contrast, other clients may continue to use coping skills developed during therapy, and continue to get better over the ensuing months. A third limitation is that there is evidence, from many studies, that clients start to improve as soon as they have made an appointment to see a therapist, probably because they feel more hopeful and are proud of themselves for taking action. As a consequence, measuring symptoms at the first session will underestimate the overall effectiveness of therapy – if the data were collected at the first point of contact (i.e. before meeting a therapist), a higher degree of benefit would almost certainly be recorded.

In response to these difficulties, it makes sense to consider some strategies for augmenting the standard data collection model:

- Administering a brief telephone measure during the first contact with the agency, or mailing out a questionnaire (and return envelope) with an information pack immediately following first contact.
- Asking clients to complete measures just before the start of every session. If a client completes a measure at the end of sessions, their answers will likely be coloured by a short-term relief effect and having spent an hour with a nice person; if they take the questionnaires home they will often forget to fill them in. Completing a measure at the start of a session may also make a positive contribution to outcome – many clients report that filling in a scale just before a session helps them to collect their thoughts, identify priorities and self-monitor change.
- Asking clients at the start of therapy if they would be willing to complete a mailed or online follow-up questionnaire at some point following the end of therapy. It is likely that many of them will not complete this measure, but at least some follow-up data are better than none. Also, by that stage, a lot of information is available about clients, so it is possible to make detailed comparisons to determine whether those who did complete follow-up scales were representative of the sample as a whole.

Of these strategies, the single most valuable and important one is weekly completion of scales. If a client drops out of therapy, the last questionnaire they completed can be used as a measure of change achieved up to that point.

Attention also needs to be paid to the processing of data. If clients are completing a questionnaire every week, it is costly, time-consuming and unnecessary to enter all of that information onto a database, if in the end all that is being analysed is the difference between start-of-therapy and end-of-therapy scores. It may be sensible to store forms until the end, and just enter the information from the last measure (this issue does not arise if the client is completing scales on a PC, tablet or laptop). However, it would be useful to record each time a measure is completed as a means of checking on the efficiency with which therapists or administrators are collecting data. Therapists and administrators are busy people with many other tasks to fulfil, and thus may need support and encouragement to persevere with data collection. Connell, Grant and Mullin (2006) found major differences across therapy agencies in relation to the proportion of clients who completed practice-based measures.

A further issue that calls for consideration on the part of novice researchers, or counselling and psychotherapy agencies seeking to evaluate the effectiveness of their practice, is the size of the sample of cases being collected. Most agencies who evaluate client outcomes try to collect all the data on all clients. This can be a stretch, and lead to missing and incomplete data, if the admin system is over-burdened. It may make sense to focus a particular effort on all clients who start therapy during a specific time period. It is important to avoid creating a system that would lead readers of eventual research reports to be suspicious that the inclusion criteria being used have subtly or unconsciously produced a situation of cherry-picking the best clients. In most agencies, it is relatively straightforward to collect intake/pre-therapy data on >95 per cent of clients, with gaps in data more likely to occur later in the client treatment trajectory. Possessing intake data on (virtually) all clients makes it possible to demonstrate that a smaller group of intensively studied clients are representative of the client population as a whole. A focus on a specific group of clients or therapists also makes it easier to invest time and effort on collecting high-quality information on client and therapist characteristics.

Allied to the choice of sample is the question of the timing of a practice-based study. An effectiveness study on a new therapy service may well produce different results compared to an analysis of that service two or three years later. There is often an initial burst of enthusiasm for a new service that may then diminish over time. Conversely, there may be early teething problems that get ironed out. The effectiveness of a team of therapists may be quite different at a time of funding cuts and management conflict, compared with a period of funding stability and inspiring and supportive leadership. These are all contextual factors that need to be taken into account when designing a study and reporting/interpreting findings.

Analysing data

In any practice-based study, it is important to provide as much factual information as possible on clients, therapists, attendance rates and social/organisational context. This information is invaluable in making it possible for readers to assess the relevance and generalisability of the study to their own practice setting, and to compare the findings of the study with other comparable projects. It is always useful to take some time to think about potentially relevant information that might be available in agency files rather than having been collected specifically for the purposes of a study. For example, Self et al. (2005) used client postcodes to generate estimates of social deprivation in their analysis of rates of unplanned endings in routine therapy in an NHS clinic. It is usually helpful to use tables to present this information in an accessible manner.

It is also valuable to provide readers with information about the number of clients who approached the agency, the number/percentage of those who underwent assessment, the number/percentage who started therapy, through to the number/percentage who completed end-of-therapy measures, and to provide information, if available, on why the numbers reduced at each stage. For example, some people who underwent assessment may have decided not to proceed with therapy, while in other cases the assessor may have deemed them unsuitable for therapy. At key points in this flow-diagram or chart where there is a major drop-off in numbers (for example 100 clients start therapy and complete CORE, while only 40 complete CORE at the end of therapy), it is usual to carry out an analysis of the representativeness of those who were retained, in relation to age, gender, earlier score, and so on.

There are two basic strategies that are generally employed in practice-based studies for reporting outcome: *effect size* (ES) and *clinical change* – these techniques are described in the following section.

Comparisons between subgroups of clients (for example those who saw a CBT therapist versus those who saw a person-centred therapist) can be accomplished by using the appropriate version of analysis of variance. If a sufficiently large data-set has been assembled, more complex forms of statistical analysis, such as linear modelling, will come into play. Further discussion of issues and options around analysing practice-based data can be found in Barkham, Hardy and Mellor-Clark (2010), Boswell (2020), Leach and Lutz (2010) and Watson et al. (2021).

Box 12.2   Illusory mental health: a challenge for interpretation of practice-based outcome data

Some clients may enter therapy because they have been encouraged to do so by significant others in their life, or because they are weary of the struggle to cope with recurring personal difficulties. Despite the fact of being in the therapy room, they may nevertheless find it hard to acknowledge their vulnerability and distress, because they cope by maintaining an image of being emotionally 'well'. Shedler, Mayman and Manis (1993) described this profile as a form of 'illusory mental health'. It seems likely that around 10 per cent of clients who attend therapy exhibit such a pattern, manifested in low levels of symptoms as recorded on outcome measures such as CORE (Stänicke & McLeod, 2021). This phenomenon represents a considerable challenge for the interpretation of practice-based outcome data: it can be hard to know whether a client who entered counselling with a low symptom score, and then gets worse, has in fact deteriorated, or is instead an illusory mental health case who has been helped. At the present time, there is no agreed strategy for addressing this methodological issue. One approach is to only analyse outcomes for those clients whose intake scores are in the 'clinical' range. The drawback here is that a substantial minority of clients, who have real needs, are thereby being excluded from research.

Statistical techniques for the analysis of practice-based outcome data

Practice-based outcome studies involve the administration of a standardised scale for measuring some aspect of functioning before therapy, at the end of therapy and, if possible, also at follow-up. Historically, analysis of change has relied on the use of a test of statistical significance to determine whether the change that has been observed is so small as to have been due to chance factors, or is in fact statistically meaningful (i.e. the differences found would be very unlikely to be the result of chance variations). However, if the sample of cases is large enough, a statistically significant result can be produced even when the actual amount of change in each case is slight. Statistically significant change is therefore not a particularly informative approach for practice-based research, because statistically significant change does not necessarily translate into meaningful clinical change. In order to provide a way of indicating the degree of change that has been produced by an intervention, an *effect size* (ES) calculation can be made. Effect size is a technique for conveying magnitude of change across a group of subjects or research participants, as a standardised metric (e.g. *small*, *medium* or *large* effects), and is widely employed in counselling and psychotherapy research. Although the actual formula is a bit more complex than this, ES is usually defined as the difference between the means of experimental (treatment) and control (no treatment) groups, divided by the standard deviation of the control group (or the pooled sample of experimental and control groups taken together). As a rough guide, ES reflects the proportion of a standard deviation (SD) represented by the shift that has been observed (Ellis, 2010; Schäfer & Schwarz, 2019). An ES of 0.2 (i.e. a shift of one-fifth of an SD) is considered small, an ES of 0.3 to 0.7 is considered medium and an ES of greater than .8 is considered large. Many therapy studies record large effect sizes.

A further approach to reporting on the effectiveness of a counselling or psychotherapeutic intervention is to estimate the proportion of individual cases that have improved or recovered, using concepts of *clinical significance* and *reliable change*. Clinically significant change is essentially defined as taking place when the client moves from the dysfunctional to the functional range during the course of therapy. However, this change also needs to occur at a magnitude that is sufficient to be credible or meaningful. This is assessed through the calculation of *reliable* change, defined in terms of sufficient number of points on the scale to enable confidence that the change is unlikely to be due to random fluctuations in scores. Estimation of reliable change uses a formula that takes into account the underlying reliability of the measure being used. Cut-off points for 'clinical' and 'non-clinical' scores can be established by administering a scale, in its development phase, to groups of people known to represent clinical and non-clinical populations. The advantage of analysing effectiveness research data in terms of clinically significant change is that it yields information on the proportions of clients who have achieved practice-relevant outcomes: *recovered* (reliable and clinical change recorded for that client), *improved* (reliable change, but not sufficient to move the client into the 'normal' range), *unchanged*, and *deteriorated* (reliable level of increase in symptoms). Although there remains some debate within the research community concerning the most appropriate techniques for determining cut-off points, and estimating reliable and clinical change levels (Atkins et al., 2005; Evans, Margison & Barkham, 1998; Seidel, Miller & Chow, 2014; Wise, 2004), the principle of reporting defining what is clinically significant has been widely accepted within the counselling and psychotherapy research community. Published clinical significance/reliability indicators are available for all widely used therapy measures, including in studies that have used such metrics.

Outcome analysis drawing on concepts of ES and clinical significance has opened up a wealth of possibilities for grassroots practice-based outcome research: comparison of rates of change with outcomes recorded in other studies and clinics; analysis of change in individual cases; the capacity to calculate the relative effectiveness of different therapists. Studies that do not report such data are open to criticism that they may be concealing poor outcome results behind broad-brush statistical significance analyses.

Using benchmarking and comparison groups

Practice-based outcome studies do not usually involve the use of comparison groups, such as clients on waiting lists, or those who have been randomly assigned to different treatment conditions. As a result, one of the limitations of this form of research is that it is open to the criticism that any changes in client problems that have been observed might have occurred in the absence of therapy. This issue can be addressed by comparing the outcomes recorded in a naturalistic pre-post comparison study with some kind of relevant *benchmark*. A benchmark consists of information about improvement rates that have been demonstrated in samples of the general population, or in clients who have received a form of therapy that is generally accepted (on the basis of RCT evidence) to be effective.

One source of benchmarking data comprises studies of the 'natural history' of psychological problems in the general population. Examples of such studies include Fairburn et al. (2000), Jokela et al. (2011) and Wittchen and Fehm (2003). Some practice-based studies (Collins et al., 2012; Swift et al., 2010) have sought to develop their own local estimates of the stability of problems by collecting information from individuals within their community who were not actively seeking help for psychological difficulties. However, although it is useful to be able to refer to research into the natural course of a disorder, this strategy is not without its problems. For example, it is clear that at least some client groups have a tendency to improve over time, for example those who have sought help and been placed in a waiting list. Also, it could reasonably be argued that those who seek counselling and psychotherapy represent a special subgroup of the population – the ones who continue to get worse over the course of their lives are those who passively accept their condition and do not seek help. Finally, being able to demonstrate that people who might have become a bit worse have in fact got a bit better does not take us very far – what most readers of research studies want to know is how the levels of gain that have been recorded compare with gains associated with other forms of therapy. For these reasons, the most convincing approach to benchmarking is to compare naturalistic pre-post data with the findings of tightly controlled RCT studies.

The practice of benchmarking practice-based data against RCT findings is discussed in detail by Minami et al. (2007) and Weersing (2005). Making a credible benchmark comparison involves taking account of a number of factors, such as the demographic characteristics of clients, client diagnoses or presenting problems, the length of therapy and the measures used. It is unlikely that an exact match can be attained in which a community sample of clients seen in routine practice could be precisely mapped on to a sample of clients from an RCT. Nevertheless, it is usually possible to make some kind of comparison that will add to the generalisability of a practice-based study. An example of how this is done can be found in Weersing and Weisz (2002), who compared the outcome statistics obtained in relation to therapy with depressed young people who were seen in their community therapy centre with findings from RCT studies of CBT for depression in similar samples. Another influential example has been a study by Minami et al. (2008).

An alternative form of benchmarking consists of comparisons with other practice-based research. For example, outcome rates are available for very large samples of clients who have completed the CORE-OM (see for example Connell et al., 2007; Mullin et al., 2006). An example of how this type of benchmark data can be used is found in Armstrong (2010), who was able to identify differences between the outcomes obtained by the novice counsellors in his own study and the higher effect sizes reported in practice-based studies of the work of fully trained and experienced counsellors. Mellor-Clark et al. (2013) provide a comprehensive review of benchmarking criteria associated with the use of the CORE outcome evaluation system in Employee Assistance Programmes (EAPs) and workplace counselling services.

Benchmarking studies that represent current good practice in respect of how to handle the issues discussed above include Hogue, Dauber and Henderson (2017), Kodet et al. (2019) and Quirk et al. (2020). Further discussion of the issues associated with the use of therapy benchmarks can be found in Delgadillo, McMillan and Leach (2014).

A key principle of practice-based research is that data collection should involve the least possible disruption to the way therapy is routinely conducted. This means that a random assignment of clients to different treatment conditions is not possible. However, in some circumstances it may be possible to use clients as their own 'controls'. If they have been invited to complete a symptom measure at the time of their first contact with a service, and then perhaps have needed to wait to begin therapy, then the waiting period can be regarded as a 'baseline' that provides information on the stability of their problems prior to commencing therapy. Some practice-based studies have used a comparison between symptom measures administered at the start of this wait period, and then at the first therapy session, to provide a quasi-control group (Balfour and Lanman, 2012; Gibbard and Hanley, 2008).

In conclusion, careful use of benchmarking and comparison groups makes it possible to address, at least in part, the criticism that practice-based naturalistic studies lack meaningfulness because they do not provide any indication of what might have happened to clients if they had not received therapy. At the same time, it is clear that benchmarking is not a straightforward process, and is a methodological strategy that needs to be applied with care and sensitivity.

Exercise 12.3   Power and control in practice-based outcome research

Knowledge is power. Within the practice-based outcome studies that you have read about, or the study that you are planning or carrying out, whose interests are best served by the data that are being collected, the way that these data are analysed and the way that analysis is disseminated? In what ways might the power dynamics of practice-based research influence or compromise the results of such studies? What strategies might be deployed to change these power dynamics?

What can go wrong?

Practice-based outcome research almost certainly comprises the domain of therapy research that is associated with the largest repository of un-analysed (or under-analysed) and un-published data. There are many counselling and psychotherapy services around the world that collect outcome data from clients, and then either publish a limited analysis of those data in annual reports or do nothing with the information that they accumulate. To some extent, this dissemination gap is due to the lack of resources within these organisations, in terms of the skills and knowledge needed to produce research articles. In some settings, there can also be reluctance to open up the work of an organisation to public scrutiny. It is also the case, once routine outcome statistics have been collected, that a therapy organisation quickly realises that the information that is available to them is virtually impossible to interpret because of missing data. It is very frustrating to put a lot of effort in collecting practice-based data, only to discover that end-of-therapy information has only been obtained for 50 per cent of clients. It is not possible to have confidence in effectiveness estimates where information about a significant proportion of clients is lacking. For this reason, when designing a practice-based study, it is essential to implement as many as possible of the attrition-prevention strategies described in an earlier section of this chapter.

An area of weakness in some practice-based outcome studies has been the absence of contextual detail – information about who clients are, who therapists are and what kind of organisation or institution it is that brings them together. The absence of such information undermines the basic philosophical rationale of this type of inquiry which is to analyse actual practices.

Other options: variants on a basic practice-based outcome design

As with any type of research study, there are several ways in which practice-based outcome investigations can be extended and adapted. The most obvious way of extending a practice-based outcome study is to look at the results, consider how the service might be improved, introduce some strategies to enhance service quality and use the next set of outcome data to evaluate whether these new ideas have had a positive effect. There are, however, few clear-cut examples of this type of action research approach. Buckroyd (2003) described a project in which client waiting time was identified as an issue, and the impact of new client contract procedures was assessed using analysis of practice-based data. Richardson and Reid (2006) used practice-based data in an action research cycle to develop a form of CBT that was tailored to the needs of older clients in a particular therapy service. Action research/ quality enhancement studies are relevant and motivating for practitioners, and have the potential to make a real difference to local services.

A further variant on practice-based outcome research is to analyse the outcomes associated with the work of specific therapists within a clinic. An early example of this type of study can be found in a paper by the pioneer of psychoanalysis in Norway, Harald Schjelderup, who published an analysis of the effectiveness of his treatment of clients with psychoneuroses (Schjelderup, 1955). This is in fact a remarkable piece of writing, one that is interesting, illuminating and honest. A similar project was published by the American psychologist Paul Clement, who analysed the characteristics and outcomes of 683 clients seen over a 26-year period of private practice (Clement, 1994). A brief update of results from the next 14 years of practice is provided in Clement (2007).

The routine collection of practice-based data provides a basis for the strategic selection of cases for further scrutiny. If background information about the client and therapist, and weekly monitoring data, are available, then it is possible to conduct a systematic case study on the basis of an in-depth follow-up interview with the client. Cases can be selected on the grounds of theoretical and practical interest; for example, comparison of good-outcome and poor-outcome cases, or closer examination of the experience of members of client groups who are under-represented.

It is possible to use qualitative interviews to supplement findings from quantitative practice-based measures. Client accounts of what has been helpful or unhelpful about a service, or the ways in which they have been able to use counselling to move on in their lives, have the possibility to humanise practice-based data as well as making it possible to explain trends in the quantitative data. An example of how this can be done can be found in a study of a counselling service for individuals with visual impairment, published by Hodge et al. (2012). Some practice-based researchers have sought to incorporate qualitative data in the form of client written responses to open-ended items included in client satisfaction questionnaires distributed at the end of therapy. This strategy has its value, as a means of unearthing new ideas – it functions along the lines of the old-fashioned workplace 'suggestion box'. However, it is hard to evaluate the significance of a suggestion made by (say) one in one hundred clients. The main function of this type of ultra-brief qualitative data is to generate ideas that can then be explored in an action research cycle, or through further analysis of the existing quantitative practice-based data-set.

How to get published

Practice-based outcome studies have been published in many leading journals. As a result, there do not appear to be any barriers to publishing studies of this type as long as these are well designed and adequately reported. The level of methodological sophistication of practice-based outcome studies continues to rise, year on year, in response to the development of strategies such as benchmarking and techniques for estimating clinically significant and reliable change. It is therefore essential, when planning and writing a practice-based study, to look at recent papers. At the present time, there do not exist any guidelines on how practice-based outcome study reports should be structured and what they should include. This means that there remains a considerable degree of variability in the quality of practice-based outcome articles, with some potentially interesting and valuable papers proving rather frustrating to read. It would be useful for both readers and authors if a consensus could be achieved around the reporting of practice-based outcome study investigations. When deciding on a journal outlet for a practice-based outcome paper, it is important to keep in mind that the major international research journals, such as *Journal of Counseling Psychology*, are only likely to publish large-sample studies that explore issues of general theoretical interest (e.g. sudden gains in therapy, the relative effectiveness of different therapists). Practice-based outcome articles that focus on evaluating and discussing the work of a particular therapy agency or clinic are better sent to a national rather than international journal to make these more accessible to colleagues within a specific and local professional community.

Conclusions

Practice-based outcome research provides opportunities for researchers who are interested in making a contribution to enhancing the effectiveness of therapy within the clinic or agency with which they are employed or affiliated. It is a form of research that allows for a wide range of issues and questions to be pursued. In relation to the wider evidence base for therapy practice, it is essential that more well-designed studies of this kind are published.

Suggestions for further reading

Useful sources for developing a deeper understanding of the rationale for practice-based research, the development of this approach and associated critical methodological issues include:

Barkham, M., Hardy, G. E., & Mellor-Clark, J. (eds) (2010). *Developing and Delivering Practice-based Evidence: A Guide for the Psychological Therapies*. Chichester: Wiley-Blackwell.

Boswell, J. F. (2020). Monitoring processes and outcomes in routine clinical practice: a promising approach to plugging the holes of the practice-based evidence colander. *Psychotherapy Research*, 30(7), 829–842.

Duncan, C. and McInnes, B. (2020). Quantitative research with outcome measures. In S. Bager-Charleson & A. McBeath (eds), *Enjoying Research in Counselling and Psychotherapy Qualitative, Quantitative and Mixed Methods Research* (pp. 195–212). London: Palgrave Macmillan.

Green, D. and Latchford, G. (2012). *Maximising the Benefits of Psychotherapy: A Practice-based Evidence Approach*. Oxford: Wiley-Blackwell.

Holmqvist, R., Philips, B., & Barkham, M. (2015). Developing practice-based evidence: benefits, challenges, and tensions. *Psychotherapy Research*, 25(1), 20–31.

Online resources

The online resource site (https://study.sagepub.com/doingresearch4e) includes learning activities based on examples of practice-based research in a range of settings.

13

Carrying Out a Systematic Case Study

Introduction

The practice of counselling and psychotherapy involves working with cases. A case can be understood as comprising the entirety of an episode of therapy, from first contact with a service through to follow-up. From the earliest writings of Freud, Jung and their colleagues, case study knowledge has played a central role in the development of therapy theory, practice and training. The case study method provides an opportunity to explore the complex interactions between different aspects of the process of therapy, investigate the ways in which these processes unfold over time, and examine the links between specific processes and events in therapy and the eventual outcome of treatment. Case study research also makes it possible to consider the influence of contextual factors, such as the setting within which therapy takes place and the cultural and social worlds of client and therapist. Case studies tend to be viewed by practitioners as meaningful and interesting, and as a result this kind of research can make an important contribution to bridging the gap between research and practice.

What is a systematic case study?

Traditionally, within the counselling and psychotherapy literature, case studies were written by the therapist in the case, based solely on their personal notes and reflections. While this type of *clinical case study* has certainly produced a wealth of fascinating and informative case examples, this type of report struggles to achieve the standards of methodological rigour that have been established in other areas of therapy research. For example, it is highly likely that therapists are selective about what they write in their notes or recall about a case, and that they would have a tendency to interpret the process of a case in line with their pre-existing theoretical assumptions. As a result, there has emerged a general agreement within the field that it is not possible to regard traditional clinical case studies as reliable and valid forms of research-based evidence.

The concept of a *systematic case study* refers to single-case investigations that draw on a range of methodological strategies that seek to enhance rigour and credibility within this form of inquiry. Systematic case study research is based on three key methodological principles:

- a 'rich case record' (Elliott, 2002) is compiled, incorporating as many sources of information as possible on the case, for example from questionnaires, interviews, session transcripts and therapist notes. This approach allows for triangulation of themes across different types of information;
- the information collected on the case is analysed by a group or team of researchers, following a clearly explained set of procedures. This methodological strategy serves to overcome the possibility that the results of the case study will merely reflect the pre-existing theoretical ideas or beliefs of the therapist;
- the case is written up in accordance with a structure and guidelines that ensure the reader is fully informed about all relevant aspects of the treatment, and how the data were collected and analysed. This strategy is designed to prevent a selective reporting of findings.

The extent to which each of these principles is reflected in a particular case study will depend on the aims of the project, and what is possible in a specific situation. The type of information that has been used in many recent systematic case study reports is well within the scope of most practitioners and students to collect. This type of case analysis can be employed to explore a wide spectrum of research questions within the field of counselling and psychotherapy.

Exercise 13.1 Using case study methods to explore your research question

Reflect on how you might investigate your research question by using each of the case study approaches introduced in this chapter. What would the study look like? What would be the advantages and limitations of different case study designs? What might be the unique insights yielded by each approach?

Why would I want to do this kind of research?

Systematic case study research is an attractive option for novice researchers. It is possible to integrate this type of inquiry into routine practice. Analysing rich case data represents a good way of learning about the strengths and limitations of qualitative and quantitative methodologies. Case study research is ethically sensitive, because of the higher risk of disclosing the identity of participants, and so offers a good grounding in the handling of ethical issues. Working with a group of colleagues to analyse case data is generally an enjoyable and stimulating experience. Finally, the discipline of looking closely at what happens in an individual case inevitably leads to new understandings around the nature of the therapy process, and the links between theory and practice.

Box 13.1 Ghent case study archive

An important resource for case study researchers is the Single Case Archive established at the University of Ghent as a searchable database of all published psychotherapy case studies (https://singlecasearchive.com). Registering as a user allows access to full-text copies of articles. The website also carries articles about case study methodology.

What kind of skills and support would I need?

Carrying out the kind of study described in this chapter requires familiarity with both qualitative and quantitative methods. However, case study research does not usually generate a sufficient volume of quantitative data to require analysis using a package such as SPSS. It is necessary to be able to draw on colleagues at various points in the process of conducting a systematic case study. For example, if the focus of the case study is your own work with a client, it is best for any follow-up interview(s) with that client to be carried out by another person. It is also necessary to be able to call on the inputs of other people during the phase of analysing data, and to be able to draw on experienced and informed supervision around ethical issues. It is also useful to receive research supervision from someone who believes in the contribution of case-based methodology and has experience in using this approach.

Basic principles of systematic case-based inquiry

As with any form of research, it is necessary to find one's way into the appropriate mind-set. This is particularly important in relation to case study research, because it is probable that the researcher will have been exposed to various types of scepticism about the value of this approach. There still exist experienced and highly regarded researchers in counselling/psychotherapy and allied disciplines who believe that case study research does not comprise a valid form of inquiry, and at best acts as a source for illustrative examples and teaching materials. Developing an informed grasp of the principles and logic of systematic case-based inquiry is essential not only to do work, but to be able to defend and justify one's work to colleagues. Key reading in relation to this task is a classic, widely read paper by Flyvbjerg (2006) that provides a succinct and powerful rationale for the value of single case research.

Thinking like a case study researcher

To carry out a good piece of case study research it is necessary to be clear about the potential role of case study inquiry within the overall range of methodologies that are currently available to therapy researchers. It is not sensible to operate on the assumption that case study research can answer every question and is all that we need to be doing. Instead, it is necessary to be able to understand the strengths and also the limitations of this approach. Case study research is particularly well suited to describing and analysing how therapy processes and interventions actually operate in practice, understanding how these processes unfold over time and taking account of how what happens in therapy is shaped by the context within which it takes place. Case studies also make it possible to conduct intensive initial analyses of phenomena, which can function as a platform for further studies with large samples. Case study inquiry is also a valuable means of developing and refining theories. On the other hand, case study research is not good at estimating the general effectiveness of therapy over a large sample of clients. There are also many research questions that address the relationship between a small number of factors/variables ('To what extent does early therapeutic alliance predict outcome?', 'How do clients respond to different types of therapist self-disclosure?') that are much easier to investigate by aggregating data across a large sample. In addition, there are many research questions that do not require data about a whole case, and can be explored perfectly well by collecting data at one point in time. The logic of case-based inquiry is explained in more detail by Fishman (1999), Flyvbjerg (2001, 2006) and McLeod (2010).

Types of question that can be addressed using case study methodology

There are basically four different types of research question that can be investigated using case study methods: pragmatic, narrative, outcome-oriented and theory-building. These approaches can be placed along a dimension of methodological complexity. Pragmatic case studies are associated with relatively limited data collection and analysis requirements, while outcome and theory-building case studies generally call for extensive pre-planning around data collection and analysis. Narrative case studies lie between these extremes.

Pragmatic case studies

A pragmatic case study represents an invaluable means of contributing to professional knowledge (Chapter 11): the act of sharing practice-based understanding and experience with colleagues. The key purpose of this kind of study is to document how therapy has been conducted with a particular client, in a way that will support the learning of other members of the professional community. A pragmatic case study addresses questions such as: 'What strategies and methods did the therapist use in this case?'; 'How were therapeutic methods adapted and implemented this case?'; 'Which therapeutic strategies and interventions made a positive contribution to outcome, and which ones were harmful or hindering?' The primary goal of a pragmatic case study is to generate a detailed representation of how a specific therapy approach has been deployed with a specific client. A pragmatic case study is similar in many respects to the kind of traditional case report written by a therapist, for example in its reliance on information from therapist notes. However, pragmatic case study methodology, as defined by Fishman (1999, 2017), goes beyond traditional case studies, in demanding a higher level of evidence (e.g. transcripts or verbatim notes of sessions, and data from symptom measures) and a more rigorous standard of reporting and reviewing. A large number of pragmatic case studies have been published in the online open access journal *Pragmatic Case Studies in Psychotherapy* and in the *Clinical Case Studies* journal. Pragmatic case studies are also published in a range of other therapy journals – see, for example, Budge (2015), Challenor (2017) and Sarantakis (2020). As well as documenting what different types of therapy look like in practice, pragmatic case studies can also be used to explore theoretical issues raised in cases that do not conform to the change process that would be expected by adhering to a predetermined theory or protocol. An example of this kind of extended use of pragmatic case study design is Kramer (2009), that showed how an established model of CBT for PTSD was individualised to accommodate the preferences of the client. Another valuable extension of pragmatic case study methodology has been its use in describing how therapy is carried out in different cultural settings – see, for example, Murase (2015).

Narrative case studies

Narrative case studies aim to tell the story of the case, from the perspective of the client or therapist (or both). These case studies explore questions such as: 'What was it like to be the client or therapist in this case?'; 'What was the meaning of this therapeutic encounter?' A narrative case study represents the application of qualitative methods in the context of case study inquiry. Generally, a narrative case study is based on interviews with the client and/or therapist that are then analysed using a standard method of phenomenological or thematic analysis. Examples of narrative case studies based on client or therapist interviews include Conti et al. (2017), Gundel, Bartholomew and Scheel (2020), Tilden et al. (2005), Quinn, Schofield and Middleton (2012) and Wendt and Gone (2016). Some narrative case studies have also been co-written by the therapist and client together (Blunden, 2020; Etherington 2000). In a narrative case study, careful attention to the experiences of therapy participants has the potential to yield important new insights that can enrich our appreciation of the process and meaning of therapy. The narrative case study approach is highly flexible, in allowing case data to be collected retrospectively, rather than needing to be planned and negotiated in advance.

Outcome-oriented case studies

Outcome-oriented case study research is concerned with one central question: 'How effective has therapy been in this case?' This type of research is particularly relevant in relation to establishing the potential effectiveness of a new form of therapy, an established approach applied to a new population, or an innovative technique incorporated as an adjunct to an existing approach. In such situations, there may be ethical and practical barriers to conducting a large-scale study. This kind of case study also supports and encourages innovation, by making it possible to evaluate a new technique fairly rapidly. There are basically two types of single case design that have been developed to undertake outcome-oriented research. The first is the tradition of 'n = 1' single case design that has its origins in behavioural psychology and CBT. The key feature of such a study is the application of repeated measures (e.g. the client rating their symptom level or occurrence of a behavioural problem every week or even every day), leading to a time series analysis. An excellent introduction to this approach is available in Morley (2017). Examples of n = 1 studies that illustrate how this approach can be used to explore different aspects of outcome in a range of clinical settings are Banting and Lloyd (2017), Ellett (2013), Halldorsson and Salkovskis (2017) and Jones and Hurrell (2019). This kind of case study project is particularly relevant to situations in which clients are already completing change measures on a routine basis. Typically, in addition to time-series analysis of quantitative case data, such studies also incorporate a narrative account of what happened in therapy.

While N = 1 studies are well suited to single-case investigations where a specific tangible outcome or therapy goal can be identified in advance, it is not appropriate for case studies where goals and outcomes are more diffuse. The Hermeneutic Single Case Efficacy Design (HSCED; Elliott, 2002) is an approach to case-based outcome analysis that has been developed to make it possible to collect information from multiple outcome sources, including client and therapist accounts and qualitative techniques as well as quantitative measures. The key features of an HSCED study are: (i) collecting multiple sources of data; (ii) interview with the client (at end of therapy or after a certain number of sessions, and/or at follow-up) to enable the client perspective to be taken into account; and (iii) a 'quasi-judicial' approach to data analysis. This form of analysis includes three main steps. First, all of the data collected on the case is independently interpreted from both an 'affirmative' stance (constructing an argument that the client has significantly improved, and that observed changes can be attributed to therapy) and a 'sceptic' stance (constructing an argument that either the client has not improved, or that any observed positive changes can be attributed to factors other than therapy). Second, there is a dialogue between affirmative and sceptic interpretations. Third, a panel of external judges decide which interpretation is more credible.

Although the HSCED process is demanding for the researcher, it tends to be a rewarding and interesting learning experience, particularly if competing teams of judges are employed. Classic examples of HSCED studies are Elliott et al. (2009), Stephen, Elliott and Macleod (2011) and Thurston, Thurston and McLeod (2012). As well as answering the question 'Did this case demonstrate a good outcome?', the in-depth case analysis that is required in this type of study also makes it possible to generate new theoretical insights. For example, the Elliott et al. (2009) 'case of George' has stimulated further research into the phenomenon of paradoxical outcome (different outcome estimates produced by different data sources; Stänicke & McLeod, 2021). A series of HSCED case studies on the outcomes of transactional analysis psychotherapy for depression (Widdowson, 2012) supported the development of a new theoretical model (Widdowson, 2014) and treatment manual (Widdowson, 2015). The HSCED approach to systematic outcome-oriented single case research has been widely applied, and has generated a second-generation critical literature that offers suggestions for refining this methodology (Benelli et al., 2015; Wall et al., 2017).

Theory-building case studies

Theory-building case study research seeks to explore questions such as: 'How can the process of therapy in this case be understood in theoretical terms?' In a theory-oriented case study, data from a single case are used to test and refine an existing theoretical model or build a new theoretical framework. Case methods have an important part to play in theory construction because a single, or small number, of observations can refute a theory or require it to be modified. In addition, therapy theories tend to consist of complex sets of concepts and if–then statements that refer to interacting process that unfold over the course of time in single cases. Such theories can only be tested and refined in the context of observations from whole cases, rather than slivers of data abstracted from cases.

In the field of therapy research, the principles of theory-building case study research have been articulated by Stiles (2007). The process begins with some kind of preliminary theoretical statement. Case data are then collected that represent potential points of contact between the theory and the case. For example, if the aim is to use a case analysis to arrive at a better understanding of the role of case formulation, the researcher needs to make sure that as much information as possible about formulation episodes can be collected (e.g. client and therapist reflections on what happened, ratings of helpfulness, transcripts of relevant segments of client-therapist interaction). The researcher (or, more usually, a team of researchers) then analyses the case in terms of the extent to which observations correspond to theoretical predictions. It is usually then necessary to adjust the theory in the light of discoveries associated with observations that are not consistent with the theory.

A substantial programme of systematic theory-building research has been carried out by Bill Stiles and his colleagues, around the development of the assimilation model of therapeutic change (Stiles, 2011). Examples of theory-building research conducted by this group are Gray and Stiles (2011) and Meystre et al. (2014). Another notable theory-building case series consists of three studies on therapist immediacy (Hill et al., 2008; Kasper, Hill & Kivlighan, 2008; Mayotte-Blum et al. 2012). An example of a theory-building case study that sought to develop a model of how therapy might be successful with clients who are highly suicidal and distrustful of therapists, triggered by observing such a case within a larger study, is Halvorsen et al. (2016). A case study by Avdi and Seikkula (2019) makes a distinctive theoretical contribution in opening up important new directions for research by showing how physiological and non-verbal interaction data can be combined with verbal sources of information.

It is important to realise that pragmatic, narrative, outcome-oriented and theory-building case designs do not represent entirely separate categories. It is possible to combine two questions or aims within one case study. For example, it is relatively straightforward to add a theory-building dimension to an outcome-oriented, pragmatic or narrative case study, by using the discussion section of the paper to explore theoretical implications. However, it is still essential to be clear about what constitutes the primary goal of the study, and which question is of secondary importance.

Also, when writing up a case study, it is vital to be clear about the aims of the investigation, so that readers understand what the researcher was trying to achieve.

Box 13.2 Case studies within RCTs

Case studies can contribute to the creation of practice-relevant knowledge by complementing and supplementing large-scale randomised clinical trials (RCTs) through providing in-depth analysis of theoretically interesting cases. In addition, case studies can provide clinical, contextual and cultural detail that is hard to accommodate within the kind of statistical analysis typical of RCTs. The rationale for incorporating case studies into RCTs, along with several examples of this approach, can be found in Fishman et al. (2017). Additional examples include an analysis of Dahl et al. (2017) of contrasting good- and poor-outcome cases from an RCT on transference-informed therapy, and the detailed presentation by Lunn, Daniel and Poulsen (2016) of a good-outcome case from a study of psychotherapy for bulimia, selected from the arm of the study that recorded slightly less satisfactory results.

Ethical rigour

Ethical issues represent a major barrier to case study research. In an article reporting a research study that has collected quantitative data on 100 clients, it is virtually impossible to imagine any scenario in which the identity of any individual participant could be disclosed. By contrast, in a detailed report on a single case there are many ways in which the identity of the client and therapist might become apparent, particularly to people who already know them, such as colleagues and family members. There are also significant ethical issues associated with the experience of reading about one's own therapy, or reading about what one's own therapist truly thought and felt about you. It can be coercive to ask a client during therapy, or at the end of therapy, to give permission for their experiences to be used in a case study. There are also ethical risks around the possibility that a therapist might act differently if he or she believes that his or her work is going to be analysed in detail by a team of researchers.

These ethical issues act as a barrier to case study research because they can lead gatekeepers such as agency managers to refuse permission to collect case study data, and make clients reluctant to agree to take part in such a study. A further barrier consists of the possibility that the client might withdraw permission to use the data at a late stage. Finally, some case study researchers can become paralysed by their moral responsibility towards the client or therapist, and avoid publishing their work.

There are a number of ethical procedures that can be applied to overcome these issues:

- an informed consent procedure that begins before the client ever meets the therapist;
- the therapist is not involved in negotiations around consent;

- use of an independent advocate to represent the interests of the client;
- process consent, in which agreement is checked at each stage, up to the point of final publication;
- the client being able to read and approve what is written about them;
- disguising any identifying information.

Further discussion of these procedures can be found in McLeod (2010).

While recognising and being vigilant about these ethical issues, it is also important to acknowledge that some clients will welcome the opportunity to tell their story and will find it personally helpful and meaningful to take part in a case study project. Case study research has the potential to be ethically benign. However, it also has the potential to be an upsetting and unhelpful experience for some participants.

Choosing a case

There is a lot of work involved in collecting, analysing and writing up case study material, and there is no one in the therapy world who has ever published more than a handful of cases. It is therefore necessary to choose cases for analysis in a purposeful manner. There are two broad case-selection strategies that can be used:

- *Typical cases* are of interest because they represent what 'usually' happens in a particular type of therapy. Some way of defining 'typicality' needs to be identified. For example, in a counselling agency where outcome data are collected on all clients, it may be possible to look at the whole range of clients and find a specific case that reflects the average severity score at intake and end of therapy, and has received the average number of clients. In many other research situations, there may be no evidence-based criteria that can be used to establish typicality. Sometimes the only option will be to start with the first client who agrees to take part in the project, and assume that what is observed in the therapy received by this person represents a reasonable approximation of typicality.
- *Theoretically interesting cases* are of interest because they allow the researcher to focus attention on some aspect of therapy that is of particular relevance to their research question. For example, good-outcome cases provide opportunities to identify what happened when a specific form of therapy worked well. Poor-outcome cases create opportunities for understanding how a form of therapy might be improved. Unusual, surprising or anomalous cases also allow a researcher to test existing theories, and come up with new ideas. An important subtype of theoretically interesting cases consists of cases in which a new approach to therapy is tried, or an established approach is used for the first time with a new client group.

Selecting cases for intensive case study research is not an exact science. For example, any particular case is likely to be typical in some respects and not typical in others. Inviting clients and therapists to take part in a case study before therapy has commenced means that it is not possible to know whether a case will end up with a good or poor outcome. The process of analysing a case may reveal aspects that were not apparent at the point when the case was initially selected for study. In practice, the issue of case selection is often handled by therapy researchers by collecting data on more cases than they will in the end be able to analyse. Many published therapy case studies are taken from the work of therapy agencies, research projects or individual practitioners, in which case data are collected on several cases with the choice being made at a later stage around which case or cases will be chosen for in-depth analysis. Other case studies are based on projects in which a student or practitioner has made a commitment to collect data on a limited series of cases.

In the end, it may be useful to keep in mind that any therapy case is potentially interesting because every person is interesting and every person's story is worth hearing. However, from a research point of view, when the aim is to use intensive single-case analysis to investigate a specific question, some cases may be more interesting than others.

Collecting data that enable connections to be made across cases

One of the most important characteristics of contemporary systematic case study research is the use of strategies to facilitate connections to be made between a specific case and the wider clinical population and world of practice. It is not logically possible to generalise from a single case. However, by the judicious recording and reporting of relevant information on a case, it is possible to make comparisons between that single case and other cases, or between a single case and findings from large-scale studies.

There are two main strategies that can be used to construct an argument around the general relevance of findings from a single case. The first is to collect and report standardised factual data that will allow the case to be positioned alongside other cases. This type of information can include demographic and biographical data on the client, such as age, gender, marital status, income, education, occupation, ethnicity, previous use of therapy, and previous/current use of medication. It can also include clinical case management data, such as number of sessions, number and occurrence of missed sessions, payment status, attributes and training of the therapist, and the therapy interventions that were used. A crucial domain of information comprises scores on standard process and outcome measures, and diagnostic or other ways of categorising the client. Each of these pieces of information provides the reader with a point of connection with cases they have come across in their own practice, case studies they may have read, and the findings from other types of study.

A further strategy is to use theory as a means of building conceptual bridges between a specific case study and other cases and studies. For example, a researcher might be interested in what happens when a therapist makes use of a particular intervention or technique. Intensive analysis of the use of that intervention in a single case can be used to generate a model (or mini-theory) of how that technique was deployed by that therapist with that particular client. This model can then be tested by looking at whether it is confirmed in a subsequent case or in a different type of study such as interviews with clients who have received that intervention. Alternatively, there may be pre-existing studies that have generated guidelines for the use of that intervention. In such a scenario, the findings from the case study can be used to confirm the validity of these guidelines, or perhaps to contribute to the production of a more differentiated protocol. In any of these situations, some form of conceptualisation or model can be used to make connections between a single case and other sources of knowledge on a topic.

These forms of case study generalisation require advance planning. It is necessary to anticipate, at the planning stage of a study, possible points of connection that might be relevant at the analysis and write-up stage, to enable appropriate data to be collected from the start.

Exercise 13.2   Imagining being the client

Imagine what it might be like to be a client in a case study investigation. This could either be a case study project that you are conducting yourself, or a published study that you have read about. What would worry you about taking part? What would excite you? In what ways might these meanings shape the course of therapy, and/or the type and quality of information that you contributed to the study?

Systematic interpretation of rich case data

Analysing case study data does not consist of the application of pre-determined procedures. Analysing data that have been collected using a questionnaire such as the Beck Depression Inventory means following a series of steps: adding up the score, comparing the score against published norms, and so on. The material collected in a systematic case study is fundamentally different from this, in that it comprises a combination of qualitative and quantitative data, gathered from a range of sources. Analysing case study data needs to be understood as an advanced pattern-recognition and hypothesis-testing task. Ultimately, case study data analysis is a process of *interpretation*, of finding meaning within a complex text.

In terms of the kind of approach that has been adopted by case study researchers in recent years, interpretation of case study data makes use of two analytic processes that occur within a cycle of inquiry. One aspect of this cycle of inquiry involves an individual attempt to make sense of the data. The other aspect involves sharing and comparing interpretations with other members of a team. This activity then feeds into a further turn of the cycle of inquiry, as each individual member of the team returns to the data and looks at these again, taking into account the ideas of colleagues.

At the level of the individual who is attempting to make sense of complex case study data, there are a number of strategies that can be helpful:

- reading through the material slowly, and noting down any impressions and personal responses that arise;
- summarising the content (the topics and issues explored) within each session – the topic analysis approach (Reichelt, Skjerve & McLeod, 2018; Skjerve, Reichelt & McLeod, 2016) represents one way of doing this;
- identifying stages and significant turning points or events within the case (sometimes the turning points will be immediately apparent in quantitative data – for instance, if the client's symptom score suddenly shifts between two sessions);
- tracking a particular theme or process through the whole case (for instance, there may be recurring metaphors and images that the client uses, or there may be homework assignments that shift from one therapeutic task to the next);
- looking for areas of convergence and divergence across various data sources;
- checking that all of the information on the case has been taken into consideration.

These strategies provide ways of 'entering' the case and beginning to make sense of what it has to say. As with any interpretive activity, the researcher needs to possess some kind of conceptualisation or model of what they are looking for. At the same time, however, these ideas need to be held lightly, to allow new meaning to emerge and new learning to occur. Once patterns begin to emerge, it is important to test these out by looking for counter-examples within the data and establishing the extent to which information from different sources triangulates to provide the same conclusion.

At the level of a team of researchers working together, it is essential to establish a group culture that allows open dialogue rather than this being dominated by one or two powerful members. In practice, this is accomplished either by assembling a group of colleagues who know each other well enough to be honest with each other, or by adopting a structured way of working together. At the present time, there are three alternative models of group structure that have been adopted by teams of case study researchers:

1. The *quasi-judicial model* treats the data as if these were evidence in a court case, and divides the research team into subgroups who are given the task of developing and presenting competing interpretations of the case material. In principle, this strategy mirrors the use of 'prosecution' and 'defence' lawyers in a court case. In an outcome-oriented case study, for example, there may be an 'affirmative' team that argues the client has benefitted from therapy, and a 'sceptic' team that argues the opposite, that the case represents a poor outcome. The most fully developed version of this kind of quasi-judicial case analysis can be found in the *Hermeneutic Single Case Efficacy Design* (HSCED) approach that was devised by Elliott (2002) and which has been applied in many case study investigations. Other forms of quasi-judicial case-based inquiry are described in a special issue of the online journal *Pragmatic Case Studies in Psychotherapy* (volume 7, module 1, 2011).
2. The widely used team-based qualitative research methodology known as *Consensual Qualitative Research* (CQR) has been adapted for use in case study research by Jackson, Chui and Hill (2012). This approach involves dividing up the task of data analysis between members of a research group, whose work is then audited by an external expert.

3. The *Ward method* (Schielke et al., 2009, 2014) is a structured form of group decision-making and problem solving, which forces each member of the group to listen closely to the ideas of other members in preparation for incorporating these ideas into their own analysis of the data. The Ward method is based on an assumption that the ideas of the group will converge within three or four such cycles of co-consultation. An example of how the Ward method can be used in case study research can be found in Smith et al. (2014).

These group-centred approaches to data analysis and interpretation are informed by a belief that each member of a group will be able to contribute valuable ideas and insights, but that the ideas of any particular individual in the group are likely to be incomplete or biased in some fashion. The benefits of working together in a group are that each member is motivated to do the best they can, and will be able to point out the shortcomings of at least some of the ideas generated by other members.

In some systematic case study articles, limitations of space will mean that the individual and group-based analytic procedures that have been followed may not be explained in detail (or may not be explained at all). However, the majority of recent case study articles have made use of the kind of analytic strategies that are outlined above.

Practical aspects of carrying out a systematic case study

The planning process for a piece of case study research needs to take account of the time that will elapse while therapy is ongoing. In some situations, for example in a service that only offers time-limited therapy, it will be possible to anticipate how long this will be. In other situations the length of therapy may be indeterminate. As with any other form of research, it is necessary to identify a set of research aims and questions at the outset.

An absolutely crucial aspect of case study planning is to construct a research situation in which client, therapist and organisation feel comfortable about taking part, and are able to withdraw consent at any stage. By contrast, a research situation in which there is pressure on participants to take part, or to continue to take part, is both ethically unsound and likely to result in data that lack meaningfulness. In practice, one of the ways in which a congenial research relationship can be established is to collect data on many more cases than will ever be analysed. In that kind of scenario, it will not be a problem if a client decides to withdraw their involvement, even at the last moment. Many of the systematic case studies that have been published in recent years have emerged from projects in which all clients starting therapy at an agency are invited to contribute data. Then, at a later point, it is possible to select cases for detailed analysis based on a combination of client willingness to continue their involvement, and an informed judgement around the theoretical or practical value of the case as a piece of research.

Building this kind of climate of care involves paying a lot of attention to the process of explaining and receiving informed ethical consent. For example, if possible, clients should be asked about their 'in-principle' willingness to take part in a case study before they ever meet their therapist. Ideally, the therapist should not be involved in doing the asking at any stage, or only minimally involved, to avoid placing pressure on the client. A client needs to know that they can withdraw consent at any point, without any cost to them. All of this needs to be explained clearly, both verbally and in writing.

Usually, a systematic case study will be built around the collection of multiple sources of data, such as:

- a pre-therapy interview (or assessment notes);
- outcome measures administered on a regular basis;
- information about the process of therapy, such as client descriptions of significant events, or completion of an alliance scale;
- therapist notes;
- session recordings;
- end of therapy or the follow-up interview.

In many counselling and psychotherapy centres and clinics, much of this information will be collected on a routine basis, and it may be possible to carry out a systematic case study on virtually any client.

Information about instruments and measures that can be used to collect case data can be found in Chapter 9. It can also be helpful to look at the types of data that have been used in published case studies. One of the key choice-points, in case study research, regards the decision of whether or not to record sessions, and then transcribe some or all of these sessions. Transcribing is very time-consuming, but has the potential to yield research insights that are not accessible using other techniques. A useful compromise would be to transcribe selected sessions. For example, the first session is always interesting. The client or therapist may be able to identify certain sessions that were turning-points, and are worth looking at more closely.

It is not sensible for the researcher to analyse data while these are coming in, to avoid any temptation to influence the process of therapy. An exception to this rule occurs when the therapist is the main researcher, or a member of the research team, and some of the data are being used within therapy to track client progress. However, it is important for someone to scan or review the data as these are collected, in case the client is using questionnaires to try to communicate an intention to self-harm or engage in other forms of risky conduct.

Once the data are in, it will be helpful to gather these up in a 'case book' that can then be used as the definitive data-set for the ensuing case analysis. The process of preparing the case book involves carrying out an initial screen of the data to alter identities and change names.

It will then be necessary to assemble a research team to analyse the data, and perhaps also be involved in writing parts of the final report or article. Various models for how such a case study analysis team can be structured were introduced earlier in the chapter. It is usually a good idea if the therapist is included in the team, and there is at least one other member of the team who has actually met the client face to face (for example, through conducting an end of therapy or follow-up interview). Although there are many examples of good-quality case studies that have not made direct use of the therapist in the analysis stage, the involvement of the therapist has the potential to add depth to the study.

The final stage of a case study project is to write the article. It can be helpful if the client is willing to read a draft of the analysis and offer comments. Sometimes a client can clarify aspects of the case that were hard for outsider members of the research team to understand. Also, receiving the approval of the client can give a research team a valuable morale boost at a point when their energy for the project may be flagging. Being able to report in a paper that the client basically agreed with the analysis of the case can make the whole study more plausible to readers. However, it is always important to be mindful of the potential impact on the client of reading about their own therapy. Some clients will not want to read a draft case report.

The experience of working in a small research team to plan, collect and analyse case study data tends to be enjoyable and rewarding for participants, in terms of learning about themselves, learning about therapy and forming supportive relationships with colleagues. This kind of research can offer practitioners and students a satisfying blend of research participation and professional development.

Box 13.3   The Client Change Interview

One of the limitations of many published therapy case studies is that they provide very little information on what the client thought about the therapy. The Client Change Interview (CCI), initially developed by Robert Elliott for use in HSCED research, offers a valuable means of collecting information on the client's experience (Rodgers & Elliott, 2015). The CCI can be administered after a set number of sessions, after therapy has been completed, or at follow-up. Usually, the CCI interview will be conducted by someone other than the therapist. Clients generally report that participating in a change interview is meaningful to them, and allows them to reflect on and consolidate their learning from therapy. The CCI is a structured interview that allows the client to tell the story of their involvement in therapy. It starts with general questions such as 'What has therapy been like for you?' 'How has it felt to be in therapy?' and 'How are you doing now in general?' The interview then gradually focuses in on specific changes (helpful and unhelpful) that the informant has experienced. Important features of the interview include detailed probing around attributions for change (whether as a result of therapy or due to other life events), how likely the change would have been in the absence of therapy, how likely it is to persist. The client is encouraged to talk about disappointing and unhelpful aspects of therapy, as well as positive gains. Links to instructions for using the CCI are available in the online resource site to this book. Examples of how the CCI is used in case study research can be found in all HSCED studies, in some instances including actual interview transcripts (e.g. Elliott et al., 2009). The CCI can also be adapted to include additional questions that are specific to the aims of a particular study (Lunn, Daniel & Poulsen (2016) and as an interview schedule in qualitative studies with several participants (Poulsen, Lunn & Sandros, 2010).

What can go wrong?

There are a few things that can go wrong with case study projects. One of the pitfalls is to lack clarity about the question that is being asked, or about what it is that was found. This can lead to a case report that consists of a somewhat shapeless accumulation of descriptive information about what happened, which leaves the reader with the task of making some sense of it all. Another reason why some case studies never get completed is that the client withdraws, or there are unresolved dilemmas around ethical issues that mean the researcher is uncertain about their right to publish.

Variants

In some research situations it will be relevant, and indeed possible, to carry out a series of case studies (see, for example, Widdowson, 2012). This strategy has the advantage of making this type of research less ethically sensitive – within a series of five or six cases, each individual client will be less identifiable. Another strategy, when there are multiple cases, is to compare good-outcome and poor-outcome cases, as a means of looking at the elements of therapy that seem to contribute to success and failure. It is also possible to conduct meta-analyses of sets of case studies (Krivzov et al., 2021). These variants are discussed in more detail in McLeod (2010) and McLeod (2013b).

How to get published

Most therapy research journals are open to publishing systematic case study articles. There are two journals that specialise in case study reports: *Clinical Case Studies* and *Pragmatic Case Studies in Psychotherapy*. It is important to check out the preferred case study format used by a target journal, as a guide to structuring any article that might be submitted to them.

Suggestions for further reading

Essential reading for anyone interested in case study research is Flyvbjerg, B. (2006). Five misunderstandings about case-study research. *Qualitative Inquiry*, 12, 219–245.

Further exploration of the topics discussed in the present chapter are available in McLeod, J. (2010). *Case Study Research in Counselling and Psychotherapy*. London: Sage.

The online journal *Pragmatic Case Studies in Psychotherapy* publishes interesting cases with commentaries, and also cutting-edge articles on case study methodology.

Online resources

The online resource site includes learning tasks and supplementary reading on issues in case study methodology: https://study.sagepub.com/doingresearch4e.

14

Using Personal Experience as a Basis for Research

Autoethnography

Introduction

Within the field of research in counselling and psychotherapy, there has been a growing appreciation in recent years of the notion that the personal experience of the researcher represents a potentially distinctive and valuable source of evidence. Within this general approach to inquiry, it is possible to identify a number of different sub-traditions. There have been many useful contributions to knowledge that have consisted of therapists and clients merely writing about their own lives, or their experience of specific events, without positioning their work within a specific methodological tradition. Historically, the analysis of subjective experience as a source of psychological data, in the form of *introspection*, was the basis for early research into processes of memory and learning. In the 1970s a whole range of new genres of personal experience research began to emerge: mindful inquiry, reflexive action research, transpersonal research, dialogal research, heuristic inquiry and narrative inquiry. These approaches to the use of subjectivity and personal experience for scientific purposes have been largely subsumed into a wide-ranging methodological perspective known as *autoethnography*. The present chapter provides an introduction to carrying out an autoethnographic research study, as well as exploring the use of other types of personal experience writing.

What is an autoethnographic study?

Personal experience research involves the researcher (or each member of a group of researchers) making a systematic effort to document, analyse and communicate their own personal or subjective experience of a topic or phenomenon. The main rationale for this approach is that an individual who is undertaking research of this kind will be better able to produce an account that is more authentic and richly described than anything that would emerge from interviews, questionnaires or other long-established data collection strategies. In addition, a personal experience study may be carried out in situations in which data would otherwise be hard to collect.

The concept of *autoethnography* refers to a fusion of two different knowledge traditions: autobiography and ethnography. In an autobiography, a person seeks to contribute to knowledge by recounting the story of their own life. By contrast, ethnography can be understood as the use of participant observation, initially employed by social anthropologists, as a means of learning about the 'way of life' or culture of a group of people. Although these traditions can be viewed as distinct from each other, it is also clear that these overlap in many ways. An autobiography may focus on a person, but that individual story always conveys important insights into the culture or cultures within which that person has lived. Similarly, for an ethnographic researcher, the experience of studying another culture becomes an episode (sometimes a dramatic, vivid and life-changing episode) in the autobiography of their own life-story: in an important sense, their understanding of that culture is based in their own subjective experience of entering that social world and living within it. Autoethnography, as an approach to knowledge, has grown and developed in that intersecting space between autobiography and ethnography.

All autoethnographic research tends to demonstrate a set of core methodological features (Chang, 2016): (i) concern to establish the authenticity and trustworthiness of personal experience data; (ii) explanation of the research process; (iii) sensitivity to ethical issues arising from data collection and reporting; (iv) analysis and interpretation of the social and cultural meaning of the writer's experience; (v) engagement with existing knowledge and scholarly traditions, with the aim of exploring theoretical issues and extending observational evidence. Within that broad framework, it is possible to identify different styles of autoethnographic inquiry that have been developed:

Analytic-evocative. Analytic autoethnography (Anderson, 2006) uses analysis of personal experience as a means of addressing academic questions. By contrast, evocative autoethnography (Bochner & Ellis, 2016) aims to elicit an emotional response in its audience, by enabling them to enter into areas of private experience being recounted by the writer, with less concern for academic objectives. In practice most autoethnographic reports comprise a mixture of analytic and evocative material. Nevertheless, the analytic-evocative distinction is valuable as a way of characterizing the range of possibilities associated with this methodology.

Individual-collective. Most autoethnographic studies that have been published are single-author pieces that report on the experience or life of an individual person. In recent years, there has been a movement in the direction of collective, group or co-autoethnography in which two or more participants work together to develop a shared autoethnographic account of an area of experience (Chang, Ngunjiri & Hernandez, 2016; Sawyer & Norris, 2012). The advantages of collective autoethnography are that sharing of personal experience allows for dialogue that enables further layers of recollection and meaning to emerge. There is also a supportive dimension to collective autoethnography, in contrast to the potentially isolating experience of constructing personally reflective inquiry on one's own. On the other hand, it is important to acknowledge that there is usually a collective or collaborative element in single-authored autoethnographic projects, in the form of talking to colleagues, research supervisors and others about the work as it progresses. Collective autoethnography seeks to build on and formalise such practices.

Written-performed. Most autoethnographic studies are disseminated through a written report of some kind. It is obvious, to anyone who has reflected on the nature of autoethnography and other personal experience methodologies, that written reports in fact represent rather limited and restricted ways to communicate the kind of insight and understanding that can be generated by this form of inquiry. As a result, some autoethnographers have developed ways to present their work in formats such as objects, pictures and displays, videos, poems, performance art and theatrical enactments (Pendzik, Emunah & Johnson, 2016), or have written papers in the style of performable scripts with characters and dialogue. In some contexts, such events and scripts may be intended to function as a therapeutic experience for both performers and audiences.

Further information about principles and styles of autoethnographic inquiry can be found in introductory textbooks such as Holman Jones, Adams and Ellis (2016) and Poulos (2021).

Why would I want to do this kind of research?

There are several reasons why it is desirable for novice and practitioner researchers to undertake this kind of research. First, it is possible to use this approach to generate practically useful knowledge – several examples of practice-oriented autoethno-graphic studies are provided later in this chapter. Second, the experience of conducting an autoethnographic study represents a good way to learn about the limitations of mainstream methodologies such as interview-based qualitative research or the use of measures: it becomes pretty obvious, quite quickly, that there exist levels of awareness and knowing that are not tapped by standard approaches. Third, most people who undertake personal experience research report that there is a great deal of personal learning and development arising from this kind of work (see, for example, Etherington, 2004; Matthews, 2019a,b). Fourth, there is an aesthetic and creative dimension to personal experience research that can be highly satisfying. Fifth, participation in autoethnographic inquiry has the potential to contribute to the development of therapeutic skills such as self-awareness/reflexivity, ethical sensitivity and the use of writing for therapeutic purposes.

Exercise 14.1   Choosing a topic

If you are thinking about undertaking an autoethnographic study, then what aspect or episode from your life would you wish to explore? What might be the effect on you, and those around you, of systematically analysing and writing about that issue?

What kind of skills and support would I need?

In the end, the success of an autoethnographic study will depend to a large extent on the capacity of the researcher to write about their experience in a direct and authentic manner. As a result, anyone who has difficulty in expressing their feelings in words, or who becomes anxious or emotionally incapacitated at the prospect of undertaking a sustained piece of writing, might want to think carefully before committing themself to a mainly autoethnographic dissertation or thesis. Similarly, doing an autoethnography requires a willingness to be known, at a personal level, which may not be congenial to some people. It is also important to take account of the potential implications of an autoethnographic inquiry for other people who might be part of the author's personal story. For example, writing about one's personal experience of therapy involves describing one's therapist. It is only sensible to embark on such a study if one has confidence in being able to approach the therapist (or others who might be mentioned in the study) for their approval.

Autoethnography is probably the form of therapy research that most heavily depends on the establishment of a strong supportive relationship between the researcher and research supervisor (or equivalent mentor or consultant if the study is not being conducted in an academic context). Good autoethnographic research is somewhat risky, and requires courage, and it is important to have someone who is close to the process who can be trusted. Analysing or making sense of material that is generated in an autoethnographic project (such as personal diaries, artefacts or descriptions of events) involves the rational part of the researcher observing and interpreting the emotional or spontaneous side of their way of being. This can be a hard thing to accomplish, and it would be useful to have someone else who is able to function as an external reference point. This is particularly necessary when the focus of the research is concerned with highly sensitive or upsetting experiences. Finally, there are many moral and ethical complexities associated with autoethnographic research arising from the depth of disclosure that can occur. As in any area of research, good practice in ethical problem solving involves consulting others and looking at the issue from a range of perspectives.

Exercise 14.2   Conducting an autoethnographic study

Reflect on how you might investigate your research question by conducting an autoethnographic study. What would your study look like? What might be the unique or distinctive insights yielded by this approach?

A step-by-step guide to conducting an autoethnographic study

Before beginning an autoethnographic study, or indeed in advance of deciding to use this methodology at all, it will be necessary to do some reading on the background to the approach, the underlying methodological principles that inform this kind of work, and the ways in which personal experience research differs from other types of qualitative inquiry. The items listed in the Suggestions for Further Reading section at the end of this chapter provide a good starting point for entry into this literature.

The practical reality of conducting a personal experience study can be divided into four broad stages: deciding on a question or focus; addressing ethical issues; generating data; and writing.

Deciding on a question or focus

As with any research study, an autoethnographic study needs to be organised around a question that is being explored or answered. Ultimately, the aim of autoethnographic or personal experience research will be to *describe* an episode or area of experience in a person's life. Some examples of autoethnographic studies are outlined below. It can be seen that, although they address different topics, all of them were trying to answer the question of 'What was it like to …?' Philosophically, autoethnographic research is a *phenomenological* approach to knowledge, which seeks to establish the essential structure or features of an area of experience. An appreciation of this philosophical stance is helpful as a way of recognising the strength of autoethnography, compared with other qualitative methods such as interviewing. When interviewing another person, the researcher can only push so far – it is difficult or impossible to know if the informant has more to give, or what might be required to encourage them to go further. By contrast, when the subject of inquiry is one's own personal experience, or personal story, the researcher has the capability, if they are willing, to take the question as far as it will go. The level of disclosure required in autoethnographic research tends to shape the question that the researcher selects for investigation. The research topic needs to be something around which the researcher has a meaningful and detailed story to tell. At the same time, it has to be a topic where the researcher can live with the fact that others will learn about previously hidden, and possibly embarrassing, aspects of their experience. Another factor to take into consideration, when choosing a topic for autoethnographic research, is the issue of whether there is an existing literature on that theme. It may be informative to construct a free-standing account of personal experience that does not connect up with any published theory or research studies. However, such an account would usually be classified as an autobiography, short story or novel. To be classified as a piece of research, links need to be made with the research literature. This is not an argument that research is 'better' or 'worse', or more or less useful, than art. It can all be useful (or otherwise) – it is just that these are different genres of writing.

Addressing ethical issues

The routine ethical issues that arise in all research have been discussed in Chapter 5. Autoethnography raises additional ethical issues because the subject of the research is being overtly identified through the name of the author. This means that the usual procedures to maintain confidentiality are not applicable. There are two areas of risk – to researchers, and to other people (e.g. family members or colleagues) mentioned in autoethnographic reports. The risks to authors are that they may not know what they are letting themselves in for, both in terms of embarking on a process of rigorous self-exploration, and in eventually publishing their story. What may seem a brave and authentic piece of writing, within the safe environment of a university department, may over time become a source of regret, as readers of the research find meaning that the author had not consciously intended. Another risk to researchers can occur in the later stages of projects, when they become aware of the personal sensitivity of the material, but are under pressure to complete a study. There can be a tendency, in such circumstances, to publish material that may later be regretted on grounds of being too disclosing. The risk to other people is that it is very easy for a family member, colleague, therapist, or whoever else was part of the writer's life, to recognise themselves in the eventual dissertation or article. While it is possible, and desirable, to collect formal consent from such participants, there is relatively little scope to disguise what is written about them. As a consequence, there are many possibilities for upsetting people. A study by Harder, Nicol and Martin (2020) of post-publication experiences of authors of autoethnographies provides valuable insight into these issues. The possibility of risk to self and others places a significant demand on supervisors of autoethnographic research. In addition, there is a broader moral requirement around honest reporting. The nature of these ethical issues, and strategies for dealing with them, have been thoroughly examined in several sources: Chatham-Carpenter (2010), Emmerich (2019), Lapadat (2017), Sieber and Tolich (2013) and Tolich (2010).

Generating data

The most interesting and rewarding part of an autoethnographic project tends to be the stage of generating data or compiling a text. This phase of the study takes the form of a journey of systematic self-exploration. Most autoethnographic research is grounded in a period of sustained writing, during which the researcher captures in words as much of the target experience as they can. Writing can take place in diaries and journals, scraps of paper, participation in writing workshops, or through using writing exercises such as those in Wright and Bolton (2012) and other sources. Many personal experience researchers will use techniques to augment their awareness of events, such as writing poetry, generating images and metaphors, recording dreams and meditation. Some researchers will invite other people to interview them. There are many creative ways of using artefacts such as photographs, music, documents and objects. These artefacts can represent or symbolise something that happened at the time of the original experience, or can be used to trigger memories of that experience. As with any form of qualitative research, the aim is to assemble a text that forms the basis for analysis and interpretation.

Writing

The hardest part of an autoethnographic study is writing the paper or dissertation. Good personal experience writing has an aesthetic quality to it, is vivid and memorable, and has an emotional impact. One of the ways in which these objectives are accomplished is to use writing to 'show' as well as to 'tell'. Other than producing a screenplay or theatre script, any form of writing will always include a significant amount of reporting or telling. Autoethnographic writing tries to minimise the amount of explanatory writing, in order to give more space to passages that convey the here-and-now 'lived experience' of key aspects of the topic being studied. This can be quite challenging for students or therapists who have been trained and socialised in the use of 'prosaic' and scientific modes of professional communication. Many autoethnographic articles use photographs or poetry as a contrast to prosaic writing. A further challenge is that an autoethnographic article or dissertation tends to move back and forward between lived experience, reflection and theory. This means that this type of article is unlikely to conform to the normal structure of a journal research article. Authors will also often use different fonts, areas of the page, columns and colours to mark out the distinct 'voices' or positions being conveyed in a study. Done well, autoethnographic writing is powerful and memorable. Done not so well, it can be hard to follow.

Compared with other research methodologies, there are fewer rules or guidelines associated with autoethnography and other personal experience approaches. Nevertheless, as with any research writing, or indeed any successful professional writing, it helps to develop a routine or discipline, reflected in such factors as setting aside specific blocks of time for writing and finding or creating the right kind of writing environment.

Examples of autoethnographic research

The best way to develop an appreciation of the possibilities of autoethnographic research is to read actual studies that have used this approach. Listed below are some autoethnographic studies that are particularly relevant to the field of counselling and psychotherapy. These fall into two broad categories – studies of various aspects of professional practice, and studies of the experience of problems and treatments.

There are several autoethnographic studies and accounts of various aspects of what it is like to be a client (Borck, 2011; Brooks, 2011; Fox, 2014; McKenzie, 2015), or a therapist (Bright et al., 2012; Falzon et al., 2020; Hayward, 2020; Olson, 2015; Råbu et al., 2021 Rober & Rosenblatt, 2017; Speciale, Gess & Speedlin, 2015; Stirling, 2020; Whybrow, 2013; Wright, 2009; Wyatt, 2013), or to work together in therapy (Etherington, 2000; McMillan & Ramirez, 2016) or supervision (King & Jones, 2019). Autoethnographic studies have also explored the experience of training and development (Chigwedere, 2019; Fetherston, 2002; Meekums, 2008; McIlveen, 2007), therapy landscapes (Liggins, Kearns & Adams, 2013), and the professional experiences of therapists with marginalised identities (Hargons et al., 2017; Speciale, Gess & Speedlin, 2015).

Another category of therapy-relevant autoethnographic inquiry encompasses studies that explore therapeutic or other healing and learning processes associated with specific disorders or life experiences. Examples include accounts of coping with loss (Matthews, 2019a, 2019b; McKenzie, 2015; Stirling, 2016), caring for an elderly relative (Wilkinson & Wilkinson, 2020), childhood sexual abuse (Barley, 2020a, 2020b; Gildea, 2020a, 2020b), psychosis (Stone, 2009), obsessive-compulsive disorder (Brooks, 2011; Fox, 2014), stress arising from being a woman working in a university (Campbell, 2018; Leitch, 2006), pregnancy loss (Sheach Leith, 2009), breast cancer (Sealy, 2012), being a victim of violent crime (Borawski, 2007), mental illness in the workplace (Kidd & Finlayson, 2010), depression (Smith, 1999), father–son relationships (Sparkes, 2012), medically unexplained symptoms (Hills et al., 2018) and being a Holocaust survivor (Hanauer, 2012, 2021). Many of these studies highlight the author's belief in the value of writing (or particular forms of writing, such as poetry) as a means of coming to terms with adverse life experiences.

These exemplar studies have been selected to offer an introduction to the diverse territory of autoethnographic research. Each study makes a meaningful contribution to knowledge, by using individual cases and lives to illustrate shared aspects of the experience of being a person, and how that experience relates to theoretical and cultural themes. These studies also exemplify the many different ways in which autoethnographic studies can be carried out and written up. Most of these are based on the experiences of the author alone, while others make use of a group of co-researchers. Studies also differ in the extent to which the method is explained, and connections to theory and previous research are discussed.

Exercise 14.3   Writing about personal experience

Once you have read a few of the studies listed in the preceding sections, take some time to reflect on how they came across to you as a reader. What were the writing strategies that seemed more or less effective? What were the writing styles that you could imagine using within your own study?

What can go wrong?

The things that can go wrong in autoethnography and other forms of personal experience inquiry are rather different from the things that tend to go wrong in other types of research. Generally, research projects do not work out because of missing data and a breakdown in co-operation between the researcher and potential informants or research sites. These problems do not arise in autoethnography because the researcher is completely in charge of the data. What goes wrong instead is that sometimes the researcher gets stuck because it becomes too emotionally painful or revealing to proceed with the study. Another way in which autoethnography can go wrong arises from difficulty in finding the right tone and style in the ultimate written dissertation or article. Effective autoethnographic reports will seem effortless – they flow, are easy to read and carry impact. But a lot of work needs to go on behind the scenes to allow this to happen.

Other types of personal experience research

Similar to autoethnographic inquiry are books and articles where someone writes about their experience of being a therapist or client, without labelling the piece as autoethnography, adhering to any particular methodological tradition, or trying to make connections with theory. The counselling and psychotherapy literature includes many fascinating first-person accounts of the experience of working as a therapist (Comas-Dias, 2010; Marzillier, 2010; Schulz, 2018), being an academic leader in the field (Kaslow, 2020), the experience of receiving therapy (Anonymous, 2011; Curtis, 2011; Freeman, 2011; Geller, Norcross & Orlinsky, 2005) and the experience of specific events in therapy as described in the books of Jeffrey Kottler and articles such as Callahan and Ditloff (2007). Most of these books, articles and chapters fulfil the criteria for autoethnographic research, and could readily be repackaged as autoethnographic studies.

A related genre of research comprises autobiographical accounts written by individuals who self-define as survivors of psychiatric services, or as being in recovery (see, for example, Broer & Chandler, 2020; Leigh, 2013). There are also significant points of overlap between autoethnography and various types of collective writing groups (Lieblich, 2013) and the many different forms of reflexivity and confessional writing undertaken by qualitative social science researchers (Sparkes, 2020).

A direction that is inevitable within autoethnography and personal experience research is the development of efforts to use evidence from this type of research within meta-analyses and literature reviews. At the present time relatively few autoethnographic studies have been published on any specific topic, which limits the possibilities around meta-analysis. However, as time goes on it is certain that multiple personal experience accounts of a whole range of therapy-relevant issues will be produced, and it will be possible to look at the extent to which these studies support and confirm findings from other types of research, and the degree to which these challenge and extend the conclusions of mainstream research.

How to get published

In relation to publishing an autoethnographic study, or similar type of investigation, it is important to be aware that this is a relatively new methodology. As a result, some academic researchers, journal editors and reviewers have little understanding of its potential, and may be wary of recommending such articles for publication. It is also important to be aware that autoethnographic methodology challenges deeply held beliefs about the necessity for researchers to be objective and detached. A leading British autoethnographer, Andrew Sparkes, has written about how, at various points in his (very successful) academic career, he has had to respond to accusations that the research carried out by his students and himself was 'self-indulgent' (Sparkes, 2002, 2013). In similar fashion, Delamont (2009) characterised much autoethnographic work as 'narcissistic' and 'self-obsessional'. This article is note-worthy because it makes clear that Delamont (2009) is not a 'positivist' researcher who believes that the only phenomena worth studying are those that are measura-ble. On the contrary, Delamont (2009) passionately believes in the central role of researcher reflexivity, but argues that this kind of self-awareness should be used to produce more in-depth understandings of the cultural groups or individuals who are being studied (i.e. other people) rather than as a basis for the researcher to write about themselves.

A development that has been very useful in supporting the 'publishability' of autoethnographic studies has been the formulation of criteria for quality and rigour in this genre of research. Following a review of such criteria, Le Roux (2017) sug-gests that there exists a broad consensus that autoethnographic work should be assessed in terms of six key dimensions:

- *subjectivity*: the researcher is visible in the report, through writing about personal experience;
- *self-reflexivity*: the researcher actively and closely engages in a process of making sense of the significance of their personal experience, and placing it within its cultural and historical context;
- *resonance*: the audience or reader is able to connect with the writer's story at an emo-tional level;
- *credibility*: the research should be trustworthy and honest;
- *contribution*: the study should make a contribution to knowledge, and inform the reader;
- *ethical integrity*: adherence to standards of ethical good practice.

For anyone planning to publish their autoethnographic research in an academic journal, it is helpful to read a paper by Sparkes (2020) in which he reflects on his extensive experience as a journal editor and reviewer charged with making decisions on whether or not to recommend autoethnographic manuscripts for publication.

In light of the experimental and emergent nature of autoethnographic research, it is necessary to be realistic and strategic about how prospective articles are written and where they are submitted. Most of the autoethnographic studies cited in the present chapter have been published in general qualitative research journals rather than in specialist therapy journals. An implication of this is that these studies are therefore unlikely to be reviewed by individuals with knowledge and experience of therapy. As a result, authors may find themselves underplaying specific therapy-focused themes in their articles, in order to connect with a wider readership, or may not be challenged by reviewers to make better links between the therapy dimension of their articles and current theory and research in psychotherapy.

Suggestions for further reading

Valuable sources for learning about recent developments and debates within the field of autoethnographic inquiry include Turner, L., Short, N., Grant, A., & Adams,

T. (eds) (2018) *International Perspectives on Autoethnographic Research and Practice*. Abingdon: Routledge, and the *Journal of Autoethnography*.

Online resources

The online resource site (https://study.sagepub.com/doingresearch4e) includes learning activities on ethical issues in therapy research.

15

Disseminating the Findings of your Research Study

Introduction

One of the fundamental differences between formal research and the kind of informal personal reflection on practice that is part of supervision and training is that the products of research are disseminated and become part of a general stock of knowledge and understanding. Usually, the findings of research are disseminated in written form. Although some researchers are beginning to experiment with other media such as video and theatre performance, the main way of passing on research remains through written articles, chapters, reports and books. The aim of these notes is to offer some guidelines for getting into print. Many therapists complete research in the context of studying for a degree, and initially write up their results in a Master's or doctoral dissertation. Others may carry out research as part of the audit and evaluation function of their agency or clinic, and their work remains hidden within internal memos and reports. It is important for therapists who wish to continue their professional development to the stage of making an impact on their peers, of claiming their own authority and professional voice, to go beyond this and publish in the public realm. Here is how to do it.

There are four main types of publication outlet: journals, conferences, books and monographs. These are discussed in turn.

Exercise 15.1   Formulating a dissemination strategy

It is important to think about what you want to accomplish through disseminating your work. The following sections of this chapter introduce a range of alternative publishing outlets. Before reading these sections, take some time to reflect on your hopes, fears and goals around publication. Who will be your audience? What do you want for yourself? In what ways might publication serve to further the interests of your research participants?

Publishing in journals

There is a huge international journals industry which is largely invisible to those outside the academic world. Advances in desktop publishing and printing have made it much cheaper to produce journals. Whereas commercial magazines need to pay authors for every word that they publish, the contributors to professional and academic journals do not usually get paid, and in many journals the editor will receive an honorarium rather than a salary. Moreover, many journals enjoy subscriptions income tied in to the membership of professional bodies. For example, all members of the British Association for Counselling and Psychotherapy receive the journals *Therapy Today* (a professional journal) and *Counselling and Psychotherapy Research* (a peer-reviewed international research journal), paid for out of their membership dues. Professional and academic journals can survive with quite limited subscription bases (around 1,000 would appear to be sufficient for a viable journal). Publishing companies therefore like publishing journals, which provide a steady income, low outgoings and a vehicle for promoting their book sales. The economics of the journals publishing industry have a number of implications for anyone wishing to get into print:

- There are *lots* of journals. If you cannot get your article accepted by a mainstream journal there will be some other niche journal, somewhere, that will in all likelihood be glad to have it.
- Most journals are run on a shoestring. People who review articles for journals are not paid. There is unlikely to be anyone paid to have the time to polish up your grammar, spelling and use of references, or to give you general advice. You also have to meet their deadlines (e.g. for proofreading) and follow their instructions.

- You must only submit your article to one journal at a time. If everyone were to submit their work to three or four journals simultaneously, the editing and reviewing system would collapse under the strain.
- You will not be paid. Normally, if you have an article accepted in a journal you will get a free copy of the journal (the one with your paper in it) and access to a PDF copy of your paper.

Beyond these points, it is important to realise that the last decade has seen a gradual shift in the direction of open access publishing, in which journals are not kept behind online paywalls or library walls, only accessible to those who are members of a university or are willing to pay. Instead, in an attempt to make knowledge more available to all (including those in developing countries, and practitioners or members of the public not affiliated to a university) there has been a move in the direction of an open access model in which all content is available to anyone at any time, with publishers' expenses being covered by fees paid by authors for publication. In reality these fees are mainly paid by the university in which the author works, or by the funding body that has grant support for the study to be carried out. Most journals who charge authors fees do so on a sliding scale, with higher fees for authors in leading universities, and lower fees for practitioners and some others. In addition, because the costs of running a journal are significantly reduced by use of online technology, there exists a growing number of open access journals that do not charge publication fees because they are operated by groups of volunteers or by a professional association. This revolution in journal publishing has also opened up new possibilities in relation to pre-publication 'preprints', open reviewing, post-review comments and other innovative features. A useful introduction to these developments can be found in Nosek and Bar-Anan (2012). One of the points they emphasise is that such changes are, on the whole, good news for practitioners, because they make it easier for them to get hold of articles that may be relevant to their work.

A broad distinction can be made between *professional* and *research/academic* journals, although there are also some journals which straddle this divide. Professional journals are mainly concerned with publishing articles about professional issues. In the counselling and psychotherapy world such journals include *Therapy Today, Psychotherapy Networker, American Psychologist* and *The Psychologist*. These journals are the official organs of professional associations. Although they may include excellent learned articles on theory and practice, they seldom carry original research, and they also tend to include fairly lengthy sections on announcements, meetings of professional committees and general professional business. In addition, they carry a lot of advertising for courses and conferences. By contrast, academic journals such as *Counselling and Psychotherapy Research, British Journal of Guidance and Counselling, Counselling Psychology Quarterly, Journal of Counseling Psychology* and *Psychology and Psychotherapy* will carry mainly research reports, reviews of the research literature, and articles on theory and methodology. These do not cover professional business, and include only limited advertising.

Box 15.1   Publication policies of professional and academic journals

Professional journals

publication criteria weighted towards topicality, interest value, readability;

may commission articles;

decision to publish often made by the editor;

broad readership;

more flexibility over writing style;

national readership.

Academic journals

publication criteria weighted towards research rigour;

publication almost wholly responsive to submissions sent in;

decision to publish always arrived at through peer review;

limited circulation but more likely to be held in libraries as a permanent record;

likely to be available online;

abstracted in databases;

strict writing style conventions and format;

international readership.

In deciding which journal to submit work to, it is essential to get hold of an actual copy of the journal. Look at the kind of articles that are published in the journal, and choose one which carries articles that are similar in style and content to the one you intend to write. Inside the cover of every journal or on its website it is possible to find some sort of 'mission statement' describing the type of papers the journal would like to receive. Sometimes this statement can be misleading, because editorial policies can outgrow the original journal remit, so it is always important to look at a few recent issues to get a feel for the territory that the journal has carved out for itself. The journal website will include other vital information, including:

- the minimum and maximum length for articles;
- guidelines for preparing articles, for example referencing conventions, policy on gender neutral language, ethical consent process, and rules on the use of subheadings, notes,

tables, diagrams, photographs and figures: most journals will require that articles are submitted with the author's name and address on a separate page and mentions of the author's name redacted from the text (to facilitate anonymous reviewing);

- how to submit an article using the journal portal;
- publication dates and deadlines, acceptance rates.

It is essential to follow these instructions as far as you can. A paper that at least *looks* as though it has been carefully prepared in accordance with the guidelines laid down by a journal will be viewed more favourably. One of the hardest things is ensuring that references are laid out exactly according to the requirements of a particular journal. There are many referencing formats in use, some of which may differ only in their use of full stops and capital letters. Bibliographic software packages such as Endnote can be invaluable in constructing reference lists, because they can transform a set of references from one format to another.

Many therapy journals have adopted the style manual of the American Psychological Association, which comprises a highly detailed set of guidelines regarding all aspects of journal layout, structure, and so on (APA, 2020; Appelbaum et al., 2018; Cooper, 2020; Levitt, 2020).

There are other aspects of the house style of a journal that tend not to be explained in their instructions for authors sections, and can only be discovered by looking at articles published in the journal itself. Most research journals expect articles to be structured around a series of subheaded sections: Abstract; Introduction (including a brief literature review) leading into a statement of the research question(s) or hypothesis; Methods/Procedures; Results; Discussion; References (see Chapter 2). However, specific journals may deviate from this structure slightly or use different terminology. Qualitative studies are notoriously difficult to fit into this kind of linear format, and it is worth looking at how your particular target journal handles qualitative material.

The length of a research paper can be between 2,000 and 10,000 words. It is essential to check the recommended word limit imposed in a target journal before submitting your paper to it. Journal editors usually have many papers waiting to be published, and only have a fixed number of pages/words that they can use in each issue. They are therefore unlikely to accept articles that are unnecessarily long (i.e. padded out). If you have carried out a small-scale study, editors will like it if you send in a brief paper, perhaps titled as an 'exploratory study' or 'early returns from ...', and so on. Some journals publish short research reports in a separate section.

The normal procedure is to send in your article through the journal's online portal with a short covering letter. Very soon you will receive a brief acknowledgement of receipt of the article. Very occasionally editors may return an article at this point if it is clearly inappropriate for the journal, too long or otherwise unsuitable. However, most articles will be sent off at this point for independent peer review. This means that anything that identifies the author(s) needs to have been deleted from the paper. Typically a paper will be reviewed by three experts nominated by the editor. Although some journals allow the author to nominate preferred (and non-preferred) reviewers, the final decision always stands with the editor. Reviewers are customarily given three to four weeks to prepare their (anonymous) reports, although it is not uncommon for them to take much longer. The standard practice is for reviewers to make ratings on the overall quality of the paper and its suitability for the journal. They will also write a brief report on the paper, which may be quite brief (five or six lines) or more lengthy (two or three pages in some cases). The ratings may or may not be sent to the author(s), depending on journal policy, but the report will almost always be sent on, accompanied by a covering letter (email) from the editor. This letter will either reject the paper, perhaps recommending other journals that might consider it, or will suggest alterations that need to be carried out. It is unusual for papers to be accepted for publication without any rewriting at all. An analysis of the kinds of things that reviewers of therapy articles are looking for can be found in Oddli, Kjøs and McLeod (2020).

At this point many would-be authors can become dispirited. Having opened their decision email from the journal, they are faced with three critical and cryptic sets of anonymous comments, some of which may contradict each other or may be personally wounding. This experience can seem like an invitation to low self-esteem, frustrated rage and depression. Personally, I have often had to banish such reports to the outer reaches of my office or laptop for several days (or longer!) before being able to read them in a balanced and constructive fashion. It is helpful to remind oneself of what is happening in these circumstances. Reviewers are not being asked to be therapeutic or supportive, but to help the editor produce the best-quality work for their journal. If an editor does not want to publish a paper at this stage, they will say so very clearly. Therefore, any invitation to resubmit a paper is an acknowledgement that it has the potential to make the grade.

What is often really helpful, on receipt of a rejection or heavily conditional offer to resubmit, is to go through the feedback with a colleague who is more experienced, and not personally invested in the manuscript. It is then also valuable to break down the reviewer and editor comments into a series of action points.

If you receive what you believe to be a mistaken review, there is very little to be gained by arguing with the editor. If the editor has made a decision to reject your paper, it may be worth sending them a brief email pointing out what you have learned from the reviews, and how you think you would be able to address review-ers' criticisms if given a chance to resubmit. In these circumstances, sometimes editors may be willing to reconsider, particularly if the initial reviews had included some positive comments. In reality, authors rarely take this course of action. Most of the time, the best policy is to lick your wounds, cut your losses, learn from failure, improve the paper and then send it to another journal.

Once the rewriting has been done it is usual to send it in along with a covering letter which explains briefly how the main points made by reviewers have been addressed. The best way to do this is to use your list of action points, and briefly explain how each of them has been dealt with. It may be necessary to explain why some of these points have *not* been addressed – reviewers can be wrong! There is little advantage in writing a long answer to a reviewer, explaining why you have analysed data in a certain way, and so on. At the end of the day, the reviewer is a proxy for the readers of the journal – your rationale for using a particular approach to analyse your data needs to be visible to *them* (i.e. in the text itself), not just to the reviewers. Again, there will be a waiting period while the paper is being considered. Some journals may permit further rounds of revisions. Once the paper has been accepted you will receive proofs to correct and permissions documents to sign, usually within a few days. Once these formalities have been completed your article will be published online for anyone to read. Typically, there is a substantial delay while it takes its place in the queue of articles for publication in an actual issue of the journal. This does not matter because for all practical purposes as soon as it appears on the journal website your work is in the public domain, and will be picked up by search engines.

It is clear that this whole process takes time. It is not uncommon for 12 months to elapse between submitting an article to an academic journal and seeing it in print. Some professional journals do not employ such elaborate review procedures, and can turn around articles more quickly. Less popular or new journals may not receive many papers and thus may be in a position to process an article quickly.

It is sensible to be on the alert for upcoming special issues of journals. Editors or the editorial boards of many journals like to reserve one or two editions each year for symposia or collections of articles on specific topics or themes. Notification of these special issues is usually advertised in the journal about two years ahead, with a deadline for submission of articles around 12 months ahead of the eventual publication date. It can be easier to get an article accepted for a special edition (there is less competition) and once published it will receive more attention, since anyone interested in the topic will seek out that issue of the journal, even if it is not a journal that they would normally read.

A valuable general guide to publishing articles in counselling and psychotherapy journals is available in Giordano, Schmit and Schmit 2021.

Box 15.2   Becoming a reviewer

A good way to learn about the review process is to become a reviewer. Most journals are open to offers to conduct reviews. Some encourage experienced reviewers to invite students or junior colleagues to co-review manuscripts with them, and may organise training (e.g. in the margins of research conferences) for new reviewers. Being involved in writing reviews makes it possible to see research papers from a different perspective. Also, once your review has been submitted, you will be sent the feedback written by other reviewers, and the editor's overview, which provide invaluable insights into the evaluative criteria and general ways of thinking about knowledge that are in circulation within the research community.

Box 15.3   Feedback is valuable

The whole structure of contemporary science is built around an assumption that knowledge creation is a collective endeavour and that the system of anonymous peer review leads to better work and more intelligible articles. Although everyone knows that on some occasions reviewers get it wrong, there is a general appreciation that on the whole the system works well enough. The significance of critical reviewer feedback may be particularly difficult for new researchers who up to that point have operated within a largely supportive research bubble within a university department or clinic. In most European countries, PhD candidates are required to submit their work for publication as they go along, with the final thesis or dissertation comprising three or four published articles along with an overview. This approach means that students have an opportunity to learn how to handle potentially harsh criticism while they are in an environment that will help them to deal with it.

Conferences

For many researchers, giving a paper at a conference represents a good way to get started in their writing career. The dates and venues of conferences are advertised about nine months in advance in relevant professional journals, or on the internet, along with a call for papers. For most conferences, the act of submitting a paper merely involves writing an abstract (i.e. a 300-word summary). It is easier to get a conference submission accepted (and generally a more satisfactory experience for all concerned) if papers are organised into panels of three to five presentations on a core theme. In advance of a conference submission deadline, there may be considerable contact between researchers around collaborating on joint panel submissions. A few conferences will demand to see the whole of the paper at the submission point, but this is rare. When the time for the conference comes round, a formal paper may or may not need to be written. Some people at conferences will actually read out papers, but this form of presentation is almost always boring and static. Presentations where the speaker talks freely around powerpoint slides tend to be better received. At a conference, ordinary speakers will have 20 minutes for their talk, plus 10 minutes for questions (keynote lectures are allowed longer), which puts pressure on the presenter to express their ideas crisply and succinctly – a good discipline. Following the conference, the journal of the professional association responsible for the event will publish the title (and sometimes also the abstract) of each paper, along with the name and address of the presenter. It is quite common to receive several requests for copies of a conference paper. The people who want to read the paper are likely to be interested enough in it to give feedback if asked. Useful feedback can also be received during the conference itself, either through formal questions asked after the paper, or less formally in the bar or round the dinner table. If you have actually written a paper in advance of a conference, it would be useful to take 10–20 copies to the event to distribute to people interested in your work.

Another format that is widely employed at conferences is the *poster* presentation. Researchers will display their work on a poster, and during a session of the conference (and/or during lunch breaks, etc.) are encouraged to stand beside it to answer questions. This can be a very rewarding way of meeting other people with similar research interests. This can be less terrifying and more convivial than actually standing up in a room and delivering a paper. Conference organisers usually provide guidelines around size of posters. Contributing a paper or poster at a conference can be a useful way of achieving some degree of dissemination of research, and getting the material into the public domain. It is also an excellent way to rehearse ideas that can be later worked up into a published article. As a means of building a professional network, it is valuable to be able to provide copies of a handout or summary of your poster that includes your email address.

Publishing a book

Most journal articles are between 2,500 and 7,000 words in length. A book can be anything between 50,000 and 100,000 words. There is therefore much more work entailed in writing a book, compared with writing a paper. Also, it is unusual, nowadays, to see book-length research reports in the field of counselling and psychotherapy. Nevertheless, there may be situations where the only way to do justice to a piece of research is to give it the space made possible by a book. Examples of some widely read counselling and psychotherapy research books that have appeared in recent years are listed at the end of this section.

Unlike a research paper, which is written and then sent off to a journal, no one would be expected to write a research book and send it off cold to a publisher. The procedure is to submit a proposal to the publisher, which is then reviewed by two or three academic referees. Just as in deciding on which journal to approach with an article, it is important to investigate the previous work published by an imprint. A book proposal is more likely to be accepted if it fits into the publisher's existing portfolio. A good proposal will include the following information:

- a title and general outline or aims;
- a synopsis of each chapter, and possibly one or two sample chapters;
- information about the previous writing experience of the author(s) – if they have limited experience, then a sample chapter should be included;
- the anticipated readership for the book;
- how the book compares with other texts in the same field;
- some indication of the timescale for finishing the manuscript.

Most publishers provide guidelines that specify the kind of information they want to see included in a proposal. As with journal article submissions, the process of getting a book proposal accepted may take some time and involve changes to the original conception. Once a publisher accepts a proposal, they will issue a contract and may pay a small advance on future royalties. (It is perhaps important to stress here that the earnings from academic or research books are meagre.) The publisher will allocate an editor to the book, who can be treated as an ally. Book editors cajole and encourage their authors, and are willing to discuss the project quite openly. Editors also put a great deal of work into ensuring that the final copy of the book is as near perfect as it can be.

One of the crucial factors that needs to be understood in relation to book publishing is that publishers are partly interested in the quality of a book but are much more interested in whether it will *sell*. As explained earlier, the economics of journal publishing are fairly stable. Books, on the other hand, are more hit or miss. It is not unusual for academic or research-focused books to struggle to break even. Publishers continually seek to be reassured that there is a market for a proposed book. The idea that a book will be bought by large numbers of students on courses in different colleges and universities (preferably all around the globe) is the kind of thing that publishers like to hear.

It is worth noting that publishers are traditionally cautious about edited collections, conference proceedings or unreconstituted doctoral dissertations. The latter are often far too dry and technical to work in book form, and multi-author edited books can be fragmented and inconsistent. Obviously many edited books are published every year in the counselling and psychotherapy domain, but many of these are put together by highly experienced academic editors. For example, in the UK, Professor Windy Dryden has edited many counselling and psychotherapy books. Close examination of these books will reveal the extent to which he has provided a clear structure and aims for the authors he has included.

Being invited to contribute to an edited book is a good way of getting published for the first time, or building an academic reputation. One of the ways of being asked to write a book chapter is to become known, for example by giving talks and conference papers.

Publishing a monograph

A monograph can be defined as an academic text that is shorter than a book (around 30,000 words), and is not usually published by a commercial company. Many university departments support their own monograph series, as do some voluntary and public sector agencies. Indeed, with the ready availability of desktop publishing and printing, any individual or group can produce their own monograph-length reports. There are many research projects which produce substantial reports, for example an end-of-project report to a funding body, which do not translate easily into journal articles. If such monographs are advertised in the appropriate professional journals, they can easily generate sales that are sufficient to cover costs. It is not difficult to get an ISBN number which will ensure that the monograph eventually finds its way into bibliographic listings. Some publishers have developed monograph imprints to support the dissemination of longer research reports.

Although paper copies of such monographs are produced, the main circulation is through e-books held within university libraries.

Box 15.4 Contrasting ways of reporting the same research study

It is useful to keep in mind that it is possible to publish different pieces on the same study. An interesting example of how one author adapted her writing style to meet the contrasting opportunities associated with different publication outlets can be found in the work of Susan Morrow. The first paper (1995) is a formal, technical research article. The 2006 chapter focuses mainly on the way that the study was carried out. The 2009 chapter highlights the personal meaning of the study for the author, and the relationships that developed through the research process. Note, also, the time lag involved in producing these items.

Morrow, S. L., & Smith, M. L. (1995). Constructions of survival and coping by women who have survived childhood sexual abuse. *Journal of Counseling Psychology*, *42*, 4–33.

Morrow, S. L. (2006). Honor and respect: feminist collaborative research with sexually abused women. In C. T. Fischer (ed.), *Qualitative Research Methods for Psychologists: Introduction through Empirical Examples*. New York: Academic Press.

Morrow, S. L. (2009). A journey into survival and coping by women survivors of childhood sexual abuse. In L. Finlay & K. Evans (eds), *Relational-centred Research for Psychotherapists: Exploring Meanings and Experiences*. Chichester: Wiley-Blackwell.

Other ways of getting the message across

Because of the domination of research by academics, it is natural to assume that research outputs must always take the form of written texts. We live in a literate professional culture, in which authority is associated with written authorship. From a therapy perspective, however, it is clear that experiential learning is, most of the time, a more powerful medium for communication and learning than reading and writing could ever be. There are many ways of using research findings. At academic conferences and professional seminars, it is not unusual for findings of research studies to be presented as pieces of performance art or theatre. In other settings, research can be translated into workshops or video documentaries. In the context of the day-to-day work of counselling and psychotherapy agencies and clinics, the results of research can be incorporated into protocols and training manuals. The impact of practitioner research depends, in the long run, not only on the adoption of a diversity of methodologies, but also on the exploration of a multiplicity of channels of communication and learning. Knoll and Fitzpatrick (2020) have described the extent to which adoption within the profession of feedback and monitoring measures required a lot more than just publishing studies with positive findings. An inspiring paper by Granek and Nakash (2016) discusses how these researchers actively promoted their work through workshops and talks to professional colleagues. In more established and better funded areas of science, there exists a sophisticated structure of knowledge exchange and promotion of public awareness. Examples of this include magazines such as *New Scientist* and *Scientific American*, newspaper articles, museum exhibitions, TV documentaries, and so on.

Conclusions

Being able to find an audience for one's research, and being able to add one's own small piece to the vast mosaic of research evidence, is a satisfying experience and a significant personal milestone. It represents the culmination of a research journey. The message of this chapter is that, although disseminating research presents fresh challenges and calls for the development or refinement of new skills, it is almost always possible, with persistence, to find a home in the literature for any study that has been conducted with care and integrity.

Suggestions for further reading

Everyone finds writing difficult. The single most frequent factor in research articles not being published and book proposals not being accepted is that they are not written in a style appropriate to that outlet, or are hard to follow. In addition, many excellent pieces of research are not submitted for publication at all, because the additional labour of re-writing is too much for the author to contemplate. In response to these factors, there exists an extensive literature on how to ease the pain of writing, and how to write for different audiences. Rather than attempt to condense this material in the present chapter, it has been placed on the online resource site.

Online resources

The online resource site includes additional material that provides advice and guidance around different aspects of the process of writing scientific papers in general, as well as specific requirements around different types of therapy research study: https://study.sagepub.com/doingresearch4e.

References

Adler, J. M. (2012). Living into the story: agency and coherence in a longitudinal study of narrative identity development and mental health over the course of psychotherapy. *Journal of Personality and Social Psychology*, 102, 367–389.

Adler, J. M. (2019). Stability and change in narrative identity: introduction to the special issue on repeated narration. *Qualitative Psychology*, 6(2), 134–145.

Agee, J. (2009). Developing qualitative research questions: a reflective process. *International Journal of Qualitative Studies in Education*, 22, 431–447.

Agnew-Davies, R., Stiles, W. B., Hardy, G. E., et al. (1998). Alliance structure assessed by the Agnew Relationship Measure (ARM). *British Journal of Clinical Psychology*, 37, 155–172.

Aherne, C., Coughlan, B., & Surgenor, P. (2018). Therapists' perspectives on suicide: a conceptual model of connectedness. *Psychotherapy Research*, 28(5), 803–819.

Anderson, L. (2006). Analytic autoethnography. *Journal of Contemporary Ethnography*, 35, 373–395.

Angus, L., Levitt, H., & Hardtke, K. (1999). The Narrative Processes Coding System: research applications and implications for psychotherapy practice. *Journal of Clinical Psychology*, 55(10), 1255–1270.

Anjum, R. L., Copeland, S., & Rocca, E. (eds) (2020). *Rethinking Causality, Complexity and Evidence for the Unique Patient*. A CauseHealth resource for health professionals and the clinical encounter. New York: Springer.

Anker, M. G., Sparks, J. A., Duncan, B. L., Owen, J. J., & Stapnes, A. K. (2011). Footprints of couple therapy: client reflections at follow-up. *Journal of Family Psychotherapy*, 22(1), 22–45.

Anonymous (2011). Lessons learned from a long-term psychoanalysis on the telephone. *Journal of Clinical Psychology*, 67, 818–827.

APA (2020). *Publication Manual of the American Psychological Association*. 7th edn. Washington, DC: American Psychological Association.

Appelbaum, M., Cooper, H., Kline, R. B., Mayo-Wilson, E., Nezu, A. M., & Rao, S. M. (2018). Journal article reporting standards for quantitative research in psychology: the APA Publications and Communications Board task force report. *American Psychologist*, 73(1), 3–25.

Archer, R., Forbes, Y., Metcalfe, C., & Winter, D. (2000). An investigation of the effectiveness of a voluntary sector psychodynamic counselling service. *British Journal of Medical Psychology*, 73, 401–412.

Areán, P. A., Ly, K. H., & Andersson, G. (2016). Mobile technology for mental health assessment. *Dialogues in Clinical Neuroscience*, 18(2), 163–175.

Armstrong, J. (2010). How effective are minimally trained/experienced volunteer mental health counsellors? Evaluation of CORE outcome data. *Counselling and Psychotherapy Research*, 10(1), 22–31.

Asfeldt, M., & Beames, S. (2017). Trusting the journey: embracing the unpredictable and difficult to measure nature of wilderness educational expeditions. *Journal of Experiential Education*, 40(1), 72–86.

Ashworth, M., Shepherd, M., Christey, J., et al. (2004). A client-generated psychometric instrument: the development of "PSYCHLOPS". *Counselling and Psychotherapy Research*, 4, 27–31.

Atkins, D. C., Bedics, J. D., McGlinchey, J. B., & Beauchaine, T. P. (2005). Assessing clinical significance: Does it matter which method we use? *Journal of Consulting and Clinical Psychology*, 73(5), 982–989.

Audet, C. T., & Everall, R. D. (2010). Therapist self-disclosure and the therapeutic relationship: A phenomenological study from the client perspective. *British Journal of Guidance & Counselling*, 38(3), 327–342.

Avdi, E., & Seikkula, J. (2019). Studying the process of psychoanalytic psychotherapy: discursive and embodied aspects. *British Journal of Psychotherapy*, 35(2), 217–232.

Bacha, K., Hanley, T., & Winter, L.A. (2020). 'Like a human being, I was an equal, I wasn't just a patient': service users' perspectives on their experiences of relationships with staff in mental health services. *Psychology and Psychotherapy: Theory, Research and Practice*, 93, 367–386.

Bachelor, A., Laverdière, O., & Gamache, D. (2007). Clients' collaboration in therapy: self-perceptions and relationships with client psychological functioning, interpersonal relations, and motivation. *Psychotherapy: Theory, Research, Practice, Training*, 44, 175–192.

Baker, E., Gwernan-Jones, R., Britten, N., McCabe, C., Gill, L., Byng, R., & Gask, L. (2019). Using interpersonal process recall to understand empowerment processes in a collaborative care intervention for people with a diagnosis of psychosis. *Psychosis*, 11(4), 350–361.

Balfour, A., & Lanman, M. (2012). An evaluation of time-limited psychodynamic psychotherapy for couples: a pilot study. *Psychology and Psychotherapy: Theory, Research and Practice*, 85: 292–309.

Balkin, R. S., & Lenz, A. S. (2021). Contemporary issues in reporting statistical, practical, and clinical significance in counseling research. *Journal of Counseling & Development*, 99(2), 227–337.

Banting, R., & Lloyd, S. (2017). A case study integrating CBT with narrative therapy externalizing techniques with a child with OCD: how to flush away the Silly Gremlin. A single-case experimental design. *Journal of Child and Adolescent Psychiatric Nursing*, 30(2), 80–89.

Barker, C., Pistrang, N., & Elliott, R. (2016). *Research Methods in Clinical Psychology: An Introduction for Students and Practitioners*. 3rd edn. Chichester: Wiley-Blackwell.

Barkham, M., Hardy, G. E., & Mellor-Clark, J. (eds) (2010). *Developing and Delivering Practice-based Evidence: A Guide for the Psychological Therapies*. Chichester: Wiley-Blackwell.

Barkham, M., Margison, F., Leach, C., et al. (2001). Service profiling and outcomes benchmarking using the CORE OM: toward practice based evidence in the psychological therapies. *Journal of Consulting and Clinical Psychology*, 69, 184–196.

Barkham, M., Mellor-Clark, J., & Connell, J. (2006). A core approach to practice-based evidence: a brief history of the origins and applications of the CORE-OM and CORE System. *Counselling and Psychotherapy Research*, 6, 3–15.

Barley, K. D. (2020a). Finding a good book to live in: a reflective autoethnography on childhood sexual abuse, literature and the epiphany. *The Qualitative Report*, 25(2), 487–503.

Barley, K. D. (2020b). Life is like a box of Derwents – an autoethnography colouring in the life of child sexual abuse. *The Qualitative Report*, 25(2), 504–524.

Barrett-Lennard, G. (2014). *The Relationship Inventory – a Complete Resource and Guide*. London: Wiley-Blackwell.

Beaty, R. E., Seli, P., & Schacter, D. L. (2019). Thinking about the past and future in daily life: an experience sampling study of individual differences in mental time travel. *Psychological Research*, 83(4), 805–816.

Beck, A. T., Steer, R. A., & Garbin, M. G. (1988). Psychometric properties of the Beck Depression Inventory: twenty-five years of evaluation. *Clinical Psychology Review*, 8, 77–10.

Benelli, E., De Carlo, A., Biffi, D., & McLeod, J. (2015). Hermeneutic Single Case Efficacy Design: a systematic review of published research and current standards. *Testing, Psychometrics, Methodology in Applied Psychology*, 22, 97–133.

Bentley, N., Hartley, S., & Bucci, S. (2019). Systematic review of self-report measures of general mental health and wellbeing in adolescent mental health. *Clinical Child and Family Psychology Review*, 22(2), 225–252.

Berg, A. L., Sandahl, C. and Clinton, D. (2008). The relationship of treatment preferences and experiences to outcome in generalized anxiety disorder (GAD). *Psychology and Psychotherapy: Theory, Research and Practice*, 81: 247–259.

Biddle, L., Cooper, J., Owen-Smith, A., et al. (2013). Qualitative interviewing with vulnerable populations: individuals experiences of participating in suicide and self-harm based research. *Journal of Affective Disorders*, 145, 356–362.

Billsborough, J., Mailey, P., Hicks, A., Sayers, R., Smith, R., Clewett, N., ... & Larsen, J. (2014). 'Listen, empower us and take action now!': reflexive-collaborative exploration of support needs in bipolar disorder when 'going up' and 'going down'. *Journal of Mental Health*, 23(1), 9–14.

Bimont, D., & Werbart, A. (2018). "I've got you under my skin": Relational therapists' experiences of patients who occupy their inner world. *Counselling Psychology Quarterly*, 31(2), 243–268.

Binder, P. E., Holgersen, H., & Nielsen, G. H. S. (2009). Why did I change when I went to therapy? A qualitative analysis of former patients' conceptions of successful psychotherapy. *Counselling and Psychotherapy Research*, 9(4), 250–256.

Binder, P. E., Holgersen, H., & Nielsen, G. H. (2010). What is a good outcome in psychotherapy? A qualitative exploration of former patients' point of view, *Psychotherapy Research*, 20: 285–294.

Binder, P. E., Moltu, C., Hummelsund, D., Sagen, S. H., & Holgersen, H. (2011). Meeting an adult ally on the way out into the world: adolescent patients' experiences of useful psychotherapeutic ways of working at an age when independence really matters. *Psychotherapy Research*, 21(5), 554–566.

Bjelland, I., Dahl, A. A., Haug, T. T., et al. (2002). The validity of the Hospital Anxiety and Depression Scale: an updated literature review. *Journal of Psychosomatic Research*, 52, 69–77.

Blanchard, M., & Farber, B. A. (2016). Lying in psychotherapy: Why and what clients don't tell their therapist about therapy and their relationship. *Counselling Psychology Quarterly*, 29(1), 90–112.

Blanchard, M., & Farber, B. A. (2020). "It is never okay to talk about suicide": Patients' reasons for concealing suicidal ideation in psychotherapy. *Psychotherapy Research*, 30(1), 124–136.

Bloor, M., Frankland, J., Thomas, M., et al. (2000). *Focus Groups in Social Research*. London: Sage.

Blunden, N. (2020). "And we are a human being": coproduced reflections on person-centred psychotherapy in plural and dissociative identity. *Psychotherapy and Politics International*, e1578.

Bochner, A., & Ellis, C. (2016). *Evocative Autoethnography: Writing Lives and Telling Stories*. London: Routledge.

Bolger, E. (1999). Grounded theory analysis of emotional pain. *Psychotherapy Research*, 9(3), 342–362.

Borawski, B. M. (2007). Reflecting on adversarial growth and trauma through autoethnography. *Journal of Loss and Trauma*, 12: 101–110.

Borck, C. R. (2011). The ontology of epistemological production: cases in ethnography and psychotherapy. *Qualitative Inquiry*, 17, 404–411.

Borg, M., Veseth, M., Binder, P. E., & Topor, A. (2013). The role of work in recovery from bipolar disorders. *Qualitative Social Work*, 12(3), 323–339.

Borrill, J., & Foreman, E. I. (1996). Understanding cognitive change: a qualitative study of the impact of cognitive-behavioural therapy on fear of flying. *Clinical Psychology and Psychotherapy*, 3, 62–74.

Boswell, J. F. (2020). Monitoring processes and outcomes in routine clinical practice: a promising approach to plugging the holes of the practice-based evidence colander. *Psychotherapy Research*, 30(7), 829–842.

Bowens, M., & Cooper, M. (2012). Development of a client feedback tool: a qualitative study of therapists experiences of using the Therapy Personalisation Form. *European Journal of Psychotherapy and Counselling*, 14, 47–62.

Bowie, C., McLeod, J., & McLeod, J. (2016). 'It was almost like the opposite of what I needed': a qualitative exploration of client experiences of unhelpful therapy. *Counselling and Psychotherapy Research*, 16(2), 79–87.

Bowling, A. (2001). *Measuring Disease: A Review of Disease-Specific Quality of Life Measurement Scales*. 2nd edn. London: Open University Press.

Bowling, A. (2017). *Measuring Health: A Review of Quality of Life Scales*. 4th edn. London: Open University Press.

Bowman, L., & Fine, M. (2000). Client perceptions of couples therapy: helpful and unhelpful aspects. *American Journal of Family Therapy*, 28(4), 295–310.

Braakmann, D. (2015). Historical paths in psychotherapy research. In O. Gelo, A. Pritz, & B. Rieken (eds), *Psychotherapy Research: Foundations, Process and Outcome* (pp. 39–66). Vienna: Springer-Verlag.

Bracken-Roche, D., Bell, E., Macdonald, M. E., & Racine, E. (2017). The concept of 'vulnerability' in research ethics: an in-depth analysis of policies and guidelines. *Health Research Policy and Systems*, 15(1), 8–19.

Brann, P., Lethbridge, M. J., & Mildred, H. (2018). The young adult Strengths and Difficulties Questionnaire (SDQ) in routine clinical practice. *Psychiatry Research*, 264, 340–345.

Brattland, H., Høiseth, J. R., Burkeland, O., Inderhaug, T. S., Binder, P. E., & Iversen, V. C. (2018). Learning from clients: a qualitative investigation of psychotherapists' reactions to negative verbal feedback. *Psychotherapy Research*, 28(4), 545–559.

Braun, V., & Clarke, V. (2006). Using thematic analysis in psychology. *Qualitative Research in Psychology*, 3, 77–101.

Braun, V., & Clarke, V. (2013). Successful qualitative research: a practical guide for beginners. London: Sage.

Braun, V., & Clarke, V. (2016). (Mis)conceptualising themes, thematic analysis, and other problems with Fugard and Potts' (2015) sample-size tool for thematic analysis. *International Journal of Social Research Methodology*, 19(6), 739–743.

Braun, V., & Clarke, V. (2019). Reflecting on reflexive thematic analysis. *Qualitative Research in Sport, Exercise & Health*, 11(4), 589–597.

Braun, V., & Clarke, V. (2021a). Can I use TA? Should I use TA? Should I not use TA? Comparing reflexive thematic analysis and other pattern-based qualitative analytic approaches. *Counselling and Psychotherapy Research*, 21(1), 37–47.

Braun, V., & Clarke, V. (2021b). One size fits all? What counts as quality practice in (reflexive) thematic analysis? *Qualitative Research in Psychology*, 18(3), 328–352.

Braun, V., & Clarke, V. (2021c). To saturate or not to saturate? Questioning data saturation as a useful concept for thematic analysis and sample-size rationales. *Qualitative Research in Sport, Exercise and Health*, 13(2), 201–216.

Braun, V., Clarke, V., Hayfield, N., & Terry, G. (2019). Thematic analysis. In P. Liamputtong (ed.), *Handbook of Research Methods in Health Social Sciences* (pp. 843–860). Cham: Springer.

Bright, F. A. S., Boland, P., Rutherford, S. J., et al. (2012). Implementing a client-centred approach in rehabilitation: an autoethnography. *Disability and Rehabilitation*, 34, 997–1004.

Brinkmann, S. (2017). *Philosophies of Qualitative Research*. New York: Oxford University Press.

British Psychological Society (2017). Ethics guidelines for Internet-mediated research, https://beta.bps.org.uk/sites/beta.bps.org.uk/files/Policy%20-%20Files/Ethics%20Guidelines%20for%20Internet-mediated%20Research%20%282017%29.pdf.

Broer, T., & Chandler, A. (2020). Engaging experience: mobilising personal encounters with mental ill-health in social science. *Social Theory & Health*, 18, 103–109.

Brooks, C. F. (2011). Social performance and secret ritual: battling against Obsessive-Compulsive Disorder. *Qualitative Health Research*, 21, 249–261.

Bruner, J. S. (1990). *Acts of Meaning*. Cambridge, MA: Harvard University Press.

Bryant, A., & Charmaz, K. (eds) (2019). *The SAGE Handbook of Current Developments in Grounded Theory*. Thousand Oaks, CA: Sage.

Buckroyd, J. (2003). Using action research to develop an assessment system in a voluntary sector counselling service. *Counselling and Psychotherapy Research*, 3, 278–284.

Budge, S. L. (2015). Psychotherapists as gatekeepers: an evidence-based case study highlighting the role and process of letter writing for transgender clients. *Psychotherapy*, 52(3), 287–297.

Burgess, S., Rhodes, P., & Wilson, V. (2013). Exploring the in-session reflective capacity of clinical psychology trainees: an interpersonal process recall study. *Clinical Psychologist*, 17(3), 122–130.

Burleson Daviss, W., Birmaher, B., Melhem, N. A., Axelson, D. A., Michaels, S. M., & Brent, D. A. (2006). Criterion validity of the Mood and Feelings Questionnaire for depressive episodes in clinic and non-clinic subjects. *Journal of Child Psychology and Psychiatry*, 47(9), 927–934.

Burton, L., & Thériault, A. (2020). Hindering events in psychotherapy: a retrospective account from the client's perspective. *Counselling and Psychotherapy Research*, 20(1), 116–127.

Butler, A. E., Copnell, B., & Hall, H. (2019). Researching people who are bereaved: managing risks to participants and researchers. *Nursing Ethics*, 26(1), 224–234.

Caccia, J. & Watson, J.P. (1987). A counselling centre and a psychiatric out-patient clinic. *Bulletin of the Royal College of Psychiatrists*, 11, 182–184.

Cahill, J., Stiles, W. B., Barkham, M., et al. (2012). Two short forms of the Agnew Relationship Measure: The ARM-5 and ARM-12. *Psychotherapy Research*, 22, 241–255.

Cairns, M. (2014). Patients who come back: Clinical characteristics and service outcome for patients re-referred to an IAPT service. *Counselling and Psychotherapy Research*, 14(1), 48–55.

Calin-Jageman, R. J. & Cumming, G. (2019). The new statistics for better science: ask how much, how uncertain, and what else is known. *The American Statistician*, 73, suppl., 271–280.

Callahan, J. L., & Dittloff, M. (2007). Through a glass darkly: Reflections on therapist transformations. *Professional Psychology: Research and Practice*, 38(6), 547–553.

Campbell, E. (2018). Reconstructing my identity: an autoethnographic exploration of depression and anxiety in academia. *Journal of Organizational Ethnography*, 7(3), 235–246.

Carey, T. A., & Stiles, W. B. (2016). Some problems with randomized controlled trials and some viable alternatives. *Clinical Psychology and Psychotherapy*, 23, 87–95.

Carr, A., & Stratton, P. (2017). The SCORE family assessment questionnaire: a decade of progress. *Family Process*, 56(2), 285–301.

Carroll, M. & Shaw, E. (2012). *Ethical Maturity in the Helping Professions: Making Difficult Life and Work Decisions*. Melbourne: PsychOz.

Chadwick, P., Kaur, H., Swelam, M., et al. (2011). Experience of mindfulness in people with bipolar disorder: a qualitative study. *Psychotherapy Research*, 21: 277–285.

Challenor, J. (2017). 'Not dead … abandoned' – a clinical case study of childhood and combat-related trauma. *European Journal of Psychotherapy & Counselling*, 19(1), 6–21.

Chang, D. F., & Berk, A. (2009). Making cross-racial therapy work: a phenomenological study of clients' experiences of cross-racial therapy. *Journal of Counseling Psychology*, 56, 521–536.

Chang, D. F., & Yoon, P. (2011). Ethnic minority clients perceptions of the significance of race in cross-racial therapy relationships. *Psychotherapy Research*, 21, 567–582.

Chang, H. (2016). Autoethnography in health research: growing pains? *Qualitative Health Research*, 26, 443–451.

Chang, H., Ngunjiri, F., & Hernandez, K. A. C. (2016). *Collaborative Autoethnography*. New York: Routledge.

Charmaz, K. (2014). *Constructing Grounded Theory*. 2nd edn. Thousand Oaks, CA: Sage.

Charmaz, K., & Thornberg, R. (2021). The pursuit of quality in grounded theory. *Qualitative Research in Psychology*, 18(3), 305–327.

Chatham-Carpenter, A. (2010). 'Do thyself no harm': protecting ourselves as autoethnographers. *Journal of Research Practice*, 6 (1), M1.

Chigwedere, C. (2019). Writing the 'self' into self-practice/self-reflection (SP/SR) in CBT: learning from autoethnography. *The Cognitive Behaviour Therapist*, 12, e38.

Clarke, H., Rees, A., & Hardy, G. E. (2004). The big idea: Clients' perspectives of change processes in cognitive therapy. *Psychology and Psychotherapy: Theory, Research and Practice*, 77(1), 67–89.

Clarke, V., & Braun, V. (2018). Using thematic analysis in counselling and psychotherapy research: a critical reflection. *Counselling and Psychotherapy Research*, 18(2), 107–110.

Clarke, V., Hayfield, N., Moller, N., & Tischner, I. (2017). Story completion tasks. In V. Braun, V. Clarke, & D. Gray (eds), *Collecting Qualitative Data: A Practical Guide to Textual, Media and Virtual Techniques*. Cambridge: Cambridge University Press.

Clement, P. W. (1994). Quantitative evaluation of 26 years of private practice. *Professional Psychology: Research and Practice*, 25, 173–176.

Clement, P. W. (2007). Story of Hope: successful treatment of Obsessive Compulsive Disorder. *Pragmatic Case Studies in Psychotherapy*, 3(4), 1–36.

Collins, J., Gibson, A., Parkin, S., Parkinson, R., Shave, D., & Dyer, C. (2012). Counselling in the workplace: How time-limited counselling can effect change in well-being. *Counselling and Psychotherapy Research*, 12(2), 84–92.

Colson, N. (2015). *Online Research Methods for Psychologists*. London: Palgrave Macmillan.

Comas-Dias, L. (2010). On being a Latina healer: voice, consciousness, and identity, *Psychotherapy Theory, Research, Practice, Training*, 47: 162–168.

Connell, J., Barkham, M., Stiles, W. B., et al. (2007). Distribution of CORE-OM scores in a general population, clinical cut-off points, and comparison with the CIS-R. *British Journal of Psychiatry*, 190, 69–74.

Connell, J., Grant, S., & Mullin, T. (2006). Client initiated termination of therapy at NHS primary care counselling services. *Counselling and Psychotherapy Research*, 6. 60–67.

Constantino, M.J., Boswell, J.F. & Coyne, A.E. (2021). Patient, therapist, and relational processes. In M. Barkham, L. Castonguay, & W. Lutz (ed.) *Bergin and Garfield's Handbook of Psychotherapy and Behavior Change*, 7th edn. New York: Wiley.

Conti, J., Calder, J., Cibralic, S., Rhodes, P., Meade, T., & Hewson, D. (2017). 'Somebody else's roadmap': lived experience of Maudsley and family-based therapy for adolescent anorexia nervosa. *Australian and New Zealand Journal of Family Therapy*, 38(3), 405–429.

Cooper, H. (2020). *Reporting Quantitative Research in Psychology: How to Meet APA Style Journal Article Reporting Standards*. 2nd edn. Washington, DC: American Psychological Association.

Cooper, M. (2005). Therapists' experiences of relational depth: a qualitative interview study. *Counselling and Psychotherapy Research*, 5, 87–95.

Cooper, M. (2008). *Essential Research Findings in Counselling and Psychotherapy: The Facts are Friendly*. London: Sage.

Cooper, M. (2014). Goals Form. www.pluralisticpractice.com

Cooper, M., & Norcross, J. C. (2016). A brief, multidimensional measure of clients' therapy preferences: the Cooper–Norcross Inventory of Preferences (C-NIP). *International Journal of Clinical and Health Psychology*, 16(1), 87–98.

Cooper, M., McLeod, J., Ogden, G. S., Omylinska-Thurston, J., & Rupani, P. (2015). Client helpfulness interview studies: a guide to exploring client perceptions of change in counselling and psychotherapy. Unpublished manuscript retrieved from https://www.researchgate.net/profile/Mick_Cooper.

Crawford, M. J., Thana, L., Farquharson, L., Palmer, L., Hancock, E., Bassett, P., ... & Parry, G. D. (2016). Patient experience of negative effects of psychological treatment: results of a national survey. *The British Journal of Psychiatry*, 208(3), 260–265.

Crits-Christoph, P., & Connolly Gibbons, M.B. (2021). Process-outcome research. In M. Barkham, L. Castonguay, & W. Lutz (ed.) *Bergin and Garfield's Handbook of Psychotherapy and Behavior Change*, 7th edn. New York: Wiley.

Cumming, G. (2014). The new statistics: why and how. *Psychological Science*, 25, 7–29.

Curtis, R. A. (2011). Speaking freely: my experiences in individual psychotherapies, group therapies, and growth groups. *Journal of Clinical Psychology*, 67, 794–805.

D'Aniello, C., Piercy, F. P., Dolbin-MacNab, M. L., & Perkins, S. N. (2019). How clients of marriage and family therapists make decisions about therapy discontinuation and persistence. *Contemporary Family Therapy*, 41(1), 1–11.

Da Silva, G. (1990). Borborygmi as markers of psychic work during the analytic session. *International Journal of Psychoanalysis*, 71, 641–659.

Dahl, H. S. J., Ulberg, R., Marble, A., Gabbard, G. O., Røssberg, J. I., & Høglend, P. (2017). Beyond the statistics: a case comparison study of Victor and Tim. *Psychoanalytic Psychology*, 34(4), 461–473.

Danchev, D., & Ross, A. (2014). *Research Ethics for Counsellors, Nurses and Social Workers*. London: Sage.

De Fina, A., Georgakopoulou, A., & Barkhuizen, G. (eds) (2015). *The Handbook of Narrative Analysis*. Chichester: Wiley Blackwell.

De Smet, M. M., Meganck, R., Van Nieuwenhove, K., Truijens, F. L., & Desmet, M. (2019). No change? A grounded theory analysis of depressed patients' perspectives on non-improvement in psychotherapy. *Frontiers in Psychology*, 10, 588.

De Smet, M. M., Meganck, R., De Geest, R., Norman, U. A., Truijens, F., & Desmet, M. (2020). What "good outcome" means to patients: understanding recovery and improvement in psychotherapy for major depression from a mixed-methods perspective. *Journal of Counseling Psychology*.

Deane, F. P., Spicer, J., & Todd, D. M. (1997). Validity of a simplified target complaints measure. *Assessment*, 4, 119–130.

Deeks, J.J., Dinnes, J., D'Amico, R. et al. (2003). Evaluating non-randomised, intervention studies. *Health Technology Assessment*, 7 (27).

Delamont, S. (2009). The only honest thing: autoethnography, reflexivity and small crises in fieldwork. *Ethnography and Education*, 4, 51–63.

Delgadillo, J., McMillan, D., & Leach, C. (2014) Benchmarking routine psychological services: a discussion of challenges and methods. *Behavioural and Cognitive Psychotherapy*, 42, 16–30.

Denzin, N., & Lincoln, Y. (eds) (2017). *The SAGE Handbook of Qualitative Research*. 5th edn. Thousand Oaks, CA: Sage.

Derogatis, L. R., & Melisaratos, N. (1983). The Brief Symptom Inventory: an introductory report. *Psychological Medicine*, 13, 595–605.

Di Malta, G., Evans, C., & Cooper, M. (2020). Development and validation of the relational depth frequency scale. *Psychotherapy Research*, 30(2), 213–227.

Di Malta, G., Oddli, H. W., & Cooper, M. (2019). From intention to action: a mixed methods study of clients' experiences of goal-oriented practices. *Journal of Clinical Psychology*, 75(10), 1770–1789.

Diamond, I. R., Grant, R. C., Feldman, B. M., et al. (2014). Defining consensus: a systematic review recommends methodologic criteria for reporting of Delphi studies. *Journal of Clinical Epidemiology*, 67(4), 401–409.

Dos Santos, O., & Dallos, R. (2012). The process of cross-cultural therapy between white therapists and clients of African-Caribbean descent. *Qualitative Research in Psychology*, 9(1), 62–74.

Downs, S.H. & Black, N. (1998). The feasibility of creating a checklist for the assessment of the methodological quality both of randomised, and non-randomised, studies of health care interventions. *Journal of Epidemiology and Community Health*, 52, 377–384.

Draucker, C. B., Martsolf, D. S., & Poole, C. (2009). Developing distress protocols for research on sensitive topics. *Archives of Psychiatric Nursing*, 23(5), 343–350.

Duncan, B. L., Miller, S. D., Sparks, J. A., et al. (2003). The Session Rating Scale: preliminary psychometric properties of a "working" alliance measure. *Journal of Brief Therapy*, 3: 3–12.

Dyregrov, K. M., Dieserud, G., Hjelmeland, H. M., Straiton, M., Rasmussen, M. L., Knizek, B. L., & Leenaars, A. A. (2011). Meaning-making through psychological autopsy interviews: the value of participating in qualitative research for those bereaved by suicide. *Death Studies*, 35(8), 685–710.

Egeli, N. A., Brar, N., Larsen, D. J., & Yohani, S. C. (2014). Intersections between hope and vulnerability in couples' experiences of the reflecting team process. *Journal of Couple & Relationship Therapy*, 13(3), 198–218.

Egeli, N. A., Brar, N., Larsen, D. J., & Yohani, S. (2015). Couples' experiences of vulnerability when participating in the reflecting team process: a case study. *Canadian Journal of Counselling and Psychotherapy*, 49(1).

Ellett, L. (2013). Mindfulness for paranoid beliefs: evidence from two case studies. *Behavioural and Cognitive Psychotherapy*, 41(2), 238–242.

Elliott, R. E. (2002). Hermeneutic Single Case Efficacy Design. *Psychotherapy Research*, 12, 1–23.

Elliott, R. E., Fischer, C. T., & Rennie, D. L. (1999). Evolving guidelines for the publication of qualitative research studies in psychology and related fields. *British Journal of Clinical Psychology*, 38, 215–229.

Elliott, R., Hill, C. E., Stiles, W. B., Friedlander, M. L., Mahrer, A. R., & Margison, F. R. (1987). Primary therapist response modes: Comparison of six rating systems. *Journal of Consulting and Clinical Psychology*, 55(2), 218–223.

Elliott, R. E., Partyka, R., Wagner, J., et al. (2009). An adjudicated Hermeneutic Single Case Efficacy Design study of experiential therapy for panic/phobia. *Psychotherapy Research*, 19, 543–557.

Elliott, R., Shapiro, D. A., & Mack, C. (1999). *Simplified Personal Questionnaire Procedure*. Toledo, OH: University of Toledo, Department of Psychology.

Elliott, R. E., Slatick, E., & Urman, M. (2001). Qualitative change process research on psychotherapy: alternative strategies. *Psychologische Beiträge*, 43, 111–125.

Elliott, R., & Timulak, L. (2021). *A Generic Approach to Descriptive-Interpretive Qualitative Research*. Washington, DC: American Psychological Association.

Elliott, R., Wagner, J., Sales, C. M. D., Rodgers, B., Alves, P., & Café, M. (2016). Psychometrics of the personal questionnaire: a client-generated outcome measure. *Psychological Assessment*, 28, 263–278.

Ellis, P. D. (2010). *The Essential Guide to Effect Sizes: Statistical Power, Meta-analysis, and the Interpretation of Research Results*. Cambridge: Cambridge University Press.

Ellison, W. D., Trahan, A. C., Pinzon, J. C., Gillespie, M. E., Simmons, L. M., & King, K. Y. (2020). For whom, and for what, is experience sampling more accurate than retrospective report? *Personality and Individual Differences*, 163, 110071.

Elton, M. (2021). *Talking It Better: From Insight to Change in the Therapy Room*. Monmouth: PCCS Books.

Emmerich, N. (2019). *The Ethical "I" in Research: Autoethnography and Ethics*. Thousand Oaks, CA: Sage.

Etherington, K. (2000). *Narrative Approaches to Working with Adult Male Survivors of Child Sexual Abuse: The Client's, the Counsellor's and the Researcher's Story*. London: Jessica Kingsley.

Etherington, K. (2004). *Becoming a Reflexive Researcher: Using Our Selves in Research*. London: Jessica Kingsley.

Evans, C., Margison, F., & Barkham, M. (1998). The contribution of reliable and clinically significant change methods to evidence-based mental health. *Evidence-Based Mental Health*, 1(3), 70–72.

Evans, C., Mellor-Clark, J., & Margison, F. (2000). CORE: Clinical Outcomes in Routine Evaluation. *Journal of Mental Health*, 9, 247–255.

Fairburn, C. G., Cooper, Z., Doll, H. A., et al. (2000). The natural course of bulimia nervosa and binge eating disorder in young women. *Archives of General Psychiatry*, 57, 659–665.

Falzon, R., Galea, C., Galea, R., Galea, S., & Muscat, M. (2020). Reflecting on Maltese school-based counselling practices: an autoethnographic collaborative writing project. *Counselling and Psychotherapy Research*, 20(1), 81–91.

Fenner, P. (2011). Place, matter and meaning: extending the relationship in psychological therapies. *Health and Place*, 17, 851–857.

Fetherston, B. (2002). Double bind: an essay on counselling training. *Counselling and Psychotherapy Research*, 2: 108–125.

Field, A. (2017). *Discovering Statistics Using IBM SPSS Statistics*. 5th edn. London: Sage.

Finlay, L. (2002). Negotiating the swamp: The opportunity and challenge of reflexivity in research practice. *Qualitative Research*, 2, 209–230.

Finlay, L. (2011). *Phenomenology for Therapists: Researching the Lived World*. Oxford: Wiley-Blackwell.

Finlay, L. (2012). Five lenses for the reflexive interviewer. In J. F. Gubrium, J. A. Holstein, A. B. Marvasti, & K. D. McKinney (eds), *The SAGE Handbook of Interview Research: The Complexity of the Craft* (pp. 317–333). Thousand Oaks, CA: Sage.

Finnegan, M., & O'Donoghue, B. (2019). Rethinking vulnerable groups in clinical research. *Irish Journal of Psychological Medicine*, 36(1), 63–71.

First, M. B. (2014). Structured clinical interview for the DSM (SCID). In R.L. Cautin & S.O. Lilienfeld (eds). *The Encyclopedia of Clinical Psychology*. New York: Wiley.

Fischer, C.T. (2009). Bracketing in qualitative research: conceptual and practical matters. *Psychotherapy Research*, 19: 583–590.

Fishman, D. (1999). *The Case for a Pragmatic Psychology*. New York: New York University Press.

Fishman, D. B. (2017). The pragmatic case study in psychotherapy: a mixed methods approach informed by psychology's striving for methodological quality. *Clinical Social Work Journal*, 45(3), 238–252.

Fishman, D., Messer, S. D., Edwards, D. J. A., & Dattilio, F. M. (2017). *Case Studies within Psychotherapy Trials: Integrating Qualitative and Quantitative Methods*. New York: Oxford University Press.

Fitzpatrick, L., Simpson, J., & Smith, A. (2010). A qualitative analysis of mindfulness-based cognitive therapy (MBCT) in Parkinson's disease. *Psychology and Psychotherapy: Theory, Research and Practice*, 83, 179–192.

Fleet, D., Burton, A., Reeves, A., & DasGupta, M. P. (2016). A case for taking the dual role of counsellor-researcher in qualitative research. *Qualitative Research in Psychology*, 13(4), 328–346.

Flückiger, C., Hilpert, P., Goldberg, S. B., Caspar, F., Wolfer, C., Held, J., & Vîslă, A. (2019). Investigating the impact of early alliance on predicting subjective change at posttreatment: an evidence-based souvenir of overlooked clinical perspectives. *Journal of Counseling Psychology*, 66(5), 613–625.

Flyvbjerg, B. (2001). *Making Social Science Matter: Why Social Inquiry Fails and How It Can Succeed Again*. New York: Cambridge University Press.

Flyvbjerg, B. (2006). Five misunderstandings about case-study research. *Qualitative Inquiry*, 12, 219–245.

Fogarty, M., Bhar, S., & Theiler, S. (2020). Development and validation of the gestalt therapy fidelity scale. *Psychotherapy Research*, 30(4), 495–509.

Fowler, J. C., Hilsenroth, M. J., & Handler, L. (2000). Martin Mayman's early memories technique: bridging the gap between personality assessment and psychotherapy. *Journal of Personality Assessment*, 75(1), 18–32.

Fox, R. (2014). Are those germs in your pocket, or am I just crazy to see you? An autoethnographic consideration of obsessive-compulsive disorder. *Qualitative Inquiry*, 20(8), 966–975.

Freeman, A. (2011). Mannys legacy: paying forward my personal therapy. *Journal of Clinical Psychology*, 67, 789–793.

Fried, A., & Fisher, C. B. (2017). Ethical issues in child and adolescent psychotherapy research. In J. R. Weisz & A. E. Kazdin (eds), *Evidence-based psychotherapies for children and adolescents*. 3rd edn (pp. 449–465). New York: Guilford Press.

Frost, N. (2016). *Practising Research: Why You're Always Part of the Research Process Even When You Think You're Not*. London: Palgrave Macmillan.

Fugard, A. J., & Potts, H. W. (2015). Supporting thinking on sample sizes for thematic analyses: a quantitative tool. *International Journal of Social Research Methodology*, 18(6), 669–684.

Gabbay, J., & le May, E. (2011). *Practice-based Evidence for Health Care: Clinical Mindlines*. London: Routledge.

Gabriel, L., & Casemore, R. (eds) (2009). *Relational Ethics in Practice: Narratives from Counselling and Psychotherapy*. London: Routledge.

Galasiński, D., & Kozłowska, O. (2013). Interacting with a questionnaire: respondents' constructions of questionnaire completion. *Quality & Quantity*, 47(6), 3509–3520.

Gauntlett, D. (2018). *Making Is Connecting: The Social Power of Creativity, from Craft and Knitting to Digital Everything*. 2nd edn. Cambridge: Polity Press.

Geller, J. D., Norcross, J. C. and Orlinsky, D. E. (eds) (2005). *The Psychotherapists Own Psychotherapy: Patient and Clinician Perspectives*. New York: Oxford University Press.

Gibbard, I., & Hanley, T. (2008). A five-year evaluation of the effectiveness of person-centred counselling in routine clinical practice in primary care. *Counselling and Psychotherapy Research*, 8, 215–222.

Gibbs, G. R. (2014). Using software in qualitative analysis. In U. Flick (ed.), *The SAGE Handbook of Qualitative Data Analysis* (pp. 277–294). Thousand Oaks, CA: Sage.

Gibson, A., Cooper, M., Rae, J., & Hayes, J. (2020). Clients' experiences of shared decision making in an integrative psychotherapy for depression. *Journal of Evaluation in Clinical Practice*, 26(2), 559–568.

Gibson, K., & Cartwright, C. (2014). Young clients' narratives of the purpose and outcome of counselling. *British Journal of Guidance & Counselling*, 42(5), 511–524.

Gibson, K., Cartwright, C., & Read, J. (2016). 'In my life antidepressants have been …': a qualitative analysis of users' diverse experiences with antidepressants. *BMC Psychiatry*, 16(1), 1–7.

Gilbert, N., Barkham, M., Richards, A., et al. (2005). The effectiveness of a primary care mental health service delivering brief psychological interventions: a benchmarking study using the CORE system. *Primary Care Mental Health*, 3, 241–251.

Gildea, I. J. (2020a). Speaking from the black hole: representing the experiences of survivors of childhood sexual abuse (CSA) in cultural pedagogies of meaning-making. *Feminist Media Studies*, 1–18.

Gildea, I. J. B. (2020b). The emergency stage: flashbacks and poetry: an autoethnographic approach. *Journal of Poetry Therapy*, 33(2), 110–122.

Gilligan, C. (2015). The Listening Guide method of psychological inquiry. *Qualitative Psychology*, 2(1), 69–77.

Giordano, A. L., Prosek, E. A., Schmit, M. K., & Wester, K. L. (2020). "We are still here": Learning from Native American perspectives. *Journal of Counseling & Development*, 98(2), 159–171.

Giordano, A. L., Schmit, M. K., & Schmit, E. L. (2021). Best practice guidelines for publishing rigorous research in counseling. *Journal of Counseling & Development*, 99(2), 123–133.

Giorgi, A. (2009). *The Descriptive Phenomenological Method in Psychology: A Modified Husserlian Approach*. Pittsburgh, PA: Duquesne University Press.

Glaser, B.G., & Strauss, A. (1967). *The Discovery of Grounded Theory*. Chicago: Aldine.

Glasman, D., Finlay, W. M. L., & Brock, D. (2004). Becoming a self-therapist: using cognitive-behavioural therapy for recurrent depression and/or dysthymia after completing therapy. *Psychology and Psychotherapy: Theory, Research and Practice*, 77, 335–351.

Goldfried, M. R. (2011). Generating research questions from clinical experience: therapists' experiences in using CBT for panic disorder. *The Behavior Therapist*, 34(4), 57–62.

Goldfried, M. R., Newman, M. G., Castonguay, L. G., Fuertes, J. N., Magnavita, J. J., Sobell, L., & Wolf, A. W. (2014). On the dissemination of clinical experiences in using empirically supported treatments. *Behavior Therapy*, 45, 3–6.

Gonçalves, M., Ribeiro, A. P., Mendes, I. et al. (2011). Tracking novelties in psychotherapy process research: the innovative moments coding system. *Psychotherapy Research*, 21: 497–509.

Goodman, R. D., & Gorski, P. C. (eds) (2015). *Decolonizing "Multicultural" Counseling through Social Justice*. New York: Springer.

Gordon, J., & Patterson, J. A. (2013). Response to Tracy's under the "Big Tent" establishing universal criteria for evaluating qualitative research. *Qualitative Inquiry*, 19(9), 689–695.

Göstas, M. W., Wiberg, B., & Kjellin, L. (2012). Increased participation in the life context: a qualitative study of clients' experiences of problems and changes after psychotherapy. *European Journal of Psychotherapy & Counselling*, 14(4), 365–380.

Göstas, M. W., Wiberg, B., Neander, K., et al. (2013). Hard work in a new context: clients experiences of psychotherapy. *Qualitative Social Work*, 12: 340–357.

Granek, L. (2017). Emotional aspects of conducting qualitative research on psychological topics. *Qualitative Psychology*, 4(3), 281–286.

Granek, L., & Nakash, O. (2016). The impact of qualitative research on the "real world" knowledge translation as education, policy, clinical training, and clinical practice. *Journal of Humanistic Psychology*, 56(4), 414–435.

Gray, M. A., & Stiles, W. B. (2011). Employing a case study in building an Assimilation Theory account of Generalized Anxiety Disorder and its treatment with Cognitive-Behavioral Therapy. *Pragmatic Case Studies in Psychotherapy*, 7(4), 529–557.

Greenberg, L.S. & Pinsof, W.M. (eds) (1986). *The Psychotherapeutic Process: A Research Handbook*. New York: Guilford Press.

Gross, C. (2016). Scientific misconduct. *Annual Review of Psychology*, 67, 693–711.

Guillemin, M., & Gillam, L. (2004). Ethics, reflexivity and ethically important moments in research. *Qualitative Inquiry*, 10, 261–280.

Gundel, B. E., Bartholomew, T. T., & Scheel, M. J. (2020). Culture and care: an illustration of multicultural processes in a counseling dyad. *Practice Innovations*, 5(1), 19.

Gupta, N., Simms, E. M., & Dougherty, A. (2019). Eyes on the street: Photovoice, liberation psychotherapy, and the emotional landscapes of urban children. *Emotion, Space and Society*, 33, 100627.

Halldorsson, B., & Salkovskis, P. M. (2017). Treatment of obsessive compulsive disorder and excessive reassurance seeking in an older adult: a single case quasi-experimental design. *Behavioural and Cognitive Psychotherapy*, 45(6), 616–628.

Hallgren, K. A. (2012). Computing inter-rater reliability for observational data: an overview and tutorial. *Tutorials in Quantitative Methods for Psychology*, 8(1), 23–35.

Halstead, J. E., Leach, C., & Rust, J. (2007). The development of a brief distress measure for the evaluation of psychotherapy and counseling (sPaCE). *Psychotherapy Research*, 17(6), 656–672.

Halvorsen, M. S., Benum, K., Haavind, H., & McLeod, J. (2016). A life-saving therapy: the theory-building case of "Cora". *Pragmatic Case Studies in Psychotherapy*, 12, 158–193.

Hamill, M., Reid, M., & Reynolds, S. (2008). Letters in cognitive analytic therapy: the patients experience. *Psychotherapy Research*, 18, 573–583.

Hanauer, D. I. (2012). Growing up in the unseen shadow of the kindertransport: a poetic-narrative autoethnography. *Qualitative Inquiry*, 18(10), 845–851.

Hanauer, D. I. (2021). Mourning writing: a poetic autoethnography on the passing of my father. *Qualitative Inquiry*, 27(1), 37–44.

Hänninen, V., & Valkonen, J. (2019). Losing and regaining grip: depression and everyday life. *Sage Open*, 9(1), 2158244018822371.

Hanson, J. (2005). Should your lips be zipped? How therapist self-disclosure and non-disclosure affects clients. *Counselling and Psychotherapy Research*, 5(2), 96–104.

Hanssen, I., van der Horst, N., Boele, M., van Bennekom, M. L., Regeer, E., & Speckens, A. (2020). The feasibility of mindfulness-based cognitive therapy for people with bipolar disorder: a qualitative study. *International Journal of Bipolar Disorders*, 8(1), 1–12.

Harder, R., Nicol, J. J., & Martin, S. L. (2020). "The power of personal experiences": post-publication experiences of researchers using autobiographical data. *The Qualitative Report*, 25(1), 238–254.

Hardy, G. E., Bishop-Edwards, L., Chambers, E., Connell, J., Dent-Brown, K., Kothari, G., & Parry, G. D. (2019). Risk factors for negative experiences during psychotherapy. *Psychotherapy Research*, 29(3), 403–414.

Hargons, C., Lantz, M., Reid Marks, L., & Voelkel, E. (2017). Becoming a bridge: collaborative autoethnography of four female counseling psychology student leaders. *The Counseling Psychologist*, 45(7), 1017–1047.

Harvey, N., & Holmes, C. A. (2012). Nominal group technique: an effective method for obtaining group consensus. *International Journal of Nursing Practice*, 18(2), 188–194.

Hatcher, R. L., & Barends, A. W. (1996). Patients' view of the alliance in psychotherapy: exploratory factor analysis of three alliance measures. *Journal of Consulting and Clinical Psychology*, 64(6), 1326–1336.

Hatcher, R. L., & Gillaspy, J. A. (2006). Development and validation of a revised short form of the Working Alliance Inventory. *Psychotherapy Research*, 16: 12–25.

Hayward, B. A. (2020). Mental health nursing in bushfire-affected communities: an autoethnographic insight. *International Journal of Mental Health Nursing*, 29(6), 1262–1271.

Heron, K. E., Everhart, R. S., McHale, S. M., & Smyth, J. M. (2017). Using mobile-technology-based ecological momentary assessment (EMA) methods with youth: A systematic review and recommendations. *Journal of Pediatric Psychology*, 42(10), 1087–1107.

Hill, C. E. (ed.) (2012). *Consensual Qualitative Research: A Practical Resource for Investigating Social Science Phenomena*. Washington, DC: American Psychological Association.

Hill, C. E., & Knox, S. (2021). *Essentials of Consensual Qualitative Research*. Washington, DC: American Psychological Association.

Hill, C. E., Sim, W., Spangler, P., Stahl, J., Sullivan, C., & Teyber, E. (2008). Therapist immediacy in brief psychotherapy: case study II. *Psychotherapy*, 45, 298–315.

Hills, J., Lees, J., Freshwater, D., & Cahill, J. (2018). Psychosoma in crisis: an autoethnographic study of medically unexplained symptoms and their diverse contexts. *British Journal of Guidance and Counselling*, 46 (2), 135–147.

Hodge, S., Barr, W., Bowen, L., et al. (2012). Exploring the role of an emotional support and counselling service for people with visual impairments. *British Journal of Visual Impairment*, 31, 5–19.

Hofmann, M., & Barker, C. (2017). On researching a health condition that the researcher has also experienced. *Qualitative Psychology*, 4(2), 139–148.

Hogue, A., Dauber, S., & Henderson, C. E. (2017). Benchmarking family therapy for adolescent behavior problems in usual care: fidelity, outcomes, and therapist performance differences. *Administration and Policy in Mental Health and Mental Health Services Research*, 44(5), 626–641.

Hollway, W., & Jefferson, T. (2013). *Doing Qualitative Research Differently: Free Association, Narrative and the Interview Method*. 2nd edn. London: Sage.

Holman Jones, S., Adams, T.E., & Ellis, C. (eds) (2016). *Handbook of Autoethnography*. New York: Routledge.

Hong, Q. N., Fàbregues, S., Bartlett, G., Boardman, F., Cargo, M., Dagenais, P., ... & Pluye, P. (2018). The Mixed Methods Appraisal Tool (MMAT) version 2018 for information professionals and researchers. *Education for Information*, 34(4), 285–291.

Horowitz, L. M., Turan, B., Wilson, K. R., et al. (2008). Interpersonal theory and the measurement of interpersonal constructs. In G. J. Boyle, G. Matthews, & D. H. Saklofske (eds), *SAGE Handbook of Personality Theory and Assessment: Vol. 2. Personality Measurement and Testing*. London: Sage.

Hou, J.-M., & Skovholt, T. M. (2020). Characteristics of highly resilient therapists. *Journal of Counseling Psychology*, 67(3), 386–400.

Hovland, R. T., & Moltu, C. (2019). Making way for a clinical feedback system in the narrow space between sessions: navigating competing demands in complex healthcare settings. *International Journal of Mental Health Systems*, 13(1), 68.

Howard, K. I., Krause, M. S., Caburney, C. A., & Noel, S. B. (2001) Syzygy, science, and psychotherapy: the Consumer Reports study. *Journal of Clinical Psychology*, 57, 865–874.

Huber, J., Nikendei, C., Ehrenthal, J. C., Schauenburg, H., Mander, J., & Dinger, U. (2019). Therapeutic Agency Inventory: Development and psychometric validation of a patient self-report. *Psychotherapy Research*, 29(7), 919–934.

Hulley, S. B., et al. (eds) (2007). *Designing Clinical Research: An Epidemiologic Approach*. New York: Lippincott Williams and Wilkins.

Humble, Á. M. (2019). Computer-aided qualitative analysis software. In P. Atkinson, S. Delamont, A. Cernat, J. W. Sakshaug, & R. A. Williams (eds), *SAGE Research Methods Foundations*. www.doi.org/10.4135/9781526421036825663

Hundt, N. E., Smith, T. L., Fortney, J. C., Cully, J. A., & Stanley, M. A. (2019). A qualitative study of veterans' mixed emotional reactions to receiving a PTSD diagnosis. *Psychological Services*, 16(4), 687–692.

Hunter, R. F., Gough, A., O'Kane, N., McKeown, G., Fitzpatrick, A., Walker, T., ... & Kee, F. (2018). Ethical issues in social media research for public health. *American Journal of Public Health*, 108(3), 343–348.

Iacono, V. L., Symonds, P., & Brown, D. H. (2016). Skype as a tool for qualitative research interviews. *Sociological Research Online*, 21(2), 1–12.

Iphofen, R., & Tolich, M. (eds). (2018). *The SAGE Handbook of Qualitative Research Ethics*. Thousand Oaks, CA: Sage.

Jackson, J. L., Chui, H. T., & Hill, C. E. (2012). The modification of Consensual Qualitative Research for Case Study Research: an introduction to CQR-C. In C.E. Hill (ed.), *Consensual Qualitative Research: A Practical Resource for Investigating Social Science Phenomena*. Washington, DC: American Psychological Association.

Jacobson, N. C., Newman, M. G., & Goldfried, M. R. (2016). Clinical feedback about empirically supported treatments for obsessive-compulsive disorder. *Behavior Therapy*, 47(1), 75–90.

Jaffe, A. E., DiLillo, D., Hoffman, L., Haikalis, M., & Dykstra, R. E. (2015). Does it hurt to ask? A meta-analysis of participant reactions to trauma research. *Clinical Psychology Review*, 40, 40–56.

Janesick, V. J. (2016). *"Stretching" Exercises for Qualitative Researchers*. 4th edn. Thousand Oaks, CA: Sage.

Jennings, L., & Skovholt, T. M. (1999). The cognitive, emotional, and relational characteristics of master therapists. *Journal of Counseling Psychology*, 46(1), 3–11.

Jimenez-Arista, L. E., Holzapfel, J., Shanholtz, C. E., & Tracey, T. J. (2020). The incremental validity of the sPaCE scale in predicting treatment outcome. *Measurement and Evaluation in Counseling and Development*, 53(3), 149–164.

Johansson, C., & Werbart, A. (2020). Am I really bipolar? Personal accounts of the experience of being diagnosed with Bipolar II Disorder. *Frontiers in Psychology*, 11, 2430.

Jokela, M., Singh-Manoux, A., Shipley, M. J., et al. (2011). Natural course of recurrent psychological distress in adulthood. *Journal of Affective Disorders*, 130, 454–561.

Jones, E. E. (1985). Manual for the psychotherapy process Q-sort. Unpublished manuscript, University of California, Berkeley, CA.

Jones, S., & Hurrell, E. (2019). A single case experimental design: how do different psychological outcome measures capture the experience of a client undergoing CBT for chronic pain? *British Journal of Pain*, 13(1), 6–12.

Jonsen, K., Fendt, J., & Point, S. (2018). Convincing qualitative research: what constitutes persuasive writing? *Organizational Research Methods*, 21(1), 30–67.

Jordan, M. (2014). Moving beyond counselling and psychotherapy as it currently is – taking therapy outside. *European Journal of Psychotherapy & Counselling*, 16(4), 361–375.

Karakurt, G., Dial, S., Korkow, H., et al. (2013). Experiences of marriage and family therapists working with intimate partner violence. *Journal of Family Psychotherapy*, 24, 1–16.

Kaslow, N. J. (2020). My life as a female leader in the Academy: lessons learned. *Women & Therapy*, 43(1–2), 18–43.

Kasper, L. B., Hill, C. E., & Kivlighan, D. M. (2008). Therapist immediacy in brief psychotherapy: Case study I. *Psychotherapy*, 45, 281–297.

Kastrani, T., Deliyanni-Kouimtzi, V., & Athanasiades, C. (2015). Greek female clients' experience of the gendered therapeutic relationship: an interpretative phenomenological analysis. *International Journal for the Advancement of Counselling*, 37(1), 77–92.

Keeney, S., Hasson, F., & McKenna, H. (2010). *The Delphi Technique in Nursing and Health Research*. Oxford: Wiley Blackwell.

Kerr, C. E., Josyula, K., & Littenberg, R. (2011). Developing an observing attitude: an analysis of meditation diaries in an MBSR clinical trial. *Clinical Psychology & Psychotherapy*, 18(1), 80–93.

Kidd, J.D., & Finlayson, M. P. (2010). Mental illness in the nursing workplace: A collective autoethnography. *Contemporary Nurse*, 36(1–2), 21–33.

King, A. (2011). When the body speaks: tummy rumblings in the therapeutic encounter. *British Journal of Psychotherapy*, 27, 156–174.

King, K. M., & Jones, K. (2019). An autoethnography of broaching in supervision: joining supervisee and supervisor perspectives on addressing identity, power, and difference. *The Clinical Supervisor*, 38(1), 17–37.

Kinney, P. (2017). Walking interviews. *Social Research Update*, 67, 1–4.

Klein, M. H., Mathieu-Coughlan, P., & Kiesler, D. J. (1986). The Experiencing Scales. In L. S. Greenberg and W. M. Pinsof (eds), *The Psychotherapeutic Process: A Research Handbook*. New York: Guilford.

Kleiven, G. S., Hjeltnes, A., Råbu, M., & Moltu, C. (2020). Opening up: clients' inner struggles in the initial phase of therapy. *Frontiers in Psychology*, 11, 3554.

Klinger, R. S., Ladany, N., & Kulp, L. E. (2012). It's too late to apologize: therapist embarrassment and shame. *The Counseling Psychologist*, 40(4), 554–574.

Knoll, M., & Fitzpatrick, M. (2020). Dissemination in psychotherapy: The case of progress monitoring measures. *Canadian Psychology*.

Knox, R. (2008). Clients experiences of relational depth in person-centred counselling. *Counselling and Psychotherapy Research*, 8, 118–124.

Knox, S., Adrians, N., Everson, E., et al. (2011). Clients' perspectives on therapy termination. *Psychotherapy Research*, 21, 154–167.

Knox, S., DuBois, R., Smith, J., et al. (2009). Clients' experiences giving gifts to therapists. *Psychotherapy: Theory, Research, Practice, Training*, 46, 350–361.

Knox, S., Goldberg, J. L., Woodhouse, S. S., et al. (1999). Clients' internal representations of their therapists. *Journal of Counseling Psychology*, 46, 244–256.

Kodet, J., Reese, R. J., Duncan, B. L., & Bohanske, R. T. (2019). Psychotherapy for depressed youth in poverty: benchmarking outcomes in a public behavioral health setting. *Psychotherapy*, 56(2), 254–262.

Kongara, S., Douglas, C., Martindale, B., & Summers, A. (2017). Individual psychodynamic therapy for psychosis: a Delphi study. *Psychosis*, 9(3), 216–224.

Kramer, U. (2009). Individualizing exposure therapy for PTSD: the case of Caroline. *Pragmatic Case Studies in Psychotherapy*, 5(2), 1–24.

Kraus, D., & Castonguay, L. G. (2010). Treatment Outcome Package (TOP) – Development and use in naturalistic settings. In M. Barkham, G. E. Hardy, & J. Mellor-Clark (eds), *Developing and Delivering Practice-based Evidence: A Guide for the Psychological Therapies*. Chichester: Wiley-Blackwell.

Kraus, D. R., Castonguay, L., Boswell, J. F., et al. (2011). Therapist effectiveness: implications for accountability and patient care. *Psychotherapy Research*, 21: 267–276.

Krause, K., Midgley, N., Edbrooke-Childs, J., & Wolpert, M. (2020). A comprehensive mapping of outcomes following psychotherapy for adolescent depression: the perspectives of young people, their parents and therapists. *European Child & Adolescent Psychiatry*.

Krause, M., Espinosa-Duque, H. D., Tomicic, A., Córdoba, A. C., & Vásquez, D. (2018). Psychotherapy for depression from the point of view of economically disadvantaged individuals in Chile and Colombia. *Counselling and Psychotherapy Research*, 18(2), 178–189.

Krivzov, J., Baert, F., Meganck, R., & Cornelis, S. (2021). Interpersonal dynamics and therapeutic relationship in patients with functional somatic syndromes: A metasynthesis of case studies. *Journal of Counseling Psychology* 68(5), 593–607.

Kroenke, K., Spitzer, R. L., & Williams, J. B. (2001). The PHQ-9: validity of a brief depression severity measure. *Journal of General Internal Medicine*, 16: 606–613.

Krueger, R. A., & Casey, M. A. (2008). *Focus Groups: A Practical Guide for Applied Research*. 4th edn. Thousand Oaks, CA: Sage.

Kuhnlein, I. (1999). Psychotherapy as a process of transformation: the analysis of posttherapeutic autobiographical narrations. *Psychotherapy Research*, 9, 274–288.

Kverme, B., Natvik, E., Veseth, M., & Moltu, C. (2019). Moving toward connectedness – a qualitative study of recovery processes for people with borderline personality disorder. *Frontiers in Psychology*, 10, 430.

Kwan, B., & Rickwood, D. J. (2015). A systematic review of mental health outcome measures for young people aged 12 to 25 years. *BMC Psychiatry*, 15, 279. https://doi.org/10.1186/s12888-015-0664-x

Kwan, B., & Rickwood, D. J. (2021). A routine outcome measure for youth mental health: clinically interpreting MyLifeTracker. *Early Intervention in Psychiatry*, 15(4), 807–817.

Kwan, B., Rickwood, D. J., & Telford, N. R. (2018). Development and validation of MyLifeTracker: a routine outcome measure for youth mental health. *Psychology Research and Behavior Management*, 11, 67.

Lajoie, C., Fortin, J., & Racine, E. (2020). Lived experiences of participation in mental health research in Canada: breaking the glass wall. *Disability & Society*.

Lajoie, C., Poleksic, J., Bracken-Roche, D., MacDonald, M. E., & Racine, E. (2020). The concept of vulnerability in mental health research: a mixed methods study on researcher perspectives. *Journal of Empirical Research on Human Research Ethics*, 1556264620902657.

Lakeman, R., McAndrew, S., MacGabhann, L., & Warne, T. (2013). 'That was helpful ... no one has talked to me about that before': research participation as a therapeutic activity. *International Journal of Mental Health Nursing*, 22(1), 76–84.

Lambert, M. J. (2015). Progress feedback and the OQ-system: The past and the future. *Psychotherapy*, 52(4), 381–390.

Landes, S. J., Smith, B. N., & Weingardt, K. R. (2019). Supporting grass roots implementation of an evidence-based psychotherapy through a virtual community of practice: a case example in the Department of Veterans Affairs. *Cognitive and Behavioral Practice*, 26(3), 453–465.

Lapadat, J. C. (2017). Ethics in autoethnography and collaborative autoethnography. *Qualitative Inquiry*, 23(8), 589–603.

Larsen, D., Flesaker, K., & Stege, R. (2008). Qualitative interviewing using Interpersonal Process Recall: investigating internal experiences during professional–client conversation. *International Journal of Qualitative Methods*, 7, 18–37.

Lave, J., & Wenger E. (1991). *Situated Learning: Legitimate Peripheral Participation*. Cambridge: Cambridge University Press.

Lavik, K. O., Veseth, M., Frøysa, H., Binder, P. E., & Moltu, C. (2018). What are "good outcomes" for adolescents in public mental health settings? *International Journal of Mental Health Systems*, 12(1), 3.

Law, D. (2011). *Goals and Goal Based Outcomes (GBOS): Some Useful Information*. London: CAMHS Press.

Law, D., & Cooper, M. (eds) (2017). *Working with Goals in Psychotherapy and Counselling*. New York: Oxford University Press.

Le Roux, C. S. (2017). Exploring rigour in autoethnographic research. *International Journal of Social Research Methodology*, 20(2), 195–207.

Leach, C., & Lutz, W. (2010). Constructing and disseminating outcome data at the service level: case tracking and benchmarking. In M. Barkham, G. E. Hardy, & J. Mellor-Clark (eds), *Developing and Delivering Practice-based Evidence: A Guide for the Psychological Therapies*. Chichester: Wiley-Blackwell.

Leech, N. L., Onwuegbuzie, A. J., & O'Conner, R. (2011). Assessing internal consistency in counseling research. *Counseling Outcome Research and Evaluation*, 2(2), 115–125.

Leigh, J. (2013). Effective counselling methods and strategies, based on my personal experiences, for victims of trauma and abuse. *Asia Pacific Journal of Counselling and Psychotherapy*, 4(2), 175–184.

Leitch, R. (2006). Outside the spoon drawer, naked and skinless in search of my professional esteem. The tale of an "academic pro". *Qualitative Inquiry*, 12, 353–364.

Lenz, A. S. (2020). Estimating and reporting clinical significance in counseling research: Inferences based on percent improvement. *Measurement and Evaluation in Counseling and Development*, 53(4), 289–296.

Leonidaki, V., Lemma, A., & Hobbis, I. (2016). Clients' experiences of dynamic interpersonal therapy (DIT): opportunities and challenges for brief, manualised psychodynamic therapy in the NHS. *Psychoanalytic Psychotherapy*, 30(1), 42–61.

Lepper, G., & Riding, N. (2006). *Researching the Psychotherapy Process: A Practical Guide to Transcript-Based Methods*. Basingstoke: Palgrave Macmillan.

Leuzinger-Bohleber, M., Solms, M., & Arnold, S.E (eds) (2020). *Outcome Research and the Future of Psychoanalysis: Clinicians and Researchers in Dialogue*. New York: Routledge.

Levitt, H. M. (2020). *Reporting Qualitative Research in Psychology: How to Meet APA Style Journal Article Reporting Standards*. Revised edn. Washington, DC: American Psychological Association.

Levitt, H. M. (2021). *Essentials of Critical-Constructivist Grounded Theory Research*. Washington, DC: American Psychological Association.

Levitt, H. M., Bamberg, M., Creswell, J. W., Frost, D. M., Josselson, R., & Suárez-Orozco, C. (2018). Journal article reporting standards for qualitative primary, qualitative meta-analytic, and mixed methods research in psychology: The APA Publications and Communications Board task force report. *American Psychologist*, 73(1), 26–46.

Levitt, H. M., Butler, M., & Hill, T. (2006). What clients find helpful in psychotherapy: developing principles for facilitating moment-to-moment change. *Journal of Counseling Psychology*, 53, 314–324.

Levitt, H., Kannan, D., & Ippolito, M. R. (2013). Teaching qualitative methods using a research team approach: Publishing grounded theory projects with your class. *Qualitative Research in Psychology*, 10(2), 119–139.

Levitt, H. M., McLeod, J., & Stiles, W. B. (2021). The conceptualization, design, and evaluation of qualitative methods in research on psychotherapy. In M. Barkham, L. Castonguay, & W. Lutz (eds), *Bergin & Garfield's Handbook of Psychotherapy and Behavior Change*. 7th edn (pp. 51–86). New York: Wiley.

Levitt, H. M., Motulsky, S. L., Wertz, F. J., Morrow, S. L., & Ponterotto, J. G. (2017). Recommendations for designing and reviewing qualitative research in psychology: promoting methodological integrity. *Qualitative Psychology*, 4, 2–22.

Levitt, H. M., & Piazza-Bonin, E. (2016). Wisdom and psychotherapy: studying expert therapists' clinical wisdom to explicate common processes. *Psychotherapy Research*, 26(1), 31–47.

Levitt, H. M., Pomerville, A., & Surace, F. I. (2016). A qualitative meta-analysis examining clients' experiences of psychotherapy: a new agenda. *Psychological Bulletin*, 142(8), 801–830.

Levitt, H. M., Surace, F. I., Wu, M. B., Chapin, B., Hargrove, J. G., Herbitter, C., Lu, E. C., Maroney, M. R., & Hochman, A. L. (2021). The meaning of scientific objectivity and subjectivity: from the perspective of methodologists. *Psychological Methods*.

Levy, R. A., Ablon, J. S., & Kächele, H. (eds) (2012). *Psychodynamic Psychotherapy Research: Evidence-Based Practice and Practice-Based Evidence*. New York: Humana.

Lieblich, A. (2013). Healing plots: Writing and reading in life-stories groups. *Qualitative Inquiry*, 19(1), 46–52.

Liggins, J., Kearns, R. A., & Adams, P. J. (2013). Using autoethnography to reclaim the 'place of healing' in mental health care. *Social Science & Medicine*, 91, 105–109.

Lilienfeld, S. O., Wood, J. M., & Howard, N. (2000). The scientific status of projective techniques. *Psychological Science in the Public Interest*, 1, 27–66.

Lilliengren, P., & Werbart, A. (2005). A model of therapeutic action grounded in the patients view of curative and hindering factors in psychoanalytic psychotherapy. *Psychotherapy: Theory, Research, Practice, Training*, 3, 324–399.

Limberg, D., Gnilka, P. B., & Broda, M. (2021). Advancing the counseling profession by examining relationships between variables. *Journal of Counseling & Development*, 99(2), 145–155.

Lind, M., Jørgensen, C. R., Heinskou, T., et al. (2019). Patients with borderline personality disorder show increased agency in life stories after 12 months of psychotherapy. *Psychotherapy*, 56(2), 274–283.

Lindhiem, O., Bennett, C. B., Orimoto, T. E., & Kolko, D. J. (2016). A meta-analysis of personalized treatment goals in psychotherapy: a preliminary report and call for more studies. *Clinical Psychology: Science and Practice*, 23(2), 165–176.

Lindgren, A., Werbart, A., & Philips, B. (2010). Long-term outcome and post-treatment effects of psychoanalytic psychotherapy with young adults. *Psychology and Psychotherapy: Theory, Research and Practice*, 83(1), 27–43.

Linstone, H. A., & Turoff, M. (2002). *The Delphi Method: Techniques and Applications.* Boston, MA: Addison-Wesley.

Llewelyn, S. (1988). Psychological therapy as viewed by clients and therapists. *British Journal of Clinical Psychology*, 27, 223–238.

Lloyd, C. E., Duncan, C., & Cooper, M. (2019). Goal measures for psychotherapy: a systematic review of self-report, idiographic instruments. *Clinical Psychology: Science and Practice*, 26(3), e12281.

Lobe, B., Morgan, D., & Hoffman, K. A. (2020). Qualitative data collection in an era of social distancing. *International Journal of Qualitative Methods*, 19, 1609406920937875.

Løvgren, A., Røssberg, J. I., Engebretsen, E., & Ulberg, R. (2020). Improvement in psychodynamic psychotherapy for depression: a qualitative study of the patients' perspective. *International Journal of Environmental Research and Public Health*, 17(18).

Lunn, S., Daniel, S. I., & Poulsen, S. (2016). Psychoanalytic psychotherapy with a client with bulimia nervosa. *Psychotherapy*, 53(2), 206–215.

Lupton, E. (2011). *Graphic Design Thinking: Beyond Brainstorming.* New York: Princeton Architectural Press.

Lutz, W., de Jong, K., Rubel, J. E., & Delgadillo, J. (2021). Measuring, predicting and tracking change in psychotherapy. In M. Barkham, W. Lutz, & L. Castonguay (eds), *Bergin & Garfield's Handbook of Psychotherapy and Behavior Change.* 7th edn. New York: Wiley.

Macaskie, J., Lees, J., & Freshwater, D. (2015). Talking about talking: interpersonal process recall as an intersubjective approach to research. *Psychodynamic Practice*, 21(3), 226–240.

MacCormack, T., Simonian, J., Lim, J., et al. (2001). Someone who cares: a qualitative investigation of cancer patients experiences of psychotherapy. *Psycho-Oncology*, 10, 52–65.

Macdonald, W., Mead, N., Bower, P., et al. (2007). A qualitative study of patients' perceptions of a minimal psychological therapy. *International Journal of Social Psychiatry*, 53, 23–33.

MacFarlane, P., Anderson, T., & McClintock, A. S. (2017). Empathy from the client's perspective: a grounded theory analysis. *Psychotherapy Research*, 27(2), 227–238.

Mackrill, T. (2007). Using a cross-contextual qualitative diary design to explore client experiences of psychotherapy. *Counselling and Psychotherapy Research*, 7: 233–239.

Mackrill, T. (2008). Solicited diary studies of psychotherapeutic practice – pros and cons. *European Journal of Psychotherapy and Counselling*, 10, 5–18.

Malterud, K. (2011). *Kvalitative metoder i medisinsk forskning: En innføring* [Qualitative methods in medical research: An introduction]. 3rd edn. Oslo: Universitetsforlaget.

Malterud, K., Siersma, V. D., & Guassora, A. D. (2016). Sample size in qualitative interview studies: guided by information power. *Qualitative Health Research*, 26(13), 1753–1760.

Maple, M., Wayland, S., Sanford, R., Spillane, A., & Coker, S. (2020). Carers' motivations for, and experiences of, participating in suicide research. *International Journal of Environmental Research and Public Health*, 17(5), 1733.

Marriott, M., & Kellett, S. (2009). Evaluating a cognitive analytic therapy service; practice-based outcomes and comparisons with person-centred and cognitive-behavioural therapies. *Psychology and Psychotherapy: Theory, Research and Practice*, 82(1), 57–72.

Marshall, R. D., Spitzer, R. L., Vaughan, S. C., Vaughan, R., Mellman, L. A., MacKinnon, R. A., & Roose, S. P. (2001). Assessing the subjective experience of being a participant in psychiatric research. *American Journal of Psychiatry*, 158(2), 319–321.

Maruish, M. E. (Ed.). (2017). *Handbook of Psychological Assessment in Primary Care Settings*. New York: Taylor & Francis.

Marzillier, J. (2010). *The Gossamer Thread: My Life as a Psychotherapist*. London: Karnac.

Matthews, A. (2019a). Orientation. *Journal of Loss and Trauma*, 24(7), 650–663.

Matthews, A. (2019b). Writing through grief: using autoethnography to help process grief after the death of a loved one. *Methodological Innovations*, 12(3).

Mayotte-Blum, J., Slavin-Mulford, J., Lehmann, M., et al. (2012). Therapeutic immediacy across long-term psychodynamic psychotherapy: an evidence-based case study. *Journal of Counseling Psychology*, 59(1), 27–40.

McAleavey, A. A., Castonguay, L. G., & Goldfried, M. R. (2014). Clinical experiences in conducting cognitive-behavioral therapy for social phobia. *Behavior Therapy*, 45(1), 21–35.

McCaslin, M. L. & Scott, K. W. (2003). The five-question method for framing a qualitative research study. *The Qualitative Report*, 8, 447–461.

McIlveen, P. (2007). The genuine scientist-practitioner in vocational psychology: An autoethnography. *Qualitative Research in Psychology*, 4(4), 295–311.

McKenna, P. A., & Todd, D. M. (1997). Longitudinal utilization of mental health services, a time-line method, nine retrospective accounts, and a preliminary conceptualization. *Psychotherapy Research*, 7, 383–396.

McKenzie, E. A. (2015). An autoethnographic inquiry into the experience of grief after traumatic loss. *Illness, Crisis & Loss*, 23(2), 93–109.

McKenzie, K., Murray, G. C., Prior, S., & Stark, L. (2011). An evaluation of a school counselling service with direct links to Child and Adolescent Mental Health (CAMH) services. *British Journal of Guidance & Counselling*, 39(1), 67–82.

McLeod, J. (2001). An administratively created reality: some problems with the use of self-report questionnaire measures of adjustment in counselling/psychotherapy outcome research. *Counselling and Psychotherapy Research*, 1, 215–226.

McLeod, J. (2010). *Case Study Research in Counselling and Psychotherapy*. London: Sage.

McLeod, J. (2011). *Qualitative Research in Counselling and Psychotherapy*. 2nd edn. London: Sage.

McLeod, J. (2013a). *An Introduction to Research in Counselling and Psychotherapy*. London: Sage.

McLeod, J. (2013b). Increasing the rigor of case study evidence in therapy research. *Pragmatic Case Studies in Psychotherapy*, 9, 382–402.

McLeod, J. (2016). *Using Research in Counselling and Psychotherapy*. London: Sage.

McLeod, J., Johnston, J., & Griffin, J. (2000). A naturalistic study of the effectiveness of time-limited counselling with low-income clients. *European Journal of Psychotherapy, Counselling & Health*, 3(2), 263–277.

McLeod, J., Levitt, H. M., & Stiles, W. B. (2021). Qualitative Research: Contributions to theory, policy and practice. In M. Barkham, L. Castonguay, & W. Lutz (eds) *Bergin & Garfield's Handbook of Psychotherapy and Behavior Change*. 7th edn (pp. 351–384). New York: Wiley.

McLeod, J., & Lynch, G. (2000). 'This is our life': strong evaluation in psychotherapy narrative. *European Journal of Psychotherapy, Counselling & Health*, 3(3), 389–406.

McLeod, Julia. (2021). How students use deliberate practice during the first stage of counsellor training. *Counselling and Psychotherapy Research*.

McLeod, Julia., Thurston, M., & McLeod, J. (2014). Case study methodologies. In A. Vossler and N. Moller (eds), *The Counselling and Psychotherapy Research Handbook*. London: Sage.

McMillan, C., & Ramirez, H. E. (2016). Autoethnography as therapy for trauma. *Women & Therapy*, 39(3–4), 432–458.

McMullen, L. M., & Herman, J. (2009). Women's accounts of their decision to quit taking antidepressants. *Qualitative Health Research*, 19, 1569–1579.

McPherson, S., Rost, F., Sidhu, S., & Dennis, M. (2020). Non-strategic ignorance: considering the potential for a paradigm shift in evidence-based mental health. *Health*, 24(1), 3–20.

Meekums, B. (2008). Embodied narratives in becoming a counselling trainer: an autoethnographic study. *British Journal of Guidance & Counselling*, 36(3), 287–301.

Mellor-Clark, J., Barkham, M., Connell, J., et al. (1999). Practice-based evidence and standardized evaluation: informing the design of the CORE system. *European Journal of Psychotherapy, Counselling and Health*, 2, 357–374.

Mellor-Clark, J., Twigg, E., Farrell, E., et al. (2013). Benchmarking key service quality indicators in UK Employee Assistance Programme Counselling: a CORE System data profile. *Counselling and Psychotherapy Research*, 13, 14–23.

Meystre, C., Kramer, U., De Roten, Y., Despland, J.-N., & Stiles, W. B. (2014). How psychotherapeutic exchanges become responsive: a theory-building case study in the framework of the assimilation model. *Counselling and Psychotherapy Research*, 14(1), 29–41.

Midgley, N., & Holmes, J. (2018). Psychoanalytic perspectives on the research interview. In K. Stamenova & R. D. Hinshelwood (eds), *Methods of Research into the Unconscious: Applying Psychoanalytic Ideas to Social Science*. London: Routledge.

Miller, S. D., Duncan, B. L., & Hubble, M. A. (2005). Outcome-informed clinical work. In J. C. Norcross and M. R. Goldfried (eds), *Handbook of Psychotherapy Integration*. New York: Oxford University Press.

Minami, T., Wampold, B., Serlin, R. C., et al. (2007). Benchmarks for psychotherapy efficacy in adult major depression. *Journal of Consulting and Clinical Psychology*, 75, 232–243.

Minami, T., Wampold, B., Serlin, R.C., et al. (2008). Benchmarking the effectiveness of psychotherapy treatment for adult depression in a managed care environment: a preliminary study. *Journal of Consulting and Clinical Psychology*, 76, 116–124.

Moltu, C., Stefansen, J., Nøtnes, J. C., Skjølberg, Å., & Veseth, M. (2017). What are "good outcomes" in public mental health settings? A qualitative exploration of clients' and therapists' experiences. *International Journal of Mental Health Systems*, 11(1), 1–10.

Moltu, C., Stefansen, J., Svisdahl, M., & Veseth, M. (2012). Negotiating the coresearcher mandate – service users' experiences of doing collaborative research on mental health. *Disability and Rehabilitation*, 34(19), 1608–1616.

Moore, S. (2006). Voluntary sector counselling: Has inadequate research resulted in a misunderstood and underutilised resource? *Counselling and Psychotherapy Research*, 6(4), 221–226.

Morley, S. (2017). *Single Case Methods in Clinical Psychology: A Practical Guide*. London: Routledge.

Morrow, S. L. (2005). Quality and trustworthiness in qualitative research in counseling psychology. *Journal of Counseling Psychology*, 52(2), 250–260.

Morrow, S. L., & Smith, M. L. (1995). Constructions of survival and coping by women who have survived childhood sexual abuse. *Journal of Counseling Psychology*, 42(1), 24–33.

Mullen, P. R., Fox, J., Goshorn, J. R., & Warraich, L. K. (2021). Crowdsourcing for online samples in counseling research. *Journal of Counseling & Development*, 99(2), 221–226.

Mullin, T., Barkham, M., Mothersole, G., et al. (2006). Recovery and improvement benchmarks for counselling and the psychological therapies in routine primary care. *Counselling and Psychotherapy Research*, 6, 68–80.

Murase, K. (2015). The art of communication through drawing: the case of "Mr. R," a young man professing misanthropy while longing for connection with others. *Pragmatic Case Studies in Psychotherapy*, 11(2), 81–116.

Mustakova-Possardt, E., Lyubansky, M., Basseches, M., & Oxenberg, J. (eds) (2014). *Toward a Socially Responsible Psychology for a Global Era*. New York: Springer.

Neal Kimball, C., & Turner, S. (2018). Nurturing the apprentice: an immersion training in qualitative research. *Qualitative Psychology*, 5(2), 290–299.

Nezu, A. M., & Nezu, C. M. (2007). Ensuring treatment integrity. In A. M Nezu and C. M. Nezu (eds), Evidence-based outcome research: a practical guide to conducting randomized controlled trials for psychosocial interventions. Cary, NC, USA: Oxford University Press.

Ng, F. Y., Townsend, M. L., Miller, C. E., Jewell, M., & Grenyer, B. F. (2019). The lived experience of recovery in borderline personality disorder: a qualitative study. *Borderline Personality Disorder and Emotion Dysregulation*, 6(1), 1–9.

Nilsson, T., Svensson, M., Sandell, R., et al. (2007). Patients' experiences of change on cognitive-behavioral therapy and psychodynamic therapy: a qualitative comparative study. *Psychotherapy Research*, 17, 553–566.

Nødtvedt, Ø. O., Binder, P. E., Stige, S. H., Schanche, E., Stiegler, J. R., & Hjeltnes, A. (2019). "You feel they have a heart and are not afraid to show it": exploring how clients experience the therapeutic relationship in Emotion-Focused Therapy. *Frontiers in Psychology*, 10, 1996.

Norcross, J. C., Koocher, G. P., & Garofalo, A. (2006). Discredited psychological treatments and tests: a Delphi poll. *Professional Psychology: Research and Practice*, 37(5), 515–523.

Norcross, J. C., & Lambert, M. J. (eds) (2019). *Psychotherapy Relationships that Work. Volume 1: Evidence-Based Therapist Contributions*. 3rd edn. New York: Oxford University Press.

Norcross, J. C., & Wampold, B. E. (eds) (2019). *Psychotherapy Relationships that Work. Volume 2: Evidence-Based Responsiveness*. 3rd edn. New York: Oxford University Press.

Nosek, B. A., & Bar-Anan, Y. (2012). Scientific utopia: 1. Opening scientific communication. *Psychological Inquiry*, 23, 217–243.

Oddli, H. W., Kjøs, P., & McLeod, J. (2020). Negotiating credibility: the peer review process in clinical research. *Qualitative Psychology*, 7(1), 59–75.

Oei, T. P., & Shuttlewood, G. J. (1999). Development of a satisfaction with therapy and therapist scale. *Australian & New Zealand Journal of Psychiatry*, 33(5), 748–753.

Ogrodniczuk, J. S., Sochting, I., Piper, W. E., & Joyce, A. S. (2012). A naturalistic study of alexithymia among psychiatric outpatients treated in an integrated group therapy program. *Psychology and Psychotherapy: Theory, Research and Practice*, 85(3), 278–291.

Olson, M. (2015). An auto-ethnographic study of "open dialogue": the illumination of snow. *Family Process*, 54(4), 716–729.

Osborn, M., & Smith, J. A. (2008). The fearfulness of chronic pain and the centrality of the therapeutic relationship in containing it: An interpretative phenomenological analysis. *Qualitative Research in Psychology*, 5(4), 276–288.

Osborne, T. L. (2018). *Practice-Based Research: How to Conduct Meaningful Research in Your Practice Setting*. New York: Routledge.

Osborne, T. L., & Luoma, J. B. (2018). Overcoming a primary barrier to practice-based research: access to an institutional review board (IRB) for independent ethics review. *Psychotherapy*, 55(3), 255–262.

Oswald, A. G. (2019). Improving outcomes with qualitative data analysis software: a reflective journey. *Qualitative Social Work*, 18(3), 436–442.

Owen, J., Reese, R. J., Quirk, K., & Rodolfa, E. (2013). Alliance in action: A new measure of clients' perceptions of therapists' alliance activity. *Psychotherapy Research*, 23(1), 67–77.

Owen, J., Wampold, B. E., Kopta, M., Rousmaniere, T., & Miller, S. D. (2016). As good as it gets? Therapy outcomes of trainees over time. *Journal of Counseling Psychology*, 63(1), 12–19.

Palmieri, G., Evans, C., Hansen, V., Brancaleoni, G., Ferrari, S., Porcelli, P., ... & Rigatelli, M. (2009). Validation of the Italian version of the clinical outcomes in routine evaluation outcome measure (CORE-OM). *Clinical Psychology & Psychotherapy*, 16(5), 444–449.

Paquin, J. D., Tao, K. W., & Budge, S. L. (2019). Toward a psychotherapy science for all: conducting ethical and socially just research. *Psychotherapy*, 56(4), 491–502.

Parkinson, S., Eatough, V., Holmes, J., Stapley, E., & Midgley, N. (2016). Framework analysis: a worked example of a study exploring young people's experiences of depression. *Qualitative Research in Psychology*, 13(2), 109–129.

Paterson, C. (1996). Measuring outcome in primary care: a patient-generated measure, MYMOP, compared to the SF-36 health survey. *British Medical Journal*, 312: 1016–1020.

Paz, C., Adana-Díaz, L., & Evans, C. (2020). Clients with different problems are different and questionnaires are not blood tests: a template analysis of psychiatric and psychotherapy clients' experiences of the CORE-OM. *Counselling and Psychotherapy Research*, 20(2), 274–283.

Pearson, D., & Vossler, A. (2016). Methodological issues in focus group research: the example of investigating counsellors' experiences of working with same-sex couples. *Counselling Psychology Review*, 31(1).

Pendzik, S., Emunah, R., & Johnson, D. R. (eds) (2016). *The Self in Performance. Autobiographical, Self-Revelatory, and Autoethnographic Forms of Therapeutic Theatre*. New York: Palgrave Macmillan.

Perren, S., Godfrey, M., & Rowland, N. (2009). The long-term effects of counselling: the process and mechanisms that contribute to ongoing change from a user perspective. *Counselling and Psychotherapy Research*, 9, 241–249.

Philips, B., Werbart, A., Wennberg, P., & Schubert, J. (2007). Young adults' ideas of cure prior to psychoanalytic psychotherapy. *Journal of Clinical Psychology*, 63(3), 213–232.

Pittig, A., Kotter, R., & Hoyer, J. (2019). The struggle of behavioral therapists with exposure: self-reported practicability, negative beliefs, and therapist distress about exposure-based interventions. *Behavior Therapy*, 50(2), 353–366.

Ponterotto, J. G. (2005). Qualitative research in counseling psychology: a primer on research paradigms and philosophy of science. *Journal of Counseling Psychology*, 52, 126–136.

Ponterotto, J. G., Park-Taylor, J., & Chen, E. C. (2017). Qualitative research in counselling and psychotherapy: history, methods, ethics, and impact. *The SAGE Handbook of Qualitative Research in Psychology* (pp. 496–517). 2nd edn. London: Sage.

Poulos, C. N. (2021). *Essentials of Autoethnography*. Washington, DC: American Psychological Association.

Poulsen, S., Lunn, S., & Sandros, C. (2010). Client experience of psychodynamic psychotherapy for bulimia nervosa: an interview study. *Psychotherapy: Theory, Research, Practice, Training*, 47(4), 469–483.

Pratt, T. C., Reisig, M. D., Holtfreter, K., & Golladay, K. A. (2019). Scholars' preferred solutions for research misconduct: results from a survey of faculty members at America's top 100 research universities. *Ethics & Behavior*, 29(7), 510–530.

Prosek, E. A., & Gibson, D. M. (2021). Promoting rigorous research by examining lived experiences: A review of four qualitative traditions. *Journal of Counseling & Development*, 99(2), 167–177.

Proulx, K. (2008). Experiences of women with Bulimia Nervosa in a mindfulness-based eating disorder treatment group. *Eating Disorders*, 16: 52–72.

Pugach, M. R., & Goodman, L. A. (2015). Low-income women's experiences in outpatient psychotherapy: a qualitative descriptive analysis. *Counselling Psychology Quarterly*, 28(4), 403–426.

Puvimanasinghe, T., Denson, L. A., Augoustinos, M., & Somasundaram, D. (2015). Vicarious resilience and vicarious traumatisation: experiences of working with refugees and asylum seekers in South Australia. *Transcultural Psychiatry*, 52(6), 743–765.

Quinn, M. C., Schofield, M. J., & Middleton, W. (2010). Permission to speak: therapists' understandings of psychogenic nonepileptic seizures and their treatment. *Journal of Trauma & Dissociation*, 11(1), 108–123.

Quinn, M. C., Schofield, M. J. & Middleton, W. (2012). Successful psychotherapy for psychogenic seizures in men. *Psychotherapy Research*, 22(6), 682–698.

Quirk, K., Owen, J., Reese, R. J., Babins-Wagner, R., & Berzins, S. (2020). Benchmarking community-based couple therapy: considering measurement reactivity. *Family Process*.

Råbu, M., & McLeod, J. (2018). Wisdom in professional knowledge: why it can be valuable to listen to the voices of senior psychotherapists. *Psychotherapy Research*, 28(5), 776–792.

Råbu, M., McLeod, J., Haavind, H., Bernhardt, I. S., Nissen-Lie, H., & Moltu, C. (2021). How psychotherapists make use of their experiences from being a client: Lessons from a collective autoethnography. *Counselling Psychology Quarterly*, 34(1), 109–128.

Råbu, M., & Moltu, C. (2021). People engaging each other: a dual-perspective study of interpersonal processes in useful therapy. *Journal of Contemporary Psychotherapy*, 51(1), 67–75.

Radcliffe, K., Masterson, C., & Martin, C. (2018). Clients' experience of non-response to psychological therapy: a qualitative analysis. *Counselling and Psychotherapy Research*, 18(2), 220–229.

Raymond, T. (2017). Hearing peristalsis: theory, interpretation and practice in biodynamic psychotherapy. *Body, Movement and Dance in Psychotherapy*, 12(1), 5–20.

Redhead, S., Johnstone, L., & Nightingale, J. (2015). Clients' experiences of formulation in cognitive behaviour therapy. *Psychology and Psychotherapy: Theory, Research and Practice*, 88, 453–467.

Reichelt, S., Skjerve, J., & McLeod, J. (2018). Topic-focused analysis in a case of integrative psychotherapy with a father fearing his own anger. *European Journal of Psychotherapy & Counselling*, 20(2), 134–163.

Rennie, D. L. (2000). Experiencing psychotherapy, grounded theory studies. In D. Cain and J. Seeman (eds), *Handbook of Research in Humanistic Psychotherapies*. Washington, DC: American Psychological Association.

Rennie, D. L., & Fergus, K. D. (2006). Embodied categorizing in the grounded theory method: methodical hermeneutics in action. *Theory and Psychology*, 16: 483–503.

Revell, S., & McLeod, J. (2017). Therapists' experience of walk and talk therapy: a descriptive phenomenological study. *European Journal of Psychotherapy and Counselling*, 19(3): 267–289.

Reynolds, F., Lim, K. H., & Prior, S. (2008). Narratives of therapeutic art-making in the context of marital breakdown: older women reflect on a significant mid-life experience. *Counselling Psychology Quarterly*, 21(3), 203–214.

Rezaie, L., Heydari, S., Paschall, E., Khazaie, H., Sadeghi Bahmani, D., & Brand, S. (2020). A mixed-method modified Delphi study toward identifying key elements of psychotherapy in Iran. *International Journal of Environmental Research and Public Health*, 17(7), 2514.

Rice, L. N., & Wagstaff, A. K. (1967). Client voice quality and expressive style as indexes of productive psychotherapy. *Journal of Consulting Psychology*, 31(6), 557–563.

Richardson, L. & Reid, C. (2006). I've lost my husband, my house and I need a new knee … why should I smile?: action research evaluation of a group cognitive behavioural therapy program for older adults with depression. *Clinical Psychologist*, 10, 60–66.

Riva, J., Malik, K. M. P., Burnie, S. J., et al. (2012). What is your research question? An introduction to the PICOT format for clinicians. *Journal of the Canadian Chiropractic Association*, 56, 167–171.

Rober, P., & Rosenblatt, P. C. (2017). Silence and memories of war: an autoethnographic exploration of family secrecy. *Family Process*, 56(1), 250–261.

Roberts, J. (1996). Perceptions of the significant other of the effects of psychodynamic psychotherapy, implications for thinking about psychodynamic and systems approaches. *British Journal of Psychiatry*, 168, 87–93.

Rodgers, B. (2006). Life space mapping: preliminary results from the development of a new method for investigating counselling outcomes. *Counselling and Psychotherapy Research*, 6(4), 227–232.

Rodgers, B. (2018). More than just a measure: exploring clients' experiences of using a standardised self-report questionnaire to evaluate counselling outcomes. *New Zealand Journal of Counselling*, 38, 90–112.

Rodgers, B., & Elliott, R. (2015). Qualitative methods in psychotherapy outcome research. In O. Gelo, A. Pritz, & B. Rieken (eds), *Psychotherapy Research: Foundations, Process and Outcome* (pp. 228–251). Vienna: Springer-Verlag.

Rogers, C. R. (1985). Toward a more human science of the person. *Journal of Humanistic Psychology*, 25, 7–24.

Rogers, C.R. & Dymond, R.F. (eds) (1954). *Psychotherapy and Personality Change*. Chicago, IL: University of Chicago Press.

Rogers, K. D., Young, A., Lovell, K., & Evans, C. (2013). The challenges of translating the clinical outcomes in routine evaluation–outcome measure (CORE-OM) into British sign language. *Journal of Deaf Studies and Deaf Education*, 18(3), 287–298.

Rupani, P., Cooper, M., McArthur, K., Pybis, J., Cromarty, K., Hill, A., ... & Turner, N. (2014). The goals of young people in school-based counselling and their achievement of these goals. *Counselling and Psychotherapy Research*, 14(4), 306–314.

Ryan, S., Hislop, J., & Ziebland, S. (2017). Do we all agree what "good health care" looks like? Views from those who are "seldom heard" in health research, policy and service improvement. *Health Expectations*, 20(5), 878–885.

Sagen, S. H., Hummelsund, D., & Binder, P. E. (2013). Feeling accepted: a phenomenological exploration of adolescent patients' experiences of the relational qualities that enable them to express themselves freely. *European Journal of Psychotherapy & Counselling*, 15(1), 53–75.

Sales, C., & Alves, P. C. (2012). Individualized patient-progress systems: why we need to move towards a personalized evaluation of psychological treatments. *Canadian Psychology*, 53(2), 115–121.

Sandberg, J., Gustafsson, S., & Holmqvist, R. (2017). Interpersonally traumatised patients' view of significant and corrective experiences in the psychotherapeutic relationship. *European Journal of Psychotherapy & Counselling*, 19(2), 175–199.

Sandell, R. (1987a). Assessing the effects of psychotherapy. II. A procedure for direct rating of psychotherapeutic change. *Psychotherapy and Psychosomatics*, 47, 37–43.

Sandell, R. (1987b). Assessing the effects of psychotherapy. III. Reliability and validity of 'Change after Psychotherapy'. *Psychotherapy and Psychosomatics*, 47, 44–52.

Sandell, R. (2015). Rating the outcomes of psychotherapy using the Change after Psychotherapy (CHAP) scales. Manual and commentary. *Research in Psychotherapy: Psychopathology, Process and Outcome*, 18, 32–49.

Sandell, R., & Wilczek, A. (2016). Another way to think about psychological change: experiential vs. incremental. *European Journal of Psychotherapy & Counselling*, 18(3), 228–251.

Sandelowski, M., & Leeman, J. (2012). Writing usable qualitative health research findings. *Qualitative Health Research*, 22, 1404–1413.

Sarantakis, N. P. (2020). Rediscovering meaning when entering "older age": a counseling case study based on a lifespan development and a pluralistic approach. *Practice Innovations*, 5(1), 1.

Sawyer, R. D., & Norris, J. (2012). *Duoethnography*. Oxford: Oxford University Press.

Saxon, D., Ivey, C., & Young, T. (2008). Can CORE assessment data identify those clients less likely to benefit from brief counselling in primary care? *Counselling and Psychotherapy Research*, 8(4), 223–230.

Schäfer, T., & Schwarz, M. A. (2019). The meaningfulness of effect sizes in psychological research: differences between sub-disciplines and the impact of potential biases. *Frontiers in Psychology*, 10, 813.

Scheeres, K., Wensing, M., Knoop, H., et al. (2008). Implementing cognitive behavioral therapy for chronic fatigue syndrome in a mental health center: a benchmarking evaluation. *Journal of Consulting and Clinical Psychology*, 76: 163–171.

Schielke, H. J., Fishman, J. L., Osatuke, K., et al. (2009). Creative consensus on interpretations of qualitative data: the Ward method. *Psychotherapy Research*, 19, 558–565.

Schielke, H. J., Fishman, J. L., Osatuke, K., & Stiles, W. B. (2014). Creative consensus on interpretations of qualitative data: the Ward Method. In W. Lutz & S. Knox (eds). *Quantitative and Qualitative Methods in Psychotherapy Research* (pp. 299–308). London: Routledge.

Schindler, A., Hiller, W., & Witthöft, M. (2013). What predicts outcome, response, and drop-out in CBT of depressive adults? A naturalistic study. *Behavioural and Cognitive Psychotherapy*, 41(3), 365–370.

Schjelderup, H. (1955). Lasting effects of psychoanalytic treatment. *Psychiatry*, 18, 109–133.

Schnellbacher, J., & Leijssen, M. (2009). The significance of therapist genuineness from the client's perspective. *Journal of Humanistic Psychology*, 49, 207–228.

Schulz, J. (2018). Thirteen ways of looking at a clinic. In K.T. Galvin (ed). *Routledge Handbook of Well-Being* (pp. 292–316). London: Routledge.

Sealy, P. A. (2012). Autoethnography: reflective journaling and meditation to cope with life-threatening breast cancer. *Clinical Journal of Oncology Nursing*, 16, 38–41.

Seidel, J. A., Miller, S. D., & Chow, D. L. (2014). Effect size calculations for the clinician: Methods and comparability. *Psychotherapy Research*, 24(4), 470–484.

Seidler, Z. E., Rice, S. M., Ogrodniczuk, J. S., Oliffe, J. L., Shaw, J. M., & Dhillon, H. M. (2019). Men, masculinities, depression: implications for mental health services from a Delphi expert consensus study. *Professional Psychology: Research and Practice*, 50(1), 51–59.

Self, R., Oates, P., Pinnock-Hamilton, T., et al. (2005). The relationship between social deprivation and unilateral termination (attrition) from psychotherapy at various stages of the health care pathway. *Psychology and Psychotherapy: Theory, Research and Practice*, 78, 95–111.

Shahar, G. (2013). An integrative psychotherapist's account of his focus when treating self-critical patients. *Psychotherapy*, 50(3), 322–325.

Sharpe, D., & Faye, C. (2009). A second look at debriefing practices: madness in our method? *Ethics & Behavior*, 19(5), 432–447.

Sheach Leith, V. M. (2009). The search for meaning after pregnancy loss: an autoethnography. *Illness, Crisis and Loss*, 17, 201–221.

Shedler, J., Mayman, M., & Manis, M. (1993). The illusion of mental health. *American Psychologist*, 48, 1117–1131.

Sieber, J. E. & Tolich, M. B. (2013). *Planning Ethically Responsible Research*. 2nd edn. Thousand Oaks, CA: Sage.

Sim, J., Saunders, B., Waterfield, J., & Kingstone, T. (2018). Can sample size in qualitative research be determined a priori? *International Journal of Social Research Methodology*, 21(5), 619–634.

Simonsen, G., & Cooper, M. (2015). Helpful aspects of bereavement counselling: an interpretative phenomenological analysis. *Counselling and Psychotherapy Research*, 15(2), 119–127.

Skjerve, J., Reichelt, S., & McLeod, J. (2016). Topic change processes in psychotherapy: a case study approach. *Qualitative Research in Psychology*, 13, 271–288.

Small, C., Pistrang, N., Huddy, V., & Williams, C. (2018). Individual psychological therapy in an acute inpatient setting: service user and psychologist perspectives. *Psychology and Psychotherapy: Theory, Research and Practice*, 91(4), 417–433.

Smink, W., Sools, A. M., van der Zwaan, J. M., Wiegersma, S., Veldkamp, B. P., & Westerhof, G. J. (2019). Towards text mining therapeutic change: A systematic review of text-based methods for Therapeutic Change Process Research. *Plos One*, 14(12), e0225703.

Smith, B. (1999). The abyss: exploring depression through a narrative of the self. *Qualitative Inquiry*, 5(2), 264–279.

Smith, E. B., & Luke, M. M. (2021). A call for radical reflexivity in counseling qualitative research. *Counselor Education and Supervision*, 60(2), 164–172.

Smith, J. A. (2011a). Evaluating the contribution of interpretative phenomenological analysis. *Health Psychology Review*, 5(1), 9–27.

Smith, J. A. (2011b). We could be diving for pearls: the value of the gem in experiential qualitative psychology. *Qualitative Methods in Psychology Bulletin*, 12, 6–15.

Smith, J. A., Flowers, P., & Larkin, M. (2009). *Interpretative Phenomenological Analysis: Theory, Method and Research*. London: Sage.

Smith, K., Shoemark, A., McLeod, J., et al. (2014). Moving on: a case analysis of process and outcome in person-centred psychotherapy for health anxiety. *Person-Centered and Experiential Psychotherapies*, 13, 111–127.

Smith, L. T. (2021). *Decolonising Methodologies: Research and Indigenous Peoples*. 2nd edn. London: Zed Books.

Snape, C., Perren, S., Jones, L., & Rowland, N. (2003). Counselling – Why not? A qualitative study of people's accounts of not taking up counselling appointments. *Counselling and Psychotherapy Research*, 3(3), 239–245.

Solstad, S. M., Kleiven, G. S., Castonguay, L. G., & Moltu, C. (2021). Clinical dilemmas of routine outcome monitoring and clinical feedback: a qualitative study of patient experiences. *Psychotherapy Research*, 31(2), 200–210.

Søndergaard, D. M. (2019). Psychology, ethics, and new materialist thinking: using a study of sexualized digital practices as an example. *Human Arenas*, 2(4), 483–498.

Sørensen, K. D., Wilberg, T., Berthelsen, E., & Råbu, M. (2020). Subjective experience of the origin and development of avoidant personality disorder. *Journal of Clinical Psychology*, 76(12), 2232–2248.

Sparkes, A. C. (2002). Autoethnography: self indulgence or something more? In A. Bochner and C. Ellis (eds), *Ethnographically Speaking: Autoethnography, Literature, and Aesthetics* (pp. 209–32). London: Altamira.

Sparkes, A. C. (2012). Fathers and sons: in bits and pieces. *Qualitative Inquiry*, 18, 174–185.

Sparkes, A.C. (2013). Autoethnography: self-indulgence or something more? In P. Sikes (ed.), *Autoethnography* (pp. 175–194). London: Sage.

Sparkes, A. C. (2020). Autoethnography: accept, revise, reject? An evaluative self reflects. *Qualitative Research in Sport, Exercise and Health*, 12(2), 289–302.

Speciale, M., Gess, J., & Speedlin, S. (2015). You don't look like a lesbian: a coautoethnography of intersectional identities in counselor education. *Journal of LGBT Issues in Counseling*, 9(4), 256–272.

Spitzer, R. L., Kroenke, K., Williams, J. B., et al. (2006). A brief measure for assessing generalized anxiety disorder: the GAD-7. *Archives of Internal Medicine*, 166(10): 1092–1097.

Stänicke, E., & McLeod, J. (2021). Paradoxical outcomes in psychotherapy: theoretical and methodological perspectives, research agenda and practice implications. *European Journal of Psychotherapy and Counselling*.

Stänicke, E., Strømme, H., Killingmo, B., & Gullestad, S. E. (2015). Analytic change: assessing ways of being in a psychoanalytic follow-up interview. *The International Journal of Psychoanalysis*, 96(3), 797–815.

Stapley, E., Target, M., & Midgley, N. (2017). The journey through and beyond mental health services in the United Kingdom: a typology of parents' ways of managing the crisis of their teenage child's depression. *Journal of Clinical Psychology*, 73(10), 1429–1441.

Steinmann, R., Gat, I., Nir-Gottlieb, O., Shahar, B., & Diamond, G. M. (2017). Attachment-based family therapy and individual emotion-focused therapy for unresolved anger: qualitative analysis of treatment outcomes and change processes. *Psychotherapy*, 54(3), 281–291.

Stephen, S., Elliott, R., & Macleod, R. (2011). Person-centred therapy with a client experiencing social anxiety difficulties: a hermeneutic single case efficacy design. *Counselling and Psychotherapy Research*, 11(1), 55–66.

Stewart, R. E., Stirman, S.W., & Chambless, D.L. (2012). A qualitative investigation of practicing psychologists' attitudes toward research-informed practice: implications for dissemination strategies. *Professional Psychology: Research and Practice*, 43, 100–109.

Stiles, W. B. (1993). Quality control in qualitative research. *Clinical Psychology Review*, 13, 593–618.

Stiles, W. B. (2001). Assimilation of problematic experiences. *Psychotherapy*, 38, 462–465.

Stiles, W. B. (2007). Theory-building case studies of counselling and psychotherapy. *Counselling and Psychotherapy Research*, 7(2), 122–127.

Stiles, W. B. (2011). Coming to terms. *Psychotherapy Research*, 21, 367–384.

Stiles, W. B., Barkham, M., Mellor-Clark, J., et al. (2008). Effectiveness of cognitive-behavioural, person-centred, and psychodynamic therapies in UK primary-care routine practice: replication in a larger sample. *Psychological Medicine*, 38, 667–688.

Stiles, W. B., Barkham, M., Twigg, E., et al. (2006). Effectiveness of cognitive-behavioural, person centred, and psychodynamic therapies as practiced in UK National Health Service settings. *Psychological Medicine*, 36, 555–566.

Stiles, W.B., Gordon, L.E., & Lani, J.A. (2002). Session evaluation and the Session Evaluation Questionnaire. In G. S. Tryon (ed.), *Counseling Based on Process Research: Applying what we Know*. Boston, MA: Allyn & Bacon.

Stiles, W. B., Leach, C., Barkham, M., Lucock, M., Iveson, S., Shapiro, D. A., ... & Hardy, G. E. (2003). Early sudden gains in psychotherapy under routine clinic conditions: practice-based evidence. *Journal of Consulting and Clinical Psychology*, 71(1), 14–22.

Stirling, F. J. (2016). Yoga and loss: an autoethnographical exploration of grief, mind, and body. *Illness, Crisis & Loss*, 24(4), 279–291.

Stirling, F. J. (2020). Journeying to visibility: an autoethnography of self-harm scars in the therapy room. *Psychotherapy and Politics International*, e1537.

Stone, B. (2009). Running man. *Qualitative Research in Sport and Exercise*, 1, 67–71.

Stone, C., & Elliott, R. (2011). Clients' experience of research within a research clinic setting. *Counselling Psychology Review*, 26(4), 71–86.

Stratton, P., Bland, J., Janes, E., & Lask, J. (2010). Developing an indicator of family function and a practicable outcome measure for systemic family and couple therapy: the SCORE. *Journal of Family Therapy*, 32(3), 232–258.

Strømme, H., Gullestad, S. E., Stänicke, E., & Killingmo, B. (2010). A widened scope on therapist development: designing a research interview informed by psychoanalysis. *Qualitative Research in Psychology*, 7(3), 214–232.

Suh, C. S., Strupp, H. H., & O'Malley, S. S. (1986). The Vanderbilt process measures: the Psychotherapy Process Scale (VPPS) and the Negative Indicators Scale (VNIS). In L.S. Greenberg & W.M. Pinsof (eds), *The Psychotherapeutic Process: A Research Handbook*. New York: Guilford.

Sündermann, O., See, C., & Veale, D. (2019). The delivery of psychotherapy – A Delphi study on the dimensions of psychotherapy delivery and a proposal for reporting guidelines. *Clinical Psychology & Psychotherapy*, 26(4), 483–491.

Sussman, S. (2001). The significance of psycho-peristalsis and tears within the therapeutic relationship. *Counselling and Psychotherapy Research*, 1: 90–100.

Sutton-Brown, C. A. (2014). Photovoice: a methodological guide. *Photography and Culture*, 7(2), 169–185.

Swift, J. K., Callahan, J. L., Cooper, M., & Parkin, S.R. (2019). Preferences. In J. C. Norcross & M. J. Lambert (eds), *Psychotherapy Relationships that Work: Volume 2: Evidence-Based Therapist Responsiveness* (pp. 156–185). New York: Oxford University Press.

Swift, J. K., Callahan, J. L., Heath, C. J., Herbert, G. L., & Levine, J. C. (2010). Applications of the psychotherapy phase model to clinically significant deterioration. *Psychotherapy: Theory, Research, Practice, Training*, 47(2), 235–248.

Swift, J. K., Christopherson, C. D., Bird, M. O., Zöld, A., & Goode, J. (2020). Questionable research practices among faculty and students in APA-accredited clinical and counseling psychology doctoral programs. *Training and Education in Professional Psychology*.

Swift, J. K., Tompkins, K. A., & Parkin, S. R. (2017). Understanding the client's perspective of helpful and hindering events in psychotherapy sessions: a micro-process approach. *Journal of Clinical Psychology*, 73(11), 1543–1555.

Szkodny, L. E., Newman, M. G., & Goldfried, M. R. (2014). Clinical experiences in conducting empirically supported treatments for generalized anxiety disorder. *Behavior Therapy*, 45(1), 7–20.

Tarabi, S. A., Loulopoulou, A. I., & Henton, I. (2020). "Guide or conversation?" The experience of Second-Generation Pakistani Muslim men receiving CBT in the UK. *Counselling Psychology Quarterly*, 33(1), 46–65.

Tarescavage, A. M., & Ben-Porath, Y. S. (2014). Psychotherapeutic outcomes measures: a critical review for practitioners. *Journal of Clinical Psychology*, 70(9), 808–830.

Tauri, J. M. (2018). Research ethics, informed consent and the disempowerment of First Nation peoples. *Research Ethics*, 14(3), 1–14.

Teo, T. (2015). Are psychological "ethics codes" morally oblique? *Journal of Theoretical and Philosophical Psychology*, 35, 78–89.

Thompson, M. N., Cole, O. D., & Nitzarim, R. S. (2012). Recognizing social class in the psychotherapy relationship: a grounded theory exploration of low-income clients. *Journal of Counseling Psychology*, 59(2), 208–220.

Thompson, V. L. S., Bazile, A., & Akbar, M. (2004). African Americans perceptions of psychotherapy and psychotherapists. *Professional Psychology: Research and Practice*, 35, 19–26.

Thurston, J., & Cooper, M. (2014). Helpful processes in psychological therapy for patients with primary cancers: a qualitative interview study. *Counselling and Psychotherapy Research*, 14(2), 84–92.

Thurston, M., Thurston, A., & McLeod, J. (2012). Counselling for sight loss: using Hermeneutic Single Case Efficacy Design methods to explore outcome and common factors. *Counselling Psychology Review*, 27, 56–70.

Tilden, B., Charman, D., Sharples, J., & Fosbury, J. (2005). Identity and adherence in a diabetes patient: transformations in psychotherapy. *Qualitative Health Research*, 15(3), 312–324.

Tolich, M. (2010). A critique of current practice: ten foundational guidelines for autoethnographers, *Qualitative Health Research*, 20, 1599–610.

Tolich, M. (2016). *Qualitative Ethics in Practice*. New York: Routledge.

Tomicic, A., Martinez, C. & Krause, M. (2015). The sound of change: A study of the psychotherapeutic process embodied in vocal expression. Laura Rice's ideas revisited. *Psychotherapy Research*, 25(2), 263–276.

Toto-Moriarty, T. (2013). A retrospective view of psychodynamic treatment: perspectives of recovered bulimia nervosa patients. *Qualitative Social Work*, 12(6), 834–848.

Toukmanian, S. G., & Rennie, D. L. (eds) (1992). *Psychotherapy Process Research: Paradigmatic and Narrative Approaches*. London: Sage.

Trachsel, M., & Grosse Holtforth, M. (2019). How to strengthen patients' meaning response by an ethical informed consent in psychotherapy. *Frontiers in Psychology*, 10, 1747.

Truax, C.B., & Carkhuff, R.R. (1967). *Toward Effective Counseling and Psychotherapy: Training and Practice*. Chicago: Aldine.

Trudeau, K. (2007). Explanation of the CONSORT statement with application to psychosocial interventions. In A. M. Nezu and C. M. Nezu (eds), *Evidence-based Outcome Research: A Practical Guide to Conducting Randomized Controlled Trials for Psychosocial Interventions*. Cary, NC: Oxford University Press.

Truijens, F. L., Desmet, M., De Coster, E., Uyttenhove, H., Deeren, B., & Meganck, R. (2019). When quantitative measures become a qualitative storybook: a phenomenological case analysis of validity and performativity of questionnaire administration in psychotherapy research. *Qualitative Research in Psychology*.

Tufford, L., & Newman, P. (2010). Bracketing in qualitative research. *Qualitative Social Work*, 11(1), 80–96.

Tuval-Mashiach, R. (2017). Raising the curtain: the importance of transparency in qualitative research. *Qualitative Psychology*, 4, 126–138.

Ulberg, R., Amlo, S., & Høglend, P. (2014). Manual for transference work scale: a microanalytical tool for therapy process analyses. *BMC Psychiatry*, 14(1), 291.

Ulberg, R., Amlo, S., Critchfield, K. L., Marble, A., & Høglend, P. (2014). Transference interventions and the process between therapist and patient. *Psychotherapy*, 51(2), 258–282.

Unsworth, G., Cowie, H., & Green, A. (2012). Therapists' and clients' perceptions of routine outcome measurement in the NHS: A qualitative study. *Counselling and Psychotherapy Research*, 12(1), 71–80.

Valkonen, J., Hanninen, V., & Lindfors, O. (2011). Outcomes of psychotherapy from the perspective of the users. *Psychotherapy Research*, 21, 227–240.

van der Vaart, R., Witting, M., Riper, H., Kooistra, L., Bohlmeijer, E. T., & van Gemert-Pijnen, L. J. (2014). Blending online therapy into regular face-to-face therapy for depression: content, ratio and preconditions according to patients and therapists using a Delphi study. *BMC Psychiatry*, 14(1), 355.

van Grieken, R. A., Beune, E. J., Kirkenier, A. C., Koeter, M. W., van Zwieten, M. C., & Schene, A. H. (2014). Patients' perspectives on how treatment can impede their recovery from depression. *Journal of Affective Disorders*, 167, 153–159.

Van Manen, M. (2014). *Phenomenology of Practice: Meaning-Giving Methods in Phenomenological Research and Writing*. London: Routledge.

van Rijn, B., & Wild, C. (2016). Comparison of transactional analysis group and individual psychotherapy in the treatment of depression and anxiety: routine outcomes evaluation in community clinics. *Transactional Analysis Journal*, 46(1), 63–74.

Vasileiou, K., Barnett, J., Thorpe, S., & Young, T. (2018). Characterising and justifying sample size sufficiency in interview-based studies: systematic analysis of qualitative health research over a 15-year period. *BMC Medical Research Methodology*, 18(1), 148.

Veseth, M., Binder, P. E., Borg, M., & Davidson, L. (2012). Toward caring for oneself in a life of intense ups and downs: a reflexive-collaborative exploration of recovery in bipolar disorder. *Qualitative Health Research*, 22(1), 119–133.

Veseth, M., Binder, P. E., Borg, M., & Davidson, L. (2016). Recovery in bipolar disorders: experienced therapists' view of their patients' struggles and efforts when facing a severe mental illness. *Journal of Psychotherapy Integration*, 26(4), 437–451.

Veseth, M., Binder, P. E., Borg, M., & Davidson, L. (2017). Collaborating to stay open and aware: service user involvement in mental health research as an aid in reflexivity. *Nordic Psychology*, 69(4), 256–263.

Vollmer, B., Grote, J., Lange, R., & Walker, C. (2009). A therapy preferences interview: empowering clients by offering choices. *Psychotherapy Bulletin*, 44, 33–37.

von Below, C. (2020). "We just did not get on": young adults' experiences of unsuccessful psychodynamic psychotherapy – a lack of meta-communication and mentalization? *Frontiers in Psychology*, 11, 1243.

Vulcan, M. (2016). "I'm a translating body": therapists' experiences working with children diagnosed with autism spectrum disorder. *Journal of Psychotherapy Integration*, 26(3), 326–337.

Wall, J. M., Kwee, J. L., Hu, M., & McDonald, M. J. (2017). Enhancing the hermeneutic single-case efficacy design: bridging the research–practice gap. *Psychotherapy Research*, 27(5), 539–548.

Ward, E. C. (2005). Keeping it real: a grounded theory study of African American clients engaged in counseling at a community mental health agency. *Journal of Counseling Psychology*, 52, 471–481.

Wasserstein, R. L., Schirm, A. L., & Lazar, N. A. (2019). Moving to a World Beyond "p < 0.05". *American Statistician*, 73, 1–19.

Watson, J. C., Ho, C.-M., & Boham, M. (2021). Advancing the counseling profession through intervention research. *Journal of Counseling & Development*, 99(2), 134–144.

Weatherhead, S., & Daiches, A. (2010). Muslim views on mental health and psychotherapy. *Psychology and Psychotherapy: Theory, Research and Practice*, 83, 75–89.

Weersing, V. R. (2005). Benchmarking the effectiveness of psychotherapy: program evaluation as a component of evidence-based practice. *Journal of the American Academy of Child and Adolescent Psychiatry*, 44, 1058–1062.

Weersing, V. R., & Weisz, J. R. (2002). Community clinic treatment for depressed youth: benchmarking usual care against CBT clinical trials. *Journal of Consulting and Clinical Psychology*, 70, 299–310.

Wendt, D. C., & Gone, J. P. (2016). Integrating professional and indigenous therapies: an urban American Indian narrative clinical case study. *The Counseling Psychologist*, 44(5), 695–729.

Werbart, A., Annevall, A., & Hillblom, J. (2019). Successful and less successful psychotherapies compared: three therapists and their six contrasting cases. *Frontiers in Psychology*, 10, 816.

Werbart, A., Bergstedt, A., & Levander, S. (2020). Love, work, and striving for the self in balance: anaclitic and introjective patients' experiences of change in psychoanalysis. *Frontiers in Psychology*, 11, 144.

Werbart, A., Levin, L., Andersson, H., et al. (2013). Everyday evidence: outcomes of psychotherapies in Swedish public health services. *Psychotherapy*, 50, 119–130.

Werbart, A., & Wang, M. (2012). Predictors of not starting and dropping out from psychotherapy in Swedish public service settings. *Nordic Psychology*, 64, 128–146.

Wertz, F. J. (2005). Phenomenological research methods for counseling psychology. *Journal of Counseling Psychology*, 52(2), 167–177.

Wertz, F. J. (2015). Phenomenology: methods, historical development, and applications in psychology. In J. Martin, J. Sugarman & K. L. Slaney (eds), *The Wiley Handbook of Theoretical and Philosophical Psychology: Methods, Approaches, and New Directions for Social Sciences* (pp. 85–101). Chichester: Wiley-Blackwell.

Wertz, F. J., Charmaz, K., McMullen, L. M., Josselson, R., Anderson, R., & McSpadden, E. (2011). *Five Ways of Doing Qualitative Analysis: Henomenological Psychology, Grounded Theory, Discourse Analysis, Narrative Research, and Intuitive Inquiry*. New York: Routledge.

West, A. (2010). Supervising counsellors and psychotherapists who work with trauma: a Delphi study. *British Journal of Guidance & Counselling*, 38(4), 409–430.

West, A. (2011). Using the Delphi Technique: experience from the world of counselling and psychotherapy. *Counselling and Psychotherapy Research*, 11(3), 237–242.

Westbrook, D., & Kirk, J. (2005). The clinical effectiveness of cognitive behaviour therapy: Outcome for a large sample of adults treated in routine practice. *Behaviour Research and Therapy*, 43(10), 1243–1261.

Wester, K. L., Wachter Morris, C. A., Trustey, C. E., Cory, J. S., & Grossman, L. M. (2021). Promoting rigorous research using innovative qualitative approaches. *Journal of Counseling & Development*, 99(2), 189–199.

Wheeler, A. J., & McElvaney, R. (2018). 'Why would you want to do that work?' The positive impact on therapists of working with child victims of sexual abuse in Ireland: a thematic analysis. *Counselling Psychology Quarterly*, 31(4), 513–527.

Whybrow, D. (2013). Psychiatric nursing liaison in a combat zone: an autoethnography. *Journal of Psychiatric and Mental Health Nursing*, 20: 896–901.

Widdowson, M. (2012). TA treatment of depression: a hermeneutic single-case efficacy design study-case three: 'Tom'. *International Journal of Transactional Analysis Research*, 3(2), 15–27.

Widdowson, M. (2014). Avoidance, vicious cycles, and experiential disconfirmation of script: two new theoretical concepts and one mechanism of change in the psychotherapy of depression and anxiety. *Transactional Analysis Journal*, 44(3), 194–207.

Widdowson, M. (2015). *Transactional Analysis for Depression: A Step-by-Step Treatment Manual*. London: Routledge.

Wilkinson, S., & Wilkinson, C. (2020). Performing care: emotion work and 'dignity work' – a joint autoethnography of caring for our mum at the end of life. *Sociology of Health & Illnes*, 42(8), 1888–1901.

Williams, M., & Haverkamp, B. E. (2010). Identifying critical competencies for psychotherapeutic practice with eating disordered clients: a Delphi study. *Eating Disorders*, 18(2), 91–109.

Willutzki, U., Ülsmann, D., Schulte, D., & Veith, A. (2013). Direkte Veränderungsmessung in der Psychotherapie. Der Bochumer Veränderungsbogen-2000 (BVB-2000) [Direct measurements of change on psychotherapy. The Bochum Change Questionnaire 2000 (BCQ-2000)]. *Zeitschrift für Klinische Psychologie und Psychotherapie*, 42(4), 256–268.

Wilson, J., & Giddings, L. (2010). Counselling women whose lives have been seriously disrupted by depression. *New Zealand Journal of Counselling*, 30(2), 23–39.

Wise, E. A. (2004). Methods for analysing psychotherapy outcomes: a review of clinical significance, reliable change and recommendations for future directions. *Journal of Personality Assesssment*, 82, 50–59.

Wittchen, H.-U., & Fehm, L. (2003). Epidemiology and natural course of social fears and social phobia. *Acta Psychiatrica Scandinavica*, 108, 4–18.

Wolcott, H.F. (1990). *Writing up Qualitative Research*. London: Sage.

Wong, G., & Breheny, M. (2018). Narrative analysis in health psychology: A guide for analysis. *Health Psychology and Behavioral Medicine*, 6(1), 245–261.

Wood, A. W., Dorais, S., Gutierrez, D., Moore, C. M., & Schmit, M. K. (2021). Advancing the counseling profession through contemporary quantitative approaches. *Journal of Counseling & Development*, 99(2), 156–166.

Woodward, L. E., Murrell, S. A., & Bettler Jr, R. F. (2005). Stability, reliability, and norms for the Inventory of Interpersonal Problems. *Psychotherapy Research*, 15(3), 272–286.

Wright, J. (2009). Autoethnography and therapy: writing on the move. *Qualitative Inquiry*, 15(4), 623–640.

Wright, J., & Bolton, G. (2012). *Reflective Writing in Counselling and Psychotherapy*. London: Sage.

Wyatt, J, (2013). Ash Wednesdays: an autoethnography of (not) counselling. In N. Short, L. Turner, & A. Grant (eds), *Contemporary British Autoethnography* (pp. 127–137). Rotterdam: Sense Publishers.

Yalom, I. (2001). *The Gift of Therapy: An Open Letter to a New Generation of Therapists And Their Patients*. London: Platkus.

Zigmond, A. S., & Snaith, R. P. (1983). The hospital anxiety and depression scale. *Acta Psychiatrica Scandinavica*, 67, 361–370.

Index